Wildlife
of India

Bikram Grewal
Manjula Mathur
& Tripta Sood

Additional Information
Birds: Clement M. Francis & Savio Fonseca
Mammals: Rohit Charkravarty
Reptiles: Indraneil Das & Abhijit Das
Butterflies: Peter Smetacek
Insects: Meenkashi Venkataraman
Trees & Shrubs: Pradeep Sachdeva & Vidya Tongbram

Princeton University Press
Princeton and Oxford

Published in 2022 in the United States and Canada by
Princeton University Press
41 William Street, Princeton, New Jersey 08540
press.princeton.edu

This edition of *Wildlife of India* is published by arrangement with
John Beaufoy Publishing Ltd

ISBN 978-0-691-21770-3
Library of Congress Control Number 2021948774

Edited and indexed by Krystyna Mayer
Cartography and design by Alpana Khare Graphic Design, New Delhi
Project management by Rosemary Wilkinson

Printed and bound in Malaysia by Times Offset (M) Sdn. Bhd.

10 9 8 7 6 5 4 3 2 1 0

CONTENTS

Geographical Regions of India

Bhanu Singh

Western Himalayas

The Indian region is characterized by great variations in geographical features that in turn impact its climate. From the high Himalayas to the north, and the arid Thar Desert in the north-west, to the great alluvial plains of the Ganges, the Brahmaputra river, and the Deccan Plateau in the south with its western and eastern boundaries, the Western and Eastern Ghats, the geographical diversity is immense. This in turns leads to climatic variations in temperature and rainfall. The Thar Desert in the north-west gets very low rainfall, while Mawsynram in Meghalaya receives the heaviest rainfall from the south-west monsoon. Unlike in more temperate regions, most of India has high temperatures that encourage continuous plant growth and insect activity – a boon for birds and herbivores, and the carnivores that prey on them.

The Indian region has 10 distinct geographical areas, namely the Western Himalayas; Eastern Himalayas; North-east; North-west including the Thar Desert; Deccan Plateau; Western Ghats; Eastern Ghats; Central Highlands; Northern Plains; Islands: Andaman and Nicobar, and Lakshadweep.

The **Western Himalayas** include the Kashmir, Himachal and Uttaranchal Himalayas, in the states of Himachal and Uttarkhand and Union territories of Kashmir and Ladakh.

The Kashmir Himalayas comprise a series of ranges such as Karakoram, Ladakh, Zanskar and Pir Panjal. Between the Great Himalayas and the Pir Panjal range lies the famed valley of Kashmir. The Ladakh cold desert lies between the Great Himalayas and Karakoram range. Some of the important passes of this region are the Zoji La on the Great Himalayas, Banihal on the Pir Panjal, and Khardung La on the Ladakh range. Important freshwater lakes include the Dal and the Wular in Kashmir, and saltwater lakes such as Pangong Tso and Tso Moriri in Ladakh. The region is famous for its scenic beauty and picturesque landscape.

The Himachal and Uttaranchal Himalayas lie between the river Ravi in the west and Kali in the east. The three Himalayan ranges in this region are the Great Himalayan, Lesser Himalayan and Shivalik ranges, running from the north to south. The region has some of the prettiest hill stations and cantonment towns such as Mussoorie, Simla, Dalhousie, Landsdowne and Ranikhet. The distinguishing features of the region are the 'dun formations', the largest being Dehra dun, and other notable ones being Harike dun, Chandigarh-Kalka dun, Nalagarh dun and Kota dun. The famous Valley of Flowers is situated in this region.

The Ladakh plateau has an average elevation of 5,300m. Here, birds such as Bar-headed Geese and Brown-headed Gulls breed in summer. Mountain ungulates such as the Himalayan Tahr, Asiatic Ibex and Bharal and their predator, the Snow Leopard, live in the high plateaux of Ladakh, Lahaul and Spiti. In Himachal and Uttarakhand, trees of oak, chestnut, Deodar, Chir Pine, walnut and spruce grow at lower elevations, while at 3,000–4,000m, forests of silver fir, junipers, birches and rhododendrons occur. Near the treeline, mosses and lichens form part of the tundra vegetation.

Tree ferns, Eastern Himalayas

Vaidehi Gunjal

Birds in the Western Himalayas include the beautiful Himalayan Monal and Cheer Pheasant, a number of laughingthrushes, and many types of babbler. In the alpine zone, butterflies such as the Clouded Yellow, Alpine Large White and Meadow Blue are typical, while at lower elevations tortoiseshells, Red Helens, Common Peacocks and Blue Sapphires are seen.

The **Eastern Himalayas** comprise the northern part of Bengal, Sikkim and Arunachal Pradesh. This is a region of high mountain peaks, such as the Kanchenjunga, and deep valleys. Coniferous trees grow at higher altitudes, and at lower elevations humid tropical vegetation such as wild bananas, tree ferns, orchids and screw-pines flourishes. Bird life gets richer, with more species of fulvettas, wren-babblers and laughingthrushes. Mammals such as the Asian Elephant roam in the forests of North Bengal and Arunachal Pradesh. The Red Panda is an endangered animal that lives in the montane forests of the northern part of Bengal, Sikkim and Arunachal Pradesh. The butterfly fauna also gets richer, with the Golden Birdwing, Great Mormon, Hill Jezebel and Kohinoor being seen.

Sikkim

5

Naga Hills

The **North-east** includes the states of Assam, Arunachal Pradesh, Nagaland, Manipur, Mizoram, Meghalaya and Tripura. The region has low hills, such as the Patkai, Naga, Khasi, Manipur and Mizo hills, which are separated from each other by many small rivers. The mighty Brahmaputra River flows through Assam and Arunachal Pradesh. Due to high annual precipitation of more than 2,000mm, evergreen and semi-evergreen trees flourish. At higher elevations, coniferous forests of oak, magnolia, rhododendron, cherry, maple, fern and bamboo occur. In the tropical zone, the vegetation comprises cinnamon, giant bamboo and ferns. Also found here is *Nepenthes khasian*, a carnivorous pitcher plant plant endemic to Meghalaya. The bird life has a strong affinity with the Indo-Chinese subregion.

This region is the most famous butterfly hotspot in India. More than half of the Indian butterfly species are found here. The Kaiser-i-Hind, Bhutan Glory, Constable and Popinjay are among the famous butterflies seen here.

The Indian Rhinoceros, Pygmy Hog, Asian Elephant and Western Hoolock Gibbon are some of the endemic mammals in the region.

Arunachal Pradesh

Brahmaputra River

Thar Desert

Great Indian Bustard

The **North-west** includes Punjab, Haryana and Rajasthan. The latter has the Great Indian Desert of Thar, which merges into the salty desert of the Rann of Kutch in Gujarat. It lies to the north-west of the Aravalli hills and is a land of undulating topography dotted with longitudinal and crescent-shaped dunes of sand. These sand dunes form 52 per cent of the desert. They extend in parallel lines, sometimes up to 3km long. They have a shifting nature due to wind action. Crests of the dunes are covered by perennial grasses.

The northern part of the desert slopes towards Sindh and the southern part towards the Rann of Kutch. Most of the rivers are ephemeral. Luni is the only significant river that flows in the southern part of the desert. Low precipitation and high evaporation makes this a water-deficient region. Even the temporary streams that flow contain brackish water, which is used to make salt.

Desert vegetation is mainly stunted scrub. Drought-resistant trees occasionally dot the landscape. On the hills grow acacias and euphorbias. The Khejri tree *Prosopis cineraria* grows throughout the plains.

The iconic bird of the Thar Desert is the Great Indian Bustard. It is making its last stand for survival. Captive breeding of the bustard is being undertaken under the supervision of the Forest Department. Desert birds such as Greater Hoopoe-larks and Black-crowned Sparrow-larks ensure that the desert is a lively ecosystem. The Blackbuck, much eulogized in romantic ballads, Chinkara, Desert Cat and Desert Fox are the important mammalian species.

The Saw-scaled Viper and Indian Cobra are the two most venomous snakes of the region. A mention must be made of the Asiatic Lion of Gir in the Junagadh district of Gujarat. Enthusiastic conservation efforts have ensured its survival after a severe decline not so long ago.

Deccan Plateau

The **Deccan Plateau** is a large triangular plateau situated in the peninsular region of India. It is bound on the west by the Western Ghats, in the east by the Eastern Ghats and by the Satpura range in the north. The North Deccan includes the Maharashtra plateau and Satpura range. The South Deccan comprises the Karnataka and Telangana plateaux. Most of the rivers in the Deccan drain towards the Bay of Bengal, with the exception of the Tapti river. The vegetation in the central and southern parts of the plateau is mainly dry deciduous forests, within the states of Maharashtra and Telangana, extending into adjacent parts of Madhya Pradesh, Chattisgarh and Andhra Pradesh. In the west are thorn-scrub forests that lie in the rain-shadow area of the Western Ghats. In the more humid eastern part of the Deccan plateau, moist deciduous forests occur.

Most of the natural forest in this region has been cleared for firewood or as grazing land, or as a result of river damming, but large areas of remaining forest are home to the Chinkara, Blackbuck, Gaur, Wild Buffalo, Tiger, Asiatic Wild Dog and Sloth Bear. About 300 bird species include the globally threatened

Gaur, Central Indian forest

Jerdon's Courser, rediscovered in 1986. The Nagarjunasagar-Srisailam Tiger Reserve in Telangana and Andhra Pradesh is the largest tiger reserve in India.

The **Western Ghats**. The two ends of peninsular India consist of the Western and Eastern Ghats. The Western Ghats stretch from South Gujarat to Kanyakumari in Tamil Nadu. The western slopes of the Western Ghats receive very heavy rainfall from the south-west monsoon. The forests in the Western Ghats are evergreen, semi-evergreen and montane. Mahogany, Shisham (Indian Rosewood) and Indian Ebony are the expensive timbers of evergreen forests. Semi-evergreen forests have trees of White Cedar, Hillock and Kail. Deciduous trees of Teak, Sal, Shisham, Mahua, Amla and Sandalwood grow on the eastern slopes of the Western Ghats, which receive less rainfall than the western slopes. The Nilgiri hills of Tamil Nadu and Karnataka, and the Annamalai hills of Kerala, have montane forests of shola with magnolias, laurels, cinchonas and wattles interspersed with grassland.

The region is a biodiversity hotspot of mammals, birds and butterflies. Due to the high elevation and humidity, several endemic laughingthrushes, barbets, hornbills and flycatchers are found here that have an affinity with birds of north-east India. Some of the endemic birds of the Western Ghats are the Nilgiri Laughingthrush, Palani

Malabar Gliding Frog

Laughingthrush, Wayanad Laughingthrush, Nigiri Sholakili, Nilgiri Flycatcher and Malabar Parakeet. The endemic mammals are no less spectacular. The Nilgiri Tahr is a montane goat that has made the Eravikulam National Park known the world over. The Nilgiri, Annamalai and Palni hills in the states of Tamil Nadu and Kerala have montane grassland mixed with thick forests at a height of 1,200–2,500m that is the preferred habitat of the mountain goat. The Nilgiri Langur, with a dark, glossy body and a golden head, lives in the Nilgiri hills and Kodagu in Karnataka. The Lion-tailed Macaque is a denizen of tropical moist evergreen forests of Kerala, Tamil Nadu and Karnataka. The Silent Valley National Park has played a crucial role in the conservation of this mammal.

Nilgiri Hills

The Purple Frog and Malabar Gliding Frog are some of the endemic amphibians of the Western Ghats. The Hump-nosed Viper, Malabar Pit Viper and Large-scaled Pit Viper are a few of the reptiles of the region. The area is renowned for its endemic butterflies – the Malabar Banded Peacock, Malabar Tree Nymph, Malabar Raven and Malabar Rose, to name a few.

Painted Jezebel

Yellow-throated Bulbul

The Eastern Ghats is an area of low hills that run parallel to the east coast of India. This is an area of lower rainfall than that of the Western Ghats. The vegetation is moist and dry deciduous. The flagship bird of the Eastern Ghats is the shy Yellow-throated Bulbul, which can be seen in Hampi in Karnataka, the Gingee hills in Tamil Nadu, and Telangana. The butterfly diversity is not as great as in the Western Ghats. However, notable butterflies are the Painted Jezebel, White Tiger and Baronet.

The **Central Highlands** is a geographical region formed by two parallel ranges of hills, the Vindhya and Satpura ranges. They are divided by the Narmada river valley. The area slopes from the east, north-east to the west, south-west. The Vindhyas lie to the north of the Narmada river and extend from Jobat in Gujarat to Sasaram in Bihar through the Malwa plateau and Kaimur ranges. The Satpuras stretch south of the Narmada river and are composed of several contiguous ranges that include the Rajpipla hills, Nimar Plateau, and Pachmarhi and Mahadeo hills. The general elevation of the Vindhyas is 450–600m, while the Satpuras rise above 900m.

The Central Highlands form a watershed area for several rivers, the Narmada, Chambal, Betwa, Ken, Sone and Tapti. The natural vegetation here is Sal forests in the east and Teak forests in the west.

Bird life in the Central Highlands is not as rich as in the Eastern Himalayas or Western Ghats. The Painted Spurfowl, Lesser Adjutant, Malabar Pied Hornbill, White-bellied Minivet, Indian Vulture and Forest Owlet are some of the endemic and threatened species found here. Among mammalian species, the Tiger is the apex predator. Six Project Tiger Reserves are located in the region.

Forest in Central India

Indian Eagle Owl

Indian Leopards

Gangetic Dolphin

Indian Spotted Deer

Gangetic Plain

The **Northern Plains** are formed by the alluvial deposits of the Indus, Ganges and Brahmaputra rivers. This region extends from the plains at the foothills of the Shiwaliks to the Sunderban delta adjoining Bangladesh. The region also has the terai, a swampy area that has natural vegetation and forests, and a varied wildlife, including birds such as the Bengal Florican and Swamp Francolin.

Dry deciduous forests are seen in the eastern parts of Uttar Pradesh and Bihar. Tendu, Flame of the Forest, Laburnum, Ber and Khair are the common trees of these forests. The Golden Champak and Red Silk Cotton grow on the eastern side towards Bengal, and mangroves are common in the Sunderban Delta.

Mammals seen in the Corbett Tiger Reserve and Rajaji National Park include the Tiger, Asian Elephant, Sambar, Indian Spotted Deer, Indian Leopard and Sloth Bear.

In the Northern Plains some common butterfly species are the Plain Tiger, Lime butterfly, Blue Pansy, Peacock Pansy, Grass Yellow and Mottled Emigrant. In the Sundarbans, butterflies such as the Tree Nymph and Spotted Black Crow can be seen. The Tiger is the apex predator in the Sunderbans. The Gangetic Dolphin is a mammal of deep rivers such as the Ganges and Brahmaputra, but is threatened by rampant fishing, pollution, damming and mining.

The **Islands** comprise the Andaman and Nicobar group in the Bay of Bengal and the Lakshadweep islands in the Arabian Sea. The former is a fascinating ecosystem for many endemic birds, butterflies and fish. The islands have tropical rainforests and mangroves in the creeks and estuaries. Birds endemic to the Andaman and Nicobar group include the Andaman Serpent Eagle, Nicobar Serpent Eagle, Andaman Shama, Andaman Bulbul and Nicobar Megapode. The region is very rich in spectacular butterfly species such as the Andaman Clubtail, Andaman Birdwing and Andaman Viscount, to mention a few.

The Lakshadweep islands, a group of 36 coral atolls off the coast of Kerala, are an important breeding habitat for offshore birds.

Andaman Barn Owl

Crab-eating Macque

Andaman Islands

Wildlife Habitats in India

While many common animal species are spread over large areas of India, others are limited to specific habitats. Some birds of coniferous forests are found only in that habitat, while desert birds are restricted to the deserts of north-west India. The habitats can be divided into wetlands, marine environments, forests, grassland and agriculture. India also has desert, marine, island and montane habitats. There is considerable overlap within the habitats, and several species need different habitats at different times for summering, wintering, feeding and breeding.

Wetlands

Wetlands in the form of shallow ponds, inland jheels (lakes), marshes and rivers are rich habitats for birds. The Indian region supports abundant wetlands of different types, including mountain lakes, freshwater and brackish marshes, water-storage reservoirs, village ponds and flooded forests. Many are temporary, appearing after monsoon rains but drying up before the next rains. Shallow lagoons, jheels and lakes are frequented by pelicans, cormorants, herons, ducks and wading birds, some of which can be seen picking their way along the water's edge probing for food. Huge numbers of migratory waterfowl congregate at jheels during the winter months. Bitterns, crakes and jacanas hide among the reed beds. Raptors such as Ospreys, Western Marsh Harriers and Greater Spotted Eagles haunt the waterbodies to prey on the waterfowl.

Wetland degradation, pollution, rampant fishing, dam building and the draining of marshland to meet the needs of providing food for a rapidly growing population have reached alarming proportions and are affecting populations of birds such as the Indian Skimmer. Among the remaining wetlands of repute are Harike in Punjab, Chilika Lake in Odisha and the Keoladeo

Coastal environment

Ghana Sanctuary in Bharatpur in Rajasthan. The wetlands of Assam support the rare and endangered White-winged Wood Duck.

India's rivers and lakes are homes to many important and endangered mammalian species. The Gangetic Dolphin, which lives in the deep waters of the Ganges and Brahmaputra, is threatened by pollution, dam building and fishing activities. The Mugger Crocodile lives in rivers and lakes in India. Large populations occur in the Ganges in the states of Bihar and Jharkhand, in the Chambal river in Rajasthan and in the Narmada river in Madhya Pradesh. The reptile faces threats from illegal poaching for its skin and meat, and from drowning due to entanglement in fishing nets. Small populations of the Indian Gharial, a long-nosed, fish-eating crocodile, survive precariously in the Ganges, Gandaki, Kosi, Ramganga, Chambal and Mahanadi rivers. It is threatened by poaching and commercial fishing.

Marine environments are aquatic environments with high levels of dissolved salts, found in or near oceans. They have unique biotic (living) and abiotic (non-living) factors. Biotic factors include plants, animals and microbes, and abiotic factors include sunlight, oxygen, nutrients dissolved in the water, proximity to land, depth and temperature.

Mangroves

Marine environments comprise estuaries, salt marshes, mangrove forests, coral reefs and open ocean. An estuary is a coastal zone where rivers meet oceans. Here nutrients of oceans mix with those of rivers and are among the most productive places on Earth. Salt marshes occur where oceans meet land. Marshes are flooded at high tide and the ground is generally wet and salty. These areas have low-growing shrubs and bushes. Another coastal ecosystem is mangrove forests in tropical areas. The roots of mangroves filter out the salt and stay above water. Fish, crabs, shrimps, reptiles and amphibians live among a mangrove's roots, while its canopy and branches provide perches and nesting sites for birds.

Coral reefs are built from the exoskeletons secreted by coral polyps. This ecosystem is very diverse and hosts sponges, molluscs, fish, turtles, sharks and dolphins. Coral diversity in the Andaman and Nicobar

15

Islands, and Lakshadweep Islands, is well known. Beyond the coral reefs lies the open ocean inhabited by whales, dolphins, sharks and octopuses. Peninsular India is surrounded by large expanses of oceans, with the Arabian Sea on its west, the Bay of Bengal on its east and Indian Ocean to the south.

The marine environment in India includes the mangrove ecosystem of the Sunderbans in West Bengal, and the Godavari and Mahanadi deltas in Andhra Pradesh and Odisha respectively, which support rare bird and other animal species. The Western Reef Egret, seldom seen inland, feeds on molluscs and crustaceans near the seashore. Greater and Lesser Flamingoes are the avian showstoppers, which turn up in winter in the creeks near Mumbai such as Sewri and Thane. Several kingfishers, such as Collared, Brown-winged and Ruddy, live in this habitat but are rare now. Oceanic birds such as boobies, petrels and skuas are passage migrants and accidental visitors to India's shores. Breeding colonies of Sooty Terns and Brown Noddies were common a few decades ago on Pitti island of the Lakshadweep archipelago, but they are under threat from egg collectors.

The endangered Fishing Cat has all but disappeared from the Kolkata wetlands due to loss of habitat and hunting.

Forest is an ecosystem that comprises soil, trees, insects, birds and humans as its interacting units. Since a forest is a large and complex system, it supports a huge biodiversity. In India, there are broadly two forest types, temperate and tropical. Temperate forests are found at an altitude of 1,000–3,000m and occur in the higher hill ranges of northeastern India, in hilly areas of West Bengal and in Uttaranchal in northwestern India. Evergreen broadleaved trees such as oaks and chestnuts are predominant. Chir, Deodar and pine are the other important trees of temperate forests. Tropical forests include different types of forest such as mangroves, tropical rainforests, dry deciduous forests and moist deciduous forests. Mangrove forests are found in the Sunderban delta, Andaman and Nicobar Islands, and western India. Tropical rainforests are found in the Andaman and Nicobar Islands, the Western Ghats, the coastline of peninsular India and the great Assam region of the north-east.

Young tigress in a mixed forest in Northern India

Grassland in the north-east

Nilgai, Central India

Deciduous forests are found in the drier areas of the Central Highlands of the Vindhya and Satpura ranges and in the rain-shadow area of the Eastern Ghats.

Forest birds generally remain in the forest canopy and are difficult to see. They can be seen more easily at the edges of forest clearings where the sun can penetrate and there is adequate insect activity. Birds in coniferous forests form mixed hunting parties of tits, warblers, laughingthrushes, minlas and sibias, and can be seen as they fly around restlessly looking for food. Deciduous forests have their special birds such as the Forest Owlet, endangered vultures, minivets and babblers. Forests in India are home to many mammals such as the Tiger, Asiatic Lion, Asian Elephant, Indian Leopard, Sloth Bear, and several species of deer and antelope.

Grassland is one of the major ecosystems in the world, covering close to one-third of the Earth's terrestrial surface. It occurs where the vegetation is dominated by grasses and there are few or no trees in the area. Grassland is found where there is not enough regular rainfall to support the growth of a forest, but enough to avoid a desert from forming.

Grassland occupies nearly 24 per cent of the geographical area of India. The major types of grassland in India are the alpine moist meadows of the Great Himalayas, the steppes of the Trans Himalayas, 'Chaurs' of the Himalayan foothills, 'Terai' grassland of the Gangetic and Brahmaputra floodplains, 'Phumdis' or floating grassland in Manipur, 'Banni' and 'Vidis' in Gujarat, plateau and valley grassland in the Satpura and Maikal hills, dry grassland in Andhra Pradesh and Tamil Nadu, and 'Shola' grassland of the Western Ghats.

This ecosystem is important because it supports agriculture, is an important source of carbon storage, and is a very important habitat for plants, birds and mammals. Many rare species, such as the Indian Rhinoceros in Assam, Pygmy Hog, Hispid Hare, Wild Buffalo, Indian Hog Deer, Swamp Deer in terai grassland, and Nilgiri Tahr in shola grassland, are found here.

Grassland is under tremendous pressure

from over-grazing and conversion to agriculture. The Great Indian Bustard that inhabits the dry, short grassland of western India is on the brink of extinction, and the Lesser Florican survives in scattered pockets in the monsoon grassland of western India due to loss of grassland. Birds such as the Bengal Florican, Swamp Francolin, Swamp Prinia, Bristled Grassbird and Finn's Weaver are also facing grave threats to their survival.

This is one of the most neglected ecosystems in India and is under threat for economic gains. Much natural grassland, such as the wet grassland of terai and the shola grassland of the Western Ghats and dry grassland of the Deccan, is being converted to plantations. Over-grazing, uncontrolled growth of invasive species and climate change are further increasing the threat to this habitat.

Agricultural habitats are used by several birds. The needs of the ever-growing human population of India put huge pressures on animal habitats. Forests are being cleared and marshes are drained in the name of development. Some birds, such as the stately Sarus Crane, India's only resident crane, are seen in agricultural fields in North and Peninsular India. The Sarus Crane is not harmed by farmers, despite its depredations of crops and harvests. Pond Herons, or paddy

Sarus Crane

birds as they are sometimes called, are regular fixtures in inundated rice fields, waiting to catch the fish that lurk in the shallow water. Francolins and quails make their homes in agricultural fields. The Great Indian Bustard lives on the fringes of cultivated areas and faces disturbances as its fragile habitat gets progressively diminished.

Pepper plantation, South India

Climate of India

Climate determines the vegetation and habitat of birds, mammals and other animals. Climate has an impact on the flowering and fruiting of trees, the seeding of grasses and the abundance of invertebrates and vertebrates. Due to the size of the Indian subcontinent there is much variation in climate. Three factors affect climate:

1. Latitude, which has a direct bearing on the temperature of a place. The closer you go to the equator or the tropics, the hotter it is.
2. Altitude, which determines temperature; it gets cooler the higher you climb. Altitude also determines the amount of rainfall that any place receives. The Himalayas and Western Ghats obstruct the rain-bearing clouds of the south-west monsoon coming over the seas and thus get the heaviest precipitation.
3. Monsoon rainfall.

India has a cold season, a hot season and the monsoons. The cool winter season is from November to February, the hot, dry season from March to June, the hot, wet season from July to September and the warm post-monsoon period from October to November.

The south-west monsoon picks up moisture from the Arabian Sea and reaches the west coast of India in June, depositing heavy rainfall on the windward side of the Western Ghats. Another branch of the south-west monsoon advances over the Bay of Bengal, laden with moisture, and gives heavy rainfall to Bengal and the Eastern Himalayas. Mawsynram is the wettest place in the world, with an annual rainfall of over 1,000mm. The monsoon current travels up the Gangetic Plain, bringing much-needed rainfall to the hot, dusty plains. Delhi and surrounding areas receive rainfall in July. By the time the monsoon clouds reach the Thar Desert, they have lost much of their moisture. Thus, northwestern India is an area of deficient rainfall.

The north-east monsoon hits the southeastern coast of India from October to December but the rainfall is milder. The monsoons in India vary from year to year, and when rainfall is insufficient, wildlife suffers and breeding cycles can get disrupted.

India also gets some rainfall from cyclonic storms originating in the Bay of Bengal before the onset of the south-west monsoon. The north of India receives convectional rainfall from storms called the 'northern disturbances', when temperatures soar in summer.

In much of peninsular India and the north-east, the temperature range is small. In northern India the range is greater. Delhi, in winter, may have temperatures of 5 °C or lower, while in May and June temperatures can rise to 45 °C degrees centigrade. In the Thar Desert, the range of temperature is even more extreme. In winter temperatures reach freezing point, while in summer they may peak at 50 °C and beyond. The variation in diurnal temperature in the desert region is also huge.

In the Himalayas, the climate is temperate, which is the ideal condition for growth of flora and fauna. In the highest peaks of the Himalayas, snow is perpetual.

Monsoons start off a season of nesting

Clement M Francis

Enjoying the Forest

Forests are one of the most critical and renewable natural resources. They have played an important socio-economic role in the lives of forest communities for centuries. So intertwined are forests and religious beliefs in India that forest gods have been revered for thousands of years. Many Indian temples are situated deep in the interiors of forests. People make pilgrimages on foot to pay obeisance to the deities enshrined in these holy places of worship, for instance at Sabarimala in Kerala.

Forests act as mighty sponges that absorb carbon emissions. They are the source of great

Sacred grove

rivers. Forests purify that which flows through them, and the gurgling streams provide healthy, potable water to drink, untampered by pollutants. The rivers that flow through virgin pristine forests carry rich alluvial soil that is used for cultivation of crops. Without doubt, we would perish if our forests were denuded.

When you travel to wildernesses and experience oneness with them, you feel a sense of spiritual regeneration and uplift that no religious beliefs and dogmas can give to their followers. Anyone who has stayed in the old forest rest houses that dot the landscape of Corbett Tiger Reserve in Uttarakhand cannot forget the atmosphere of the forest at night – the blinking of the glow-worms, the repetitive, chunk-chunk calls of nightjars, the hooting of forest owls and the sudden, piercing alarm call of a deer warning that a predator is on the move. It is a truly mystical experience.

Nowadays, forests are magnets of tourism. Many people throng to them to see the big cats and often come away disappointed when they fail to see them. Forests are to be enjoyed for themselves and when you visit them without harbouring any expectations, you come away fulfilled in different ways. You may

Mottled Wood Owl

uniquely rewarding. The different bird vocalizations in the form of bird calls and songs, when heard in the precincts of prime forests, can add to the thrill. Birdwatching requires you to be patient, attentive and inconspicuous in the forest. All you need is a pair of binoculars and a field guide – it is easy to spend many enjoyable hours ticking off the birds that you are able to spot. Lakes, waterholes and fruiting trees in the forest are vantage points from where birds can be seen without being intruded upon.

Enjoyment of the peace and tranquility of a forest can give solace to many. By being silent and unobtrusive in a forest, we enable Mother Nature to unfold her many secrets. Forests are best enjoyed in solitude with a spirit of compassion for all their inhabitants. Nurturing love and respect for forests will make us truly evolved human beings.

Black Rajah

not see a Tiger but could be lucky enough to observe a rare mammal such as the Honey Badger. Many people have seen Tigers in the wild in India, but only a handful of them have ever set eyes on a Honey Badger. Some of us may be lucky to come across a fascinating predator, the endangered Asiatic Wild Dog. For some, the sighting of a Brown Fish Owl or the less commonly seen Mottled Wood Owl will prove to be a delight. For butterfly watchers, after a long, weary ride in the forest, it will be that sudden flicker on a bush that will make their hearts skip a beat and their joy will know no bounds when it turns out to be a Gaudy Baron or Black Rajah.

Another way to enjoy a forest is to watch the birds that dwell in it. The immense variety of bird life in India and the colourful plumage of many species make birdwatching a very rewarding hobby. The diversity of different forest habitats such as coniferous, evergreen, deciduous, shola and scrub, and the resultant bird diversity, make this hobby

Honey Badger

21

How to Behave in the Forest

When you visit a forest sanctuary or national park, there are some rules, written and unwritten, which should be second nature for anyone with a genuine love of wildlife.

One important rule concerns maintaining proper decorum in the forest. Posing with a selfie stick with a Tiger in the background, to the squeals and shouts of other occupants in a safari vehicle, is not desirable. Watch out: the Tiger may take this chance to charge at you and come too close for comfort.

Crowding an animal to get the 'perfect' photograph does not give it a chance to get away to its safe haven. It causes tremendous stress and disrupts the animal's natural behaviour such as feeding, hunting and courting. Safari vehicles have sometimes been seen reversing to a Tiger to enable photographers to get a 'close' shot. These shoddy tactics can have dangerous consequences. Examples of such human behaviour include:

- Safari jeep seen reversing to a Tiger in Corbett Tiger Reserve, provoking a charge.
- Chasing European Rollers in Hesaraghatta, near Bangalore.
- Hassling Leopards in Kabini, Nagarhole.
- Crowding Tigers in Tadoba, Pench and Ranthambhore.
- Chasing Leopards in Jhalana, near Jaipur.

Another important rule is that on no account should anyone get off a safari vehicle while visiting a forest sanctuary or Tiger reserve. A wild animal coming across a human on foot would be alarmed and interpret it as a danger to itself or its young ones, if they are nearby. It may be forgiven if it decides to attack. As an example, a video was in circulation a few years ago in which a safari guide was filmed getting off a safari jeep in Ranthambhore Tiger Reserve, provoking a charge from a Tiger that was sitting nearby. Such misplaced bravado not only endangered the individual's life but also the lives of those in the vehicle. Some wildlife photographers have gained notoriety for their idea that animals are their 'models' and that they exist for their photographic pleasure. This selfish and insensitive attitude can traumatize animals in the wild. The Great Indian Bustard is one of India's rarest birds and lives in open grassland in western India. When it spots someone hundreds of metres away, it does not feed, court or mate while the 'threat' persists. As a result of disturbances caused to the bird by unethical photographers, the Ministry of Environments and Forests has issued a circular banning photography of the bustard during its breeding season, when it is most vulnerable.

Photographers often converge on a location where an important animal has been 'discovered' in order to get that perfect photograph, which they hope will get them accolades and praise. In the process, they end up damaging the habitat and scaring away their 'prey'. The actions of overenthusiastic weekend photographers have caused damage to Hesaraghatta grassland, on the outskirts of Bangalore. Likewise, crowding by photographers in vehicles and on foot with utter disregard for ground-nesting and wading birds that roost on the sandy beaches has caused damage to salt pans and coastal areas.

One important objective of wildlife photographers is to 'shoot' nocturnal animals. They flash powerful torches at owls in the Andaman Islands and Slender Lorises in the forests of Tamil Nadu, to cite examples, in order to get that crisp shot and many 'likes' on social media. In fact, these animals have very sensitive eyes and can be temporarily blinded by powerful torches and flashes.

Handling reptiles and amphibians for photography is to be frowned upon. If a snake has just eaten, handling it may cause it to regurgitate its food. Handling amphibians for photography may lead to spreading of bacterial and fungal infection to them from human hands. The vilest practices are employed by photographers. Snakes are sometimes nailed to the ground to obtain pictures of Short-toed Snake Eagles and other raptors 'capturing' and devouring their prey; amphibians are refrigerated to stun them into immobility, causing their deaths after the photographers have done their unethical job and moved on.

Playing bird calls in forests is a common practice of some guides to make birds come out of the bushes and give the delighted photographer a chance to tick them off a 'must photograph' list. Indiscriminate use of bird calls causes serious psychological strain to birds and may disrupt their breeding behaviour. Patience, discretion and a good knowledge of bird behaviour and habitats will help people to see birds in their natural environments and enable a photographer to get a natural shot.

Mobile phone usage has been banned in wildlife sanctuaries and parks. Some visitors 'manage' to carry their mobile phones into a park and pester the guide in the safari vehicle to seek information about the presence of animals like big cats. The ringing of phones and people talking on them disturbs wildlife and people who have to come to enjoy nature. People who carry phones into wildlife sanctuaries should be fined on the spot by the Forest Department.

Speeding in national parks and Tiger reserves is noticed when the driver of a safari vehicle gets news of a Tiger in another location from his associates. He then drives at break-neck speed to get there. He is a danger to both the animals in the forest and the 'animals' in the vehicle. At such times, good sense must prevail and the driver should be advised to stick to the speed limits. Another reason for speeding is that the vehicle may have lingered too long in a forest to get a last chance at Tiger spotting and is now rushing to exit the park gate by the specified time. Remember, only animals can speed in the jungle.

The thirst for wildlife photography is growing at an alarming pace in India. Armed with massive telephoto lenses, photographers are on the move, in India and abroad, for that Holy Grail – a perfect photograph of a rarity. Unfortunately, there is no overarching body to set standards to regulate their behaviour. The voice of decency and common sense should speak from within. Am I going beyond the limits of permissible behaviour? Am I endangering the bird and its nestlings? Is my vehicle crowding a subadult Tiger, whose innocence and inexperience is being taken advantage of? We can all get the right answer if we ask these questions sincerely enough. Senior photographers who have been doing wildlife photography for a while can also set a good example, hoping that their attitude will rub off on others. The message of ethical photography must be spread on social media and among friends. We should preach and practise what is right for the benefit of wildlife.

Birdwatching in eastern India

How to Use This Book

This book is about Indian wildlife, its birds, mammals, reptiles, insects and plants. Its aim is to aid rapid field identification, which is necessary for conservation, management and biodiversity surveys. The species described are those that an average resident or visitor to India is likely to encounter. The introductory sections cover the geography and climate of India, the variety of vegetation in different geographical regions and the resultant biodiversity.

In a two- or three-word scientific name of a species, the first word is the genus, which is a taxonomic category that ranks above species and below family, and is denoted by a capitalized Latin name, for example *Lanius*. The second word is the species name and the third where relevant is the subspecies name. If the third word is the same as the second, it indicates that this was the first subspecies to be named, e.g. for Grey-backed Shrike in north-east India the scientific name is *Lanius tephronotus tephronotus*. It was the first subspecies of Grey-backed Shrike to be named. In Ladakh the subspecies is named as *Lanius tephronotus lahulensis* denoting a different subspecies. Families are joined together in larger groups called orders. The Grey-backed Shrike would be in the order Passeriformes, which includes all small and perching birds. Names and sequences change rapidly with improved scientific knowledge.

Birds The species and their names used in this book are generally those in popular usage, and also follow official taxonomic authorities where available. For birds, we follow the Checklist of the Birds of India, whilst using some names defined by the International Ornithological Congress (IOC) World Bird List where these are more commonly used. Taxonomic science is constantly advancing, so further changes can be expected after publication of this book.

In this book many 'splits' are taken into account, for example Long-billed Vulture has become two species, namely Indian and

Birds spread

Slender-billed Vultures, and Eurasian Eagle Owl has been split into Eurasian Eagle Owl and Rock Eagle Owl.

The measurement given beside the scientific name is the bill-tip to tail-tip length. All birds in the photos are male unless otherwise specified.

Mammals India has about 410 species, which is nearly 9 per cent of the world's population of mammals. They are divided into families, of which the most prominent are Cercopithecidae (monkeys), Proboscidae (Elephant), Canidae (Wild Dog, Bengal Fox, Desert Fox), Cervidae (deer), Carnivora (Tiger, Lion), Viverridae (civets) and Sciuridae (squirrels).

Reptiles are four-limbed animals in the class Reptilia. This section discusses turtles, lizards, snakes and crocodiles.

Mammals spread

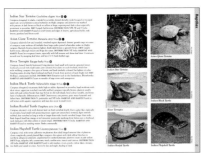

Reptiles spread

Wildlife-watching Sites spread

Butterflies and Other Insects The species descriptions include insects such as butterflies, moths, dragonflies and damselflies, aphids, grasshoppers, beetles and wasps. In the longest section, butterflies, the insects are grouped according to the current arrangement of families; measurements are the wing-tip to wing-tip length.

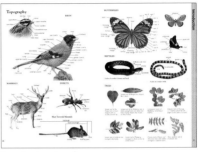

Introduction spread

Trees and Shrubs are grouped within their families. For each species, the text describes identifying features, habitats and uses; measurements are of the height.

The Wildlife Sites selected are representative of the different geographical regions with a varied biodiversity.

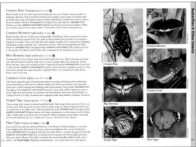

Butterflies & other Insects spread

Each description contains one or more of the symbols below, depicting their status.

V Vulnerable or endangered

i Introduced to India

e Endemic to India

n Native to India

r Resident in the area

m Seasonal migrant

♀ Female

Trees and Shrubs spread

Topography

BIRDS

eye-ring · lores
supercillium
eye-stripe
culmen
upper mandible
lower mandible
moustachial stripe
submoustachial stripe
malar stripe

crown · lores
forehead
ear-coverts
chin
throat
nape (hindneck)
mantle
scapulars
back
secondaries
tertials
rump
uppertail-coverts
lesser coverts
median coverts
breast
alula
greater coverts
primary coverts
flanks
belly
primaries
tarsus
tail (rectrices)
undertail-coverts
vent
thigh

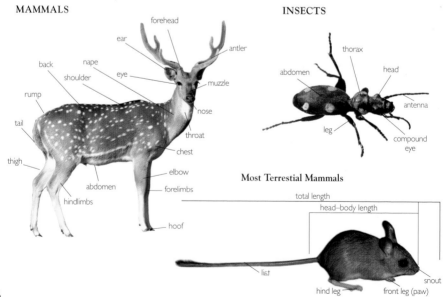

MAMMALS

forehead
ear
back
nape
shoulder
eye
muzzle
rump
nose
tail
throat
chest
thigh
elbow
abdomen
forelimbs
hindlimbs
hoof

INSECTS

thorax
head
abdomen
antenna
leg
compound eye

Most Terrestrial Mammals

total length
head–body length
tail
snout
hind leg
front leg (paw)

BUTTERFLIES

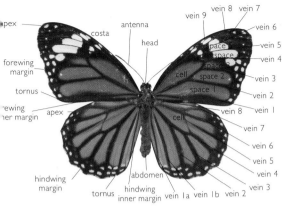

wingspan

apex
antenna
costa
head
vein 9
vein 8
vein 7
vein 6
vein 5
space
space
space 2
space 1
cell
vein 4
vein 3
vein 2
vein 1
forewing margin
tornus
rewing ner margin
apex
cell
vein 8
vein 7
vein 6
vein 5
vein 4
vein 3
hindwing margin
tornus
abdomen
hindwing inner margin
vein 1a vein 1b vein 2

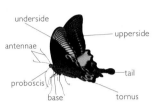

underside
upperside
antennae
tail
proboscis
base
tornus

REPTILES

midbody scale rows
temporal
frontal
supralabials
infralabials

Scales of a snake's dorsum and head.

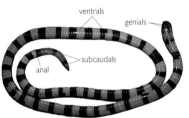

ventrals
genials
subcaudals
anal

Scales of a snake's belly.

TREES

Simple leaf of Mango tree, shaped like a lance.

Simple leaf of the Peepal tree is heart shaped with an acutely pointed tip.

Simple leaf of the Mulberry tree, in which young leaves are lobed and have varying shapes that morph as they mature.

Compound leaves of Bauhinia, comprising 2 leaflets.

Palmate leaf of Chorisia, 5–7 leaflets joined like the fingers on the palm of a hand.

Simple leaf of Jackfruit tree, arranged alternately.

Simple leaf of Plumeria, arranged in whorls at the tip of the branch.

Pinnate leaf of Neem and Tamarind trees with leaflets arranged in opposite pairs.

Thrice pinnate leaf of Drumstick tree.

Glossary

accidental Vagrant.

acute Sharply pointed.

adult Mature; capable of breeding.

aerial Making use of the open sky.

antennae Pair of sensory organs on an insect's head.

anterior Area on front part of body.

anther In plants, part of stamen containing pollen.

antlers Growth on top of head of a deer that grows annually.

aquatic Living on or in water.

arboreal Living in or climbing trees for food or shelter.

axil Point between leaf and stem from which buds emerge.

biodiversity Refers to places with many different life forms in their areas.

burrow Hole in the ground dug by animals like hares.

callosities A thick and hardened part of skin.

canine Taxonomic group that includes dogs, wolves and foxes.

canopy Leafy foliage of treetops.

carnivore Meat-eating animal.

casque Growth above bill of hornbill.

cetacean Of the mammalian order Cetacea, including whales, dolphins and porpoises.

cheek Term loosely applied to sides of head, below eye or on ear-coverts.

clutch Total number of eggs laid by a female at a time.

collar Distinctive band of colour that encircles or partly encircles neck.

compound leaf Leaf that is divided into a number of leaflets.

cone Woody, seed-bearing structure found on conifers such as pines and firs.

coverts Small feathers on birds' wings, ears and base of tail.

crepuscular Active at dawn and dusk.

crest In birds, extended feathers on head.

cryptic Camouflaged by body colour and/or shape.

cultivar Plant species created by cultivation.

deciduous Refers to plants that shed leaves in certain seasons.

depressed Flattened from top to bottom.

dimorphism Refers to distinct physical differences between sexes.

diurnal Active during day.

dorsal Upper surface, or back.

dorsum Dorsal surface of body, excluding head and tail.

ear-coverts In birds, feathers covering ear opening. Often distinctly coloured.

endangered Facing high risk of extinction.

endemic Found only in a certain area.

extinct No longer in existence.

eye-ring Contrasting ring around eye.

family Specific group of genera.

feral Escaped and living in the wild.

flank Side of body.

foraging Searching for food.

fruits Seeds of a plant.

gape Basal part of bird's bill.

genus Taxonomic group above species and below family.

Ghats Hills parallel to east and west coasts of India.

gregarious Living within a group or community.

gular Loose skin extending from throat.

hackles Long and pointed neck feathers.

herbivorous Feeding only on plant matter.

horns Growths on head of an antelope that never shed.

hybrid Refers to plant developed from cross-fertilization of two species.

infraorder Taxonomic rank below suborder.

insectivore Animal that feeds on insects.

invertebrate Animal that lacks a backbone.

iris Coloured eye membrane surrounding pupil.

jheel Shallow lake or wetland.

juvenile Immature or pre-adult.

keel Narrow prominent ridge.

lanceolate Refers to narrow and lance-shaped leaf.

larva Newly hatched, wingless stage of an animal.

linear Slender and parallel sided.

malar Stripe on side of throat.

mandible Each of the two parts of bird's bill.

mangroves Coastal salt-resistent trees or bushes.

mantle Back, between birds' wings.

marine Able to live in salt water.

mask Dark plumage around eyes and ear-coverts of birds.

mesial stripe Central throat stripe.

migration Seasonal movement between distant places.

montane Pertaining to mountains.

morph One of several distinct types of plumage in birds of the same species.

moult Seasonal shedding of plumage.

native Occurring naturally in a region.

nocturnal Active at night.

nomadic Species that move according to where there is available food and water.

nominate subspecies First subspecies to be formally named.

non-passerine All orders of birds except passerines.
nuchal crest Crest along back of neck.
nullah Dry or wet stream bed or ditch.
ocelli Brightly-coloured 'eye-like' spots.
Old World Asia, Europe and Africa.
order Taxonomic rank above family and below class.
ovate Refers to egg-shaped leaf, bract or petal.
Palearctic Old World and Arctic biogeographic zone.
palmate Refers to leaf shaped like an open hand.
parasite Organism that lives on or within another.
pelagic Ocean-going.
petal In a flower, one of the segments or divisions of the inner whorl of non-fertile parts surrounding the fertile organs, usually soft and conspicuously coloured.
pied Black and white.
pinnate Refers to compound leaf.
plankton Tiny organisms that float or swim weakly in the oceans.
plumage Feathers of a bird.
pod Elongated fruit, often cylindrical.
pollen Tiny grains that contain male sex cells produced by a flower's anthers.
postocular Area behind the eye.
predator Animal that feeds on other animals.
primaries Outer flight feathers in bird's wing.
proboscis Long, mobile feeding tube extending from front of head, seen in insects.
race Subspecies.
range Geographical area inhabited by a species.
raptors Birds of prey and vultures, excluding owls.
recurved Curved or bent.
resident Non-migratory and breeding in the same place.
reticulated Arranged like a net.
rump Lower back.
sal riverine forest Sal forests bordering rivers.
savannah Open flat land with grasses or small shrubs.
scapulars Feathers along edge of mantle in birds.
scute Thickened horny plate on turtle's shell.
secondaries Inner wing feathers of birds.
serrated With a saw-toothed edge.
sholas Tropical montane forests in valleys.
spangles Distinctive white or shimmering spots in plumage.
species Group of animals or plants reproductively isolated from other such groups.

speculum Area of colour on secondary feathers of duck's wings.
stamen Male part of flower, comprising anther and filament.
storey Level of a tree or forest.
streamers Long extensions to bird's feathers, usually of tail.
sub-apical Located below or near apex.
submontane Hills below the highest mountains.
subspecies Distinct form that does not have specific status.
substrate Underlying layer or material on which an organism lives.
supercilium Streak above eye.
talons Strong sharp claws used to seize or kill prey.
tarsus Final section of leg.
taxonomy Science of classifying organisms.
terai Alluvial stretch of land south of the Himalayas.
termen Outer margins of wings.
terminal band Broad band on tip of a bird's feathers or tail.
terrestrial Living on or spending time on the ground.
territory Area that an individual or group occupies and protects.
tertials In birds, innermost secondaries, often covering primary bases.
thorax Middle section of body of insect, between head and abdomen.
tricarinate Having three ridged keels.
underparts Undersurface of a bird from throat to vent.
underwing Undersurface of a bird's wing including the linings and flight feathers.
ungulate Animal that has hooves.
upperparts Upper surface of a bird including wings, back and tail.
vagrant Accidental, irregular.
vent Undertail area.
ventral Undersurface or belly of an animal.
vertebral Pertaining to region of backbone.
wing-coverts Small feathers on bird's wing at bases of primaries and secondaries.
wingspan Length from one wing-tip to the other when fully extended.
winter plumage In birds, plumage seen during the non-breeding winter months.

Nicobar Megapode *Megapodius nicobariensis* 43cm 🅔 🅥

Sexes alike, although female more greyish than male. Stout, short-tailed bird with powerful legs and feet, small ashy-grey head, reddish face with exposed skin and small rufous crest. Mostly dark brown with more grey than brown on underparts. Found in pairs or groups with young. Strong runner, often spending time on the ground and rarely flying. Lays eggs in mounds of rotting vegetation. **VOICE** Loud, gull-like screech and crackling *kuk … ah… kuk.* **DISTRIBUTION** Resident, Nicobar Islands. **HABITAT** Dense undergrowth of evergreen forests on sandy beaches.

Snow Partridge *Lerwa lerwa* 38cm 🅡

Rather plump bird with prominent bright red bill and legs. Upperparts blackish-grey, finely barred with rufous and white. Underparts dark chestnut, broadly streaked white, and deep chestnut breast. Dark tail barred with white tip. Sexes alike, but male has blunt spur on tarsus. Found in small groups. Nests well concealed on hillsides under rocks. **VOICE** Loud call, in breeding season similar to the Grey Francolin's (p. 32). **DISTRIBUTION** Resident; the Himalayas, 2,500–5,000m. **HABITAT** Alpine meadows, scrubby hillsides.

Himalayan Snowcock *Tetraogallus himalayensis* 55–72cm 🅡

Largish bird, overall grey, black and white, with some chestnut streaking on flanks. Sides of head and throat bordered chestnut. Dark reddish-brown band extends from behind eye to neck. Dark moustachial stripe from hindneck to collar. Upper breast barred with darker grey; white vent and undertail-coverts; yellow legs; dark grey bill; brown eyes surrounded by yellowish orbital skin. Sexes alike. The **Tibetan Snowcock** *T. tibetanus* has white cheeks, chin, throat and breast, with some irregular patches on upper breast. **VOICE** Noisy; cock utters loud whistle. **DISTRIBUTION** The Himalayas; Kashmir to Nepal. **HABITAT** Alpine meadows, rocky slopes.

Chukar Partridge *Alectoris chukar* 38cm 🅡

Plumpish, medium-sized partridge, overall greyish-brown with distinct black band running from eye to neck-base; whitish-buff face and throat; grey head and breast. Upperparts grey-buff. Black gorget across forehead and eyes, and white cheeks and throat. Flanks prominently barred; tail and lower back dark grey; buffish belly; chestnut outer-tail feathers; bright red bill and legs. Sexes similar. Occurs in small groups. **VOICE** Loud chuckle with up to a dozen notes. **DISTRIBUTION** W Himalayas to C Nepal. **HABITAT** Scrub, rock-covered hills.

Black Francolin *Francolinus francolinus* 35cm 🅡

Male jet-black, spotted and marked white and fulvous; white cheeks; chestnut collar, belly and undertail-coverts. Female browner where male is black; rufous nuchal patch; no white cheeks; pale chestnut collar. Solitary or in small parties in high grass and edges of canals. Emerges in the open in the early mornings. Sometimes cocks tail. **VOICE** Cock utters loud 3–6-note crow. **DISTRIBUTION** N and C subcontinent. **HABITAT** High grass, cultivation; prefers wetter areas along canals and rivers.

Painted Francolin *Francolinus pictus* 31cm 🅡

Medium-sized, profusely marked bird. Distinguished from female Black Francolin (above) by lack of rufous hind-collar and white spots on underside. Rufous face; chestnut head and throat. Upperparts blackish-brown; neck and underparts densely spotted white; white rump and tail finely barred with black; yellowish-orange legs. Skulking, shy and secretive; not easily flushed. Rarely flies. Roosts in trees. **VOICE** Noisy. Call a high-pitched, *khik … kheek …khee… khh.*
DISTRIBUTION Most of C India. **HABITAT** Grassland, scrub.

Nicobar Megapode

Himalayan Snowcock

Tibetan Snowcock

Black Francolin

Snow Partridge

Chukar Partridge

Painted Francolin

31

Grey Francolin *Francolinus pondicerianus* 31cm ⓪

Grey-brown and rufous above, barred and blotched; buffy-rufous below; narrow cross-bars on throat and upper breast; fine black markings on abdomen and flanks; black loop around throat encloses bright rufous-yellow throat. Sexes alike, but female smaller than male, with indistinct spur. Occurs in small parties, digging and moving amid scrub and grass. Seen on country roads, dust bathing or feeding. Quick to take to cover on being alarmed, scattering over the area. **VOICE** Loud, high-pitched call. **DISTRIBUTION** All subcontinent. **HABITAT** Open scrub, grass, cultivation.

Swamp Francolin *Francolinus gularis* 37cm ⓪ Ⓥ

Largest francolin with unusually long legs. Brown crown, beige supercilium and thin brown eye-stripes that extend to neck; upper throat and upper neck rusty-brown. Back and wings have mix of black and brown feathers with white flashes on the chest, chestnut flight feathers and outer-tail. Underparts brown longitudinally streaked with white. Blackish bill and dull brownish-red legs. **VOICE** Calls include vocal and loud *kyew … kyew … kyew … kaa … kaa* and *chukeroo*. **DISTRIBUTION** Globally threatened; breeding resident **HABITAT** Tall grassland, swamps.

Common Quail *Coturnix coturnix* 20cm ⓪ Rain Quail *C. coromandelica* 20cm

Male pale brown above, boldly streaked and marked. Blackish chin, and stripe down throat-centre and narrow stripe curving towards ear-coverts; rufous-buff breast with white streaks; whitish abdomen. Female has buff throat; breast heavily streaked with black. The more common Rain Quail, has bold black streaks on flanks. **VOICE** Fluid whistling of male a common and familiar call. **DISTRIBUTION** Resident and local migrant. Breeds in Kashmir; common in winter across India. **HABITAT** Cultivation, standing crops, grassland.

Jungle Bush Quail *Perdicula asiatica* 17cms ⓪

Very small quail with heavily barred back and whitish underparts, strongly barred with brown, and rufous head; crown slightly mottled with brown and white; white supercilium and moustache; dark eyebrow-stripe bordered with white coming down to nape; variegated wings. Upperparts mottled black, brown and yellow. Orangish-yellow legs and feet. Small spurs on feet. Female has more uniform pinkish-brown underparts. **VOICE** Call a trilling, musical *tirri … tirr*. **DISTRIBUTION** All India, to about 1,200m in the outer Himalayas. **HABITAT** Dense grass scrub.

Rock Bush Quail *Perdicula argoondah* 17cm ⓗ

Male similar to Jungle Bush Quail (above) but with white underparts barred with black; rufous stripe above pale eyebrows; vermiculated beige and black underparts; pale undertail-coverts. Female has plain rufous face, whitish chin and pale supercilium. Small coveys feed under vegetation. Nests under rock cover. Feeds on grain, seeds and leaves, sometimes insects. **VOICE** Call a musical, ascending trill. **DISTRIBUTION** W India from Haryana to S Kerala, Gujarat to Madhya Pradesh. **HABITAT** Dry semi-desert, thorny scrub.

Painted Bush Quail *Perdicula erythrorhyncha* 17cm ⓗ

Distinct-looking bird, easily recognized by big bold spots on brown upperparts, black face and white throat; rufous underparts and flanks; white scapular line and wing-coverts; black around eyes, forehead and chin; bright red bill and legs. Seen feeding in small groups on grass, seeds, weeds, grains and insects in the open, in the early mornings or late afternoons. **VOICE** Calls *kirikee … kirikee*. **DISTRIBUTION** Endemic resident: Eastern and Western Ghats, hills of C India. **HABITAT** Low, hilly scrub along forest margins.

Grey Francolin

Swamp Francolin

Common Quail

Jungle Bush Quail

Rain Quail

Painted Bush Quail

Rock Bush Quail

33

Hill Partridge *Arborophila torqueola* 28cm (r)

Plump, medium-sized game bird with black-barred brown upperparts and grey underparts with chestnut-and-white flank-streaks. Male has bright chestnut head with white-streaked black eye-stripe, throat and neck, and white gorget. Female smaller and less colourful, with brownish head and no white neck-collar. Secretive and prefers to run if disturbed. Expert flier through trees. More heard than seen. **VOICE** Call a mournful whistle, *po … eer … po … eer …*, the second syllable slightly longer. **DISTRIBUTION** The Himalayas. **HABITAT** Dense jungle undergrowth.

Rufous-throated Partridge *Arborophila rufogularis* 26cm (r)

Little-known partridge with distinctive head and throat pattern. White half collar and broad, distinct breast-band. Rufous-orange ear-coverts, throat and forehead. Black spots on ear-coverts and neck-sides. Sexes alike. **VOICE** Little known. **DISTRIBUTION** Two subspecies (*A. r. rufogularis* and *A. r. intermedia*) found in foothills of the Himalayas. **HABITAT** Grassland, scrub and agriculture.

Mountain Bamboo Partridge *Bambusicola fytchii* 28cm (r)

Distinctive, comparatively long-tailed partridge with broad buffish-white supercilium and dark eye-stripe. Warm buff ear-coverts, throat and foreneck. Rufous-and-chestnut spotting on breast, mantle and scapulars, diffusely barred tail and bold, blackish heart-shaped spotting on flanks. Shows rufous in primaries and tail-sides in flight. Sexes alike. **VOICE** Shrill and high-pitched *che-chiree-che-chiree*, repeated often. **DISTRIBUTION** Mainly NE hills, Nagaland in particular. **HABITAT** Dense grass in foothills bordering paddy fields and scrub.

Red Spurfowl *Galloperdix spadicea* 36cm (e)

Reddish-brown bird with grey face, head and neck; red facial skin, eye-patches, legs and feet; long tail and crown feathers. Sexes similar. Kerala race deeper chestnut-red. Male larger and darker than female, with darker markings with one or two spurs. Shy; runs rapidly if disturbed, rarely taking to flight. Forages in small groups of 2–5 birds in open patches. **VOICE** Loud cackling notes. Calls when flushed. **DISTRIBUTION** From Uttar Pradesh terai south across Gangetic Plain through peninsula. **HABITAT** Scrub in forested, broken hilly country.

Painted Spurfowl *Galloperdix lunulata* 32cm (e)

Colourful, medium-sized bird with dark brown upperparts, dark bill and grey legs. Black head and neck have luminous green sheen. Black tail. Male has finely white-barred black head and neck; white-spotted chestnut upperparts; underparts ochre with black flecks; mantle, rump and wing-coverts chestnut. Very shy and timid. Nests on the ground. **VOICE** Loud call of male reported. **DISTRIBUTION** Rajasthan, Madhya Pradesh and dry, forested areas of S India. **HABITAT** Dense thorn and bamboo jungles in broken hilly, rocky country.

Blood Pheasant *Ithaginis cruentus* 38cm (r)

Dissimilar to other pheasant species, resembling partridge in size and shape. White crest; black stripe above and below eye; red orbital skin. Upperparts white-streaked grey. Pale buff upper breast; rest of underparts greyish-white streaked with red. Tail streaked with grey and buff. Female evenly brown with grey nape and crest. Colour varies according to race. Feeds on the ground, scratching for food. **VOICE** Call a long-drawn squeal. **DISTRIBUTION** High Himalayas, east of C Nepal. **HABITAT** Steep hill forests.

Hill Partridge

Rufous-throated Partridge

Mountain Bamboo Partridge

Red Spurfowl

Painted Spurfowl

Blood Pheasant

Satyr Tragopan *Tragopan satyra* 76cm ⓡ ⓥ

Large, brightly coloured game bird with blue face. Male's underparts mainly white, spotted crimson. Black and white-spotted brown upperparts. Red on wings. Dark brown rump and tail. **VOICE** Call a loud, mournful *guwaa … guwaah … guwaah*. Also a *wak … wak* alarm call. Very skulking, but appears in open areas in the early morning or late evening. **DISTRIBUTION** Scarce, very local breeding resident from Uttaranchal to Arunachal Pradesh. Relatively common in Bhutan. **HABITAT** Montane forest undergrowth, particularly on slopes or in ravines.

Blyth's Tragopan *Tragopan blythii* 68cm ⓡ ⓥ

Large, brilliantly coloured game bird. Bare yellow facial skin with black band extending from bill-base to crown. Unmarked red head; rusty-red neck and breast. Pale blue horns. Upperparts brownish-red with many white ocelli. Grey-red lower breast and belly faintly spotted. Pinkish-brown legs; white-spotted red flanks. Female uniform brown with black buff and white mottling. **VOICE** Call a loud *hwaa … ouwaa … ouwaa*. **DISTRIBUTION** Globally threatened resident in Arunachal Pradesh and Nagaland. **HABITAT** Montane forests on steep slopes.

Koklass Pheasant *Pucrasia macrolopha* 61cm ⓡ

Silvery-grey and brown bird with distinct backswept crest and elongated tail. Black head; white cheek-patches; bright orange breast; male has deep green head and ear-tufts; golden-brown crest. Underparts chestnut; silver-grey flanks; dark pointed tail. Female paler with shorter crest. Feeds in pairs on steep slopes, on seeds, insects and berries. Very shy and timid, running or flying when disturbed. Courting male has interesting display. **VOICE** Call a loud *khok … kok … kok … kokha…* **DISTRIBUTION** The Himalayas, hills of NE India. **HABITAT** Steep forested hills, nullahs.

Himalayan Monal *Lophophorus impejanus* 72cm ⓡ

Sturdy bird with long, luminous green crest. Male has overall iridescent purple-blue upperparts with chestnut tail and wings. Underparts, face and foreneck brown-black; patch of metallic purple behind ear-coverts. Rear neck coppery-yellow changing to green on mantle; purple shorter tail-coverts; iridescent green longest tail-coverts. Female brown with black-and-white throat. Confiding; seen flying down hills at great speed. **VOICE** Call a wild whistling. **DISTRIBUTION** The Himalayas. **HABITAT** High forests, glades, snow patches.

Sclater's Monal *Lophophorus sclateri* Male 68cm; female 63cm ⓡ ⓥ

Medium-sized bird similar to the Himalayan Monal (above), but with blue-and-bronze colouring on head. Upperparts range from iridescent purplish-green to metallic green, blue, purple and black with white-and-black patches; velvety-black underparts. Lacks spatulate crest. Female dark brown with white throat and tail-tip. Two subspecies, based on amount of white on tail. **VOICE** Territorial, far-crying, plaintive howling. **DISTRIBUTION** Arunachal Pradesh and adjoining hills. **HABITAT** Scrub on steep hillsides.

Red Junglefowl *Gallus gallus* Male 70cm; Female 42cm ⓡ

Male glistening red-orange above, with yellow about neck; metallic black tail with long, drooping central feathers distinctive. Female has bright chestnut forehead, supercilia continuing to foreneck; reddish-brown plumage, vermiculated with fine black and buff. Seen in small parties, often several hens accompanying a cock. Shy and skulking. Emerges in clearings and on forest roads. **VOICE** Male has characteristic crow. **DISTRIBUTION** Outer Himalayas, E and C India. **HABITAT** Sal forest mixed with bamboo and cultivation patches.

Satyr Tragopan

Blyth's Tragopan

Koklass Pheasant

Himalayan Monal

Sclater's Monal

Red Junglefowl

Grey Junglefowl *Gallus sonneratii* 80cm **e**

Silvery game bird with pink legs, long tail and elongated neck. Gold streaks restricted to neck and wing-coverts; silver belly and black flight feathers. Female overall brown above and black with bold white streaks below. Wings not barred like Red Junglefowl's (p. 36). Feeds in pairs. Often seen on roads in mornings and evenings. Shy but confiding. **VOICE** Male utters loud, distinctive crow. Rather vocal when breeding. **DISTRIBUTION** Peninsula and S India, with range coinciding with Teak country. **HABITAT** Mixed deciduous forests, forest clearings.

Kalij Pheasant *Lophura leucomelanos* 65cm **r**

Male glossy black above, with steel-blue gloss; glossy tail ending in sickle-like feathers; whitish edges to rump feathers; bare scarlet around eyes; long, hairy white crest; brownish-grey underbody; lanceolate breast feathers. Female reddish-brown, scalloped paler; brown crest and bare scarlet patch around eye; brown tail. Several races. Occurs in pairs or small gatherings. Good flier. Roosts in trees at night. **VOICE** Male utters loud crowing. **DISTRIBUTION** The Himalayas, NE hill regions. **HABITAT** Forest undergrowth, clearings, terraced cultivation, habitation.

Cheer Pheasant *Catreus wallichii* 118cm **r** **v**

Male grey-brown; buff bar-tailed pheasant with long crest and red facial skin; large and very long tailed; long, backswept crest and red face; plain pale grey upper neck. Male more boldly marked than female, with black barring above and on white breast. Feeds on roots, tubers, bulbs, seeds and insects. Very wary and runs swiftly for cover when disturbed; hurtles downhill if flushed. **VOICE** Noisy before dawn and at dusk. **DISTRIBUTION** The Himalayas between NW Kashmir and C Nepal. **HABITAT** Grass-covered, steep rocky hillsides with scattered tree cover.

Grey Peacock-pheasant *Polyplectron bicalcaratum* Male 64cm; female 48cm **r**

Small, greyish-brown pheasant with short, tufted crest and long, broad tail. Male has striking purple-and-green ocelii, rimmed in white on mantle, wings and uppertail-coverts and tail. Bare pink or yellow facial skin. White throat and grey iris, bill and legs. Female similar, but smaller and less ornamented. Occurs singly or in pairs or small family groups. Rarely seen. **VOICE** Loud, guttural *hoo*. **DISTRIBUTION** Sikkim, Assam, Arunachal Pradesh. **HABITAT** Dense undergrowth in tropical forests.

Indian Peafowl *Pavo cristatus* Male 120cm; female 85cm **r**

Glistening blue neck and breast; wire-like crest and very long tail distinctive. Female lacks blue neck and breast; browner plumage; lacks long train. Familiar bird of India; solitary or in small parties, with several females and one or more males. Wary in forested areas, and rather tame and confiding around human habitation. Ever alert; gifted with keen eyesight and hearing. National bird of India. Tail feathers often illegally sold to tourists. **VOICE** Loud *may-yow* calls. **DISTRIBUTION** All India. **HABITAT** Forests, villages, cultivated country.

Green Peafowl *Pavo muticus* Male 80–300cm; female 100cm **r** **v**

Large pheasant that resembles the Indian Peafowl (above) superficially, but long train has more vivid bronze, copper and purple hues. Male has green tufted crest, and blue-and-yellow facial skin; green neck and underparts; green coverts; brown tertials and secondaries; iridescent metallic green upperparts; emerald-green tail feathers with ocelli, seen in display. Long tail and ocelli absent in female. **VOICE** Call a loud *ki ... woo*. **DISTRIBUTION** Recorded from a few areas of E and NE India. Status currently uncertain. **HABITAT** Dense forests near near streams or clearings.

Biswarup Sarpati

Grey Junglefowl

Sonu Anand

Cheer Pheasant

Garima Bhatia

Indian Peafowl

♀

Manoj Kejriwal

Kalij Pheasant

Vijay Sachen

Grey Peacock-pheasant

Francesco Veronesi

Green Peafowl

39

Lesser Whistling Duck *Dendrocygna javanica* 42cm ⓡ

Smallish, overall pale buff duck, with maroon-chestnut upperparts; crown darker grey-brown with golden-orange feather margins; chestnut uppertail-coverts; scaly pattern on back; large head, thin neck and long legs; inconspicuous yellow eye-ring. Dark brown, rounded wings with chestnut lesser wing-coverts. Sexes alike. Gregarious. Feeds on seeds and other vegetation. The larger **Fulvous Whistling Duck** *D. bicolor* is a scarce and declining breeding resident of NE India and is rare elsewhere. **VOICE** Call a wheezy, whistling call uttered in flight. **DISTRIBUTION** Largely resident species distributed unevenly. **HABITAT** Still freshwater lakes.

Bar-headed Goose *Anser indicus* 75cm ⓡ

Silvery-grey and white bird with two horseshoe-shaped, brownish-black bars on back of white head. Body overall grey; dark hindneck and lower flanks; yellow legs; black-tipped yellow bill; white neck-stripe along back of neck; white tail. **VOICE** Nasal, quite musical honking. **DISTRIBUTION** Breeds only in Ladakh within Indian limits. Winter visitor across Gangetic Plain to Assam. Less common south of the Deccan. **HABITAT** Rivers, large jheels.

Greylag Goose *Anser anser* 74–84cm ⓜ

Large goose with bluish-grey plumage with pale fringes to feathers; large darker head; thick, long neck; thick pink bill, and pink legs and feet; white uppertail-coverts; pale belly dotted black. Sexes alike. Black-speckled belly absent in juvenile. Feeds on grass. Occasionally feeds in the water on algae. Gregarious and wary. Nests on heaps of plant material lined with feathers. **VOICE** Domestic goose honk. Typical geese gaggles when feeding. **DISTRIBUTION** Winter visitor; most common in N India, rarer in S India. **HABITAT** Jheels, winter cultivation.

Knob-billed Duck *Sarkidiornis melanotos* 55–75cm ⓡ

Unmistakable because of fleshy knob (comb) on top of bill. White head and neck, speckled black; purple-green glossy back; bluish and greenish iridescence, especially prominent on secondaries; white lower neck-collar and underbody; short black bars extend on upper breast-sides and flanks. Occurs in small groups; nests in trees. **VOICE** Usually silent, but may occasionally utter some low croaking sounds. **DISTRIBUTION** All India; mostly resident, and uncommon in extreme S and NW India. **HABITAT** Swamps, rivers and lakes with scattered trees.

Ruddy Shelduck *Tadorna ferruginea* 65cm ⓡ

Whitish-buff head; orange-brown plumage; in flight, orangish body and white wing-coverts; green speculum and blackish flight feathers distinctive; black tail and ring around neck (breeding). Female has whiter head than male and lacks neck-ring. In pairs or small parties; rather wary. Rests by day on riverbanks, sandbars and edges of jheels; prefers clear, open water. **VOICE** Loud, goose-like honking, on the ground and in flight. **DISTRIBUTION** Breeds in Ladakh; winter visitor; all across India, less common in south. **HABITAT** Rivers with sandbars, large, open jheels.

White-winged Wood Duck *Asarcornis scutulata* 65–80cm ⓡ ⓥ

Large khaki, black and brown duck with whitish mottled head and neck. Lesser median coverts and inner edges of tertials whitish; secondaries bluish-grey. White edges of wings obvious in flight. Male larger than female, with whiter head. Roosts and nests on trees and in tree holes. Rarely wanders from breeding grounds. Feeds on snails, small fish and insects. **VOICE** Usually silent. **DISTRIBUTION** Globally endangered breeding resident. Now restricted to a few areas in NE India. **HABITAT** Undisturbed secluded pools and marshes in evergreen swamp forests.

Lesser Whistling Duck

Bar-headed Goose

Fulvous Whistling Duck

Knob-billed Duck

Greylag Goose

Ruddy Shelduck

White-winged Wood Duck

Cotton Teal *Nettapus coromandelianus* 32cm (r)

Tiny, pied duck with very small bill. Breeding male has green-glossed black upperparts, white underparts, black cap and breast-band, and pale grey flanks. Shows striking white wing-bars in flight. Black bill and feet. Usually in pairs or small parties. Flight very swift and low. Engages in aerobatic courtship chases. Nests in tree holes. Feeds on aquatic vegetation. **VOICE** Male utters rapid, chattering quack in flight. **DISTRIBUTION** Locally common breeding resident throughout India. **HABITAT** Inhabits well-vegetated freshwater jheels and village ponds.

Garganey *Spatula querquedula* 40cm (m)

Small, slight duck with large grey bill and flat crown. Dramatic broad white supercilium crossing to back of mottled brown head and curving downwards to neck; grey flanks; brown breast and spotted brown rear; white underparts; silvery-blue forewings seen in flight. Gregarious and social; often seen with other species. **VOICE** Male's mating call a distinctive crackling sound. **DISTRIBUTION** Abundant winter visitor. **HABITAT** Narrow or well-sheltered, shallow standing fresh water merging into grassland, floodlands or other wetlands.

Northern Shoveler *Spatula clypeata* 50cm (m)

Broad, long bill diagnostic. Male has metallic green head and neck; in flight, dark head, back-centre, rump and uppertail-coverts contrast with white of back and tail; also, dull blue upperwing-coverts against dark flight feathers; metallic green speculum. Occurs in pairs or small flocks, often with other ducks; swims slowly, with bill held very close to the water; sometimes upends. **VOICE** Loud, two-note quacking notes uttered by male. **DISTRIBUTION** Winter visitor; quite common. **HABITAT** Marshes, lakes; also vegetation-covered village ponds.

Gadwall *Mareca strepera* 50cm (m)

Medium-sized, dull grey-brown duck. Male has distinct vermiculations on scapular and back feathers; grey and brown upperparts; grey bill; orange legs. Brown head; upper and lower tail-coverts black. Long, pointed, silver-grey tertials; white secondaries with black greater secondary coverts distinctive and obvious in flight. Female lacks vermiculation; very similar plumage to male's, but more brownish on back and buffy tan on breast. **VOICE** Single-note, low call uttered by male. **DISTRIBUTION** Winter visitor; fairly abundant. **HABITAT** Marshes and small lakes.

Eurasian Wigeon *Mareca penelope* 50cm (m)

Medium-sized, plump, large-headed and short-necked duck. Breeding male has grey back, white belly and pink chest; rusty head with buff forehead; tail predominantly black. White shoulder-patch; stubby, greyish-blue bill with black tip. Male in eclipse resembles female. Female dull, mottled greyish-brown. Juvenile very similar to female. Very gregarious, often mixing with other ducks. **VOICE** Male utters haunting *wheeo* whistle. **DISTRIBUTION** Common winter visitor throughout India. Most numerous in N India. **HABITAT** Jheels, marshes, large rivers.

Indian Spot-billed Duck *Anas poecilorhyncha* 60cm (r)

Blackish-brown plumage, feathers edged paler; almost white head and neck; black cap; broad dark eye-stripe; green speculum bordered above with white; black bill tipped yellow; coral-red legs and feet. Sexes alike. Occurs in pairs or small parties; usually does not associate with other ducks. If injured, can dive and remain underwater, holding on to submerged vegetation with only bill exposed. **VOICE** Loud, duck-like quack. **DISTRIBUTION** Resident; N subcontinent, migrant in some areas. **HABITAT** Reed- and vegetation-covered jheels, shallow ponds.

Nikhil Devasar

Cotton Teal

Arpit Deomurari

Panchami Manoo Ukil

Northern Shoveler

Clement M Francis

Garganey

Bjorn Johansson

Rathika Ramasami

Gadwall

Eurasian Wigeon

Bjorn Johansson

Indian Spot-billed Duck

Panchami Manoo Ukil

Mallard *Anas platyrhynchos* 60cm (r) (m)

Large, heavy-looking duck said to be the ancestor of most domestic ducks. Male has long grey body and black rear parts. Head and neck glossy deep green; white neck-ring and dark purplish-brown breast; whitish underparts; yellow bill. Diagnostic blue patch on tops of wings bordered white; two curly feathers on tail. **VOICE** Drake's call a loud, wheezy *yheeep*; loudest when alarmed. **DISTRIBUTION** Very small numbers breed in some of Kashmir's lakes. Winter visitor: N, C India. Rare further south. **HABITAT** Marshes, lakes, swamps, rivers, streams.

Northern Pintail *Anas acuta* 60cm (m)

Slender duck with pointed tail. Male greyish above; chocolate-brown head and upper neck; thin white stripe up neck-side; bronze-green speculum. Female mottled buff-brown; pointed tail lacks longer tail-pins; whitish belly. In flight, pointed tail between feet distinctive. Highly gregarious. Very common on vegetation-covered jheels. Crepuscular and nocturnal. Characteristic hissing swish of wings as flock flies over. **VOICE** Usually quiet. **DISTRIBUTION** Winter visitor across subcontinent. **HABITAT** Vegetation-covered jheels, lagoons.

Common Teal *Anas crecca* 32cm (m)

Male greyish with chestnut head; broad metallic green band from eye to nape with yellow-white border. Black, green and buff wing speculum. Female mottled dark and light brown; pale belly and black-and-green wing speculum. A common migratory duck. Swift flier and difficult to circumvent. Feeds on aquatic plants and animals from the water's surface. Flight very fast and agile. **VOICE** *krit … kri t …*; also wheezy quack. **DISTRIBUTION** Entire subcontinent in winter. **HABITAT** Well-vegetated large rivers, jheels, coastal lagoons, swamps.

Red-crested Pochard *Netta rufina* 55cm (m)

Large duck with deep orange-crested head and red bill. Black neck and breast; pale flanks; brown back and black rear parts. Female lighter brown with pale cheeks, darker crown and dark bill. Juvenile darker with multicoloured belly. In flight, both sexes display broad white wing-bars. Nests near slow-moving rivers and clearings of open water with shrubs. Feeds actively in the early mornings and late evenings. **VOICE** Silent. **DISTRIBUTION** Rather scarce winter visitor throughout lowlands. **HABITAT** Well-vegetated large rivers and lakes.

Common Pochard *Aythya ferina* 45cm (m) (V)

Stocky, medium-sized duck with rich reddish-brown, wedge-shaped head; black breast, rear parts and tail. Grey body; large black bill with broad grey band; red eyes. Both sexes show black-bordered grey wing-bars in flight. Feeds by diving or dabbling, on aquatic plants, aquatic insects and small fish. Gregarious, forming large flocks in winter, often mixed with other diving ducks. **VOICE** Rather quiet. Female sometimes purrs in flight. **DISTRIBUTION** Common winter visitor throughout lowlands. **HABITAT** All types of open water, including village ponds.

Ferruginous Duck *Aythya nyroca* 40cm (m)

Earlier referred to as the White-eyed Pochard, this small, compact diving duck has a peaked head. Mahogany-brown, darker on back and head. Larger triangular patches of white under tail. Male bright russet-brown with sharp white iris. Long white wing-bars and belly visible in flight. Numbers declining. Usually keeps to small groups. Wary and cautious. **VOICE** Usually silent, although female makes burring sound in flight. **DISTRIBUTION** Most common in NW India. Scarce and local winter visitor elsewhere. **HABITAT** Well-vegetated jheels, ponds, canals, rivers.

Mallard

Common Teal

Common Pochard

Northern Pintail

Red-crested Pochard

Ferruginous Duck

45

Tufted Duck *Aythya fuligula* 45cm Ⓜ

Round-bodied, medium-sized diving duck with round head and very obvious head-tuft. Male glossy black with broad white flanks. Female dark brown with paler flanks. White under tail, occasionally visible in flight. Both sexes have yellow irises and black-tipped grey bills. Feeds during the day by diving. **VOICE** Rather quiet. Male has high bubbling note; female croaks. **DISTRIBUTION** Fairly common winter visitor throughout lowlands. Less common in E and S India. **HABITAT** All kinds of open water, including reservoirs.

Common Merganser *Mergus merganser* 58–72cm Ⓡ Ⓜ

Large, slender duck; big head and long, narrow, reddish-orange, serrated bill. Breeding male has glossy green domed head; bushy, mane-like feathers on back of neck; white lower neck, breast, belly and flanks; bright red feet and legs; pinkish tint to underparts; white patch on inner wing. Female has brown head with shaggy crest; grey and cream underparts. Feeds solely on fish by repeated diving. **VOICE** Male has a deep *kruu …* call. **DISTRIBUTION** Scarce; winters mainly in N India. Breeds in Ladakh and Lahaul. **HABITAT** Rests on rocks. Flight usually follows river course.

Sri Lanka Frogmouth *Batrachostomus moniliger* 23cm Ⓡ

Large-headed with huge, frog-like gape and flat, hooked and feathered bill. Male grey-brown, heavily mottled white and with white neck-bar. Female plainer orange-rufous, lightly spotted white. Hunts insects at night; roosts in thick undergrowth; perches vertically, camouflaged by its cryptic plumage. Points bill upwards when disturbed. Secretive. Lays single white egg. **VOICE** Calls include harsh *chaak*; decelerating whistle, *klok-klok*. **DISTRIBUTION** Scarce endemic breeding resident of Western Ghats. **HABITAT** Thick, wet evergreen forests.

Hodgson's Frogmouth *Batrachostomus hodgsoni* 26cm Ⓡ

Medium-sized frogmouth with large head, white gape and very broad, hooked bill. Long facial bristles. Slit-like nostrils and forwards-facing eyes. Male mottled grey-rufous with washed rufous buff with white spotted collar. Large white spots on scapulars and blackish crown. Rufous underparts roughly barred with black and white. Female has more white-spotted collar, scapulars and breast. Nocturnal. Assumes alarm posture when disturbed. **VOICE** Slightly trilled whistles, *wheow-whurree*; soft *gwdd* notes. **DISTRIBUTION** Hills of NE India. **HABITAT** Subtropical evergreen broadleaved forests.

Jungle Nightjar *Caprimulgus indicus* 30cm Ⓡ

Large, greyish-brown nightjar. Upperparts grey-brown streaked darker. White tail-tip in male; cream submoustachial stripe; large white patch on throat-sides. Brownish bill, legs and feet. Dark brown iris. Underparts grey-brown, barred darker and becoming more buff towards belly and flanks. **VOICE** Calls diagnostic. A whistling *chuckoo … chckoo* up to seven times. Also quick, repeated, mellow *tuck … tuck … tuck …* up to 50 times. **DISTRIBUTION** Resident and summer visitor from E Rajasthan, Bihar, Odisha and W peninsula. **HABITAT** Forest clearings and broken scrubby ravines.

Grey Nightjar *Caprimulgus jotaka* 32cm Ⓡ

Medium-sized nightjar with long, pointed tail; short legs; short bill with large rictal bristles; longish wings and tail. Small, dark, arrowhead-shaped markings on crown, and irregular buff spotting on nape forms indistinct collar. Roosts on tree along length of branch; remains motionless, making it difficult to see. **VOICE** Song a *kowrr … kowrr … kowrr*; guttural *tuk … tuk*. **DISTRIBUTION** The Himalayas and NE India. **HABITAT** Forest clearings.

Tufted Duck

Common Merganser

Sri Lanka Frogmouth

Hodgson's Frogmouth

Jungle Nightjar

Grey Nightjar

Jerdon's Nightjar *Caprimulgus atripennis* 28cm r

Larger than the Indian Nightjar (below). Distinguished by barred tail, rufous rear neck and wing-bars. Male has white wing-patch; plumage mainly variegated buff and brown; buff edges to scapulars; unbarred brown breast, rufous neck-band; unbroken white gorget similar to that of the Large-tailed Nightjar (below), but has shorter tail. Roosts in bushes. Like all nightjars, difficult to spot as it stays motionless during daylight hours. **VOICE** Call a series of liquid, tremulous *ch … wo … wo*. **DISTRIBUTION** C and S peninsular India. **HABITAT** Edges of forests.

Large-tailed Nightjar *Caprimulgus macrurus* 33cm r

Large, long and broad-tailed nightjar. Grey-brown upperparts streaked darker; more broadly on crown; indistinct buff collar; bright buff-edged black scapular lines; white moustache and breast-patch; small bill. Male has broad white apical tips to tail and primary patches. Roosts on the ground. Hunts flying insects at night. Erratic, stiff-winged flight. **VOICE** Quick *chunk … chunk … chunk*. **DISTRIBUTION** Fairly common resident along Gangetic Plain and throughout NE India, south to Andhra Pradesh. **HABITAT** Lowland forests, woodland.

Indian Nightjar *Caprimulgus asiaticus* 24cm r

Medium-sized, sandy-grey to brownish-grey nightjar with shortish wings and tail; boldly streaked crown; rufous-buff markings on nape forming distinct collar; bold black centres and broad buff edges to scapulars; bold rufous-buff or buff spotting on wing-coverts; pale, relatively unmarked central-tail feathers. Similar to the Large-tailed Nightjar (above), but with shorter tail. **VOICE** Call a far-carrying *chuk … chuk … chuk … ch … uk …* **DISTRIBUTION** Widespread resident; unrecorded in NW and most of NE India. **HABITAT** Open-wooded country in plains and foothills.

Savanna Nightjar *Caprimulgus affinis* 23cm r

Male has grey-brown plumage, mottled dark; buffy 'V' on back, from shoulders to about centre of back; two pairs of outer-tail feathers white, with pale dusky tips; white wing-patches. Female like male, but without white outer-tail feathers, which are barred; conspicuous rufous-buff wing-patches. Remains motionless; flies at around dusk, often flying high. Drinks often. **VOICE** Fairly loud, penetrating *sweeesh* or *schweee*. **DISTRIBUTION** Throughout area; moves considerably locally. **HABITAT** Rocky hillsides, scrub and grass country, light forests, dry streams.

Crested Treeswift *Hemiprocne coronata* 23cm r

Male bluish-grey above with faint greenish wash; chestnut sides of face and throat; grey breast, whiter below. Female similar, but lacks chestnut on head. Backwards-curving crest and long, deeply forked tail diagnostic. Found in pairs or small scattered parties. Flies by day, hawking insects; has favourite foraging areas. Graceful flight. Perches on higher dry branches. **VOICE** Calls a parrot-like *keei … ked …* Also double-note, faint scream. **DISTRIBUTION** Subcontinent south of the Himalayan foothills. Absent in NW India. **HABITAT** Open deciduous forests.

Indian Swiftlet *Aerodramus unicolor* 12cm r

Diminutive blackish-brown swiftlet with slightly forked tail visible in flight. Gregarious and colonial. Occurs in huge numbers on cliff sides and in caves. Large swarms leave before dawn and spend the day hawking insects over mountains and countryside. The **Himalayan Swiftlet** *A. brevirostris* is larger with a very obvious forked tail and looks boomerang-shaped in flight, with backswept wings. **VOICE** Roosting birds keep up incessant faint chatter. **DISTRIBUTION** Western Ghats and associated hills. **HABITAT** Caves and cliffs on rocky offshore islands.

Jerdon's Nightjar

Large-tailed Nightjar

Indian Nightjar

Savanna Nightjar

Crested Treeswift

Himalayan Swiftlet

Indian Swiftlet

49

Asian Palm Swift *Cypsiurus balasiensis* 13cm **r**

Sooty-brown plumage; typical swift wings that are long and sickle-like. Deeply forked tail distinctive, particularly in flight. Sociable small parties in open, farm-dotted country. Strong in flight. Hawks insects all day, occasionally rising very high. Roosts on undersides of palm leaves. **VOICE** Call a three-note, shrill scream, uttered very fast and always on the wing. **DISTRIBUTION** All over peninsular India, south of the Himalayan foothills. Also NE hill states. **HABITAT** Open countryside, revolving around palm trees.

Alpine Swift *Tachymarptis melba* 23cm **r**

Very long, sickle-shaped, pointed wings; dark sooty-brown above; white underbody. Broad brown band across breast diagnostic in flight. Dark undertail-coverts. Sexes alike. Loose parties dash erratically at high speed in the skies. Very strong fliers, seen higher in the sky around dusk, with many birds wheeling and tumbling, their shrill screams rending the air. Drinks at ponds and puddles by skimming over the water's surfaces. **VOICE** Calls include shrill *chirr … che … che …* screams in fast flight. **DISTRIBUTION** Ranges all over India. **HABITAT** Hill country and cliffs.

Indian House Swift *Apus affinis* 15cm **r**

Overall dark swift, with white rump and throat distinctive. Short, square tail. Highly gregarious. On the wing by day, hawking insects, and flying over human habitation, cliffs and ruins. Strong flier, exhibiting great mastery and control in fast-wheeling flight. Often utters squealing notes on the wing. Returns to safety of nest colonies in overcast weather. **VOICE** Musical squeals on the wing. Very vocal. **DISTRIBUTION** Throughout India. **HABITAT** Human habitation, cliffs and ruins.

Great Indian Bustard *Ardeotis nigriceps* Male 120cm; female 92cm **e** **V**

Male has black crown; short crest; sandy-buff upperbody, finely marked black; white below; black band on lower breast. Female smaller; breast gorget broken and only rarely full. Occurs in scattered pairs or small parties. Shy and difficult to approach. Fast runner. Hides in shade of bushes. Flies low over the ground. **VOICE** Loud *whonk …*, often audible for more than a mile. **DISTRIBUTION** Resident and local migrant; distant areas of Rajasthan, Karnataka; numbers and erstwhile range much reduced today. **HABITAT** Open grassland and scrub, semi-deserts.

Macqueen's Bustard *Chlamydotis macqueenii* 65cm **m** **V**

Overall brown bustard with prominent black stripe on neck-sides. Long wings show black and brown on flight feathers, visible in flight. Sexes similar, but female smaller than male and greyer above, with indistinct crest. Raises white feathers of head and throat, and withdraws head in flamboyant courtship display. Very wary; lurks under low cover with neck outstretched. **VOICE** Nothing recorded. **DISTRIBUTION** Rare winter visitor to semi-desert areas of NW India. **HABITAT** Semi-deserts and associated cultivation, particularly mustard fields.

Bengal Florican *Houbaropsis bengalensis* 66cm **r** **V**

Very reclusive bird known for courtship display where male shows off black-and-white plumage in aerial displays. Overall black with white wings conspicuous in flight. Long black feathers on head and neck, upright during display. Female larger than male with brownish plumage; white wing-patch visible in flight. Young birds have pale brown head, neck and breast, and white belly. **VOICE** Clicking sound in display and when flushed. **DISTRIBUTION** Globally threatened; breeding resident, now restricted to few sites in the terai and Assam. **HABITAT** Wet grassland.

Asian Palm Swift

Alpine Swift

Indian House Swift

Great Indian Bustard

Macqueen's Bustard

Bengal Florican

Lesser Florican *Sypheotides indicus* 45cm 🔴 🔵

Small, slender bustard with long, curved neck and long, thin legs. Adult male has distinct black head plumes with spatulate tips. Black head, neck and belly; brown back and wing feathers brown edged black; whitish collar and white coverts. Female larger than male and more sandy-brown with black streaks on head. Solitary or in pairs. Male displays by series of jumps from tall grass with outstretched neck and folded legs. **VOICE** Call a rattling *click* in display. **DISTRIBUTION** Globally threatened endemic breeder. Restricted to a few sites in NC India. **HABITAT** Dry, scrubby grassland.

Greater Coucal *Centropus sinensis* 50cm 🔴

Glossy bluish-black plumage; chestnut wings; blackish, long, graduated tail. Sexes alike. Female somewhat bigger than male. Solitary or in pairs. Moves amid dense growth, fanning and flicking tail often. Poor flier, lazily flying short distances. The **Lesser Coucal** *C. bengalensis* is smaller, with short, decurved bill. Local breeding resident from E Uttarakhand. **VOICE** Loud and resonant *coop … coop … coop …* call; occasionally a squeaky call. **DISTRIBUTION** Subcontinent, from the outer Himalayas to about 2,000m. **HABITAT** Forest, scrub, cultivation, near human habitation.

Sirkeer Malkoha *Taccocua leschenaultii* 45cm 🔴

Olive-brown plumage; long, graduated tail, with broad white tips to blackish outer feathers diagnostic in flight; cherry-red bill with yellow tip. Sexes alike. Solitary or in pairs. Moves mostly on the ground, in dense growth; may clamber on to some bush tops or low trees. Flight weak and short. Runs low and rat-like when disturbed. Builds its own nest. **VOICE** Fairly loud and sharp clicking notes: mostly vocal when breeding. **DISTRIBUTION** Most of subcontinent; absent in NW India and Kashmir. **HABITAT** Open jungle, scrub, ravines.

Blue-faced Malkoha *Phaenicophaeus viridirostris* 39cm 🔴

Large, dark greenish-grey cuckoo with diagnostic blue, bare and warty orbital skin. Head and upperparts dark grey, irridescent greenish-grey wings and tail. Dark grey underparts, washed rufous on abdomen. Bluish streaked throat and very long black-and-white tail. Deep brown to red iris with white eye-ring. Sexes alike. Solitary or in pairs. **VOICE** Mostly silent, croaking occasionally. **DISTRIBUTION** Resident in S India. **HABITAT** Thick thorn scrub, open forest undergrowth.

Green-billed Malkoha *Phaenicophaeus tristis* 51cm 🔴

Large, pale-billed grey cuckoo with very long black-and-white tail. Whole body greenish-grey with paler head and underparts, and graduated tail, black with white feather-tips. Bare red skin around eyes; heavy, pale apple-green curved bill. Sexes alike. Very shy. Feeds creeping with surprising manoeuvrability. Eats insects and reptiles. Flies poorly. Builds own nest. **VOICE** Rather silent but sometimes croaks quietly. **DISTRIBUTION** Scarce breeding resident of northern foothills, NE and Eastern Ghats. **HABITAT** Forested scrub undergrowth.

Chestnut-winged Cuckoo *Clamator coromandus* 45cm 🔴 🟤

Slender, long-tailed cuckoo with chestnut wings, white collar and long, erect black crest. Top of head and upperparts to tail of adult glossy metallic black; pale orange-brown throat to upper breast, breast and upper belly; white belly; blackish undertail-coverts; tail tipped white. Feathers edged paler; small crest; white underparts; rufous-edged wing-coverts, and buff edge and tip of tail. **VOICE** Call a whistling *peep … peep* in breeding season. **DISTRIBUTION** Breeds in the Himalayas and NE India, and winter visitor to S India. **HABITAT** Forests, thick scrub.

Greater Coucal

Lesser Florican

Lesser Coucal

Sirkeer Malkoha

Blue-faced Malkoha

Green-billed Malkoha

Chestnut-winged Cuckoo

Pied Cuckoo *Clamator jacobinus* 33cm 🔴 Ⓜ

Black above; noticeable crest; white in wings and white tip to long tail feathers diagnostic in flight; white underbody. Sexes alike. Young birds, seen in autumn, dull sooty-brown with indistinct crests; white areas dull fulvous. Solitary or in small parties of 4–6. Arboreal; occasionally descends to the ground to feed on insects. Arrives just before SW monsoon by end of May. Noisy and active. **VOICE** Noisy; loud, metallic *plew … piu …* call notes. **DISTRIBUTION** Chiefly SW monsoon breeding visitor. **HABITAT** Open forests, cultivation, orchards.

Asian Koel *Eudynamys scolopaceus* 42cm 🔴

Male has metallic black plumage; greenish bill and crimson eyes. Female dark brown, thickly spotted and barred white; whitish below, dark spotted on throat, barred below. Solitary or in pairs. Arboreal. Mostly silent in July–February. Fast flight. **VOICE** Familiar call of Indian countryside. Very noisy in March–June; loud *kuoo … kuooo …* whistling calls in crescendo by male; water-bubbling call by female. **DISTRIBUTION** Subcontinent. **HABITAT** Light forests, orchards, city parks, cultivation, open areas.

Asian Emerald Cuckoo *Chrysococcyx maculatus* 18cm 🔴

Tiny cuckoo with iridescent emerald-green head, neck, breast and upperparts. White upperparts barred prominently metallic green. Orange orbital skin; black-tipped yellow bill. Female has brighter rufous crown and upper mantle than male, with glossy bronze-green wash on lower mantle and wings. Rufous wash on face. Arboreal, mainly in canopy, venturing out to capture insects. **VOICE** Loud *kee … kee … kee* in flight. **DISTRIBUTION** Uttarakhand east to Arunachal Pradesh, Assam and S Assam hills. **HABITAT** Broadleaved evergreen forests, secondary growth.

Violet Cuckoo *Chrysococcyx xanthorhynchus* 18cm 🔴

Tiny, distinctive forest bird with iridescent dark purple head, upperparts and upper breast. White underparts barred deep purple; bright orange bill. White-spotted dark undertail. Female dark bronze-brown above with white underparts barred brown. Rufous outer-tail feathers; dull orange-yellow bill. Arborial. **VOICE** Calls *che … wick* in flight. Shrill trilling. **DISTRIBUTION** Arunachal Pradesh, Assam and S Assam hills. **HABITAT** Evergreen forests, secondary growth.

Banded Bay Cuckoo *Cacomantis sonneratii* 24cm 🔴

Small cuckoo with longish, curved bill. Upperparts rufous-brown, strongly barred, uniformly and regularly, dark brown. Adult male has broad white supercilium that encircles brown ear-coverts; dark eye-stripe; whitish cheeks; white-tipped tail. Whitish underparts, washed pale buff from belly to flanks, finely and uniformly barred; central-tail feathers barred and darker on each side of shaft. **VOICE** Call a shrill whistle. **DISTRIBUTION** Up east to Assam; also peninsular India. **HABITAT** Dense broadleaved forests, lightly wooded country, edges of forests.

Grey-bellied Cuckoo *Cacomantis passerinus* 23cm 🔴

Grey head with grey-brown glossy underparts. White tail-tip and patch under wing seen in flight. Grey throat and upper breast; paler, almost white below. Sexes alike. Female has hepatic phase. Bright chestnut upperparts and throat with reddish-brown wash. Cross-barred black on back. White below throat. **The Plaintive Cuckoo** C. *merulinus* of the NE is a scarce breeding resident and very similar to the Grey-bellied. **VOICE** Noisy with wide range of calls, from a plaintive, single-note *piteer* to a three-note, long-drawn call. **DISTRIBUTION** India, south from the Himalayas except the NW. **HABITAT** Open forests, gardens.

Garima Bhatia

Pied Cuckoo

♀ Gururaj Moorching

Gururaj Moorching

Asian Koel

Deboshree Gogoi

Asian Emerald Cuckoo

Biswarup Satpati

Banded Bay Cuckoo

Prassana Parab

Grey-bellied Cuckoo

Rejaul Karim

Violet Cuckoo

Panchami Manoo Ukil

Plaintive Cuckoo

Fork-tailed Drongo Cuckoo *Surniculus dicruroides* 23cm (r)

Smallish, mainly glossy black cuckoo, similar to drongo species, but with small, slimmer downcurved bill. Long black fork-cut tail and vent white barred, unlike those of drongos. White thighs and sometimes white nape-spot. No white rictal spot. Mostly arboreal. **Square-tailed** and **Fork-tailed** forms sometimes considered separate species. **VOICE** Diagnostic. Noisy during monsoon. Calls a short, whistled *pee … pee … pee … pee …* **DISTRIBUTION** Hills of S and SW India. Summer visitor to the Himalayas and NE India. **HABITAT** Forests, orchards.

Common Hawk-cuckoo *Hierococcyx varius* 35cm (r)

Ashy-grey above; dark bars on rufescent-tipped tail; dull white below, with pale ashy-rufous on breast; barred below. Sexes alike. Solitary. Arboreal. Noisy during May–September; silent after rains. The larger but similar **Large Hawk-cuckoo** *H. sparverioides* a common breeding summer visitor to the Himalayas and hills of NE India. **VOICE** Famous call notes; interpreted as *brain-fever* …, uttered untiringly in crescendo; also described as *pipeeha … pipeeha …*; very noisy in overcast weather. **DISTRIBUTION** Subcontinent; uncommon in arid zones. **HABITAT** Forests, open country.

Hodgson's Hawk-cuckoo *Hierococcyx nisicolor* 31cm (r)

Medium-sized, slaty-grey cuckoo with barred tail and rufous breast with white streaks, black chin and white throat. Iris red and bill has black tip and base. Distinguished by grey upperparts, whitish belly and grey head-sides. Shy and difficult to locate, but may sing incessantly in breeding season. **VOICE** Calls include series of paired, thin, sharp, high-pitched *gee … whiz*. **DISTRIBUTION** Summer visitor to E Himalayas, Assam and Arunachal Pradesh. **HABITAT** Decidous forests; winters in evergreen forests.

Lesser Cuckoo *Cuculus poliocephalus* 24cm (r)

Small cuckoo with longish curved bill. Upperparts rufous-brown, strongly barred, uniformly and regularly dark brown; adult male has broad white supercilium cross-barred with black, which encircles brown ear-coverts; dark eye-stripe; whitish cheeks; white-tipped tail. Whitish underparts, washed pale buff from belly to flanks, finely and uniformly barred; central-tail feathers barred and darker on each side of shaft. **VOICE** Shrill whistle. **DISTRIBUTION** N Uttar Pradesh, east to Assam. **HABITAT** Dense broadleaved forests, lightly wooded country, open forests.

Indian Cuckoo *Cuculus micropterus* 32cm (r)

Slaty-brown above; greyer on head, throat and breast; whitish below, with broadly spaced black cross-bars; broad subterminal tail-band; female often has rufous-brown wash on throat and breast. Sexes alike. Call notes most important identification clue. Solitary. Arboreal. The **Common Cuckoo** *C. canorus* differs by lacking subterminal black band and has diagnostic *cuck-koo* call. **VOICE** Very distinct call; four-noted mellow whistle, *bo … ko … ta … ko*. **DISTRIBUTION** Subcontinent. **HABITAT** Forests, orchards.

Chestnut-bellied Sandgrouse *Pterocles exustus* 28cm (r)

Male sandy-buff above, speckled brown and dull yellow; black gorget and chocolate-black belly. Female buffy above, streaked and barred darker; black-spotted breast; rufous and black-barred belly and flanks. Pointed central-tail feathers and black wing-underside distinctive in flight. Huge gatherings at waterholes in dry season; regularly arrives at water. Seen often on the ground. **VOICE** Deep, clucking *kut … ro …* call note, uttered mostly on the wing. **DISTRIBUTION** All India except north-east and extreme south. **HABITAT** Open areas, semi-deserts, fallow land.

Nitin Srinivasamurthy

Somnath Ghosh

Common Hawk-cuckoo (left)
Large Hawk-cuckoo (right)

Fork-tailed Drongo Cuckoo

Hodgson's Hawk-cuckoo

Biswarup Satpati

Lesser Cuckoo

Indian Cuckoo

Manjula Mathur

Chestnut-bellied Sandgrouse

Painted Sandgrouse *Pterocles indicus* 28cm 🔴

Small, blunt-tailed sandgrouse. Male has broad black-and-buff and chestnut breast-bands and black-and-white crown pattern; plain sandy head and neck; intensely barred black and white; plain sandy wing-coverts; plain underwings. Both sexes have barred upperparts and foreneck. Female has plainer face and finer barring on body, and plain greyish throat. Gregarious. **VOICE** Call a thick, clucking *wuko … wuko* in flight. **DISTRIBUTION** Scarce breeding resident mainly in dry parts of N and C India. **HABITAT** Dry, open woodland and thorn scrub.

Rock Pigeon *Columba livia* 33cm 🔴

Medium-sized blue-grey pigeon with darker head and neck and wing-bars, but interbreeds with domestic pigeons so several colour varieties possible. Basically blue-grey with green-purple sheen across neck. Wings darker and tail with black subterminal band. Some have white lower back. However, always has two long black bars across wing-coverts. Feeds in flocks on split grain and sprouting cereals. **VOICE** Deep, guttural *tru … troo … tru …* **DISTRIBUTION** Common breeding resident throughout India. **HABITAT** All types of habitats including cliffs and ruins.

Snow Pigeon *Columba leuconota* 35cm 🔴

Blackish-brown head separated from dull brown back by whitish collar; extensive white on lower back and three dark bands in grey wings, seen both at rest and in flight; very dark tail with white subterminal band; black bill and red feet. Sexes alike. Flocks of variable size glean on the ground. Flight very strong. Breeds in large colonies on cliffs and in rock caves. **VOICE** Call a high *coo … coo … coo*. **DISTRIBUTION** The Himalayas. **HABITAT** Open meadows, cultivation, mountain habitation, cliff faces.

Nilgiri Wood Pigeon *Columba elphinstonii* 42cm 🟢

Reddish-brown above; metallic purple-green on upper back. Grey head and underbody; whitish throat; black-and-white chessboard on hindneck diagnostic. Solitary or in small gatherings. Arboreal, but often descends to forest floor to pick fallen fruits. Strong flier, wheeling and turning among branches at high speed. **VOICE** Loud *whoo* call, followed by 3–5 eerie-sounding *whoo … whoo … whoo* notes. Characteristic call of Western Ghats forests. **DISTRIBUTION** Western Ghats. **HABITAT** Moist evergreen forests, sholas, cardamom plantations.

Oriental Turtle Dove *Streptopelia orientalis* 32cm 🔴 🟡

Large, stocky dove with grey-and-black spotted patch on neck-sides. Rufous-brown back and scapulars, with black markings diagnostic; slaty-grey lower back and rump; whitish border to roundish tail, best seen when tail fanned during landing. Sexes alike. In pairs or loose parties; occasionally solitary birds. Feeds mostly on the ground. Rests during hot hours in leafy branches. Perches on overhead wires. **VOICE** Call a deep and grating *ghur … ghroo …* **DISTRIBUTION** Several races, resident and migratory. **HABITAT** Mixed forests, cultivation, orchards.

Eurasian Collared Dove *Streptopelia decaocto* 32cm 🔴

Greyish-brown plumage; lilac wash about head and neck; black half-collar on hindneck diagnostic; broad whitish tips to brown tail feathers, seen as a terminal band when fanned during landing; dull lilac breast and ashy-grey underbody. Sexes alike. Occurs in small parties when not breeding. Often associates with other doves. Large gatherings glean in cultivated country. Strong flier; chases intruders in territory. **VOICE** Characteristic *kukkoo … kook …* **DISTRIBUTION** Most of Indian subcontient. **HABITAT** Cultivation, open scrub, dry forests.

Painted Sandgrouse

Rock Pigeon

Snow Pigeon

Nilgiri Wood Pigeon

Oriental Turtle Dove

Eurasian Collared Dove

Red Collared Dove *Streptopelia tranquebarica* 22cm **r**

Male has deep ashy-grey head, black hindneck-collar, rich wine-red back, and slaty grey-brown lower back, rump and uppertail. Whitish tips to all but central feathers. Female much like the Eurasian Collared Dove (p. 58), but smaller and more brownish. Solitary or in small parties; associates with other doves, but less commonly. Feeds on harvested grain and grass seeds. **VOICE** Quick, repeated *gru … gurgoo …* call, with more stress on first syllable. **DISTRIBUTION** Uncommon. All India south of the Himalayas. **HABITAT** Cultivation, scrub, deciduous country.

Spotted Dove *Streptopelia chinensis* 30cm **r**

Grey and pink-brown above, spotted white; white-spotted black hindneck-collar (chessboard) diagnostic; dark tail with broad white tips to outer feathers seen in flight; vinous-brown breast, merging into white on belly. Sexes alike. Young birds barred above and lack chessboard. Occurs in pairs or small parties on the ground; often settles on paths and roads. Quite tame and confiding. **VOICE** Soft, somewhat doleful *crook … cru … croo* or *croo … croo … croo.* **DISTRIBUTION** Subcontinent. **HABITAT** Open forests, scrub, human habitation, cultivation.

Laughing Dove *Streptopelia senegalensis* 26cm **r**

Pinkish grey-brown plumage with black-and-white chessboard on sides of foreneck; white tips to outer-tail feathers and broad grey wing-patches best seen in flight; small size distinctive. Sexes alike. Occurs in pairs or small flocks; associates freely with other doves in huge gatherings at harvest time. Feeds mostly on the ground, walking about silently. **VOICE** Harsh but pleasant *cru … do … do … do … do.* **DISTRIBUTION** Almost entire India to about 1,200m in the outer Himalayas; uncommon in NE states. **HABITAT** Open scrub, cultivation, human habitation.

Barred Cuckoo Dove *Macropygia unchall* 41cm **r**

Large, distinctive dove with slim body and large, graduated tail; reddish-brown upperparts and tail heavily barred with brown; male has paler unbarred buff head and underparts than female. Iridescent green on nape and crown; some barring on neck-sides and upper breast. Female has barring on upperparts and some iridescence on nape and neck-sides. Forest dweller, often seen flying between trees. **VOICE** Call a deep *croo … urmm.* **DISTRIBUTION** NE India. **HABITAT** Broadleaved tropical forests and secondary growth.

Asian Emerald Dove *Chalcophaps indica* 27cm **r**

Male has bronze emerald-green upperparts; white forehead and eyebrows; grey crown and neck; white on wing shoulder and across lower back; whitish rump diagnostic in flight; rich pinkish-brown below; coral-red bill and pink-red legs. Female has warm brown on crown and underparts; lacks white shouder-patch. Occurs in clearings or darts through trees. **VOICE** Deep, plaintive *hoo … oon …* **DISTRIBUTION** Subcontinent. **HABITAT** Forests, bamboo, clearings, foothills.

Orange-breasted Green Pigeon *Treron bicinctus* 29cm **r**

Fairly small green pigeon with blue eyes. Male has distinctive bright orange breast with lilac border above; face and forehead yellowish-green; nape and hindneck bluish-grey; unmarked green mantle. Female has yellower wash on underparts. Both have dark uppertail-coverts; central-tail feathers grey; light grey banding on tail; yellow-bordered wing-coverts. Gregarious, in both small and large groups, often with other fruit-eating birds. Arboreal and difficult to see. **VOICE** Typical green pigeon whistle; quiet gurgle. **DISTRIBUTION** The Himalayas, Eastern and Western Ghats. **HABITAT** Subtropical moist deciduous evergreen forests, well-wooded country.

Red Collared Dove

Spotted Dove

Laughing Dove

Barred Cuckoo Dove

Asian Emerald Dove

Orange-breasted Green Pigeon

♀

Grey-fronted Green Pigeon *Treron affinis* 28cm ⓔ

Small dark green pigeon with whitish forehead and pronounced grey crown. Face and brow greenish-yellow. Male has maroon mantle, uniform green breast, pale blue-grey cap, yellowish face and throat, and darker chestnut undertail-coverts. Female has green mantle. The similar **Ashy-headed Green Pigeon** *T. phayrei* has distinct grey crown and thin blue-grey bill, but lacks red base to bill. **VOICE** Fluty whistles. **DISTRIBUTION** Western Ghats. **HABITAT** Evergreen and moist deciduous forests.

Thick-billed Green Pigeon *Treron curvirostra* 27cm ⓡ

Medium-sized green pigeon. Male has greyish nape and crown; maroon mantle; brown undertail-coverts; broad bluish-green orbital skin; heavy, large bill with scarlet-red base. Female has greyish crown and nape; white mantle; green underparts. Gregarious and often found with other green pigeons. Primarily a forest bird, but often seen in forest fringes, gardens and plantations. **VOICE** Calls include musical whistles and a throaty *khoo … khoo*. **DISTRIBUTION** NE India. **HABITAT** Forest groves.

Yellow-footed Green Pigeon *Treron phoenicopterus* 33cm ⓡ

Male ashy olive-green above; olive-yellow collar, band in dark slaty tail; lilac-red shoulder-patch (mostly absent in female); yellow legs and underbody. Female duller than male. Nominate race has grey lower breast and belly. Occurs in small flocks. Mostly arboreal, rarely coming to salt-licks or cropland. Remains well hidden in foliage but moves briskly; has favourite feeding trees. **VOICE** Rich, mellow whistling notes. **DISTRIBUTION** Resident throughout India except the Himalayas and NW India. **HABITAT** Forests, orchards, city parks, cultivated village vicinities.

Pin-tailed Green Pigeon *Treron apicauda* 42cm ⓡ

Large green pigeon with long, pointed central feathers in grey tail; vivid yellow-green rump; green head, back and mantle; grey cast on upper mantle, stronger in male; pale yellow edges to wing-coverts. Male also has pale orange wash to breast, lacking in female. Both sexes have blue-grey around base of bill and eye. Strong flier in small numbers, often in mixed hunting parties. **VOICE** Call a soft whistling *ko … kiu … oi … oi …* **DISTRIBUTION** Uttarakhand to NE India. **HABITAT** Tropical, broadleaved and evergreen forests.

Wedge-tailed Green Pigeon *Treron sphenurus* 33cm ⓡ

Largish pigeon with distinctive, wedge-shaped tail; dark grey-green plumage on upperparts; maroon patch of male restricted to shoulders and lower mantle; grey upper mantle; pale orange crown and breast; only faint, narrow yellow edges to wing-coverts; yellowish-green face, throat and underparts. Often associates with other green pigeons. **VOICE** Call a melodious, whistling *hoo … whoo … huhuhu*. **DISTRIBUTION** Himachal Pradesh east to entire NE Indian region. **HABITAT** Subtropical broadleaved mixed forests, edges of forests.

Green Imperial Pigeon *Ducula aenea* 43cm ⓡ

Large forest pigeon, often confused with **Mountain Imperial Pigeon** *D. badia*, but smaller. Greyish head, neck and underbody with distinct pinkish wash; metallic bronze-green upperbody, unbanded tail; chocolate-maroon undertail; reddish legs. Sexes alike. Known for aerial display, repeatedly rising to dive with half-closed wings. Mainly arboreal. Strong flight. Has favourite feeding spots. **VOICE** Deep chuckling notes, quite pleasant sounding. **DISTRIBUTION** Forested parts of N India, from Garhwal terai eastwards; Western Ghats. **HABITAT** Evergreen forests.

Grey-fronted Green Pigeon

K S Seshadri

Thick-billed Green Pigeon

Ashy-headed Green Pigeon

Vinit Arora

Pin-tailed Green Pigeon

Yellow-footed Green Pigeon

Ramki Sreenivasan

Mountain Imperial Pigeon

Wedge-tailed Green Pigeon

Ramki Sreenivasan

Green Imperial Pigeon

Slaty-legged Crake *Rallina eurizonoides* 25cm 🔴r

Rich brown head, and short, rounded wings. Rufous head and breast; reddish-brown iris; bold, strong black-and-white barring on flanks, underparts and undertail; small white throat-patch, yellowish or greyish bill; greenish-grey legs. Sexes similar. Walks through leaf litter, foraging on berries, insects, worms and molluscs. **VOICE** Noisy mix of double notes. **DISTRIBUTION** All India. **HABITAT** Well-watered areas.

Water Rail *Rallus aquaticus* 25–28cm 🔴r

Brown upperparts streaked with black; dirty-white throat and chin with grey breast and belly barred black and white. Long red bill diagnostic. Young have distinct white barring on wings. Mostly solitary, although mate usually in the vicinity. Unobtrusive, secretive and cautious. Some consider the **Brown-cheeked Rail** *R. indicus* to be a separate species. **VOICE** Shrill squeal. **DISTRIBUTION** All India. **HABITAT** Marshes, reed beds, paddy cultivation, ponds.

Brown Crake *Zapornia akool* 28cm 🔴r

Darkish olive-brown upper body, wings and tail; white chin and throat fade into ashy-grey underparts; browner on breast, flanks and abdomen. Sexes alike, but female slightly smaller than male. Solitary or in pairs. Crepuscular. Very elusive and secretive. Feeds in the early mornings and late evenings on edges of jheels, flicking its stub tail and generally moving very suspiciously. **VOICE** Mostly silent, but utters a plaintive note and long-drawn, vibrating whistle. **DISTRIBUTION** Resident and local migrant. **HABITAT** Reed-covered marshes, dense growth on jheels.

White-breasted Waterhen *Amaurornis phoenicurus* 32cm 🔴r

White forehead and head-sides; dark slaty-grey above; silky-white below; slaty-grey breast-sides and flanks; rufous on vent and undertail-coverts. Sexes alike. Solitary or in small parties, often around village ponds and tanks. Jerks stumpy tail as it walks with long strides. Climbs trees easily, especially when breeding. **VOICE** Very noisy when breeding during rains; series of loud croaks and chuckles, the most common being a harsh *krr … khwakk*. **DISTRIBUTION** South from the Himalayan foothills. **HABITAT** Reed-covered marshes, ponds, tanks, cultivation, streams.

Black-tailed Crake *Zapornia bicolor* 25cm 🔴r

Small, red-legged, jungle-dwelling crake with sooty-grey head, neck and underparts; whitish chin; rufous-chestnut mantle and wings; charcoal-black rump, vent, tail and undertail-coverts. Pale green bill, sometimes with red base. Red iris. Generally shy. **VOICE** Call a low, hoarse *hraaa … hraaa … waak*. The **Ruddy-breasted Crake** *Z. fusca* has a chestnut face with dark olive-brown upperparts. **DISTRIBUTION** Isolated pockets in Nepal, Bhutan, Assam and Arunachal Pradesh. Often found at high altitudes. **HABITAT** Forests and dense undergrowth surrounding paddy fields; marshy streams, pools in or near forests, secondary growth.

Baillon's Crake *Zapornia pusilla* 19cm 🟠m

Very small crake with streaked black-and-white upperparts. Pale grey underparts that stretch from breast to around eyes. Pale green bill and legs. Sexes similar in appearance. Stout, well-muscled legs with three forwards-facing toes and one hind toe. Walks with bobbing head and flicking tail. **VOICE** Call a frog-like or grasshopper-like dry, rattling *trrr … trrr*. **DISTRIBUTION** Common breeding visitor to Kashmir. Scarce passage migrant and winter visitor throughout region. Much overlooked. **HABITAT** Marshes, reedy jheel edges, small ponds, wet paddy.

Slaty-legged Crake

Water Rail

Brown Crake

Brown-cheeked Rail

Black-tailed Crake

White-breasted Waterhen

Ruddy-breasted Crake

Baillon's Crake

Spotted Crake *Porzana porzana* 22cm 🅜

Stocky, short-billed crake with plain buff undertail-coverts. Black-flecked brown with dense white spotting on head, wings and breast, and white-barred flanks. Grey supercilia. Red-based yellow bill and green legs. White leading edge to wings in flight. Sexes similar. Larger than Baillon's Crake (p. 64) and lacks grey on underparts. **VOICE** Far-carrying, whipping *huit huit* heard mainly at night. **DISTRIBUTION** Scarce winter visitor in NW and W India and south to Karnataka. Probably overlooked. **HABITAT** Reed beds, swamps.

Watercock *Gallicrex cinerea* 36–43cm 🅡

Mainly blue-black bird; conical red bill an extended 'frontal shield'; green legs. Female smaller than male, with dark brown upperparts, and paler below with streaked and barred plumage; yellow bill and green legs. Probes mud for insects, small fish and seeds, but also picks food by sight. Secretive, but sometimes seen in the open. Crepuscular. **VOICE** Booming call when breeding. **DISTRIBUTION** Scarce local migrant throughout lowlands, breeding mainly in NE India. **HABITAT** Reed beds, marshes and wet paddy; also tidal estuaries when migrating.

Grey-headed Swamphen *Porphyrio poliocephalus* 45–50cm 🅡

Large rail with dusky black upperparts, broad dark blue collar, and dark blue to purple underparts. Strong red bill and frontal shield; orange-red scaly legs and feet. Long legs and elongated toes trail behind body in flight. Strong flier, readily taking to the wing when threatened. Proficient swimmer, but prefers to wander on edges of water, among reeds and on floating vegetation. **VOICE** Noisy when breeding, a mix of cackling and hooting notes. **DISTRIBUTION** Mostly resident. **HABITAT** Vegetation and reed-covered jheels, tanks.

Common Moorhen *Gallinula chloropus* 32cm 🅡

Medium-sized, striking looking waterbird. Distinctive red shield; short yellow bill; dark olive-brown upperparts; grey underparts; white centre of abdomen; bright yellowish-green legs; white trim on undertail. Sexes alike. Occurs in small feeding groups in marsh vegetation. Jerks head and tail while swimming. **VOICE** Very vocal; capable of bizarre, distinctive sounds, including a variety of clucks and chattering calls. **DISTRIBUTION** All India; breeds commonly in Kashmir. **HABITAT** Vegetation and reed-covered ponds, tanks, jheels.

Eurasian Coot *Fulica atra* 42cm 🅡

Slaty-black plumage; stout, ivory-white bill and flat forehead-shield distinctive. Sexes alike. Almost tailless, duck-like appearance. Gregarious; much more abundant in winter when numbers greatly augmented with winter visitors. Huge gatherings on jheels, ponds and placid stretches of rivers and other waterbodies. **VOICE** Chuckling sounds, loud *krark*. **DISTRIBUTION** All India; both resident and winter visitor. **HABITAT** Reed-fringed jheels, tanks, slow-moving rivers.

Sarus Crane *Grus antigone* 156cm 🅡 🅥

Grey plumage; naked red head and upper neck; young birds brownish-grey, with rusty-brown on head. Sexes alike, but female slightly smaller than male. Occurs in pairs, family parties or flocks, and feeds with other waterbirds. Known to pair for life and usually well protected in N and W-C India. Flies low. **VOICE** Very loud, far-reaching trumpeting, often a duet between a pair; elaborate dancing rituals. **DISTRIBUTION** Most common in N and C India. **HABITAT** Marshes, jheels, cultivation, village ponds.

Spotted Crake

Grey-headed Swamphen

Eurasian Coot

Vitraag Shah

Watercock

Kunan Naik

Common Moorhen

Nikhil Devasar

Sarus Crane

Demoiselle Crane *Grus virgo* 90–100cm ⓜ

Overall plumage grey; black head and neck; prominent white ear-tufts; long black feathers of lower neck fall over breast; brownish-grey secondaries, sickle-shaped and drooping over tail. Sexes alike. Huge flocks in winter, often numbering many thousands. Rests during hot hours on marsh edges and sandbanks. Flies en masse when disturbed. VOICE High-pitched, sonorous *kraak … kraak …* calls. DISTRIBUTION Winter visitor; most common in E Rajasthan, Gujarat and Madhya Pradesh. HABITAT Winter crop fields, sandy riverbanks, ponds, jheel edges.

Common Crane *Grus grus* 110–120cm ⓜ

Large, impressive crane with pale slaty-grey plumage; slight red on crown; black face, throat and white stripe on sides of head and neck; black flight feathers and dark, drooping tail plumes diagnostic; bright red or reddish-brown eye. Sexes alike. Gregarious in winter. Feeds in the mornings and evenings; rests by day. Rather shy and suspicious, and ever alert. Slow but strong flight. VOICE Call a loud, strident trumpeting *krr … oohk …* Calls on the ground and from high in the sky. DISTRIBUTION Arid plains of W India. HABITAT Cultivation of wheat and groundnuts.

Black-necked Crane *Grus nigricollis* 139cm ⓡ ⓥ

Ash-grey crane with black head and neck; dull red lores, complete crown; small white patch around eye; black wing-tips; drooping plumes; whitish underparts. Sexes alike; female slightly smaller than male. Occurs in pairs or small flocks; up to 100 birds seen together in Bhutan, where it is much revered by locals. Dancing displays begin around March. Flies high during the afternoons, calling loudly. VOICE Loud, trumpet-like call. DISTRIBUTION Ladakh, parts of Arunachal Pradesh. Breeds in Ladakh. HABITAT High-altitude marshes, lakesides, cultivation.

Little Grebe *Tachybaptus ruficollis* 22cm ⓡ

A small waterbird; squat and tailless. Plumage silky and compact; dark brown above; white in flight feathers; white abdomen. Sexes alike. Breeding: chestnut head-sides, neck and throat; black chin; blackish-brown crown and hindneck. Winter: white chin; brown crown and hindneck; rufous neck. Purely aquatic. Seen singly or in small groups. VOICE Shrill, trilling notes and an occasional click. DISTRIBUTION Subcontinent; resident in most areas. HABITAT Village tanks, deep jheels, lakes, reservoirs.

Great Crested Grebe *Podiceps cristatus* 46–51cm ⓡ ⓜ

Medium to large bird with long neck, long bill and distinctive black double crest. Black crown; white face; black line from bill-base to eye; dark brown wings with prominent white patches; satiny-white underparts; dark olive-green feet prominent in flight. Breeding adults of both sexes have reddish-orange head plumes, tipped black. Sexes similar. VOICE Loud, guttural croaks when breeding. DISTRIBUTION Scarce breeder in N mountains and Gujarat. Winter visitor to northern lowlands. HABITAT Large, deep open bodies of fresh water, rivers.

Greater Flamingo *Phoenicopterus roseus* 120–145cm ⓡ

Easily recognizable bird with long, thin, curved neck, long pink legs, and distinctive downwards bending pale pink bill with black tip. Rose-white plumage; red shoulders and black tips to wings; yellow eyes. Characteristic flight with legs and neck stretched to full length. Feeds in any shallow water, including estuaries, lakes, rivers and flooded fields. VOICE Assortment of cackles. DISTRIBUTION Breeds in Kutch; wanders widely throughout region. Sporadic in appearance. HABITAT Breeds on saline or brackish lagoons.

Demoiselle Crane

Common Crane

Ramki Sreenivasan

Black-necked Crane

Little Grebe

Savio Fonseca

Great Crested Grebe

Greater Flamingo

Savio Fonseca

Lesser Flamingo *Phoeniconaias minor* 80–90cm (r) (v)

Shorter and darker rose-pink than the Greater Flamingo (p. 68), with light pink bill tipped with black. Pale pink feathers with black primaries and secondaries; deep crimson legs; yellow-orange eyes with maroon ring. Feeds with long neck bent over and bill upside down in water. Spectacular courtship takes place throughout the year. Very sociable. **VOICE** Call a *murr-err*, *murr-err*. **DISTRIBUTION** Breeds in Kutch. Some wander particularly to east coast. **HABITAT** Prefers salt and brackish lagoons and salt pans.

Yellow-legged Buttonquail *Turnix tanki* 15cm (r)

Three-toed ground bird, resembling true quail. Female slightly bigger than male. Yellow legs and bill in both sexes. Male has blackish crown. Rufous and buff pale stripe through centre of crown; white chin and throat; buffy underparts with dark spots on breast-sides. Female like male with prominent rufous-orange nuchal collar. Single or in pairs, rarely forming coveys. Confirmed skulker; difficult to see. Moves amid dense, damp herbage. **VOICE** Female utters a loud drumming call. **DISTRIBUTION** All India. **HABITAT** Damp grassland, scrub, cultivation.

Barred Buttonquail *Turnix suscitator* 15cm (r)

Distinctive white eye, dark brown crown, black speck on white sides of head, and back speckled with white, black and brown. Pale buff on wing and shoulders seen in flight; diagnostic. Sexes alike; female slightly larger than male. Feeds on seeds, grains and small insects. **VOICE** Female utters a loud drumming during breeding. **DISTRIBUTION** India, south of the Himalayas. **HABITAT** Grass, scrub near cultivation, open forests.

Indian Thick-knee *Burhinus indicus* 40cm (r)

Sandy-brown plumage, streaked dark; whitish below breast; thickish head; long, bare yellow legs and large eye-goggles diagnostic; white wing-patch visible in flight. Sexes alike. Solitary or in pairs. Mostly seen on ground. Crepuscular and nocturnal. Quiet, sitting in the same patch where regularly seen. Colouration makes it difficult to spot. Squats tight or runs in short steps when disturbed. **VOICE** Plaintive, curlew-like call at dusk; also sharp *pick … pick*-like notes **DISTRIBUTION** Drier parts of India. **HABITAT** Light, dry forests, scrub, dry riverbanks, ravines, orchards, open areas.

Great Thick-knee *Esacus recurvirostris* 50cm (r) (v)

Sandy-grey above; thickset head and enormous-looking, somewhat upturned, black-and-yellow bill; large goggle eyes surrounded by white; two black bands on face; white below, washed grey on neck and breast; white in flight feathers visible in flight. Sexes alike. Solitary or in pairs. Mostly crepuscular and partly nocturnal, spending the day under strong sun, resting and usually difficult to spot. Wary, moving cautiously on approach. **VOICE** Harsh call note, somewhat whistle-like; wild, piping calls at night. **DISTRIBUTION** Almost all India except NE, where uncommon. **HABITAT** Dry open country, barren lands, riverbanks, rocky areas.

Eurasian Oystercatcher *Haematopus ostralegus* 40–46cm (m) (v)

Pied plumage. Black head, upperparts and breast; white below; long orange bill and pinkish legs distinctive. White on throat in winter. White rump and broad wing-bar conspicuous in flight. Sexes alike. Most common on sea coasts. Frequently associates with other shorebirds. Runs and probes mud; bill highly specialized for feeding on molluscs. **VOICE** Piping *kleeeep … in* flight. **DISTRIBUTION** Winter visitor, especially to coastal regions; most common on western seaboard. **HABITAT** Rocky and sandy coastal areas.

Lesser Flamingo

Yellow-legged Buttonquail

Barred Buttonquail

Indian Thick-knee

Great Thick-knee

Eurasian Oystercatcher

71

Ibisbill *Ibidorhyncha struthersii* 41cm ®

Grey wader with white belly, crimson, long, downcurved bill, black face and black breast-band. Short orange legs. Upperparts sandy-grey with short white wing-bars. Head, neck and breast lavender-grey with white-edged black crown and face, and white-and-black breast-bands. White below. Usually solitary. Wary, but loyal to favoured spots. Bobs when alarmed. Feeds on invertebrates. VOICE Call a high *ti … ti …, kluklu; wicka … tik … tik.* DISTRIBUTION Rare breeding resident in N mountains. HABITAT Pebble beds in fast-flowing rivers.

Black-winged Stilt *Himantopus himantopus* 25cm ®

Male jet-black mantle and pointed wings; rest of plumage glossy white. Female dark brown where male is black; black wing undersides; black spots on head; duller overall in winter. Very long, pink-red legs diagnostic; extend much beyond tail in flight. Gregarious; in large numbers, often with other waders in wetlands. Long legs enable it to enter relatively deep water; clumsy walk. Submerges head when feeding. VOICE Shrill notes in flight. DISTRIBUTION Resident and local migrant. HABITAT Marshes, salt pans, tidal creeks, village ponds.

Pied Avocet *Recurvirostra avosetta* 45cm ®

Black-and-white plumage, long, bluish legs and long, slender, upcurved bill diagnostic. In flight, long legs extend much beyond tail. Sexes alike. Usually gregarious. Often enters shallow water. Characteristic sideways movement of head when feeding; head is bent low as upcurved bill sweeps along bottom mud. Also swims and upends, duck-like. VOICE Loud, somewhat fluty *klooeet* or *kloeep* call. DISTRIBUTION Breeds in Kutch; winter visitor, sporadically over most parts of area. HABITAT Freshwater marshes, coastal tidal areas, creeks.

Northern Lapwing *Vanellus vanellus* 31cm ⓜ ⓥ

Striking black-and-white wader with wispy black crest, and black crown, face and cheek-stripe. Glossy upperparts with purplish-green iridescence. Orange undertail-coverts; black breast; pinkish legs and short dark bill. Rounded wings have white tips and white underwing-coverts. White tail has black tips. Sexes similar. Rarely mixes with other waders. Usually appears in parties. Relaxed, low, flapping flight. VOICE Characteristic shrill call. DISTRIBUTION Scarce winter visitor. HABITAT Wet grassland, jheels, river margins, fallow land.

River Lapwing *Vanellus duvaucelii* 30cm ® ⓥ

Black forehead, crown and crest drooping over back; sandy grey-brown above; black-and-white wings; black chin and throat, bordered white; grey-brown breast-band; white below with black patch on belly; black spur at bend of wing. Sexes alike. In pairs in close vicinity; often remains in hunched posture, when not easy to spot. Slow flight. Often swims and dives. VOICE Rather like that of the Red-wattled Lapwing (p. 74); also a sharp *deed … did … did.* DISTRIBUTION Breeds in parts of E and C India; may disperse in winter. HABITAT Stony river beds, sandbanks.

Yellow-wattled Lapwing *Vanellus malabaricus* 28cm ⓔ

Jet-black cap, bordered with white; sandy-brown upper body; black band in white tail; in flight, white bar in black wings; black chin and throat; sandy-brown breast; black band on lower breast; white below; yellow lappets above and in front of eyes and yellow legs diagnostic. Sexes alike. Solitary or in pairs; rarely small gatherings. Feeds on the ground, moving suspiciously. VOICE Quiet bird; quick-repeated notes when nest site is intruded upon. DISTRIBUTION From NW India south through area; absent from extreme NE India. HABITAT Dry, open country.

Ibisbill

Garima Bhatia

Black-winged Stilt

Pied Avocet

Biswarup Satpati

Northern Lapwing

River Lapwing

Savio Fonseca

Yellow-wattled Lapwing

Grey-headed Lapwing *Vanellus cinereus* 37cm (m)

Large, sandy-brown wader, striking in flight with extensive black wing-tips, white secondaries and black-banded white tail. Pale grey head, neck and breast; black breast-band; black-tipped yellow bill; long, spindly yellow legs; red iris and bare yellow lores. Sexes alike. Feeds in shallow water on insects, worms and molluscs. **VOICE** Rather quiet. **DISTRIBUTION** Local winter visitor to NE India; rare elsewhere in N India. **HABITAT** Open, usually wet grassland, jheel and river edges, fallow land.

Red-wattled Lapwing *Vanellus indicus* 30cm (r)

Jet-black head, neck and breast; bronze-brown upperbody; white below, continuing to broad bands up neck-sides towards eyes; fleshy crimson facial wattles diagnostic. Solitary or pairs when breeding; often large flocks in winter. Moves on open ground. Vigilant species, its loud cries heralding any new activity in an area. Feeds late into the evening. **VOICE** Calls include short, plaintive notes; quick-repeated notes when nest site intruded upon. **DISTRIBUTION** From NW India, south through country. **HABITAT** Dry, open country.

White-tailed Lapwing *Vanellus leucurus* 28cm (m)

Elegant-looking bird with unusually long, bright yellow legs. Upperparts greyish-brown tinged with pink and streaked black; pinkish-brown head and back; long dark bill; grey-white forehead and supercilium; ash-grey chin and throat, turning dark grey on breast; rusty-red ring around eye. Sexes alike. Occurs in small to medium-sized flocks, often with other waders. **VOICE** Mostly silent in winter except for an occasional soft, double-noted whistle. **DISTRIBUTION** Winter visitor. **HABITAT** Open, marshy areas; edges of lakes and jheels.

Pacific Golden Plover *Pluvialis fulva* 27cm (m)

Dumpy, short-billed wader with spangled yellowish upperparts, white supercilia and belly; overall golden-brown, with dark head and ear-coverts. Sexes similar. In breeding plumage, white extends from forehead to vent in broad band bordering black face and underparts. Juvenile similar to non-breeding adult, but with light barring on chest-sides and flanks. **VOICE** Call a distinct *tu … teep*. **DISTRIBUTION** Local winter visitor to all coasts. **HABITAT** Coastal mudflats, salt pans and grassland; inland on marshes and jheels.

Grey Plover *Pluvialis squatarola* 30cm (m)

Medium-sized, long-legged plover distinguished by large head and sturdy black bill. Upperparts dark greyish-brown with white edges; distinctive black axillaries visible beneath wings in flight. Upperparts pale grey above with fine mottling; whitish forehead and eyebrow; strongly barred white tail. Whitish underparts. Breeding adult boldly marked black and white. **VOICE** A loud, penetrating *pee-ou ee*. **DISTRIBUTION** Uncommon winter visitor to most coasts. Rare inland on passage. **HABITAT** Coastal, open mudflats. Inland on open jheels, flooded land and rivers.

Little Ringed Plover *Charadrius dubius* 16cm (r)

Sandy-brown above; white forehead; black bands on head and breast and white neck-ring diagnostic; white chin and throat; lack of wing-bar in flight and yellow legs and ring around eye additional clues. Sexes alike. In small numbers, often with other shorebirds; runs on the ground, on mud and drying jheels. Walks with characteristic bobbing gait, picking food from the ground. Flies rapidly, low over the ground, in zigzag flight. **VOICE** A *few … few …* whistle. **DISTRIBUTION** Resident and local migrant. **HABITAT** Riverbanks, tidal mudflats, estuaries, lake edges.

Grey-headed Lapwing

Red-wattled Lapwing

White-tailed Lapwing

Pacific Golden Plover

Grey Plover

Little Ringed Plover

Kentish Plover *Charadrius alexandrinus* 17cm ⓜ

One of the smallest plovers, paler than the Little Ringed Plover (p. 74), with longer legs and thinner bill. Pale grey-brown upperparts, crown and cheeks; incomplete breast-band; white underparts. Breeding male has small white forehead, black forecrown-band and slightly reddish hindcrown; black eye-band below slim white brow. Forages in a 'run and pause' rather than steady probing. **VOICE** Call a soft *dri ... ip*. **DISTRIBUTION** Common winter visitor; local breeding resident to most coasts and throughout lowlands. **HABITAT** Coastal sandflats, salt pans, sandbars.

Lesser Sand Plover *Charadrius mongolus* 19cm ⓜ

Small wading shorebird with greyish-brown upperparts, white belly and throat, and black forehead. Dark partial breast-band; brown face with slight pale eyebrow-stripe. White underwing and upperwing have prominent white wing-bars. Breeding adult has rusty-red feathers on head and black cheeks; thin black line separating reddish breast from white neck. Female duller than male. Bill short and dark, and long legs greenish-brown. **VOICE** Call a hard, repeated *tri ... ip*. **DISTRIBUTION** Common winter visitor. **HABITAT** Coastal sand and mudflats.

Greater Sand Plover *Charadrius leschenaultii* 22–2cm ⓜ

Relatively dull looking in non-breeding plumage. Dark lores, bill and upperwing; dusky ear-coverts; prominent white plumage on forehead, chin, throat and underparts, including underwing. In breeding, crown and breast turn dull brick-red, and area around ear changes to black. Chin and throat remain white throughout the year; nape and forehead greyish-brown year round. **VOICE** Call a trilling *trrr ... t*. **DISTRIBUTION** River and jheel margins in area. **HABITAT** Coastal sand and mudflats.

Greater Painted-snipe *Rostratula benghalensis* 25cm ⓡ

Polyandrous. Breeing female metallic olive above, thickly marked buff and black; buff stripe down crown-centre; chestnut throat, breast and neck-sides; white below breast. Breeding male duller overall; lacks chestnut. Sexes difficult to distinguish when not in breeding plumage. Crepuscular and nocturnal. Solitary or a few scattered birds. Feeds in squelchy mud but also moves on drier ground. Runs on landing. **VOICE** Common call a long-drawn, mellow note. **DISTRIBUTION** Resident throughout area. **HABITAT** Wet mud, marshes.

Pheasant-tailed Jacana *Hydrophasianus chirurgus* 30cm ⓡ

Male breeding plumage chocolate-brown and white; golden-yellow on hindneck. Dull brown and white. When not breeding, also has blackish necklace and lacks long tail. Very long toes diagnostic. Sexes alike. Solitary or in pairs when breeding; small flocks in winter. Purely aquatic, moving on vegetation-covered pond surfaces; unusually long toes enable it to walk on the lightest of floating leaves. **VOICE** Loud, mewing call when breeding. **DISTRIBUTION** Throughout region. **HABITAT** Ponds and jheels covered with floating vegetation.

Bronze-winged Jacana *Metopidius indicus* 30cm ⓡ

Glossy black head, neck and breast; glistening bronze-green back and wings; broad white stripe over eyes; chestnut rump and tail; long legs with massive toes distinctive. Sexes alike. Female slightly larger than male. Small gatherings during winter and summer. Keeps to leafy, floating growth on jheel beds and village tanks. Wary, moving slowly and silently. Flies low with long legs trailing. **VOICE** Loud harsh notes; also shrill piping call. **DISTRIBUTION** Most of India, except some NW regions. **HABITAT** Vegetation-covered jheels, ponds.

Kentish Plover

Lesser Sand Plover

Greater Sand Plover

Greater Painted-snipe

Pheasant-tailed Jacana

Bronze-winged Jacana

Eurasian Whimbrel *Numenius phaeopus* 43cm Ⓜ

Large shorebird with long, downcurved bill, long neck and long legs. Streaked brown upperparts, neck and breast; white belly and rump; dark brown crown; greyish line above eye, and dark brown line on eye-mask. Uses bill to probe deep in sand for invertebrates; also feeds on berries and insects. Aggressive nest protector. **VOICE** Call a trilling, usually seven-note whistle, *tee … tee … tee … tee … tee … tee … tee.* **DISTRIBUTION** Fairly common winter visitor to most coasts; rare inland. **HABITAT** Coastal muddy and rocky shores, mangroves.

Eurasian Curlew *Numenius arquata* 48cm Ⓜ Ⓥ

Large wader. Sexes alike. Sandy-brown upper body, scalloped fulvous and black; white rump and lower back; whitish below, streaked black; very long, downcurved bill. Runs on the ground, between tidemarks, occasionally venturing into very shallow water. A truly wild and wary bird, not easy to approach close. **VOICE** Famed scream; a wild, rather musical *cour … leeor cooodee …* with the first note longer. **DISTRIBUTION** Winter visitor; sea coasts, west to east; large inland marshes, rivers. **HABITAT** Estuaries, creeks, large remote marshes.

Bar-tailed Godwit *Limosa lapponica* 35cm Ⓜ Ⓥ

Large wader with long neck, bill and legs. Wedge-shaped white rump-patch and no wing-bars. Stockier than the Black-tailed Godwit (below), with shorter, slightly upturned bill and shorter legs. Size varies; female and eastern race larger. Non-breeding adult finely streaked brown above and on head and neck; latter turns rich orange, as do all underparts, when breeding. Back turns darker and wing-coverts silvery-grey. **VOICE** Rather quiet. Call a soft *kik … kik*. **DISTRIBUTION** Scarce winter visitor; most common on NW coasts. **HABITAT** Coastal; favours open mudflats.

Black-tailed Godwit *Limosa limosa* 40cm Ⓜ Ⓥ

Grey-brown above; whitish below; very long, straight bill; in flight, broad white wing-bars, white rump and black tail-tip distinctive. Sexes alike, but female slightly larger than male. Gregarious; often with other large waders. Quite active, probing with long bill. Wades in water, with long legs often barely visible. Fast and graceful, low flight. **VOICE** Occasional fairly loud *kwika … kwik*. **DISTRIBUTION** Winter visitor, fairly common over N India; lesser numbers towards E and S India. **HABITAT** Marshes, estuaries, creeks.

Ruddy Turnstone *Arenaria interpres* 22cm Ⓜ

Stocky, short-billed wader with distinctive pied underpart patterns visible in flight. Non-breeding birds mottled brown above with blackish breast-patch. Wedge-shaped bill and short orange legs. When breeding, upperparts rich chestnut and black, and head patterned black, grey and white. **VOICE** Rapid *tuka … tuk … tuk* in flight. **DISTRIBUTION** Scarce winter visitor to most coasts, rocky coasts and sandy flats on large rivers. **HABITAT** Mostly rocky coasts and sandy flats by large rivers.

Ruff *Calidris pugnax* 32cm Ⓜ

Medium-sized wader with long neck, small head, rather short, slightly droopy bill and medium-long orange or reddish legs. Non-breeding adult has scalloped brown-grey upperparts. Breeding male has striking ruff ranging from black or brown to orange or white, with pronounced black stripes and ear-tufts. Shows white 'U' on tail, separating dark rump and dark tail-tip in flight. **VOICE** Usually silent. **DISTRIBUTION** Abundant winter visitor mainly to W and S parts of India. **HABITAT** Marshes, jheels, stubble, cultivation, mudflats, salt pans.

Eurasian Whimbrel

Niranjan Sant

Eurasian Curlew

Bar-tailed Godwit

Manjula Mathur

Black-tailed Godwit

Ruddy Turnstone

Panchami Manoo Ukil

Ruff

Curlew Sandpiper *Calidris ferruginea* 21cm ⓜ ⓥ

Very similar to the Dunlin (below), but larger and more slender, with longer bill, neck and legs, and divided eyebrow-stripe. Obvious downcurved bill; bright white rump, white wing-stripe and white chin. Non-breeding adult greyer with distinct white supercilium. Toes extend beyond tail-tip in flight. In mixed flocks with other waders. Feeds mainly on insects and small invertebrates and worms. **VOICE** Call a trilling *chirrup* in flight. **DISTRIBUTION** Common winter visitor to most coasts. **HABITAT** Coastal mud, sandflats, salt pans, muddy jheels, sandy rivers.

Temminck's Stint *Calidris temminckii* 13–15cm ⓜ

Tiny, rather plain wader with short, fine, slightly downcurved bill and pale yellowish legs; rather parallel posture. Non-breeding adult has more uniform grey-brown upperparts, grey on breast and white underparts. Darker black-and-brown patterning on upperparts in breeding adult, with darker head and breast. In flight, differs from other stints by white outer-tail feathers. Fairly gregarious. Occurs singly or in small scattered flocks. **VOICE** High, trilling *ttrrr*. **DISTRIBUTION** All India. **HABITAT** Inland freshwater wetlands, fields, mudflats, marshes.

Sanderling *Calidris alba* 20cm ⓜ

Small, active shorebird with short, stout black bill and black legs that lack hind-toe. Breeding adult has cinnamon-red upperparts; head and breast mottled black and white. Non-breeding adult largely white; pale grey upperparts; pure white underparts; distinct dark shoulder-patch; broad white wing-bar bordered black. Sexes similar. **VOICE** Call a metallic *plit*. **DISTRIBUTION** Local winter visitor to most coasts; very rare inland. **HABITAT** Almost entirely restricted to sandy coasts.

Dunlin *Calidris alpina* 16–22cm ⓜ

Medium-sized sandpiper with bright reddish upperparts, black belly and long, drooping bill. Relatively short neck and long blackish legs. Breeding adult has black belly, and rufous back and crown. Non-breeding adult overall dull brownish-grey with whitish belly; black bill and legs. Slightly hunched appearance. **VOICE** Call a trilling *creep* in flight. **DISTRIBUTION** Locally common winter visitor to most coasts. Most common in NW India. Rare inland. **HABITAT** Coastal mudflats; inland on sandy rivers and muddy jheels.

Little Stint *Calidris minuta* 14cm ⓜ

Tiny wader. In breeding plumage, edges of back feathers, flanks and cheeks rusty-red with darker mottling; white underparts. Dark and split cap; white supercilium. Short, straight and narrow-tipped bill. Thin wing-bars. Juveniles distinct white 'V' on back, prominent in flight. White lengthways stripes on back and grey on tail feathers diagnostic. Black legs, bill and iris. Sexes similar. Swift flight. **VOICE** Call a piercing, repeated *stit … it*. **DISTRIBUTION** Abundant winter visitor. **HABITAT** Coastal mudflats, salt pans, shallow open fresh water, muddy lakes.

Eurasian Woodcock *Scolopax rusticola* 33–38cm ⓜ

Medium to small wader with intricately patterned reddish-brown upperparts and buff underparts; long, straight bill; head barred black; eyes set far back on head to give better vision. Rounded wings; bill-base flesh coloured with dark tip; legs vary from grey to pinkish. Probes the ground for food with long bill. Crepuscular; rarely active by day. Secretive and shy; difficult to see unless flushed. **VOICE** Usually silent. **DISTRIBUTION** Breeds in the Himalayas. **HABITAT** Dense forests.

Curlew Sandpiper

Temminck's Stint

Savio Fonseca

Sanderling

Dunlin

Manjula Mathur

Little Stint

Eurasian Woodcock

Ranjan Barthakur

Common Snipe *Gallinago gallinago* 28cm (r) (m)

Cryptic-coloured marsh bird; brownish-buff, heavily streaked and marked buff, rufous and black; dull white below. Sexes alike. Fast, erratic flight; whitish wing-lining distinctive, but not easily seen. Difficult to see unless flushed. Probes with long bill in mud. The similar **Pin-tailed Snipe** G. *stenura* has less pointed wings than Common's. Shorter tail and flatter flight path. VOICE Loud call when flushed. DISTRIBUTION Breeds in parts of the W Himalayas; winter visitor over subcontinent. HABITAT Marshland, paddy cultivation, jheel edges.

Terek Sandpiper *Xenus cinereus* 24cm (m)

Resembles the Common Sandpiper (below), but has long bill with dull yellow to orange base, visibly upcurved. Brownish-grey upperparts; grey face; neck and breast speckled pale grey, but other underparts white. White trailing edges to wings; black lengthways stripe over each wing. Orange legs; blackish-brown eyes. Sexes alike. VOICE Call a ringing *twoot … wee … wee*. DISTRIBUTION Rather scarce winter visitor to both coasts. HABITAT Muddy coasts, mangroves; when inland, mostly on sandy rivers or muddy jheels.

Common Sandpiper *Actitis hypoleucos* 20cm (r) (m)

Small sandpiper with markedly contrasting plumage, short bill, and brown upperparts with bib-like brown breast; white underparts with clear white sides to breast diagnostic; white eye-ring and supercilia; characteristic parallel or horizontal posture. Bobs rear end while feeding. In flight, white wing-bar, brown rump, tail centre, white sides to tail, low, quick, flick-flick-glide on bent wings distinctive. Solitary. Feeds by running along the water's edge VOICE Piping, trilling *tee … tee … tee*. DISTRIBUTION All India. HABITAT Stony mountain streams, coasts, wetlands.

Green Sandpiper *Tringa ochropus* 23cm (m)

Medium-sized sandpiper, similar to the Wood Sandpiper (p. 84), but larger and stockier; shorter legs; darker and less spotted back; more uniform white flanks. Overall brown and spotted white; blackish underwings and tail have broad black lateral stripes; white rump square. Wings dark above and below; tail white; indistinct eye-stripe; black bill with reddish base; dark brown eyes with white eye-ring. VOICE Call a ringing *tlu … eet … weet*. DISTRIBUTION Widespread winter visitor. HABITAT Well-vegetated pools, streams, mangroves, village ponds.

Common Redshank *Tringa totanus* 23cm (r) (m)

Grey-brown above; whitish below, faintly marked about breast; white rump; broad band along trailing edges of wings; orange-red legs and bill-base. In summer, browner above, marked black and fulvous, and more heavily streaked below. Sexes alike. Occurs in small flocks with other waders. Makes short dashes, probing and jabbing deep in mud. Rather alert and suspicious bird. VOICE Quite musical, fairly loud and shrill *tleu … ewh … ewh*. DISTRIBUTION Breeds in Kashmir, Ladakh; winter visitor all over. HABITAT Marshes, creeks, estuaries.

Marsh Sandpiper *Tringa stagnatilis* 23cm (m)

Distinctive wader with long, needle-like bill and very long greenish legs. Non-breeding adult has greyish-brown upperparts and white underparts; grey crown and hindneck; white eyebrow. Dark outer wing and slightly lighter inner wing. White wedge on lower back and rump visible in flight. Feeds upright with slow, graceful movements, breaking into quick dashes. VOICE Rather quiet. Call a briefly repeated *klew*. DISTRIBUTION Common winter visitor throughout lowlands. HABITAT Shallow freshwater jheels, village ponds, wet paddy, river shoals.

Common Snipe

Manjula Mathur

Terek Sandpiper

Pin-tailed Snipe

Sumit Sen

Common Sandpiper

Green Sandpiper

Common Redshank

Manjula Mathur

Marsh Sandpiper

Wood Sandpiper *Tringa glareola* 20cm Ⓜ

Grey-brown above, closely spotted with white; slender build; white rump and tail; white below; brown on breast; no wing-bar. Summer: dark olive-brown above, spotted white. Sexes alike. Occurs in small to medium-size flocks, often with other waders. Quite active, probing deep into mud or feeding at edge. **VOICE** Noisy; somewhat metallic *chiff ... chiff* calls when flushed; sometimes a loud, sharp *thuie ...* call. **DISTRIBUTION** Winter visitor to most of area. **HABITAT** Wet cultivation, marshes, tidal creeks, mudflats.

Spotted Redshank *Tringa erythropus* 33cm Ⓜ

Slightly larger, slimmer and longer legged than the Common Redshank (p. 82). No wing-bars; long, cigar-shaped white patch on back between wings, extending to rump; long red legs. Non-breeding adult has light grey, speckled upperparts and whitish underparts; paler head and neck with short white supercilium. Red lower mandible; downcurved. Breeding adult has black underparts, head and neck; dark grey upperparts, spotted white. **VOICE** Noisy. Call an explosive *chew ... it*. **DISTRIBUTION** Common winter visitor in lowlands. **HABITAT** Marshes jheels, rivers.

Common Greenshank *Tringa nebularia* 32cm Ⓜ

Medium-sized, slim wader with dark grey back and white underparts. Diagnostic long, greyish-green legs; slightly upturned, blackish-grey bill. Long neck; white rump extends into distinctive white wedge up back, visible in flight; grey streaking on head and neck; whitish tail. Breeding adult heavily streaked, spotted darker on upperparts, head, neck and upper breast. **VOICE** Call a wild, ringing *tew ... tew ... tew*. **DISTRIBUTION** Winter visitor, fairly common over most of region. **HABITAT** Marshes, estuaries.

Crab-plover *Dromas ardeola* 41cm Ⓜ

Distinctly patterned, large, ungainly wader. Overall black and white with long bluish legs; heavy, straight black bill; large white head with black-edged eye; short grey tail. Juvenile more uniform grey-brown than adult. Feeds in plover-like manner, scattered over flats or among exposed reefs, mainly on crabs but also on mudskippers. Nests in deep burrows in sandbanks. Feeds at low tide. Often confiding. **VOICE** Call a goose-like, honking *qurk ... qurk ... qurk*. **DISTRIBUTION** Very rare outside Gujarat, where regular. **HABITAT** Sandy coasts, reefs.

Indian Courser *Cursorius coromandelicus* 36cm Ⓡ Ⓥ

Bright rufous crown; white-and-black stripes above and through eyes to nape; sandy-brown above; chestnut throat and breast; black belly; long whitish legs; in flight, dark underwings. Sexes alike. Small parties occur in open country. Strictly a ground bird; runs in short spurts and feeds on the ground, suddenly dipping body when disturbed. Flies strongly for short distances. **VOICE** Soft, hen-like clucking call in flight. **DISTRIBUTION** South of the Himalayas, but distribution rather patchy; absent in NE. **HABITAT** Open scrub, fallow land, dry cultivation.

Oriental Pratincole *Glareola maldivarum* 25cm Ⓡ

Medium-sized, short-legged wader with long, narrow wings and short, forked tail. Almost identical to the **Collared Pratincole** G. *pratincola*, except brown on breast extends down to belly and merges into the white, and tail-tips shorter than wing-tips. In flight, much less contrast above and no white trailing edges. Sexes alike. Long, narrow wings. **VOICE** Tern-like *krek krek* in flight. **DISTRIBUTION** Locally common breeding resident and local migrant. **HABITAT** Open bare mud, near dry jheels; favours river sandbanks. Nests on bare ground.

Wood Sandpiper

Commom Greenshank

Indian Courser

Spotted Redshank

Arpit Deomurari

Crab-plover

Manjula Mathur

Oriental Pratincole

Panchami Manoo Ukil

Collared Pratincole

Arpit Deomurari

Small Pratincole *Glareola lacteal* 16–19cm **r**

Small, sandy-grey, short-legged wader; smallest of Indian pratincoles; striking black-and-white wing patterns in flight. Shallow-forked, squarer tail distinctive; red bill-base; black lores, buff tinge on cheeks and throat of breeding male; black-banded tail. Gregarious and mostly crepuscular. Hawks swarming insects over water. **VOICE** Shrill, harsh *tir … trit … tir … trit … tir … trit …; tuk . tuk*. **DISTRIBUTION** All India. **HABITAT** Sandy banks of large, broad rivers, lakes, marshes, wet cultivation, estuaries and mudflats.

Indian Skimmer *Rynchops albicollis* 40cm **r** **v**

Diagnostic yellowish-orange bill, with much longer lower mandible; slender, pointed wings; tern-like pied plumage, blackish-brown above, contrasting with white underbody; white forehead, neck-collar and wing-bar; red legs. Sexes alike. Characteristic hunting style, skimming over calm water, bill wide open, with longer projecting lower mandible partly submerged at an angle to snap up fish. Many rest together on sandbars. **VOICE** Call a shrill scream; twittering cries at nest colony. **DISTRIBUTION** N and C India. Uncommon. **HABITAT** Large rivers.

Slender-billed Gull *Chroicocephalus genei* 43cm **m**

Distinguished by remarkably long and slender, blood-red bill, very flat forehead, pale iris and long neck. Breeding adult usually has strong pink wash on underparts. Very similar to the Black-headed Gull (below), but lacks black hood in summer. Pale grey body; white head and breast; black tips to primary wing feathers. Dark red legs; yellow iris. Flies above the water's surface, diving on prey; probes mud for invertebrates. **VOICE** Slightly deeper than that of Black-headed. **DISTRIBUTION** Winter visitor to India. **HABITAT** Coasts, lagoons, estuaries, tidal creeks.

Brown-headed Gull *Chroicocephalus brunnicephalus* 42cm **r** **m**

Slightly larger than the Black-headed Gull (below). Summer adult has pale brown head, pearl-grey body, chocolate-brown partial hood, and red bill and legs. In non-breeding adult, mask reduced to brown ear-patch. Black-tipped primary wing feathers have large, conspicuous white spots; grey underwing; black flight feathers. Sexes alike. Light, easy flight. Swims buoyantly. Very gregarious; often with Black-headed. **VOICE** Call a deep *kraaa*. **DISTRIBUTION** Breeds in Ladakh. Common winter visitor to coasts; sometimes inland. **HABITAT** Coasts, rivers, lakes.

Black-headed Gull *Chroicocephalus ridibundus* 45cm **m**

Winter, when in India, greyish-white plumage; dark ear-patches; white outer flight feathers with black tips. Summer breeding: coffee-brown head and upper neck, sometimes acquired just before migration. Sexes alike. Highly gregarious. In large flocks on sea coasts, scavenges in harbours, and wheels over busy seaside roads and beaches. Large numbers rest on rocky ground and sand; follows boats in harbours. **VOICE** Noisy; querulous *kree … ah …* screams. **DISTRIBUTION** Winter visitor to seaboard; also strays inland. **HABITAT** Sea coasts, harbours, refuse dumps.

Gull-billed Tern *Gelochelidon nilotica* 38cm **m**

Big tern with stout black bill and long black legs. Bull-necked, gull-like mien. In breeding plumage has sleek black cap, reduced to black patch behind eye in non-breeding plumage. Pale grey above, including rump and tail. Dark trailing edges to primaries noticeable in flight. Sexes alike. Hawks for flying insects, often over dry land, but also picks fish from the water's surface. Nests on the ground. **VOICE** Normally quiet, but sometimes utters a guttural *gerr … erk*.

DISTRIBUTION All India. **HABITAT** Rivers, jheels, coasts, beaches, estuaries.

Small Pratincole

Indian Skimmer

Slender-billed Gull

Brown-headed Gull

Black-headed Gull

Gull-billed Tern

Caspian Tern *Hydroprogne caspia* 53cm 🅜

Large, gull-like tern with white body and black cap. Large, thick, brilliant red bill with black band near yellow tip. Breeding adult has black crown that becomes speckled white in non-breeding season. Pale grey upperparts; blackish outer primaries visible in flight. Juvenile has blackish crown, and black edging to back feathers. Sexes alike. Heavy, strong and determined flier. **VOICE** Call a deep, heron-like *kaarrh* in flight. **DISTRIBUTION** Migrant populations are widespread. Breeds in Gujarat. **HABITAT** Coasts, large rivers, lakes.

Greater Crested Tern *Thalasseus bergii* 47cm 🅡

Robust, dark grey-backed marine tern with powerful greenish-yellow bill. Heavily built, with dark grey upperparts and blackish wing-tips. Always has white forehead. Shaggy black cap in breeding plumage; black cap reduced in non-breeding plumage. Dark legs. Sexes alike. The **Lesser Crested Tern** *T. bengalensis* is paler grey above and has thinner orange bill. **VOICE** Coarse *kerrick*. **DISTRIBUTION** Local resident of W and S Indian coasts. **HABITAT** Seen mostly offshore, where it nests on islets.

Little Tern *Sternula albifrons* 23cm 🅡

Tiny tern with white forehead and black-tipped yellow bill. Pale grey back and wings with dark outer primaries. Forehead-patch extends to above eye. Yellow legs. In non-breeding, black bill and black crown reduced. Sexes alike. The **Sooty Tern** *Onychoprion fuscatus* is a larger black tern with white underparts, forehead and tail-streamers. **VOICE** High-pitched *kirik … kirik*. **DISTRIBUTION** Local breeder on N and S Indian coasts. Disburses widely in non-breeding season. **HABITAT** Sandy coasts, large rivers, lakes.

River Tern *Sterna aurantia* 35–38cm 🅡 🆅

Very light grey above; jet-black cap and nape when breeding; white below; narrow, pointed wings; deeply forked tail; bright yellow, pointed bill and red legs diagnostic. In winter, black on crown and nape reduced to flecks. Sexes alike. Solitary or in small flocks, flying about erratically. Keeps to riversides, calm waters and large tanks; rests on riverbanks. Noisy and aggressive, especially at nesting colonies. **VOICE** Occasional harsh, screeching note. **DISTRIBUTION** Most of India. **HABITAT** Inland waterbodies, rivers, tanks; almost completely absent on sea coasts.

Common Tern *Sterna hirundo* 35cm 🅡

Medium-sized pale tern with greyish wash to underparts and black-tipped red bill. Mantle and wings pale grey, contrasting with white rump and white, deeply forked tail. In flight shows darker tips to primaries. Black cap confined to hindcrown on breeding plumage and underparts whiter. Feeds by plunge diving. Non-breeding birds and juveniles have mottled heads. Sexes alike. **VOICE** Loud, harsh *kirrah … kirah*. **DISTRIBUTION** Both coasts of India. **HABITAT** Coastal and sometimes inland lakes and rivers.

Whiskered Tern *Chlidonias hybrida* 26cm 🅡

Black markings on crown; silvery-grey-white plumage; long, narrow wings and slightly forked, almost squarish tail; short red legs and red bill distinctive. Summer: jet-black cap and snow-white cheeks; black belly. Sexes alike. Large numbers fly about a marsh or tidal creek, leisurely but methodically, with bills pointed down. Also hunts flying insects over standing crops. **VOICE** Sharp, wild notes. **DISTRIBUTION** Breeds in Kashmir and Gangetic Plain; common in winter over area. **HABITAT** Inland marshes, wet cultivation, coastal areas, tidal creeks.

Caspian Tern

Greater Crested Tern

Dick Daniels

Little Tern

Lesser Crested Tern

Nikhil Devasar

Sooty Tern

River Tern

Manjula Mathur

Common Tern

Whiskered Tern

Panchami Manoo Ukil

89

Wilson's Storm-petrel *Oceanites oceanicus* 16–18cm (m)

Small, overall blackish-brown seabird with dark underparts and white rump. Pale wing-panels; long legs extend beyond feet in flight. Difficult to spot unless close. Often hovers over the water's surface, feeding. In small, loose groups; dense flocks seen feeding or resting on water. Distinctive fluttering and hovering flight, with wings held high. **VOICE** Peeping sound while feeding. **DISTRIBUTION** Breeds in Antarctica and distributed across all oceans in non-breeding season. Most common around SW India. **HABITAT** Seen offshore, sometimes seen from land.

Painted Stork *Mycteria leucocephala* 95cm (r) (v)

White plumage; blackish-green and white wings; blackish-green breast-band and black tail; rich rosy-pink wash on greater wing-coverts; large, slightly curved, orangish-yellow bill. Sexes alike. Common and gregarious. Feeds with bill partly submerged, ready to grab prey. When not feeding, settles hunched up outside water. Regularly soars high on thermals. **VOICE** Characteristic mandible clattering of storks. **DISTRIBUTION** Resident and local migrant. **HABITAT** Inland marshes, jheels; occasionally riversides.

Asian Openbill *Anastomus oscitans* 76–81cm (r)

Smallest stork in region. Breeding adult has white plumage, lightly washed with smoky-grey; glistening purplish-greenish black on wings and tail. Non-breeding adult grey; black scapulars, flight feathers and tail; white or grey head; characteristic open bill formed by hollow in lower mandible; pinkish-grey bill; greyish-pink lores; pink to red legs. Sexes similar. Feeds in rice fields and marshes in fresh water. **VOICE** Call a mournful *hoo-hoo*. **DISTRIBUTION** Locally common breeding resident. **HABITAT** Large wetlands; rare on coast.

Black Stork *Ciconia nigra* 95–100cm (r)

Similar to the **European White Stork** *C. ciconia*, but sturdier with wider wings. Long neck, bill and legs; short tail; black upperparts with varying green-and-purple gloss; white breast and belly; scarlet-red bill and legs, brighter in breeding and more brownish in non-breeding. Flies with neck and legs extended; white triangles on underwings visible in flight. Sexes alike, although male larger than female. Secretive. **VOICE** Voiceless. **DISTRIBUTION** Scarce winter visitor mainly to N India. **HABITAT** Prefers undisturbed, open forests and woodland, to 2,000–2,500m.

Woolly-necked Stork *Ciconia episcopus* 75–92cm (r) (v)

Large black-and-white stork with red legs; glossy black crown, back and breast; huge wings, the black parts having distinct purplish-green sheen; white neck, lower abdomen and undertail-coverts; long, stout black bill, occasionally tinged crimson. Sexes alike. In young birds, glossy black replaced by dark brown. Solitary or in small, scattered parties, feeding with other storks, ibises and egrets. **VOICE** Only clattering of mandibles. **DISTRIBUTION** Resident; subcontinent. **HABITAT** Marshes, cultivation, wet grassland.

Black-necked Stork *Ephippiorhynchus asiaticus* 140cm (r) (v)

Largest stork in region. Unmistakable, massive black bill. Overall white with glossy greenish-black head, wing-bar and tail. Iridescent purple-tinted green-blue neck; coral-red legs. White wings with broad band along length, conspicuous in flight. Sexes identical except for iris, which is yellow in female, brown in male. Occurs singly or in pairs; sometimes in family groups. Shy and wary. **VOICE** Voiceless, but clatters mandibles. **DISTRIBUTION** Increasingly rare breeding resident throughout Indian lowlands. **HABITAT** Wetlands.

Wilson's Storm-petrel

Painted Stork

Black Stork

Asian Openbill

European White Stork

Woolly-necked Stork

Black-necked Stork

Lesser Adjutant *Leptoptilos javanicus* 110–120cm 🔴 🔵

Adult has dark slaty blue-black upperparts and white underparts; white neck-base. Black underwing and undertail; bare pinkish-orange neck, with sparse grey feathers; bony plate on top of head; long, thick bill greyish to horn coloured; pale blue-grey eyes and legs. Characteristic hunched posture. Solitary and shy. Feeds on aquatic animals. **VOICE** Usually silent. **DISTRIBUTION** Globally threatened, rare, but widespread breeding resident throughout lowlands. **HABITAT** Wet areas such as mangroves, mudflats, marshes.

Greater Adjutant *Leptoptilos dubius* 150cm 🔴 🔵

Tall, greyish-white stork with almost prehistoric appearance. Breeding male has bare red head and neck (yellowish-brown in non-breeding). Large pale pink bill; pendulous gular pouch; silvery-grey wing-band and thick white neck ruff; white underparts. Dark legs. Erects nest of sticks in canopy of large trees. Sometimes eats injured ducks and carrion. **VOICE** Silent, apart from croaks and bill clattering. **DISTRIBUTION** Globally threatened and now very rare except in Assam. **HABITAT** Marshes, jheels, cultivation, urban refuse dumps.

Little Cormorant *Microcarbo niger* 50cm 🔴

Smallest and most common cormorant; short, thick neck and head distinctive; lacks gular patch. Sexes alike. Breeding adult has black plumage with blue-green sheen; silky white feathers on forecrown and sides of head; silvery grey wash on upper back and wing-coverts, speckled with black. Non-breeding adult has white chin and upper throat. Gregarious. Swims with only head and short neck exposed. Dives often. Basks with wings spread open. **VOICE** Mostly silent. **DISTRIBUTION** All India, south of the Himalayas. **HABITAT** Rivers, jheels, lakes and coasts.

Indian Cormorant *Phalacrocorax fuscicollis* 63cm 🔴

Small to medium-sized cormorant with a hooked, slender bill. Mainly black in breeding season, with white neck-plumes and whitish throat. Silvery wing-coverts; longish tail; white ear-tufts, blue eyes. White-flecked feathers on neck, blackish gular pouch and no crest. Sexes alike. Gregarious. Often found in large bodies of water and rivers. Feeds in shallow water. **VOICE** Harsh croaks at nest. **DISTRIBUTION** Throughout region. Locally common breeding resident. **HABITAT** Large freshwater wetlands, marshes, estuaries, brackish tidal creeks, mangrove swamps.

Great Cormorant *Phalacrocorax carbo* 80–100cm 🔴

Breeding adult has black plumage with metallic blue-green sheen; white facial skin and throat; bright yellow gular pouch and white thigh-patches; silky white plumes on head and neck. Non-breeding adult has no white thigh-patches; gular pouch less bright. Sexes alike. Aquatic. Gregarious species. Dives underwater in search of fish. **VOICE** Usually slient. **DISTRIBUTION** Resident in most areas of subcontinent. **HABITAT** Jheels, lakes, mountain torrents; occasionally coastal lagoons.

Oriental Darter *Anhinga melanogaster* 90cm 🔴 🔵

Long, snake-like neck, pointed bill and stiff, fan-shaped tail confirm identity. Adult black above, streaked and mottled with silvery-grey on back and wings; chocolate-brown head and neck; white stripe down sides of upper neck; white chin and upper throat; entirely black below. Highly specialized feeder. Swims low in the water with only head and neck uncovered, spearing a fish with sudden rapier-like thrusts. **VOICE** Loud croaks and squeaks. **DISTRIBUTION** Subcontinent, south of the Himalayan foothills. **HABITAT** Freshwater lakes, jheels.

Lesser Adjutant

Greater Adjutant

Tripta Sood

Little Cormorant

Indian Cormorant

Garima Bhatia

Great Cormorant

Oriental Darter

Nikhil Devasar

Black-headed Ibis *Threskiornis melanocephalus* 75cm (r) (v)

White plumage; naked black head; long, curved black bill; blood-red patches seen on underwing and flanks in flight. Breeding birds have long plumes over neck; some slaty-grey in wings. Sexes alike. In young, head and neck feathered; only face and patch around eye naked. Gregarious; feeds with storks, spoonbills, egrets and other ibises. Moves actively in water, with long, curved bill held partly open and head partly submerged as it probes nutrient-rich mud. **VOICE** Loud, booming call. **DISTRIBUTION** Resident; subcontinent. **HABITAT** Marshes, riversides.

Red-naped Ibis *Pseudibis papillosa* 68cm (r)

Glossy dark plumage; blackish-green, downcurved bill; red warts on naked black head; white shoulder-patch; brick-red legs. Sexes alike. Occurs in small parties. Spends most time on drier edges of marshes and jheels. When feeding in shallow water, often feeds with other ibises, storks and spoonbills. **VOICE** Loud 2–3-note nasal screams, uttered in flight. **DISTRIBUTION** Resident; NW India, east through Gangetic Plain; south to Karnataka. **HABITAT** Cultivated areas, edges of marshes.

Glossy Ibis *Plegadis falcinellus* 55–65cm (r)

Dark wading bird with long legs and decurved bill. Breeding adult chestnut with green-and-purple gloss; naked grey facial skin; pale blue lines border front part of face; brown eyes and bill; grey legs with red knee joints. Flies with neck and legs outstretched. Feeds in shallow water or marshy wetlands on small fish, aquatic insects, molluscs and frogs. **VOICE** Usually silent. **DISTRIBUTION** Fairly common but local breeding resident. Most frequent in N and W India. **HABITAT** All types of shallow fresh water, particularly with floating vegetation.

Eurasian Spoonbill *Platalea leucorodia* 80–93cm (r)

Snowy-white bird with long, spoon-shaped black bill and long, blackish legs. Breeding adult has orangish-yellow tip on bill, crest and yellow breast-patch. Sexes alike. Immature has paler bill than adults, and black wing-tips. Flies with neck and legs outstretched, with flapping movements interspersed with gliding. Feeds on aquatic animals by sweeping bill from side to side through water. **VOICE** Mandible clattering; short grunts when breeding. **DISTRIBUTION** Locally common breeding resident. **HABITAT** Shallow wetlands, marshes, rivers.

Yellow Bittern *Ixobrychus sinensis* 35–38cm (r)

Small bittern with dull yellowish-brown upperparts and whitish underparts streaked darker from chin to belly. Short neck; longish bill. Crown, short crest and nape black marked with buff; orangish-brown on sides of face, head and neck; deeper rufous on hindneck, greyer on forehead and supercilium; white undertail- and underwing-coverts; black tail. Solitary and usually seen in feeding flights. The **Little Bittern** *I. minutus* is common in the Kahsmir valley. **VOICE** Male's breeding call a quiet *uu … uu*. **DISTRIBUTION** Rather local breeding resident. Monsoon breeding visitor to NW India. **HABITAT** Reed beds, wet scrub.

Cinnamon Bittern *Ixobrychus cinnamomeus* 36–38cm (r)

Solitary, crepuscular bittern, overall cinnamon with darker crown. Sides of face, mantle, back and tail paler and tinged with pink; underparts rich buffy-brown with dark reddish-black central streaks down middle from chin to belly. Chin and throat whitish. Flanks pale cinnamon; vent and undertail-coverts pale buffy-brown. **VOICE** Male's breeding call a loud *kok … kok*. **DISTRIBUTION** Eastern coast, NE India, Indo-Gangetic Plain and C India. **HABITAT** Reeds in marshes.

Black-headed Ibis

Red-naped Ibis

Biswarup Sarpati

Glossy Ibis

Eurasian Spoonbill

Kunan Naik

Yellow Bittern

Little Bittern

Cinnamon Bittern

Vaidehi Gunjal

Black Bittern *Ixobrychus flavicollis* 58cm **r**

Medium-sized heron with diagnostic yellow neck-stripe. Male has dull black upperparts; buff streaks on throat; rufous-streaked, black and grey belly. Female paler than male, with more yellowish wash on underparts. Immature more streaked; upperpart feathers have buff fringes. Crepuscular, solitary and very secretive. May fly quite high to feeding sites. **VOICE** Characteristic booming call. **DISTRIBUTION** Scarce breeding resident. **HABITAT** Reed beds with bushes, and bushy margins of canals, rivers, jheels.

Black-crowned Night Heron *Nycticorax nycticorax* 58–72cm **r**

Stocky heron with short neck and legs. Black cap, upper back and scapulars; grey wings, rump and tail; stout black bill; blood-red iris; pink legs in breeding birds; creamy-white underparts. Sexes alike. Juvenile buff spotted and streaked brown. Social; nests colonially on trunks or forks of branches. **VOICE** Call a harsh raucous *quak quak*, mostly in flight. **DISTRIBUTION** Locally common breeding resident throughout lowlands. **HABITAT** All wetland types, including paddy.

Striated Heron *Butorides striata* 45cm **r**

Grey, black and dark metallic green heron. Slaty-grey above, with glossy green wash; white cheeks; very dark green forehead and crown; longish crest; grey head; neck glossy green; grey and white in wings; white chin and centre of throat; ashy-grey below. Sexes alike. Solitary, shy and sluggish. Feeds by day, but mostly crepuscular and nocturnal. Sits patiently near water. **VOICE** Redshank-like *tewn … tewm*. **DISTRIBUTION** India, south of the Himalayas. Uncommon. **HABITAT** Secluded pools, ponds near dense growth, mangroves.

Indian Pond Heron *Ardeola grayii* 46cm **r**

Common, small heron. Thickset and earthy-brown with dull green legs; bill bluish at base, yellowish at centre with black tip; neck and legs shorter than in true egrets. During breeding, has buffy-brown head and neck; white chin and upper throat; longish crest; rich maroon back; buffish-brown breast. Non-breeding birds have streaked dark brown head and neck; grey-brown back and shoulders; more white in plumage. Sexes alike. Remains motionless. Slowly stalks prey. Hunts alone and roosts in groups. **VOICE** Harsh croak, when flushed; also squeaks and chatters at nesting colony. **DISTRIBUTION** All India. **HABITAT** Marshes, jheels, riversides, roadside ditches, tidal creeks.

Cattle Egret *Bubulcus ibis* 50cm **r**

Snowy-white egret seen on and around cattle and rubbish heaps. Breeding birds have buffy-orange plumes on head, neck and back. Non-breeding birds distinguished from other egrets by yellow bill and size. Sexes alike. Widespread; abundant both around water and away from it. Attends to grazing cattle, feeding on insects disturbed by them; follows tractors; scavenges at refuse dumps and slaughter houses. **VOICE** Mostly silent except for some croaking sounds when breeding. **DISTRIBUTION** All India. **HABITAT** Cultivation, forest clearings.

Grey Heron *Ardea cinerea* 100cm **r**

Long-legged, long-necked bird of open marshes. Ashy-grey above; white crown, neck and underparts; black stripe after eye continues as long black crest; black-dotted band down centre of foreneck; dark blue-black flight feathers; golden-yellow iris at close range. Sexes alike. Mostly solitary. Usually stands motionless, head pulled in between shoulders. Characteristic flight, with head pulled back and long legs trailing. **VOICE** Loud *quaak* in flight. **DISTRIBUTION** Resident, subcontinent. **HABITAT** Marshes, tidal creeks, freshwater bodies.

Black Bittern

Manjula Mathur

Black-crowned Night Heron

Striated Heron

Garima Bhatia

Indian Pond Heron

Cattle Egret

Savio Fonseca

Grey Heron

Purple Heron *Ardea purpurea* 78–90cm **r**

Slender-necked, lanky bird. Slaty-purple above; black crown with long, drooping crest; rufous neck with prominent black stripe along length; white chin and throat; deep slaty and chestnut below breast; almost black on wings and tail. Sexes alike. Solitary. Crepuscular. Very shy but master of patience; freezes and hides amid marsh reeds. When flushed, flies with neck outstretched. Active in the early mornings. **VOICE** Harsh croak; sometime high-pitched *frannk*. **DISTRIBUTION** Widespread across India. **HABITAT** Open marshes, reed-covered lakes, riversides.

Great Egret *Ardea alba* 94–104cm **r**

Large, white heron with contrasting black feet and long black legs. Black tip to bright yellow bill; greenish-yellow patch between bill and eye; long 'S'-shaped neck prominent in flight. Breeding adult displays beautiful plumes extending from back to beyond tail. In courtship display plumes are spread into fan shape. Feeds actively at dawn and dusk, waiting motionlessly to catch prey. **VOICE** Occasional croak. **DISTRIBUTION** Resident, local migrant; common and widespread across India. **HABITAT** Marshes, jheels, rivers, estuaries.

Intermediate Egret *Ardea intermedia* 65–72cm **r**

Overall striking white bird with dark legs and thickish yellow bill. Breeding adult may have reddish or black bill; greenish-yellow gape skin; loose, filamentous breast trails and back plumes; dull yellow or pink upperparts. Sexes similar. Stalks prey in shallow water, including flooded fields. Feeds on fish, frogs, crustaceans and insects. Nests in colonies with other herons, normally on platforms of sticks, trees or shrubs. **VOICE** Usually silent. **DISTRIBUTION** Locally common breeding resident throughout lowlands and coasts. **HABITAT** Wetlands.

Little Egret *Egretta garzetta* 65cm **r**

Slender, snow-white waterbird. White plumage; black legs, yellow feet and black bill diagnostic. In breeding birds, nuchal crest of two long plumes; feathers on back and breast lengthen into ornamental filamentous feathers. Sexes alike. Small flocks feed at edge of water, sometimes wading into shallower areas. Stalks prey like typical heron, waiting patiently at the water's edge. **VOICE** Occasional croak. **DISTRIBUTION** Resident in subcontinent, to 1,600m in the outer Himalayas. **HABITAT** Inland marshes, jheels, riversides, damp irrigated areas; tidal creeks.

Western Reef Heron *Egretta gularis* 65cm **r**

Slender bird of rocky sea coasts. Two colour phases. In dark phase, slaty-black plumage; white throat and upper foreneck. In light phase, all-white plumage, like the Little Egret's (above), but habitat and more solitary nature distinctive; bill brown and yellow or bright yellow; plumes in breeding much like Little Egret's. Most active at twilight. Sometimes both phases feed side by side. Moves cautiously on tidal ooze. Settles hunched up on rock. **VOICE** Occasional croak. **DISTRIBUTION** West and east coasts. **HABITAT** Rocky and sandy coasts.

Great White Pelican *Pelecanus onocrotalus* 175cm **r**

Enormous bird with azure-blue bill with central red stripe. Bright yellow, expandable pouch extends from lower jaw to base of throat. Bare, fleshy pink face; bushy white crest; creamy-white plumage with pale pinkish wash; pink feet and yellowish tuft on breast; black primaries and undersides of secondaries. Social. Strong flier. The globally threatened **Dalmatian Pelican** *P. crispus* is a very local winter visitor. **VOICE** Grunts and croaks. **DISTRIBUTION** Resident, Rann of Kutch. Spreads in winter. **HABITAT** Large jheels, lakes, coastal lagoons.

Purple Heron

Great Egret

Little Egret

Intermediate Egret

Great White Pelican

Western Reef Heron

Dalmatian Pelican

Spot-billed Pelican *Pelecanus philippensis* 150cm (r) (V)

Whitish plumage sullied with grey-brown; pink on lower back, rump and flanks; white-tipped brown crest on back of head; black primaries and dark brown secondaries distinctive in flight; flesh-coloured gular pouch has bluish-purple wash; at close range blue spots on upper mandible and on gular pouch confirm identity. Purely aquatic. Seen singly as well as in large gatherings. VOICE Mostly silent. DISTRIBUTION Breeds in well-watered parts of S, SE and E India, but population spreads in non-breeding season. HABITAT Large jheels, lakes.

Osprey *Pandion haliaetus* 55–58cm (m)

Large bird whose long wings have a characteristic bend at the carpal joints. Underparts sharp white, with dark brown patches at carpal joints and mottled dark brown necklace. Dark eye-stripe; dark brown back; pale blue-grey feet; black bill. Solitary or in scattered pairs. Circles over water; hovers characteristically. Dives with feet dangling; often splashes into water. Carries fish to perch. VOICE Short, nasal scream; rarely calls. DISTRIBUTION Winter visitor all over India. HABITAT Lakes, rivers, coastal lagoons.

Black-winged Kite *Elanus caeruleus* 32cm (r)

Pale grey-white plumage, whiter on head, neck and underbody; short black stripe through eye; black shoulder-patches and wing-tips distinctive at rest and in flight; blood-red eyes. Sexes alike. Usually solitary or in pairs. Rests on exposed perch or flies over open scrub and grass country. Mostly hunts on the wing, regularly hovering like a kestrel to scan the ground; drops height to check when hovering, with legs held ready. VOICE High-pitched squeal. DISTRIBUTION All over subcontinent. HABITAT Open scrub and grass country, light forests.

Bearded Vulture *Gypaetus barbatus* 110–115cm (r) (V)

Large, majestic vulture with enormous wings that enable it to soar easily above the mountains. Long, diamond-shaped tail distinctive in flight. Creamy-yellow head; black eye-patches that extend below bill; short, narrow bill; black bristles under chin creating 'beard'. Neck and underparts rusty-orange; back, wings and tail dark grey-blue to black. Juvenile patchy brown. Known for unusual habit of dropping bones on to rocks to smash them open and get at the marrow. VOICE Usually silent. DISTRIBUTION The Himalayas. HABITAT High mountains.

Egyptian Vulture *Neophron percnopterus* 65cm (r) (V)

White plumage; blackish in wings; naked yellow head, neck and throat; yellow bill; thick ruff of feathers around neck; wedge-shaped tail and blackish flight feathers distinctive in overhead flight. Sexes alike. Several usually together, perched on tops of ruins or earthen mounds, or just walking on the ground. Glides a lot but rarely soars high. Sometimes with other vultures. VOICE Usually silent. DISTRIBUTION All India; plains to about 2,000m in the Himalayas. HABITAT Open country, vicinity of human habitation.

Oriental Honey Buzzard *Pernis ptilorhynchus* 57–60cm (r)

Slender head and longish neck distinctive; tail rarely fanned. Highly variable phases. Mostly darkish brown above; crest rarely visible; male has reddish-brown iris while female has yellow iris; pale brown underbody with narrow whitish bars; pale undersides of wings barred; broad dark subterminal tail-band; 2–3 more bands on tail; tarsus unfeathered. Sexes alike. Solitary or in pairs. Feeds mainly on larvae of bees and honey. VOICE High-pitched, long-drawn *weeeeeu* … DISTRIBUTION Resident and local migrant, subcontinent. HABITAT Forests, open country, cultivation.

Spot-billed Pelican

Osprey

Black-winged Kite

Bearded Vulture

Egyptian Vulture

Oriental Honey Buzzard

Black Baza *Aviceda leuphotes* 32cm (m)

White breast-band bordered with black and chestnut; rufous belly barred with buff. Secondary flight feathers show chestnut-and-white patches; chestnut markings on lower back, scapulars and greater wing-coverts. Black vent, undertail-coverts and thighs. Feeds on large insects, lizards and tree frogs. **VOICE** Vocal in flight and when perched. **DISTRIBUTION** Uncommon migrant in the Himalayan foothills, NE and S India. **HABITAT** Evergreen forests, clearings, foothills.

White-rumped Vulture *Gyps bengalensis* 75–85cm (r) (v)

Blackish-brown plumage; almost naked head has whitish ruff around base; white rump (lower back) distinctive when perched and often in flight; in overhead flight, white underwing-coverts contrast with dark underbody and flight feathers. Sexes alike. Increasingly becoming uncommon. When resting, head and neck are dug into shoulders. Soars high on thermals. Several converge on to a carcass. Basks in sun. **VOICE** Loud screeches when feeding. **DISTRIBUTION** Resident, all India. **HABITAT** Open country.

Indian Vulture *Gyps indicus* 89–103cm (r) (v)

Scruffy-looking bird with bald head, very broad wings and short tail feathers. Adult has pale yellow bill; pale eye-ring; white neck-ruff; black neck and head. Brown upperwings graduate to cream below. Dark flight feathers and tail form striking contrast to pale underparts. Cream-feathered thighs. Nests colonially exclusively on cliff ledges and buildings. **VOICE** Quiet. **DISTRIBUTION** Formerly common breeding resident except in extreme south. Now globally threatened and very local. Most frequent in large wildlife sanctuaries. **HABITAT** Open country.

Slender-billed Vulture *Gyps tenuirostris* 93–100cm (r) (v)

Overall greyish-brown vulture with sharply accentuated dome. Rather scruffy, ill-kempt appearance. Slender, snake-like neck; thin, elongated dark bill; dark cere with pale culmen; bare head and neck with wrinkled skin; dark eye-ring; underparts streaked pale. White thigh-patches visible in flight. Dark underside to flight feathers. **VOICE** Cackling screeches. **DISTRIBUTION** Resident; the lower Himalayas, from NW India through N, NE India and Ganges delta. Globally threatened. **HABITAT** Cities, towns, villages.

Himalayan Vulture *Gyps himalayensis* 125cm (r) (v)

Bulky vulture with huge wingspan. Soft white down feathers on head and upper neck; sandy-brown upperparts and ruff on lower neck; short, square black tail; buffy-white coverts; dark brown flight feathers. Tawny underparts streaked white; large, heavy yellow bill; yellow eyes; fleshy pink legs. Sexes similar. Wary and shy; takes flight if disturbed while feeding. Soars solitarily or in small flocks over mountain slopes and cliffs. **VOICE** Cackling screeches at carcass sites. **DISTRIBUTION** The Himalayas. **HABITAT** Barren, high-altitude country.

Griffon Vulture *Gyps fulvus* 93–100cm (r)

Large, carnivorous scavenger with impressive creamy-white ruff. Plain pale reddish-brown upperparts; white head and neck; yellow bill; dark flight feathers on rest of wings and tail; pale underwing-coverts with bands of white; dark grey legs and feet. Breeds colonially. Usually in pairs or small groups. **VOICE** Quiet. Grunts and hisses when feeding. **DISTRIBUTION** Common breeding resident N India and NW India. Winters widely in lowlands. **HABITAT** Mountains, semi-deserts; wanders into nearby dry plains in winter.

Black Baza

Nikhil Devasar

White-rumped Vulture

Indian Vulture

Biswapriya Rahut

Slender-billed Vulture

Himalayan Vulture

Manjula Mathur

Griffon Vulture

Red-headed Vulture *Sarcogyps calvus* 85cm 🔴 ⓥ

Male has pale iris, female's dark brown; sexes otherwise alike. Black plumage with white on thighs and breast; naked red head, neck and feet; in overhead flight, white breast, thigh-patches and grey-white band along wings distinctive; widely spread primaries. Mostly solitary but 2–4 may be seen at a carcass with other vultures; usually does not mix with the rest. **VOICE** Hoarse croak. **DISTRIBUTION** Resident, all India; uncommon. **HABITAT** Open country, village outskirts.

Cinereous Vulture *Aegypius monachus* 100–110cm ⓜ ⓥ

Large bird with long, broad, parallel wings that have prominently indented trailing edges and splayed wing-tips. Short, wedge-shaped tail; bare, buff head; dark eyes; dark facial mark; whitish legs; chocolate-brown plumage and ruff; bluish neck; blackish throat and large, dark eye-patches. Powerful horn-coloured bill; pale blue cere. Nests on small trees growing out of cliffs. Dominant over other species at carcasses. **VOICE** Usually silent. **DISTRIBUTION** Mainly scarce winter visitor to N India. **HABITAT** Open country, often near rivers.

Crested Serpent Eagle *Spilornis cheela* 75cm 🔴

Dark brown plumage; roundish, pied crest, visible when erected; pale brown below, finely spotted white. In overhead flight, dark body, white bars along wings and white tail-band confirm identity. Sexes alike; female larger than male. Solitary or in pairs. Flies over forest, often very high, calling frequently. Perches on leafy branches. Swoops down on prey, snatching it in its talons. Raises crest when alarmed. **VOICE** Characteristic call. Loud, whistling scream, *keee … kee … ke …* **DISTRIBUTION** Resident, subcontinent. **HABITAT** Forested country.

Andaman Serpent Eagle *Spilornis elgini* 65cm ⓔ ⓥ

Almost entirely dark brown eagle with bright yellow face and legs. Breast, belly and scapulars speckled white; black primary feathers finely edged white; undertail banded black and white; short, bushy crest; long wings. Juvenile paler than adults, with whiter head and dark-streaked throat; wing-coverts spotted; underparts barred buff; barring on belly; thinner bars on undertail. **VOICE** Loud, whistling scream. **DISTRIBUTION** Endemic to Andaman Islands. **HABITAT** Forested country.

Short-toed Snake Eagle *Circaetus gallicus* 65cm 🔴

Large, long-winged eagle with large head, relatively small bill and long, bare legs. Upperparts, head, throat and chest brown; white underparts, marked with dark bars and blotches. Dark flight feathers of tail marked with 3–4 dark bands; bright yellow eyes. Sexes similar; female heavier than male, with slightly longer tail. Feeds on snakes, usually eaten whole. **VOICE** Call a loud *kee yo*. **DISTRIBUTION** Scarce breeding resident in lowlands; more common and widespread winter visitor except in NE India. **HABITAT** Open country, scrubby grassland.

Changeable Hawk Eagle *Nisaetus cirrhatus* 70cm 🔴

Large, slender, crested forest eagle. Brown above; white underbody longitudinally streaked all over with brown. Prominent occipital crest; streaked whitish body, broad wings and long, rounded tail distinctive in flight. Sexes alike, but female larger than male. Different races, depending on size of crest. Solitary; occasionally in pairs. Circles high over forests. Surveys for prey from high leafy branches. **VOICE** Screaming, long-drawn cry. **DISTRIBUTION** Resident India south of the Himalayas. **HABITAT** Semi-evergreen deciduous forest clearings.

Ranjan J Saxena

Red-headed Vulture

Nitin Srinivasamurthy

Cinereous Vulture

Crested Serpent Eagle

Garima Bhatia

Andaman Serpent Eagle

Short-toed Snake Eagle

Clement M Francis

Changeable Hawk Eagle

Mountain Hawk Eagle *Nisaetus nipalensis* 72cm 🔴r

Large brown-and-white raptor with brown upperparts, rufous head and black, pale-tipped crest. Belly and underwing-coverts barred dark brown; tail has three bands and is grey-brown from above and white below. Juvenile dark brown with buff to tawny underparts, barred tail and white legs. Broad wings with curved trailing edges, held in shallow 'V' shape in flight. **VOICE** Call a high, whistling *peeo … peeo* during breeding season. **DISTRIBUTION** The Himalayas and hills of NE India. **HABITAT** Upland forests.

Black Eagle *Ictinaetus malaiensis* 70–80cm 🔴r

Almost entirely black eagle with yellow cere and feet. Brown eyes; yellow-grey bill tipped black; white patches at bases of primary feathers; extended primary feathers; long wings reach tail-tip at rest. Wings held in shallow 'V' shape with long, upturned fingers while gliding. Usually seen soaring alone or in pairs over the canopy. Seldom observed sitting. **VOICE** Rather quiet. Call a loud *kee … kee … kee* when courting. **DISTRIBUTION** Disjunct. Northern hills east of Uttarakhand, NE India, Western and Eastern Ghats. **HABITAT** Hills, mangrove forests.

Greater Spotted Eagle *Clanga clanga* 65–72cm 🔴r 🔵v

Deep brown above; somewhat paler below; often has whitish rump; soars on straight wings with drooping tips. Sexes alike, but female slightly larger than male. The **Indian Spotted Eagle** *C. hastata* is slightly smaller, with narrower wings, and paler above. Mostly solitary. Prefers vicinity of water. Sluggish behaviour. **VOICE** Loud, shrill *kaek … kaek …*, often from perch. **DISTRIBUTION** Gangetic plains, eastwards to Manipur, Madhya Pradesh and S Orissa, north Tamil Nadu. **HABITAT** Tree-covered areas in vicinity of water.

Booted Eagle *Hieraaetus pennatus* 52cm 🔴r

Two distinct colour phases. In lighter phase head paler as uppertail- and upperwing-coverts. Buffy-white wing linings, underbody and tail with blackish flight feathers distinctive. In darker phase chocolate-brown below. Pale-banded tail makes it easily identifiable in flight. Often seen alone, or sometimes in pairs hunting in concert. Pairs often roost together at night. **VOICE** Call a loud scream of several notes. **DISTRIBUTION** Breeds in the Himalayas. **HABITAT** Open country.

Tawny Eagle *Aquila rapax* 70cm 🔴r 🔵v

Large bird with variable plumage ranging from very dark brown to light brown. Blackish flight feathers and tail; light bars on wings; short, rounded tail; pale lower back; brown eyes; yellow bill with dark tip; heavily feathered legs. Female larger than male. Holds tail straight and parallel to body in flight. **VOICE** Loud crackling notes; high-pitched call. **DISTRIBUTION** Sporadically over parts of India. **HABITAT** Open country, vicinity of villages, towns and cultivation.

Steppe Eagle *Aquila nipalensis* 80cm ⬛m 🔵v

Adult overall dark brown with well-defined bars on flight and tail feathers; pale-tipped secondaries; reddish-brown patch on nape of neck; long, wide gape; small head; pale throat; dark iris; yellow legs. Juvenile resembles adult, but paler brown, with characteristic broad white band running along underside of wing. Juveniles often overwinter. **VOICE** Usually silent. **DISTRIBUTION** Winter visitor to N India. Absent in NE India. Rare in peninsular India. **HABITAT** Lightly wooded, open country, villages and towns.

Mountain Hawk Eagle

Greater Spotted Eagle

Indian Spotted Eagle

Tawny Eagle

Black Eagle

Sumit Sen

Booted Eagle

Nitin Srinivasamurthy

Steppe Eagle

Manjula Mathur

107

Eastern Imperial Eagle *Aquila heliaca* 85cm 🔵 🅥

Entirely brown or black eagle with light gold crown and neck-sides. Dark grey tail with subterminal band tipped white; white patch on shoulder; wing-coverts edged white. Pale rusty-cream undertail; yellow eyes and feet; grey bill with black tip. Long tail; large head and large feet. Spends much time in high soaring or sitting on the ground or bare trees. **VOICE** Usually silent. Gruff barking occasionally. **DISTRIBUTION** Globally threatened, scarce winter visitor mainly to NW India; very rare elsewhere. **HABITAT** Wetlands, open country.

Bonelli's Eagle *Aquila fasciata* 70cm 🔴

Large brown-and-white eagle with short, rounded wings and long tail. Dark brown back and wings; white belly and underparts mottled brown; white trailing edges to wings; black terminal band; grey-patch at carpal joint; long, feathered legs; yellow-orange eyes; yellow feet and cere. Juvenile has pale chestnut underside and hazel eyes. **VOICE** Call a shrill scream of 3–6-notes. **DISTRIBUTION** All India, sporadically from about 2,400m in the Himalayas. **HABITAT** Forests.

Crested Goshawk *Accipiter trivirgatus* 42cm 🔴

Large dark brown hawk with black mesial stripe from chin to breast. Long brown tail has four wide black bands; brownish-black head with slight crest; black neck and white throat. White undertail; breast vertically streaked rufous; belly marked with horizontal dark brown bands. Iris, legs and feet yellow. Watches prey from perch, capturing it in rapid attack. **VOICE** Call a high-pitched scream, *ke … ke … ke … ke.* **DISTRIBUTION** Fairly common breeding resident. **HABITAT** Forests.

Shikra *Accipiter badius* 32cm 🔴

Ashy-grey above; whitish below, close-barred with rust-brown; grey throat-stripe; in flight, multi-banded tail and roundish wings help in identification; golden-yellow eyes and yellow legs and feet seen at close range. Usually solitary. Hides in leafy branches. Pounces on unsuspecting prey; occasionally chases small birds. Soars over forests. **VOICE** Loud, drongo-like *titew … titew.* **DISTRIBUTION** Resident; subcontinent, to 1,600m in the Himalayas. **HABITAT** Light forests, open country, neighbourhood of villages; also cities.

Eurasian Sparrowhawk *Accipiter nisus* 35cm 🔴

Smallish sparrowhawk with long legs and short, rounded wings. Upperparts dark grey with pale underparts finely barred reddish-brown. Hooked bill; pale line above eye; white chin-patch. Female significantly larger than male, with darker, more brown upperparts and white underparts barred; yellow iris. The Himalayan resident, *A. n. melaschistos*, is blackish-grey above. **VOICE** Rather quiet. Call a rapid *kew … kew … kew … kew* when nesting. **DISTRIBUTION** Fairly common breeding resident. **HABITAT** Open wooded country, cultivation. Probably overlooked.

Northern Goshawk *Accipiter gentilis* Male 50cm; female 61cm 🔵

Large, powerful bird with short, strong wings and long tail. Upperparts brown-grey; black cap on head; distinct white supercilium; orange-red eyes; light grey underparts, finely barred on breast; throat vertically streaked. Female considerably larger than male, with browner underparts and markings on breast less defined. Juvenile brown above and pale buff to whitish below, with heavy streaking. **VOICE** Usually quiet, but pairs call chattering *yek … yek … yek.* **DISTRIBUTION** Scarce winter visitor to the Himalayas. **HABITAT** Uninhabited grassland, scrubland, cultivated areas.

Eastern Imperial Eagle

Bonelli's Eagle

Clement M Francis

Crested Goshawk

Shikra

Nitin Srinivasamurthy

Eurasian Sparrowhawk

Northern Goshawk

Kirill Lapin

Western Marsh Harrier *Circus aeruginosus* 55cm (m)

Male has dark brown plumage; dull rufous head and breast; silvery-grey wings and tail; black wing-tips (best seen in flight). Female chocolate-brown; buff on head and shoulders; like the Black Kite (below), but tail rounded (not forked). Solitary or in pairs. Sails low over marshes, grassland or cultivation; often drops to the ground, vanishing in dense grass and reed growth. Perches on mounds or edges of marshes. Very similar **Eastern Marsh Harrier** *C. spilonotus* found in the north-east from Siliguri eastwards, often overlapping with the Western. VOICE Usually silent. DISTRIBUTION Common winter visitor. HABITAT Marshes, jheels, wet cultivation.

Hen Harrier *Circus cyaneus* 44–52cm (m) (v)

Medium-sized, broad-winged harrier with short legs. Adult male has grey head, upper breast and upperparts, white underparts and black-tipped primaries. Female brown above with streaked neck and underparts, and white around eyes. In flight male shows prominent black wing-tips, and dark underwing trailing edges. Surveys the ground by flying low, then dropping sharply on prey with outstretched talons. Gregarious, communal ground rooster. VOICE Usually silent. DISTRIBUTION Winter visitor to N and NE India. HABITAT Open country, grassland.

Pallid Harrier *Circus macrourus* 40–48cm (m) (v)

Slender bird with narrow wings and tail. Light grey upperparts; dark wedges on primaries; pale grey head and underbody; lacks black secondary bars. Female has distinctive underwing pattern; pale primaries, irregularly barred and lacking dark trailing edges. VOICE Usually silent. DISTRIBUTION Widespread winter visitor; unrecorded in parts of NE India. HABITAT Open country in plains and foothills, semi-deserts, grassy slopes, cultivation, scrub-covered plains, marshes.

Pied Harrier *Circus melanoleucos* 45–49cm (r)

Slim, long-winged raptor, overall white and grey. Black head, back, throat and breast; grey tail and wings; black primaries; black band across median coverts. Female dark brown above; pale white nape-patch and rump; pale buffy-rufous below; marked underside of flight feathers. Solitary or in pairs. VOICE Usually silent. DISTRIBUTION Resident: Manas and adjoining areas in Assam. Winter visitor over parts of E India and erratically in parts of C and S India. HABITAT Grassy areas, cultivation, reedy edges of jheels.

Montagu's Harrier *Circus pygargus* 48cm (m)

Slender, medium-sized, slim bird with long, narrow wings and long tail. Extensive black marking on wing-tips; distinct black band on lateral and dorsal sides of wings. Head, breast, back and inner wings dark grey; rest of wings and tail lighter grey; narrow white rump; chestnut streaking on belly and underwing. Roosts communally in long grass; often in scattered groups. VOICE Usually silent. DISTRIBUTION Rather scarce winter visitor throughout peninsula; passage migrant through NW India; rare in E India. HABITAT Open country, cultivation.

Black Kite *Milvus migrans* 60cm (r)

Dark brown plumage; forked tail, easily seen in flight; underparts faintly streaked. Sexes alike. The **Black-eared Kite** *M. m. lineatus*, breeding in the Himalayas and wintering in N and C India, slightly larger and has conspicuous white patch on underwing, visible in overhead flight. Common and gregarious; most common near humans, thriving on the refuse generated. Roosts communally. VOICE Loud, musical whistle. DISTRIBUTION Resident, subcontinent, co-existing with the Black-eared in some localities. HABITAT Mostly neighbourhood of human habitation.

Western Marsh Harrier

Hen Harrier

Eastern Marsh Harrier

Pied Harrier

Pallid Harrier

Black Kite

Montagu's Harrier

Black-eared Kite

M V Shreeram

Clement M Francis

Clement M Francis

Gunjan Arora

111

Brahminy Kite *Haliastur indus* 48cm **r**

White head, neck, upper back and breast; rest of plumage rich rusty-chestnut; brownish abdomen and darker tips to flight feathers visible mostly in flight. Sexes alike. Young brown, like the Black Kite (p. 110), but with rounded tail. Solitary or small scattered parties. Loves water; frequently scavenges around lakes and marshes; also around villages and towns. **VOICE** Loud scream. **DISTRIBUTION** Resident and local migrant; subcontinent, absent in the Himalayas. **HABITAT** Margins of lakes, marshes, rivers, sea coasts.

White-bellied Sea Eagle *Haliaeetus leucogaster* 70cm **r**

Ash-brown and white bird with pure white head and neck, and short white tail. Black flight feathers; white underwing-coverts; pale blue-grey, hooked bill with dark tip and grey cere; dark brown eyes; pale greyish-yellow legs. Sexes similar, but female larger than male. Juvenile has dark brown upperparts and wings, **VOICE** Call a loud, goose-like honking, *hank ... hank ... hank*, typically heard during breeding season. **DISTRIBUTION** Resident on both coasts. **HABITAT** Islands, rocky coasts, large inland waterbodies, wetlands.

Pallas's Fish Eagle *Haliaeetus leucoryphus* 76–84cm **r** **v**

Upperparts dark brown with pale brown-grey head and neck, and brown underparts; dark grey bill and cere; long, rounded tail and contrasting broad white band diagnostic. Juvenile brown from above and below, with white markings on underwing. Sexes alike; female larger than male. Feeds mostly on fish caught close to the surface of water. Known to hunt in pairs and sometimes steal food from other birds. **VOICE** Call a loud, creaky *kha ... kha ...* Noisy during breeding season. **DISTRIBUTION** Resident; local migrant. **HABITAT** Jheels, large rivers.

Lesser Fish Eagle *Haliaeetus humilis* 64cm **r** **v**

Medium-sized bird; overall grey-brown plumage. Blunt, broad wings; featherless legs. Similar to the Grey-headed Fish Eagle (below), but smaller and has brown breast, white thighs and belly, and grey tail with slightly darker subterminal tail-band. Short, rounded tail; long neck and small head; large, curved talons, specialized for catching fish. Feeds on fish snatched from water. **VOICE** Loud, excitable shrieks, including wavering *kleeure*. **DISTRIBUTION** The Himalayas and SW India. **HABITAT** Forested streams, lakes.

Grey-headed Fish Eagle *Haliaeetus ichthyaetus* 69–74cm **r** **v**

Striking bird with relatively small head, longish neck and powerful grey bill. Upperparts brownish-grey and underparts white. Rounded tail; sandy-yellow eyes; long black talons; relatively short legs; tail with broad black terminal band. Female larger and heavier than male. Juvenile has white belly mottled with brown. **VOICE** Calls include *awh-awhr* and *chee-warr*, repeated. **DISTRIBUTION** Resident; from Delhi to Assam; south through peninsula. **HABITAT** Lakes and rivers in forested country.

White-eyed Buzzard *Butastur teesa* 45cm **r**

Ashy-brown above; distinct throat, white with two dark cheek-stripes and third stripe from chin; white nape-patch, white eyes and orange-yellow cere visible from close quarters; in flight, pale shoulder-patch from above; from below, pale underside of roundish wings against darkish body distinctive. Solitary or in scattered pairs. Seen on exposed perches. Seems to prefer certain sites. Soars high and does aerial displays when breeding. **VOICE** Musical, plaintive *te ... twee*.
DISTRIBUTION Resident; subcontinent. **HABITAT** Open and dry forests, cultivation.

Brahminy Kite

White-bellied Sea Eagle

Savio Fonseca

Pallas's Fish Eagle

Lesser Fish Eagle

Subharghaya Das

Grey-headed Fish Eagle

White-eyed Buzzard

Sunil Kini

Long-legged Buzzard *Buteo rufinus* 43–58cm 🔴

Largest of *Buteo* species, with many colour morphs, from pale white to dark brown, but with clear orangish tint to plumage. Tail reddish and head pale. Underwings whitish; rump mostly dark brown. Hunts mostly small and medium-sized mammals. Often seen sitting on electricity posts, pylons and other vantage points. **VOICE** Rather quiet. **DISTRIBUTION** Winters commonly in NW India; rare elsewhere. **HABITAT** Open, uncultivated areas with high bushes, trees, cliffs or hillocks are favoured nesting areas.

Common Buzzard *Buteo buteo* 51cm 🔵

Large buzzard with broad, rounded wings, and short neck and tail. Plumage highly variable, ranging from darkish brown, to russet, to pale buff. Upperparts darker; wing-tip and trailing edge of wing also darker than rest of wing feathers. Barred tail and flight feathers; streaked throat and breast. Wings held in shallow 'V' shape and tail fanned when gliding and soaring. **VOICE** Mostly silent in winter. **DISTRIBUTION** Widespread winter visitor but status uncertain. **HABITAT** Open wooded or cultivated areas.

Common Barn Owl *Tyto alba* 35cm 🔴

Dull gold-buff above, finely speckled black and white; white below, often with fine dark spots; heart-shaped white facial disc with brown edge; brownish wash between lower edges of eyes and base of pale pink bill. Sexes alike. Solitary or in pairs. Nocturnal. Perches upright. Flies silently, mostly under 4m from the ground. Pounces on prey. **VOICE** Call a long-drawn, wild shriek; variety of snoring, hissing notes. **DISTRIBUTION** Almost all India, south of the Himalayan foothills. **HABITAT** Grassland, cultivation, human habitation, town centres.

Mountain Scops Owl *Otus spilocephalus* 20cm 🔴

Seen in many morphs and individually variable. Adult has reddish-brown facial disc with pale base and dark-tipped bristles; yellow eyes; blackish cheeks and ear-coverts; paler head-sides and forehead. Dark tawny or rufous brown upperparts, darkly vermiculated. Whitish underparts, barred rufous, with small, triangular, paired black-and-white spots. Like other scops owls, completely nocturnal and difficult to spot. **VOICE** Song an eerie, gliding whistle, *whi … whoo … ee … yo*. **DISTRIBUTION** The Himalayas, NE India. **HABITAT** Dense forests.

Indian Scops Owl *Otus bakkamoena* 23–25cm 🔴

Medium-sized buffy-brown owl with large, prominent ear-tufts; buff nuchal collar edged with dark brown; finely streaked underparts; buffish scapular spots; dark orange or brown eyes, although can be yellow. Very variable in colouration: can be pale grey-brown or warm rufous-brown; legs feathered to bases of toes. Similar **Collared Scops Owl** *O. lettia* found in north of India. **VOICE** Call a subdued, frog-like *whuk*. **DISTRIBUTION** Widespread resident south of the Himalayas. **HABITAT** Forests, well-wooded areas. Often ventures into human habitation.

Oriental Scops Owl *Otus sunia* 19cm 🔴

Small, mottled brown owl with short ear-tufts. Breast heavily streaked with black; orange-yellow iris; greyish bill and feet. Cryptic, mottled plumage in three morphs: rufous, brown and grey. Prominent white scapular lines. Large, vertical ear-tufts often suppressed. Strictly nocturnal; roosts by day close to trunks in thickly foliaged trees. Nests in holes. **VOICE** Slowly repeated *wug-chug-chug*. **DISTRIBUTION** Locally common breeding resident in plains and lower hills, mainly in N, Western Ghats and S peninsular India. **HABITAT** Forests, groves, orchards.

Long-legged Buzzard

Common Buzzard

Savio Fonseca

Common Barn Owl

Mountain Scops Owl

Dushyant Prasher

Indian Scops Owl

Oriental Scops Owl

Savio Fonseca

Indian Eagle Owl *Bubo bengalensis* 48.5cm ⓡ

Brown plumage, mottled and streaked dark; prominent ear-tufts; orange eyes; legs fully feathered. Sexes alike. Solitary or in pairs. Mostly nocturnal, spending the day in leafy branch, on rock ledges or in old wells. Flies slowly but over considerable distances when disturbed. Emerges to feed around sunset, advertising arrival with characteristic call. The similar **Eurasian Eagle Owl** B. *bubo* found in Ladakh. **VOICE** Deep, booming *bu … boo …* call; snapping calls at nest. **DISTRIBUTION** Throughout area. **HABITAT** Ravines, cliffs, riversides, scrub, open country.

Spot-bellied Eagle Owl *Bubo nipalensis* 63cm ⓡ

Large, dramatic-looking bird of prey. Pallid, overall stark greyish-brown with prominent, horizontally held ear-tufts; characteristic dark heart- or chevron-shaped markings on white underparts diagnostic; dark brown primaries striped lighter; heavily barred secondaries; plain white facial disc; white supercilium; large, pale yellow bill; dark brown eyes. Nocturnal; roosts by day. **VOICE** Blood-curdling moan and scream. **DISTRIBUTION** Uttaranchal eastwards, throughout NE Indian region; also Western Ghats. **HABITAT** Dense evergreen forests.

Dusky Eagle Owl *Bubo coromandus* 58cm ⓡ

Pale grey-brown plumage, profusely spotted, streaked and marked with white; pale buffish-grey underparts with dark shaft-stripes and brown cross-bars; prominent ear-tufts, erect when alert, and dull yellow eyes diagnostic. Feathered tarsus and bristled toes. Sexes alike. Mostly in pairs. **VOICE** Call a deep, hollow, somewhat eerie hoot of 5–8 notes fading towards end; interpreted as *woo … wo … wo … wo … o … o … o*. **DISTRIBUTION** Throughout region. **HABITAT** Groves, light forests, roadside leafy trees, vicinity of human habitation.

Brown Fish Owl *Ketupa zeylonensis* 35cm ⓡ

Dull golden-buff above, finely speckled black and white; white below, often with fine dark spots; heart-shaped white facial disc with brown edge; brownish wash between lower edges of eyes and base of pale pink bill. Sexes alike. Solitary or in pairs. Nocturnal. Perches upright. Flies low. The similar **Tawny Fish Owl** K. *flavipes* has flattened ear-tufts, smallish facial disc and more tawny plumage with white patch on front of neck. **VOICE** Call a long-drawn, wild shriek. **DISTRIBUTION** South of the Himalayan foothills. **HABITAT** Grassland, cultivation, human habitation.

Mottled Wood Owl *Strix ocellata* 48cm ⓔ

Medium-sized owl with no ear-tufts. Yellowish-red upperparts, profusely mottled and vermiculated red-brown, black, white and buff; whitish facial disc with narrow chocolate-black barring forming concentric circles; white spots on crown and nape; chestnut-and-black throat, stippled white; rest of underparts whitish, barred golden-buff to orange-buff. Yellowish-brown toes and blackish talons. Sexes alike. Solitary. **VOICE** Call a loud, hooting note. **DISTRIBUTION** All India; absent in arid northwestern parts and much of NE India. **HABITAT** Forests, orchards.

Brown Wood Owl *Strix leptogrammica* 50cm ⓡ

Medium-sized owl with warm brown plumage; no ear-tufts; fulvous or rufous-brown facial disc with narrow but distinct black rim. The Himalayan S. *i. newarensis* has dark brown face with prominent white eyebrows, and striking white band across foreneck. Underparts greyish-white, heavily barred with brown. **VOICE** Calls include *hoo … hoohoohoo … (hoo)* and loud, eerie scream. **DISTRIBUTION** The Himalayas, NE India, Eastern and Western Ghats. **HABITAT**

Dense broadleaved subtropical or temperate forests.

Indian Eagle Owl

Spot-bellied Eagle Owl

Eurasian Eagle Owl

Brown Fish Owl

Dusky Eagle Owl

Tawny Fish Owl

Mottled Wood Owl

Brown Wood Owl

Collared Owlet *Glaucidium brodiei* 17cm **r**

Smallest owl in Asia. Short-tailed, dark, barred owlet with distinctive 'face' marks on hindneck; rufous or greyish upperparts; dark brown barring on mantle, wings, tail and sides of upper breast; relatively large, rounded head with tiny buffy spots and bright yellow eyes; white underparts have brown bar across throat and rufous-brown 'droplet'-shaped spots along sides. Sexes alike. **VOICE** Call a liquid *poop ... po ... poop ... poop*. **DISTRIBUTION** Locally common breeding resident: N mountains eastwards. **HABITAT** Thick forests at lower levels.

Asian Barred Owlet *Glaucidium cuculoides* 23cm **r**

Smallish, heavily barred owl with bright lemon-yellow eyes; white eyebrows; white moustache; yellowish-green bill; greyish-green cere. Upperparts overall olive-brown; nape and head finely speckled pale buff; faintly barred mantle. Underparts plainer with indistinct markings; white patch on throat; whitish barring on dark brown breast. Yellow feet. Sexes alike. Eastern race more rufous. Hunts by day. **VOICE** Call a bubbling *wowowo-wowowo*. Also, abrupt *kao ... kuk*. **DISTRIBUTION** Common breeding resident in northern hills. **HABITAT** Hill forests.

Jungle Owlet *Glaucidium radiatum* 20cm **r**

Lacks ear-tufts. Darkish brown above, barred rufous and white; flight feathers barred rufous and black; white moustachial stripe, centre of breast and abdomen; remainder of underbody barred dark rufous-brown and white. Sexes alike. Solitary or in pairs. Crepuscular. **VOICE** Noisy; musical *kuo ... kak ... kuo ... kak ...* call notes. **DISTRIBUTION** Throughout area, to 2,000m in the Himalayas; absent in extreme NE states. **HABITAT** Partial to Teak and bamboo mixed forests.

Spotted Owlet *Athene brama* 20cm **r**

No ear-tufts. Greyish-brown plumage, spotted white. Yellowish eyes; broken whitish-buff nuchal collar. Young birds more thickly marked white than adults; darkish streaks below breast. Sexes alike. Occurs in pairs or small parties; roosts by day in leafy branches and tree cavities. Active in some localities by day. Disturbed birds fly to neighbouring tree or branch and bob and stare at intruder. The **Little Owl** *A. noctua* a scarce and very local breeding resident in north-west mountains. **VOICE** Scolding and cackling notes, screeches and chuckles. **DISTRIBUTION** Throughout area. **HABITAT** Open forests, orchards, cultivation, human habitation.

Forest Owlet *Athene blewitti* 23cm **e** **v**

Thought to be extinct; rediscovered in 1997. Small, overall dark greyish-brown bird with fairly large head. Tail and wings heavily banded; almost completely white underparts; white face; unspotted brown crown; broad brown breast-band; barred flanks. Underparts white with large claws. Diurnal, shy and wary. **VOICE** Not well known, but *oh ... hu* and *kweek ... kweek* calls reported. **DISTRIBUTION** Rare endemic breeder rediscovered in extreme NW Maharashtra. **HABITAT** Open, dry deciduous forests on low hills.

Brown Hawk Owl *Ninox scutulata* 32cm **r**

Slender dark owl. Dark brown facial disc has white radial streaks; chocolate-brown crown and nape with ochre streaks; mantle and wing-coverts plain chocolate-brown; some white on back and wings; underparts have intense, drop-shaped streaks, becoming chevron shaped towards flanks; long, grey-banded tail with whitish tip; no ear-tufts; yellow eyes; feathered legs. Sexes alike. Crepuscular or nocturnal. **VOICE** Call an extended, liquid *oowup ... oowup ... oowup*.
DISTRIBUTION Locally common breeding resident. **HABITAT** Well-wooded country.

Birds

Collared Owlet

Jungle Owlet

Forest Owlet

Asian Barred Owlet

Spotted Owlet

Little Owl

Brown Hawk Owl

119

Andaman Hawk Owl *Ninox affinis* 25cm (e) (v)

Small to medium-sized brown owl with round head, greyish facial disc and no ear-tufts; yellow eyes; dull green cere; yellowish-grey bill; plain brown crown and mantle finely vermiculated ochre. Upperparts pale buffy-brown; underparts longitudinally streaked with chestnut from neck to abdomen. Distinguished by reddish-brown spotting on white underparts, and unmarked undertail-coverts. **VOICE** Call a loud, resounding *craw*. **DISTRIBUTION** Andaman Islands. **HABITAT** Forests, secondary woodland, mangroves.

Short-eared Owl *Asio flammeus* 38cm (m)

Medium-sized owl with cat-like face and tiny ear-tufts set in middle of forehead; bold facial disc; black mask around small yellow iris. Buff upperparts and breast streaked blackish; yellowish-ochre upper primaries with black tips and white trailing edges; whitish underwing with black tips and carpal crescents; long wings; slightly wedge-shaped tail. Sexes alike. Glides on stretched wings. Rests in grass clumps. Perches on posts. **VOICE** Usually silent. **DISTRIBUTION** Scarce but widespread winter visitor. **HABITAT** Dry, open country with scattered bushes.

Malabar Trogon *Harpactes fasciatus* 30cm (e)

Male has sooty-black head, neck and breast; yellow-brown back; black wings narrowly barred white; rich crimson underbody; white breast gorget. Female duller overall; lacks black on head and breast; orange-brown underbody. Long, squarish tail diagnostic. Solitary or in pairs. Strictly arboreal. Hunts flycatcher-style or flits among taller branches. Flicks tail and bends body when disturbed. **VOICE** Diagnostic, often a giveaway to bird's presence, somewhat whistling *cue ... cue ... cue* calls. **DISTRIBUTION** Peninsular India. **HABITAT** Forests.

Red-headed Trogon *Harpactes erythrocephalus* 35cm (r)

Brilliantly coloured bird with long, square-ended tail. Head and neck bright crimson; white crescent-shaped breast-band; underparts more pinkish. Golden-orange back; dark grey and black wings closely barred with white. Tail edged with black, with slim white outer borders; broad bill; weak legs. Female has ruddy-brown head and breast. Shy but inquisitive. Difficult to see. **VOICE** Call includes a scaled sequence of *chaup ... chaup ... chaup* notes. **DISTRIBUTION** Scarce breeding resident in NE India. **HABITAT** Dense broadleaved forests.

Ward's Trogon *Harpactes wardi* 38cm (r) (v)

Large, vividly coloured trogon. Male has deep pink forehead and supercilium; pale blue orbital skin; slaty-grey hindneck; maroon upper breast; rest of underparts pinkish-red; short, broad pink bill; long, broad pink tail; upperparts, head and upper breast maroon. Female has olive-brown head; bright yellow forehead; pale yellow underparts. Solitary or in pairs. Agile in hawking insects. **VOICE** Call includes dull, rapid, rising *klew ... klew ... klew*. **DISTRIBUTION** Sikkim, Arunachal Pradesh. **HABITAT** Dense broadleaved evergreen montane forests, bamboo.

Common Hoopoe *Upupa epops* 31cm (r)

Fawn-coloured plumage; black-and-white markings on wings, back and tail; black-and-white-tipped crest; longish, gently curved bill. Sexes alike. Solitary or in scattered pairs. Small, loose flocks in winter. Probes the ground with long bill, sometimes feeding with other birds. Flits among tree branches. Crest often fanned open. Becomes rather aggressive with onset of breeding season. **VOICE** Pleasant, mellow *hoo ... po ... po*. Calls have a ventriloquistic quality.
120 **DISTRIBUTION** Subcontinent. **HABITAT** Meadows, open country, garden lawns, open forests.

Andaman Hawk Owl

Short-eared Owl

Amit Sharma

Malabar Trogon

Red-headed Trogon

Manjula Mathur/Ramki Sreenivasan

Ward's Trogon

Common Hoopoe

Biswaroop Satpati

Great Hornbill *Buceros bicornis* 95–10cm **r** **v**

Black face, back and underbody; two white bars on black wings; white neck, lower abdomen and tail; broad black tail-band. Huge yellow bill with enormous concave-topped casque distinctive. Sexes alike. Occurs in pairs or small parties; occasionally large flocks. Mostly arboreal, feeding on fruiting trees. May settle on the ground to pick up fallen fruits. Noisy flight, audible from far away, consisting of alternation of flapping and gliding. **VOICE** Loud, deep barking calls; loud *tokk* at feeding sites. **DISTRIBUTION** Lower Himalayas, Western Ghats. **HABITAT** Forests.

Oriental Pied Hornbill *Anthracoceros albirostris* 88cm **r**

Black above; white face-patch, wing-tips (seen in flight) and tips to outer-tail feathers; black throat and breast; white below. Black-and-yellow bill with cylindrical blackish casque. Sexes alike. In small parties, occasionally collecting into several dozen birds on favourite fruiting trees; associates with other birds. Arboreal but often feeds on the ground. **VOICE** Loud cackles and screams; also a rapid *pak … pak … pak*. **DISTRIBUTION** Uttaranchal to extreme NE India; Eastern Ghats, south to Bastar and N Andhra Pradesh. **HABITAT** Forests, orchards, groves.

Malabar Pied Hornbill *Anthracoceros coronatus* 65cm **v** **e**

Striking, medium-sized hornbill with large creamish bill and very prominent black-and-yellow casque. Black head and neck; black orbital skin; white eye-ring; black white-tipped wings; white underparts. Female smaller than male, with pale blue orbital skin that turns pinkish in breeding. **VOICE** Call a loud *kek … kek … kek*. **DISTRIBUTION** Scarce endemic breeding resident in foothills of Western and Eastern Ghats. Probably overlaps in NC India with the Oriental Pied Hornbill (above). **HABITAT** Open forests and groves, particularly *Ficus* and other fruiting trees.

Malabar Grey Hornbill *Ocyceros griseus* 45cm **e**

Medium-sized hornbill with dark grey upperparts and paler grey-streaked underparts. Distinct very pale grey supercilium; blackish crown and eye-stripes; rufous bill graduating to yellow tip. Greyish-brown wings; white carpal patch; white-tipped primaries and tail; cinnamon vent. Feeds high in trees on fruits and small invertebrates. Nests in tree holes. **VOICE** Noisy, with squealing, laughing cry. **DISTRIBUTION** Local endemic breeding resident in Western Ghats. **HABITAT** Restricted to open broadleaved Western Ghat forests.

Indian Grey Hornbill *Ocyceros birostris* 50cm **r**

Grey-brown plumage; large, curved bill with casque diagnostic; long, graduated tail, tipped black and white. Casque smaller in female than male. Occurs in pairs or small parties. Mostly arboreal, but descends to pick fallen fruits or lizards. Noisy, undulating flight. **VOICE** Noisy; normal call a shrill squealing note; also other squeals and screams. **DISTRIBUTION** Almost throughout India, to about 1,500m in the Himalayas; absent in arid north-west regions and heavy rainfall areas of southern Western Ghats. **HABITAT** Forests, orchards, tree-covered avenues, human habitation.

Rufous-necked Hornbill *Aceros nipalensis* 100cm **r** **v**

Large, black-and-rufous hornbill with white terminal half of tail. Male and immature have head, neck and most of underparts rich orange-brown. Female has black head and underparts. Both have black upperparts with white wing- and tail-tips, bare blue skin around eyes and bill-base, and bare red chin-pouch. Bill long, thick and yellow but no casque. Arboreal, feeding mainly on fruits. **VOICE** Deep, single, far-carrying staccato *wok*. **DISTRIBUTION** Globally threatened rare breeding resident in northeastern forests. **HABITAT** Primary forests.

Great Hornbill

Malabar Pied Hornbill

Indian Grey Hornbill

Gururaj Moorching

Oriental Pied Hornbill

Savio Fonseca

Malabar Grey Hornbill

Rahul Gurung/Anand Gupta

Rufous-necked Hornbill

Wreathed Hornbill *Rhyticeros undulates* 80cm 🔴 ⓥ

Black hornbill with completely white tail. Male has white face, chestnut crown and nape, and red orbital patch; yellow pouch with black stripe. Female has blue pouch and black head. Female seals itself into tree hole while male feeds female and chicks through narrow slit. Feeds mainly on fruits, sometimes travelling in large parties to favoured sites. Roosts communally. **VOICE** Call a loud *kuk … kwek*; wings make whooshing sound in flight. **DISTRIBUTION** Fairly common breeding resident of NE Indian plains and foothills. **HABITAT** Forests with fruiting trees.

Indian Roller *Coracias benghalensis* 33cm 🔴

Pale greenish-brown above; rufous-brown breast; deep blue tail has light blue subterminal band; in flight, bright Oxford-blue wings and tail, with Cambridge-blue bands distinctive. Sexes alike. Solitary or in pairs. Perches on overhead wires. The much paler **European Roller** *C. garrulus* is a scarce winter visitor to the Himalayas and W India. **VOICE** Usually silent; occasionally harsh *khak … kak … kak …* notes; exuberant screeching notes and shrieks during courtship display, diving, tumbling and screaming wildly. **DISTRIBUTION** Almost entire subcontinent, south of the outer Himalayas. **HABITAT** Open country, cultivation, orchards, light forests.

Dollarbird *Eurystomus orientalis* 28cm 🔴

Dark greenish-brown upperparts, washed bluish-green on back and wings. Brown breast; throat and undertail glossy blue; silvery-blue 'coin' on primaries, visible in flight; pale belly and undertail-coverts; stout red bill with black tip; red legs and eye-ring. Perches high in trees. Crepuscular and sociable. Groups often hunt after dusk. Nests in tree holes. **VOICE** Call a rasping *drak … drak*. **DISTRIBUTION** Scarce breeding resident; partial migrant to NE India, Western Ghats. **HABITAT** Forest edges and clearings; also near cultivation.

Stork-billed Kingfisher *Pelargopsis capensis* 35cm 🔴

Very large, mainly blue-and-buff kingfisher with large head and huge red bill, making it appear top heavy. Dull blue upperparts, brown crown, and rich yellow-buff collar and underparts. Tail fairly long. Feet small and red. Sexes alike. Feeds on fish by diving; also eats crustaceans, reptiles, and young birds. **VOICE** Very noisy, uttering a loud, ringing, oft-repeated *kee kee kee*. **DISTRIBUTION** Fairly common breeding resident. **HABITAT** Well-wooded lakes, rivers, forest streams.

Brown-winged Kingfisher *Pelargopsis amauroptera* 36cm 🔴 ⓥ

Large brown kingfisher with bright orange head and underparts; huge red bill. Brown upperparts; blue rump and lower back. Feeds by plunging into water or on to mud from favoured perch. Will feed in sea surf, often resting within breaking waves. Rather sluggish but has powerful high flight. Sits on bare twigs in middle storey while calling. **VOICE** Calls include laughing, descendent *cha … cha … cha*. **DISTRIBUTION** Globally near threatened. Scarce breeding resident on E India's coast. **HABITAT** Coasts with mangroves and wooded estuaries.

Ruddy Kingfisher *Halcyon coromanda* 25cm 🔴 ⓜ

Overall orange-rufous bird with large coral-red bill; rufous-orange upperparts washed violet, and lighter rufous underparts; bluish-white rump, seen in flight. Juvenile has darker and browner underparts than adults, bluer rump, faint blackish barring on rufous underparts and blackish bill. Solitary or in pairs. Secretive; more heard than seen. Perches in understorey, dropping to capture prey. **VOICE** Descending, high-pitched *tititititti*. **DISTRIBUTION** E Himalayan foothills, NE India. **HABITAT** Pools and streams in dense tropical and subtropical evergreen forests, mangroves.

Wreathed Hornbill

Dollarbird

Brown-winged Kingfisher

Panchami Manoo Ukil

Indian Roller

Savio Fonseca

European Roller

Vinit Araora

Stork-billed Kingfisher

Gururaj Moorching

Ruddy Kingfisher

White-throated Kingfisher *Halcyon smyrnensis* 28cm ®

Chestnut-brown head, neck and underbody below breast; bright turquoise-blue above, often with greenish tinge; black flight feathers and white wing-patch in flight; white chin, throat and breast distinctive; coral-red bill and legs. Sexes alike. Solitary or in scattered pairs; often found far from water. **VOICE** Noisy; loud, cackling laugh; song a longish, quivering whistle, sounding as *kililililili* ... **DISTRIBUTION** Subcontinent, south of the outer Himalayas. **HABITAT** Forests, cultivation, lakes, riversides; also coastal mangroves and estuaries.

Black-capped Kingfisher *Halcyon pileata* 28cm ®

Black cap, white collar and deep blue upperbody; white throat and upper breast, and dull rufous below; in flight conspicuous white wing-patch; deep, dagger-like, coral-red bill. Sexes alike. Mostly solitary. Coastal bird. Has favoured feeding sites. Dives for fish but also takes insects from the ground. **VOICE** Call a shrill, fairly loud cackle, unmistakable once heard. **DISTRIBUTION** Both coasts. **HABITAT** Coastal areas, mangroves, estuaries; may wander inland, especially along rivers.

Collared Kingfisher *Todiramphus chloris* 24cm ®

Medium-sized, heavy-billed kingfisher with broad white collar. White underparts, sometimes washed buff; turquoise head, wings and tail. Variable dark and white markings depending on race. Upperparts bright turquoise-green; bluer on wings. Sexes alike. Juvenile has faint buff scaling on upperparts, and indistinct dark scaling on underparts and collar. Solitary or in pairs. **VOICE** Call a hard *krerk ... krerk ... krerk*. **DISTRIBUTION** Scarce breeding resident sporadically along coast. **HABITAT** Mangroves.

Common Kingfisher *Alcedo atthis* 18cm ®

Bright blue above, and greenish on wings; top of head finely banded black and blue; ferruginous cheeks and ear-coverts; white patch on neck-sides; white chin and throat and deep ferruginous underbody distinctive; coral-red legs and blackish bill. Sexes alike. Solitary or in scattered pairs. Never found away from water. Occasionally hovers over the water before diving for fish. The rarer **Blue-eared Kingfisher** *A. meninting* is often mistaken for this species, but is deeper blue with brighter orange underparts, and restricted to forest streams. **VOICE** Shrill *chichee chichee*. **DISTRIBUTION** Subcontinent. **HABITAT** Streams, lakes, canals; also coastal areas.

Oriental Dwarf Kingfisher *Ceyx erithaca* 14cm ®

Tiny forest bird. Brownish-chestnut crown; iridescent purple back and rump; deep purplish-blue of closed wings often hides back; deep blue-and-white spots on neck-sides and short chestnut tail; orangish-yellow underbody and large, bright coral-red bill striking. Sexes alike. Solitary or in pairs. **VOICE** Call a sharp, squeaky *chicheee ... or chcheee*. **DISTRIBUTION** E Garhwal through NE Indian states; Western Ghats; Nilgiris. Appears in many areas only with onset of SW monsoons. **HABITAT** Forest streams, nullahs.

Crested Kingfisher *Megaceryle lugubris* 41–43cm ®

Crested, dark grey-and-white kingfisher, much larger than the Pied Kingfisher (p. 128). Strongly barred, dark grey-and-white upperparts; untidy, white-streaked black crest, erect when alarmed; white collar; white face with black malar stripe; orange neck-patch on male, black-speckled white on female. Underparts white with grey flank barring. Strongly barred black-and-white tail. Powerful dark bill. Solitary and loyal to favoured perches. **VOICE** Quiet; occasional *kik* note.

DISTRIBUTION Breeding resident of Himalayan rivers. **HABITAT** Fast-flowing rivers.

White-throated Kingfisher

Collared Kingfisher

Oriental Dwarf Kingfisher

Black-capped Kingfisher

Savio Fonseca

Common Kingfisher

Savio Fonseca

Blue-eared Kingfisher

Savio Fonseca

Crested Kingfisher

Manoj Kejriwal

Pied Kingfisher *Ceryle rudis* 25cm ⓡ

Speckled black-and-white plumage diagnostic; black nuchal crest; double black gorget across breast in male. Female differs in having single broken breast gorget. Solitary, in pairs or in small groups. Always around water, perched on poles, tree stumps or rocks. Hovers when hunting, bill pointed down as wings beat rapidly. Dives fast, headlong on sighting fish; batters catch on perch. Calls in flight. **VOICE** Piercing, twittering *chirrruk … chirruk …* cries in flight, sounding as if the bird is complaining. **DISTRIBUTION** Subcontinent. **HABITAT** Streams, rivers, ponds.

Blue-bearded Bee-eater *Nyctyornis athertoni* 34cm ⓡ

Unmarked grass-green above; bluer on forehead; elongated blue feathers along centre of throat to breast appear beard-like, prominent when bird is calling; buffy-yellow below breast, streaked green; tail lacks long central pins; long, sickle-shaped tail. Sexes alike. Occurs in pairs or groups. Arboreal. Makes short aerial sallies after winged insects; batters prey on perch. Usually not an easy bird to see from close up. **VOICE** Harsh *korrr … korrr* croaking notes. **DISTRIBUTION** The Himalayas, Western and Eastern Ghats, NE and E India. **HABITAT** Edges of forests, clearings.

Green Bee-eater *Merops orientalis* 16–18cm ⓡ

Bright green plumage; red-brown wash about head; pale blue on chin and throat, bordered below by black gorget; slender, curved black bill; rufous wash on black-tipped flight feathers; elongated central-tail feathers distinctive. Sexes alike. Occurs in small parties. Perches freely on bare branches and overhead telegraph wires; launches graceful sorties after winged insects; batters prey against perch before swallowing it. **VOICE** Noisy; cheerful trilling notes, chiefly uttered on the wing. **DISTRIBUTION** Subcontinent. **HABITAT** Open country and cultivation, light forests.

Blue-tailed Bee-eater *Merops philippinus* 23–26cm ⓡ

Elongated central-tail feathers. Greenish above, with faint blue wash on wings; bluish rump and tail diagnostic; yellow upper throat-patch with chestnut throat and upper breast; slightly curved black bill; broad black stripe through eye. Sexes alike. The very similar **Blue-cheeked Bee-eater** M. *persicus* has dull white and blue-green cheek-patch. Usually in small flocks. **VOICE** Musical, ringing notes. **DISTRIBUTION** Breeds in N, NE India; winters in S India. **HABITAT** Open country, light forests, vicinity of water, cultivation.

Chestnut-headed Bee-eater *Merops leschenaulti* 21cm ⓡ

Grass-green plumage; chestnut-cinnamon crown, hindneck and upper back; yellow chin and throat; rufous and black gorget. Sexes alike. Occurs in small gatherings on telegraph wires or bare upper branches of trees, from where the birds launch short aerial sallies. Fast, graceful flight. Noisy when converging at roosting trees. **VOICE** Musical twittering notes, uttered on the wing, and sometimes from perch. **DISTRIBUTION** Disjunct, but widespread. **HABITAT** Vicinity of water in forested areas.

Great Barbet *Psilopogon virens* 33cm ⓡ

Bluish-black head and throat; maroon-brown back; yellowish hind-collar; green on lower back and tail; brown upper breast; pale yellow below, with thick, greenish-blue streaks; red undertail-coverts distinctive. Large yellowish bill. Sexes alike. Solitary or in small bands. Arboreal, but comes into low-fruiting bushes. Difficult to spot and mostly heard. **VOICE** Very noisy; loud, if somewhat mournful *pi … you* or *pi … oo*, uttered continuously for several minutes; one of the most familiar bird calls in the Himalayas. **DISTRIBUTION** The Himalayas. **HABITAT** Forests, orchards.

Pied Kingfisher

Blue-bearded Bee-eater

Arpit Deomurari

Green Bee-eater

Blue-tailed Bee-eater

Biswarup Satpati

Blue-cheeked Bee-eater

Manjula Mathur

Chestnut-headed Bee-eater

Great Barbet

Vinit Arora

Brown-headed Barbet *Psilopogon zeylanicus* 28cm (r)

Grass-green plumage; brownish head, neck and upper back, streaked white; bare orange patch around eye. Sexes alike. Solitary or in pairs; occasionally in small parties. Strictly arboreal; keeps to fruiting trees, often with other frugivorous birds. Difficult to spot in the canopy. Strong, undulating flight. The **Lineated Barbet** *P. lineatus* distinguished by broader white eyebrows and larger yellow eye-patches leading to bill. VOICE Noisy; *kutroo … kutroo* or *pukrook … pukrook* call. DISTRIBUTION Most of India south of the foothills. HABITAT Forests, groves; city gardens.

White-cheeked Barbet *Psilopogon viridis* 28cm (e)

Large green-and-brown barbet with light brown head streaked buff; pale yellow orbital patch; large yellowish-horn coloured bill; bright green body with unmarked wings; heavy white streaking on head, neck, mantle and underparts to upper belly; white throat. Sexes alike. Strictly arboreal. Feeds on fruits. Calls from open branches. VOICE Persistent, rather subdued *kuruk … kuruk*, usually with long guttural start-up note. DISTRIBUTION Western Ghats, S Eastern Ghats, hills of S India. HABITAT Foothill forests, parks, gardens.

Golden-throated Barbet *Psilopogon franklinii* 23cm (r)

Plump, medium-sized green barbet with distinct head pattern; yellow upper throat and greyish lower throat; red forehead and hindcrown and yellow crown centre; broad black stripe through eye; whitish cheeks. Mainly green upperparts and greenish-yellow underparts; bluish wing shoulders. Short tail. Sexes alike. Feeds mainly on fruits. Solitary or in pairs. Difficult to see in foliage. Nests in tree holes. VOICE Start-up call *krrr* followed by monotonous *pukwok … pukwok*. DISTRIBUTION Breeding resident in NE plains and hills. HABITAT Forest trees.

Blue-throated Barbet *Psilopogon asiaticus* 23cm (r)

Grass-green plumage; black, crimson, yellow and blue about head; blue chin and throat diagnostic; crimson spots on sides of throat. Sexes alike. Solitary or in pairs; sometimes small parties on fruiting trees, along with other fruit-eating birds. Strictly arboreal; keeps to canopy of tall trees. Difficult to spot but loud, monotonous calls an indicator of its presence. VOICE Calls similar to those of the Brown-headed Barbet (above). DISTRIBUTION The Himalayas east from Kashmir; to about 2,250m; also Bengal, including Kolkata. HABITAT Forests, groves.

Coppersmith Barbet *Psilopogon haemacephalus* 17cm (r)

Grass-green plumage; yellow throat; crimson breast and forehead; dumpy appearance. Sexes alike. The similar-sized **Malabar Barbet** *P. malabaricus* (e) of the Western Ghats has a crimson chin, throat, foreneck and upper breast. Solitary, in pairs or in small parties. Strictly arboreal. Feeds on fruiting trees, often with other birds. Visits flowering *Erythrina* and *Bombax* trees for flower nectar. VOICE Noisy, monotonous *tuk … tuk …* Familiar sound of the Indian countryside. DISTRIBUTION All India. HABITAT Light forests, groves, city gardens.

Yellow-rumped Honeyguide *Indicator xanthonotus* 15cm (r)

Olive-brown plumage; bright orangish-yellow forehead, cheeks and rump (lower back) diagnostic, seen also when perched, with wings drooping slightly; finch-like bill; overall appearance sparrow-like. Sexes alike. Solitary or in small scattered parties. Keeps to cliffs and rock faces around honeybee colonies; no indication of guiding humans or any other mammal to honeycomb sites. VOICE Call note a sharp *cheep …* DISTRIBUTION The Himalayas.

Overlooked species. HABITAT Rock faces and cliffs in forests; in some areas above treeline.

Brown-headed Barbet

Lineated Barbet

A V Prassana

White-cheeked Barbet

Golden-throated Barbet

Manjula Mathur

Malabar Barbet

Blue-throated Barbet

Panchami Manoo Ukil

Coppersmith Barbet

Yellow-rumped Honeyguide

Clement M Francis

Eurasian Wryneck *Jynx torquilla* 17cm ⓡ

Small, rather reptilian-looking woodpecker, the colour of tree bark. Basically grey and brown with dark eye-stripes and dark stripe running from crown to rump. Underparts barred and throat warm buff. Tail long and barred, making it look rather shrike-like in flight. Bill short and pointed. Twists neck around and often raises crown feathers. Does not drill holes or use tail as support. **VOICE** Call a high-pitched *pee … pee … pee*. **DISTRIBUTION** Breeds in Kashmir. Scarce but widespread winter visitor. **HABITAT** Breeds in scrub and cultivation.

Speckled Piculet *Picumnus innominatus* 10cm ⓡ

Olive-green above (male has some orange and black on forecrown); two white stripes on sides of head, the upper one longer; dark olive band through eyes; moustachial stripe; creamy-white below, boldly spotted with black. Sexes alike. Usually in pairs. The similar-sized **White-browed Piculet** *Sasia ochracea* is overall brown and rufous in colouration, with prominent white supercilia. **VOICE** Sharp, rapid *tsip … tsip …*; also loud drumming sound. **DISTRIBUTION** The Himalayas, foothills. Eastern and Western Ghats, from Goa south. **HABITAT** Mixed forests; fondness for bamboo jungle.

Heart-spotted Woodpecker *Hemicircus canente* 16cm ⓡ

Male has black forehead (speckled white), crown and crest; black back; broad, pale buff wing-patch with heart-shaped spots; black flight feathers; whitish-buff, olive and black below. Female has extensive buff-white on forehead; otherwise similar to male. Occurs in pairs or small parties. Active and arboreal. Perches across branch and calls often. **VOICE** Quite vocal, especially in flight; call a somewhat harsh *chirr …*; other sharp clicking and squeaky notes. **DISTRIBUTION** Western Ghats, Satpuras, SE Madhya Pradesh, Odisha, NE India. **HABITAT** Forests.

Brown-capped Pygmy Woodpecker *Yungipicus nanus* 13cm ⓡ

Small woodpecker. Male barred brown and white above; paler crown with short scarlet streak; prominent white band from just above eyes extends to neck; pale dirty-brown-white below, streaked black. The male **Grey-capped Pygmy Woodpecker** *Y. canicapillus* of the Himalayas has black upper back and white-barred lower back and rump. Male's tiny red nape mark is often invisible. Mostly in pairs. Quite active. **VOICE** Faint but shrill squeak, sounding like *clicck … rrr*. **DISTRIBUTION** Almost all India. **HABITAT** Light forests, cultivation, bamboo, orchards.

Brown-fronted Woodpecker *Dendrocoptes auriceps* 20cm ⓡ

Medium-sized Himalayan woodpecker. Overall pied; yellow crown; black upperparts barred white; black moustache extends to breast; black-streaked white underparts; deep pink vent. Male has brown forecrown with yellow centre; red rear crown; red vent. Female has entirely yellow crown. Uses tail as prop. Nests in self-made holes. **VOICE** Calls a fast, chattering *chik … chik chik … rrr* and short *chik*. **DISTRIBUTION** Locally common breeding resident in northern hills. **HABITAT** Deciduous and coniferous hill forests.

Yellow-fronted Woodpecker *Leiopicus mahrattensis* 18cm ⓡ

Male brownish-black above, spotted all over with white; golden-brown forehead and crown; small scarlet crest; pale fulvous below throat, streaked brown; scarlet patch in centre of abdomen distinctive. Female lacks scarlet crest. Solitary or in pairs. Moves in jerks along tree branches. **VOICE** Soft but sharp *clic … click … clickrrr …*; drums when breeding. **DISTRIBUTION** Common and widespread; all subcontinent, from the Himalayan foothills south; uncommon in northeastern regions. **HABITAT** Open forests, scrub, cultivation, vicinity of human habitation, gardens.

Eurasian Wryneck

Speckled Piculet

Kintoo Dhawan

Heart-spotted Woodpecker

White-browed Piculet

Ramki Sreenivasan

Grey-capped Pygmy Woodpecker

Brown-capped Pygmy Woodpecker

Garima Bhatia

Brown-fronted Woodpecker

Yellow-fronted Woodpecker

Garima Bhatia

Rufous-bellied Woodpecker *Dendrocopos hyperythrus* 20cm ⓡ

Distinct woodpecker with rufous underparts and strongly barred black-and-white upper mantle; white face and chin; black rump and central tail. Male has red crown; female has black crown spotted white. Occurs singly or in pairs. Probes bark for sap. Nests in self-made tree holes. Confiding and approachable. **VOICE** Call a short *kit*, sometimes extended excitedly. **DISTRIBUTION** NW mountains, NE India. **HABITAT** Montane forests with preference for coniferous trees.

Fulvous-breasted Woodpecker *Dendrocopos macei* 18cm ⓡ

Medium-sized pied woodpecker with heavily barred back and underparts. Male has distinct red crown; orange forehead; black and white in female. Buff belly with light barring and streaking on flanks; red undertail; whitish cheeks, partially bordered black. Feeds on invertebrates. Often props itself on tail. Locally common. Nests in self-made holes. **VOICE** Call a hard *tick*, sometimes extended into chatter. **DISTRIBUTION** Common breeding resident in N, NE India, Eastern Ghats. **HABITAT** Open broadleaved and coniferous forests.

White-bellied Woodpecker *Dryocopus javensis* 48cm ⓡ

Male has black head, upperbody and breast; white rump and underparts below breast; bright crimson crown (including forehead), crest and cheeks. Crimson restricted to nape in female. Occurs in pairs, sometimes 4–5 birds, in tall forests. Moves up along tree stems, jerkily and slowly, inspecting bark crevices for insects. Strong, lazy flight. **VOICE** Call a loud, metallic *chiank* note. Chuckling note in flight. **DISTRIBUTION** Forested areas of Western Ghats, south of Tapti river; also Bastar. **HABITAT** Tall evergreen forests.

Andaman Woodpecker *Dryocopus hodgei* 38cm ⓔ

Large blackish woodpecker, endemic to Andaman Islands. Male has red crown, crest and moustachial stripe; pale eyes and very long bill; red restricted to hindcrown and crest in female. Similar to the White-bellied Woodpecker (above), but without white on belly and differs in range. Solitary or in pairs. Feeds high in the canopy, but sometimes descends to feed. **VOICE** Shrill, sharp, two-note cries. **DISTRIBUTION** Restricted to Andaman Islands. **HABITAT** Mangroves, evergreen forests.

Greater Yellownape *Chrysophlegma flavinucha* 33cm ⓡ

Prominent yellow-crested nape and throat. Underparts dark olive-green and grey. Brownish crown; flight feathers chestnut-barred black. Shy, flushing readily if disturbed. Uses tail as prop. Nests in tree holes. Feeds on invertebrates, from the ground to the canopy. Often seen with mixed hunting species. **VOICE** Calls include loud, plaintive *keeyu* and hard *chep* note. **DISTRIBUTION** Fairly common breeding resident of N foothills, NE India, Eastern Ghats. **HABITAT** Upland broadleaved forests.

Lesser Yellownape *Picus chlorolophus* 27cm ⓡ

Medium-sized woodpecker with green upperparts; bright yellow, tufted nape. Olive-green neck and breast; whitish belly, finely barred green; black rump and tail. Adult male has green head and white throat; red markings above eye and nape; red moustachial stripe. Female has red patch above ear-coverts. Feeds on invertebrates at lower levels, including the ground. **VOICE** Noisy. Call a loud, sad *pee … oo* and descending *ke … ke … ke … ke*. **DISTRIBUTION** Common breeding resident in foothills, NE and peninsular hills. **HABITAT** Forests, plantations.

Rufous-bellied Woodpecker

Fulvous-breasted Woodpecker

White-bellied Woodpecker

Andaman Woodpecker

Lesser Yellownape

Greater Yellownape

135

Streak-throated Woodpecker *Picus xanthopygaeus* 30cm ⓡ

Male grass-green above; crimson crown and crest; orange and brown on nape; white supercilium and malar stripe; yellow rump; bold black scaly streaks on white underbody with tawny green wash on breast; throat greyer and streaked. Female has black crown and crest. Solitary or in pairs. Works up along tree stems; moves either straight up or in spirals. Taps with bill for insects. Also settles on the ground. **VOICE** Mostly silent; call an occasional *pick* …; drums on branches. **DISTRIBUTION** Subcontinent; to 1,500m in the outer Himalayas. **HABITAT** Mixed forests, plantations.

Scaly-bellied Woodpecker *Picus squamatus* 35cm ⓡ

Similar to the Streak-throated Woodpecker (above), but larger, with unstreaked throat and upper breast. Strong black moustachial stripe; white supercilium speckled black; large pale bill; distinct scaling from breast to vent; strongly barred tail. Male has red forehead, crown and nape, while female has dark slaty crown. **VOICE** Contact call a hard, repeated *quik*. Also musical, repeated *peeko … peeko*. **DISTRIBUTION** Common breeding resident in northern mountain forests east to E Nepal. **HABITAT** Coniferous and broadleaved forests; cultivated country.

Grey-headed Woodpecker *Picus canus* 32cm ⓡ

Male darkish green above; crimson forehead; black hindcrown, faint crest and nape; dark sides of head and black malar stripe; yellow rump; white-barred dark wings and blackish tail; unmarked, dull greyish-olive underbody diagnostic. Female black from forehead to nape; no crimson. Solitary or in pairs. Descends to the ground, hopping awkwardly. **VOICE** High-pitched *keek … keek …* of 4–5 notes; drums often between March and early June. **DISTRIBUTION** The Himalayas from lower foothills. **HABITAT** Forests, both deciduous and temperate.

Himalayan Flameback *Dinopium shorii* 30–32cm ⓡ

Largish woodpecker with golden upperparts. Male has black hindneck; brownish-buff throat centre with irregular border of black spots; indistinctly divided moustachial stripe; brownish-buff centre with small red patch; reddish or brown eyes; blackish bill; greenish-brown feet. Underparts boldly streaked and scalloped black, and on some, almost unmarked. Confiding. Often seen in mixed feeding flocks. Locally common. **VOICE** Call a rapid, repeated *klok … klok … klak … klok … klak*. **DISTRIBUTION** The Himalayas. **HABITAT** Mature forests.

Black-rumped Flameback *Dinopium benghalense* 30cm ⓡ

Male shining golden-yellow and black above; crimson crown and crest; black throat and head-sides, with fine white streaks; white underbody, streaked black, boldly on breast. Female has black crown spotted with white; crimson crest. Occurs in pairs. Widespread and common. Moves jerkily up and around tree stems or clings to undersides of branches. **VOICE** Noisy. Call a loud, high-pitched cackle, like laughter; drums often. **DISTRIBUTION** Subcontinent. **HABITAT** Forests, both dry and mixed deciduous, orchards, gardens, villages and other human habitation.

Greater Flameback *Chrysocolaptes guttacristatus* 33cm ⓡ

Male has crimson crown and crest; golden-olive above; white and black sides of face and throat; whitish-buff below, profusely spotted with black on foreneck, and speckled over rest of underbody; extensive crimson rump and black tail and flight feathers distinctive. Female has white-spotted black crown and crest. **VOICE** Noisy. Loud, grating scream; calls mostly in flight. **DISTRIBUTION** Uttaranchal to NE India; parts of Eastern Ghats, SE Madhya Pradesh; Western Ghats, Kerala to Tapti river; plains to about 1,500m. **HABITAT** Forests.

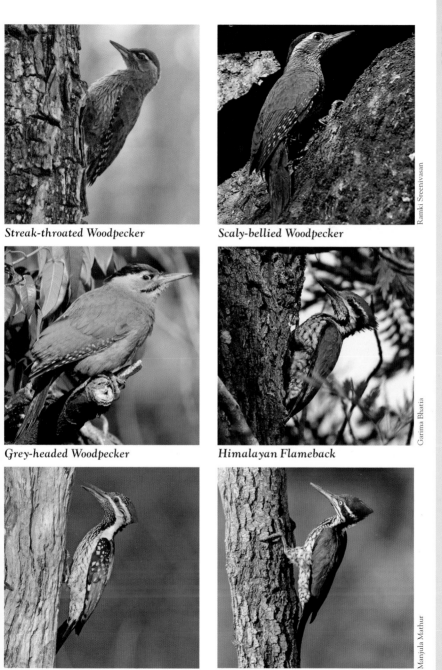

Streak-throated Woodpecker

Scaly-bellied Woodpecker

Grey-headed Woodpecker

Himalayan Flameback

Black-rumped Flameback

Greater Flameback

Ramki Sreenivasan

Garima Bhatia

Manjula Mathur

White-naped Woodpecker *Chrysocolaptes festivus* 29cm (e)

Pied woodpecker with red-crested crown in male, yellow in female. Conspicuous white nape with a contrasting black border, and a divided black horizontal stripe below the cheek. Black lines extend up from neck from nape to bill, branching to rear crown; white face. Uses tail as prop. Feeds on lower branches and sometimes on the ground. Nests in self-made tree holes. **VOICE** Thin, repeated *tee … tee … tee …* **DISTRIBUTION** Scarce breeding endemic, mostly in peninsular India. **HABITAT** Dry open woodland, plantations, shrubs.

Rufous Woodpecker *Micropternus brachyurus* 25cm (r)

Chestnut-brown plumage; fine black cross-bars on upper body, including wings and tail; paler edges to throat feathers; crimson patch under eye in male, absent in female. Sexes alike. Usually in pairs; sometimes 4–5 scattered birds close by. Mostly seen around ball-shaped nests of tree ants; clings to outsides of nests and digs for ants. Plumage often smeared with gummy substance. **VOICE** Rather vocal, loud, high-pitched 3–4 notes, *ke … ke … kr … ke …*; drums when breeding. **DISTRIBUTION** Subcontinent, south of the outer Himalayas. **HABITAT** Mixed forests.

Great Slaty Woodpecker *Mulleripicus pulverulentus* 51cm (r) (v)

Overall grey with bluish wash; ear-coverts and neck speckled with white; paler underparts; breast faintly speckled creamy-white to golden throat and upper neck; darker tail and wings. Brown iris and grey orbital ring. Male has pinkish-red patch on malar region and pink on lower throat. Long, robust bill with grey-yellow lower mandible and grey upper mandible; bluish-grey legs. Gregarious; seen in flocks. **VOICE** Loud bleating and cackle in flight. **DISTRIBUTION** The Himalayas and terai region. **HABITAT** Mature trees in tropical forests and clearings.

Collared Falconet *Microhierax caerulescens* 18cm (r)

Very small, pied falcon, with bold white supercilium and collar. Slaty-grey cheeks and crown; double-toothed bill, shortish wings and barred tail; rufous underparts; underwings white with black bars; strong, rufous-feathered legs. Half-feathered legs and powerful feet. Sexes similar. Perches on tops or edges of trees or bushes, frequently bobbing head and slowly moving tail up and down. **VOICE** Call a shrill whistle, *killi … kill.* **DISTRIBUTION** Scarce breeding resident: Himalayan foothills. **HABITAT** Clearings and edges of broadleaved tropical forests and plantations.

Common Kestrel *Falco tinnunculus* 35cm (r) (m)

Male black-streaked, ash-grey crown, sides of neck and nape; rufous mantle, black spotted; cheek-stripe; grey tail has white tip and black subterminal band; streaked and spotted buffy underbody and black talons. Female pale rufous above; streaked head and narrowly barred back; paler buff below, densely streaked. Solitary or in pairs. Often hovers. The migratory, smaller **Lesser Kestrel** *F. naumanni* is more delicate looking, with shorter wings and tail. **VOICE** Infrequent clicking sound. **DISTRIBUTION** Resident; local migrant. **HABITAT** Open country; cliff sides.

Red-necked Falcon *Falco chicquera* 35cm (r) (v)

Smallish, stout falcon, with short, blunt-ended wings, long, rounded tail and distinctive chestnut head and neck. Overall blue-grey plumage with black primary feathers; white-tipped grey tail, whitish underparts mottled and streaked black and rufous; black banding on belly. Sexes similar. Hunts from sheltered perch. Rapid, direct flight; rarely hovers. **VOICE** Calls include shrill, trilling screams. **DISTRIBUTION** Resident; all India, south of the Himalayan
foothills. **HABITAT** Prefers open country and cultivated plains with groups of trees.

White-naped Woodpecker

Great Slaty Woodpecker

Common Kestrel

Lesser Kestrel

Rufous Woodpecker

Nitin Srinivasamurthy

Collared Falconet

Tripta Sood

Red-necked Falcon

Nikhil Devasar

139

Amur Falcon *Falco amurensis* 26–30cm (m)

Small, slender falcon with long, pointed wings. Male overall dark grey, with rusty-cinnamon lower abdomen and thighs; white underwing, prominent in flight; bright orange-red legs and facial skin; orange bill-base; white claws. Female similar in size to male, with cream or rusty underparts, streaked and barred; grey upperparts; slaty-grey head; barred tail with dark tip; white cheeks and throat; dark eye-patch and moustache. Very sociable. **VOICE** Call a high-pitched *kew ... kew ...* **DISTRIBUTION** Scarce passage migrant. **HABITAT** Open country near water.

Eurasian Hobby *Falco subbuteo* 33cm (r)

Small, slender falcon with long, square-tipped tail. Upperparts and crown slaty-grey; creamy buff underparts heavily streaked black; chestnut thighs and vent; underwings and undertail barred; pale throat and cheeks; dark moustache; thin white line above eye. Sexes alike. Aerial feeder. The rarer **Oriental Hobby** *F. severus* has slaty-grey upperparts and deep black head and cheeks; rich chestnut underparts with paler throat. **VOICE** Call a hurried *ki ki ki ki.* **DISTRIBUTION** Breeds in the Himalayas; scarce passage migrant. **HABITAT** Open, wooded country often near water.

Laggar Falcon *Falco jugger* 45cm (r) (v)

Overall dark greyish-brown falcon with white head; rufous crown; narrow, dark moustache. Whitish underparts streaked densely on flanks. In flight, pale breast contrasts with darker flanks and thighs; longish tail. Sexes alike, but female larger than male. Usually in pairs. The more restricted **Saker Falcon** *F. cherrug* is difficult to identify due to its various colourations, ranging from uniform chocolate-brown, to pale buff, to almost pure white. **VOICE** Call a 2–3-note scream, mostly when breeding. **DISTRIBUTION** Resident, local migrant; all India. **HABITAT** Open country, scrub.

Peregrine Falcon *Falco peregrinus* 38–51cm (r) (m)

Fairly large, stocky falcon with pointed wings and relatively short, square tail. Upperparts bluish-grey; underparts reddish-brown with variable dark spotting and barring; barred underwings and tail; pale throat and cheeks; broad dark moustachial stripe. Yellowish-orange facial skin and legs; bluish bill, tinged yellow at base and black at tip. Sexes similar, **VOICE** Variety of calls, including loud, harsh, persistent chatter, used against intruders. **DISTRIBUTION** Resident; all India; not found in semi-arid regions. **HABITAT** Mostly rugged, mountainous areas, cliffs.

Slaty-headed Parakeet *Psittacula himalayana* 40cm (r)

Both sexes overall green, washed blue; bluish-grey head; blackish chin; wide stripe across lower cheeks; blue-green band around hindneck bordered with fine black line; base of tail green graduating to deep blue, tipped with bright yellow; red upper mandible and pale yellow lower mandible; pale yellow eyes. Male has prominent maroon patch on inner median wing-coverts and long central-tail feathers. **VOICE** Noisy, musical *tool ... tool.* **DISTRIBUTION** Common breeding resident of N hills; resident in the Himalayas to Arunachal Pradesh. **HABITAT** Hill forests.

Plum-headed Parakeet *Psittacula cyanocephala* 35cm (r)

Male has yellowish-green plumage; plum-red head; black and bluish-green collar; maroon-red wing shoulder-patch; white tips to central-tail feathers distinctive. Female dull, with greyer head than male; yellow collar; almost non-existent maroon shoulder-patch. Occurs in pairs or small parties. Arboreal, but descends into cultivation; sometimes huge gatherings. Strong, darting flight over forests. **VOICE** Loud, interrogative *tooi ... tooi ...* notes in fast flight. **DISTRIBUTION** Subcontinent south of the Himalayan foothills. **HABITAT** Forests, orchards, cultivation in forests.

Amur Falcon

Laggar Falcon

Saker Falcon

Slaty-headed Parakeet

Eurasian Hobby

Oriental Hobby

Peregrine Falcon

Plum-headed Parakeet

Red-breasted Parakeet *Psittacula alexandri* 38cm **r**

Attractive medium-sized, distinctive parakeet with rosy-pink breast; blue-grey head, black lores and broad black stripe across chin; yellow wing-patches. Male has red bill, female black. Female overall a shade paler. Long tail bluish, narrow and seemingly short. Gregarious; generally in small feeding and roosting flocks; large feeding and raiding parties can be destructive. Slower flight than in other parakeets. **VOICE** Quiet when feeding; otherwise noisy and vocal. Call a loud, nasal *kaink*. Also wailing notes. **DISTRIBUTION** N and NE foothills. **HABITAT** Open deciduous forests, secondary growth, hillside cultivation.

Malabar Parakeet *Psittacula columboides* 38cm **e**

Long-tailed, mainly blue-and-grey parakeet with bluish-grey head, breast and mantle, blue flight feathers and yellow-edged blue tail. Green patch around eyes. Both sexes have black collars; pale iris. Bluish-green collar-band absent in female, which has less green on face and forecrown than male. Juvenile has greenish head; bluish-green band under black stripe absent. Very sociable. Nests in tree holes. **VOICE** Call a hard, squeaky *screet ... screet*. **DISTRIBUTION** Endemic breeding resident restricted to Western Ghats. **HABITAT** Mainly evergreen hill forests.

Alexandrine Parakeet *Psittacula eupatria* 53cm **r**

Male has rich grass-green plumage; hooked, heavy red bill; deep red shoulder-patch; rose-pink collar and black stripe from lower mandible to collar distinctive. Female smaller and lacks collar and black chin-stripe. Yellow undertail in both sexes. Occurs both in small flocks and large gatherings. Feeds on fruiting trees in orchards and on standing crops. Strong flier. **VOICE** High-pitched *kreeak ... scream*, on the wing as well as on perch. **DISTRIBUTION** Throughout area. **HABITAT** Forests, orchards, cultivated areas, towns.

Rose-ringed Parakeet *Psittacula krameri* 42cm **r**

Male has grass-green plumage; short, hooked red bill; rosy-pink and black collar distinctive. Female lacks pink-and-black collar; instead, pale emerald-green around neck. Gregarious; large flocks a familiar sight in India. Causes extensive damage to crops, orchards and garden fruit trees; also raids grain depots and markets. Large roosting colonies, often with mynas and crows. **VOICE** Shrill *keeak ... screams*. **DISTRIBUTION** Subcontinent. **HABITAT** Light forests, orchards, towns, villages.

Vernal Hanging Parrot *Loriculus vernalis* 15cm **r**

Small, short-tailed and primarily emerald-green bird with blue patch on throat; red rump and uppertail-coverts; red bill; white eyes. Female similar to male but with little or no blue on throat. Juvenile similar to adults but has dull greyish-green on forehead and cheeks; no blue on throat; dull red rump washed green; pale orange bill; brown eye. Unique for ability to sleep upside down. Very arboreal. **VOICE** Quiet but distinctive and rapid *zzit ... zzit* in flight. **DISTRIBUTION** Scarce breeding resident of lower hills of SW, E India. **HABITAT** Forests.

Long-tailed Broadbill *Psarisomus dalhousiae* 28cm **r**

Gregarious, noisy, forest-dwelling bird with vivid plumage. Long, thin blue tail; black head; yellow face and throat-sides; blue patch on crown; yellowish-blue ear-covert patch; yellow-green bill; large eyes; bright green upperparts; blue-green underparts. Diagnostic white patch on blue underwing visible in flight. Arboreal and crepuscular. Perches upright. **VOICE** Calls include loud, repeated whistles, *tseeay ... pseeuw*. **DISTRIBUTION** Uttaranchal eastwards to entire NE Indian region. **HABITAT** Tropical and subtropical semi-evergreen and evergreen forests, bamboo.

Red-breasted Parakeet

Malabar Parakeet

Manjula Mathur

Alexandrine Parakeet

Rose-ringed Parakeet

Garima Bhatia

Vernal Hanging Parrot

Long-tailed Broadbill

Manjula Mathur

Silver-breasted Broadbill *Serilophus lunatus* 19cm ⓡ

Adult male has greyish forehead; broad black eyebrow continuing through to neck; yellow eye-ring. Black wings with blue-and-white wing-patches; ash-brown mantle; chestnut lower back; brown rump; black tail with white border. Female has broken white necklace; black thighs. Iris varies from emerald-green to sapphire-blue. **VOICE** Call a mostly squeaky *pee … ou*. **DISTRIBUTION** Scarce breeding resident, extreme NE India. **HABITAT** Lowlands, foothill forests.

Indian Pitta *Pitta brachyura* 19cm ⓡ

Multi-coloured, stub-tailed, stoutly built bird; bright blue, green, black, white, yellowish-brown and crimson; white chin, throat and patch on wing-tips and crimson vent distinctive. Sexes alike. Solitary or in pairs. Spends much time on the ground. Shows fondness for shaded, semi-damp areas. The very similar **Mangrove Pitta** *P. megarhyncha* has longer, heavier bill and dark brown crown without black coronal stripe. Different call. **VOICE** Loud, lively whistle, *wheeet … peu*; very vocal when breeding; also longish single-note whistle. **DISTRIBUTION** Almost entire subcontinent, with seasonal movement. **HABITAT** Forests, orchards; also cultivation.

Bar-winged Flycatcher-shrike *Hemipus picatus* 14cm ⓡ

Pied shrike with distinct black cap and hindneck. Brown mantle in Himalayan race (shown). Black in southern races. Long white patches on black wings showing 'V' in rear views. Tail black with white borders. Throat white, contrasting with pinkish-grey underparts. Female more brown than male. **VOICE** Noisy. Calls include persistent *tsit … it … it … tsit … it … it … , si …* and short *chip*. **DISTRIBUTION** Fairly common breeding resident in foothills, Eastern and Western Ghats. Makes altitudinal and other local movements. **HABITAT** Open forests, edges of forests.

Large Woodshrike *Tephrodornis virgatus* 23cm ⓡ

Plain, thickset, shrike-like bird with drab plumage; heavy black bill; distinct nasal tuft. Certain Himalayan and eastern races have grey crown and nape; brown mantle and upperparts; fairly broad dark mask; black bill; usually yellow eyes; breast and flanks have pale pinkish-grey wash. Female duller than male, with brown upperparts and ill-defined mask. The **Malabar Woodshrike** *T. v. sylvicola* is larger and has white outer-tail feathers. **VOICE** Tuneful *kew … kew … kew …* **DISTRIBUTION** NE India and lowlands of E India. **HABITAT** Moist evergreen broadleaved forests.

Common Woodshrike *Tephrodornis pondicerianus* 18cm ⓡ

Greyish-brown plumage; broad whitish supercilium and dark stripe below eye distinctive; white outer-tail feathers seen when bird flies. Dark stripe may be slightly paler in female than male. Sexes alike. Occurs in pairs or small parties. **VOICE** Whistling *wheet … wheet …* and interrogative, quick-repeated *whi … whi … whi … whee* thereafter. **DISTRIBUTION** Most of India; most common in low country. **HABITAT** Light forests, edges of forests, cultivation, gardens in and around human habitation.

Ashy Woodswallow *Artamus fuscus* 19cm ⓡ

Slaty-grey plumage, greyer on head; paler on rump and underbody; short, square tail, tipped white; white undertail-coverts. Somewhat heavy-looking bird, rather swallow-like in appearance, but wings much shorter and broader. Sexes alike. Small numbers in open country; perches on leaf stalks and overhead wires. Hunts flying insects. Quiet during hot hours. **VOICE** Call a harsh *chey … chey …* or *chaek … chaek …*, often uttered in flight; **DISTRIBUTION** Widespread but not continuously distributed. **HABITAT** Open country, edges of forests.

Silver-breasted Broadbill

Indian Pitta

Bar-winged Flycatcher-shrike

Mangrove Pitta

Common Woodshrike

Large Woodshrike

Malabar Woodshrike

Ashy Woodswallow

Common Iora *Aegithina tiphia* 14cm **r**

Male greenish above (rich black above, with yellowish rump, in summer breeding plumage); black wings and tail; two white wing-bars; bright yellow underbody. Female has yellow-green plumage; white wing-bars; greenish-brown wings. Occurs in pairs on leafy branches. **Marshall's Iora** *A. nigrolutea* has broad white edgings to tertials and extensive white on tail. **VOICE** Renowned vocalist; wide range of calls; commonly long-drawn *wheeeeeee* or *wheeeeeee … chu*. **DISTRIBUTION** Subcontinent; absent in arid NW Indian desert regions. **HABITAT** Forests, orchards, tree-dotted cultivation, human habitation.

White-bellied Minivet *Pericrocotus erythropygius* 15cm **r**

Rare small minivet, mostly black above with white markings on wings; white underparts with orange on breast and rump. Long tail. Female greyish-brown above, with white underparts and grey breast. Juvenile similar to female, but has some scaling and barring, particularly on crown, some mottling on breast and white tips on wing-coverts. **VOICE** Call *tseep … tseep* in flight. **DISTRIBUTION** Rare breeding resident of NC Indian lowlands and Gujarat. **HABITAT** Open dry woodland, thorn scrub.

Small Minivet *Pericrocotus cinnamomeus* 15cm **r**

Male has dark grey head, back and throat; orange-yellow patch on black wings; black tail; flame-orange breast; orange-yellow belly and undertail. Female paler above; orange rump; dusky white throat, breast tinged with yellow; yellowish belly and undertail. Occurs in pairs or small flocks. Keeps to tree tops, actively moving amid foliage. Flutters and flits about in untiring hunts for small insects. **VOICE** Soft, low *swee … svee …* notes uttered as birds hunt in foliage. **DISTRIBUTION** Most of India; absent in arid parts of Rajasthan. **HABITAT** Forests, groves, gardens.

Long-tailed Minivet *Pericrocotus ethologus* 20cm **r**

Male has glossy blue-black upperparts, hood, chin and throat; scarlet rump; scarlet underparts; black wings with bright scarlet patches on secondaries and inner greater coverts forming 'U' shape; long tail with red outer-tail feathers. Female yellow on forehead and supercilium; grey cheeks; greenish-yellow-grey mantle, back and rump; pale yellow throat graduating to orange-yellow on breast and flanks. **VOICE** Whistle-like *pee … ru*. **DISTRIBUTION** Common breeding resident, N hills eastwards; winters in plains. **HABITAT** Broadleaved and coniferous hill forests.

Scarlet Minivet *Pericrocotus speciosus* 22–23cm **r**

Male has glistening black head and upper back; deep scarlet lower back and rump; black-and-scarlet wings and tail; black throat, scarlet below. Female has rich yellow forehead and supercilium; grey-yellow above; yellow-and-black wings and tail; bright yellow underbody. Occurs in pairs or small parties. **VOICE** Pleasant two-note whistle; also longer, whistling warble. **DISTRIBUTION** The Himalayas, hills of C and E India. The recently split **Orange Minivet** *P. flammeus* found south of Gujarat through Western Ghats. **HABITAT** Forests, gardens, groves.

Rosy Minivet *Pericrocotus roseus* 18cm **r** **m**

Grey-brown underparts. Male has pinkish-red patch on wings and tail; reddish rump; silvery-white face; pale grey crown and nape; blackish-brown wings and long tail. Pale buffy-pink underparts. Female has yellow underparts with yellow-olive rump. Feeds in the canopy on invertebrates in small parties; less active than other minivets. **VOICE** Whirring trill. **DISTRIBUTION** Winters in NE India. Also Eastern Ghats. **HABITAT** Forests, woodland, glades.

Common Iora

White-bellied Minivet

Marshall's Iora

Long-tailed Minivet

Orange Minivet

Small Minivet

Scarlet Minivet

Rosy Minivet

147

Large Cuckooshrike *Coracina macei* 30cm ⓡ

Medium-sized bird. Adult male has light grey upperparts and tail; dark mask over eye; paler grey throat and breast; white belly and vent. Several racial variations. Females of Himalayan and northeastern races told from other females by pale grey unbarred throat and upper breast; barred below. Solitary or in pairs or dispersed groups. Arboreal, sometimes descending to feed. Active feeder. **VOICE** Noisy, parrot-like screech. **DISTRIBUTION** Himachal to Arunachal Pradesh, S Assam hills. **HABITAT** Open and secondary forest growth, forest edges, scrub forests, plantations.

Black-winged Cuckooshrike *Lalage melaschistos* 24cm ⓡ

Smallish cuckooshrike, darkest of the cuckooshrikes. Adult male has dark grey head, mantle and breast; black wings; paler grey belly and vent; tail feathers tipped white, giving impression of large white spots. Female paler grey; faint barring on underside; sometimes has white ring above and below eye. Solitary or in pairs. Gregarious. Arboreal, occasionally descends to ground. **VOICE** *tutwee ... tutwee ... tutwee ...; peeoo ... peeoo ... peeoo*. **DISTRIBUTION** Breeding resident in N mountains; winters lower down. **HABITAT** Open forest edges, forest groves.

Black-headed Cuckooshrike *Lalage melanoptera* 20cm ⓡ

Male has grey plumage; black head, wings and tail, latter white tipped, except on middle feathers; pale grey below breast, whiter on abdomen and vent. Female has brown plumage; whitish-buff below barred dark brown to abdomen; lacks black head. Solitary or in pairs; only occasionally several together. Probes foliage for insects; methodically checks foliage before flying off. **VOICE** Song is a series of clear, loud whistles. **DISTRIBUTION** Across E and S India, W Uttar Pradesh; Himalayan race found in Punjab, Himachal and Uttarakhand. **HABITAT** Forests, gardens, groves.

Brown Shrike *Lanius cristatus* 19cm ⓜ

Uniformly rufous-brown upperparts; black band through eye with white brow over it. Pale creamy underside with warmer rufous flanks; rufous tail. Wings brown without any white 'mirror'. Solitary. Keeps lookout from conspicuous perch or tree stump for prey on the ground, often returning to same perch after hunting. Territorial. **VOICE** Harsh chattering; grating call; sometimes sings in low, chirruping tone with bill closed. **DISTRIBUTION** Winter visitor to peninsular India. **HABITAT** Open country, cultivation, forest edges, scrub, gardens.

Isabelline Shrike *Lanius isabellinus* 17cm ⓡ ⓜ

Small shrike with rather plain sandy-brown plumage. Adult male has rufous lower rump and tail; dark face-patch; fine white supercilium; white patches on primaries; buff underparts. Several racial variations can be paler. White wing-patch absent in female and juvenile. Sits on prominent patch in open. Catches food from perch, and sometimes impales it on thorns. **VOICE** Noisy, grating *kereek ... kereek*. **DISTRIBUTION** Common winter visitor to NW India; vagrant elsewhere. **HABITAT** Dry thorn scrub and edges of fields, often near water.

Bay-backed Shrike *Lanius vittatus* 18cm ⓡ

Deep chestnut-maroon back; broad black forehead-band, continuing through eyes to ear-coverts; grey crown and neck; small white patch on blackish wings; white rump distinctive; black wings with white in outer flight feathers; white underbody; fulvous on breast and flanks. Sexes alike. Solitary or in scattered pairs. Keeps lookout from perch on tree stump, overhead wire or bush top. Pounces once potential prey is sighted. **VOICE** Harsh *churr*. **DISTRIBUTION** Subcontinent; absent in NE India. **HABITAT** Open country, forests, scrub.

Krishna Prajapati CC

Large Cuckooshrike

Ramki Sreenivasan

Black-winged Cuckooshrike

Clement M Francis

Black-headed Cuckooshrike

Clement M Francis

Brown Shrike

Isabelline Shrike

Ramki Sreenivasan

Bay-backed Shrike

Long-tailed Shrike *Lanius schach* 25cm 🔴

Pale grey from crown to middle of back; bright rufous from then on to rump; black forehead; band through eye; white 'mirror' in black wings; whitish underbody, tinged pale rufous on lower breast and flanks. Sexes alike. Mostly solitary. Boldly defends feeding territory. Keeps lookout from conspicuous perch. **VOICE** Noisy; harsh mix of scolding notes, shrieks and yelps; excellent mimic. **DISTRIBUTION** Three races; undergo considerable seasonal movement. **HABITAT** Open country, cultivation, vicinity of human habitation, gardens.

Grey-backed Shrike *Lanius tephronotus* 25cm 🔴

Large shrike with dark grey uppeparts; black mask; yellowish flanks; long tail; rufous uppertail-coverts and belly; similar to the Long-tailed Shrike (above), but darker grey, no rufous on upperparts and grey forehead; larger head and bill. Usually lacks white primary patch on blackish wings. Breeds at high altitudes. **VOICE** Call a grating shriek; mimics other birds. **DISTRIBUTION** Local, common breeding summer visitor to the Himalayas from Ladakh eastwards. **HABITAT** Open areas, usually with trees; also high-altitude steppes.

Great Grey Shrike *Lanius excubitor* 25cm 🔴

Includes the Indian subspecies *lahtora*, previously known as the Southern Grey Shrike. Bluish-grey above; broad black stripe from bill through eye; black wings with white mirrors; black-and-white tail; unmarked white underbody. Sexes alike. Mostly in pairs in open areas. Remains perched upright on bush tops or overhead wires or flies low, uttering a harsh scream. Batters and tears prey before swallowing it. **VOICE** Harsh, grating *khreck* … call. **DISTRIBUTION** Drier areas of N, NW, S and C India. **HABITAT** Open country, semi-deserts, scrub, edges of cultivation.

Himalayan Shrike-babbler *Pteruthius ripleyi* 16cm 🔴

Strikingly patterned, with short, shrike-like bill, hooked at end; male has broad white supercilium over and behind eye; bluish-black crown, nape and ear-coverts; grey mantle, back and rump; rufous-chestnut panel on black wings; white-tipped primaries and secondaries; white underparts, with pinkish wash on flanks. Mostly solitary. Arboreal. **Blyth's Shrike-babbler** *P. aeralatus* distinguished by orange stripes towards wing-tips. **VOICE** *Churrs* in alarm. Song *chyip … chyip … chyip*. **DISTRIBUTION** The Himalayas. **HABITAT** Broadleaved evergreen forests; mixed forests.

Maroon Oriole *Oriolus traillii* 28cm 🔴

Adult male has maroon body, and black head and wings. Deep scarlet-red tail; strong, decurved grey-blue bill; startling white iris. Female has blackish upperparts; dull maroon back; white underparts heavily streaked maroonish-brown. Occurs in pairs or singly. Well hidden in canopy. **VOICE** Most commonly a cat-like, squawking *meow*. Also, fluty *pi … lio … ilo*. **DISTRIBUTION** Locally common breeding resident in N and NE hills. Moves lower down to foothills and nearby plains in winter. **HABITAT** Subtropical or tropical moist lowland forests.

Black-hooded Oriole *Oriolus xanthornus* 25cm 🔴

Golden-yellow plumage; black head diagnostic; black-and-yellow wings and tail; deep pink-red bill seen at close quarters. Sexes alike. Active and lively; moves a lot in forests and birds chase one another. Rich colours striking against green or brown of forests. Visits fruiting and flowering trees. **VOICE** Very vocal. Assortment of melodious and harsh calls; fluty two- or three-note *tu … hee* or *tll … yow … yow …* more common; also single, mellow note. **DISTRIBUTION** Subcontinent, to about 1,000m in the Himalayan foothills. **HABITAT** Forests, orchards, gardens.

Long-tailed Shrike

Great Grey Shrike

Maroon Oriole

Grey-backed Shrike

Himalayan Shrike-babbler

Blyth's Shrike-babbler

Black-hooded Oriole

Indian Golden Oriole *Oriolus kundoo* 25cm 🔴 Ⓜ

Male has bright golden-yellow plumage; black stripe through eye; black wings and centre of tail. Female yellow-green above; brownish-green wings; dirty-white below, streaked brown. Young male much like female. Solitary or in pairs; arboreal. **VOICE** Fluty whistle of 2–3 notes, interpreted as *pee … lo … lo*; rich, mellow song when breeding, somewhat mournful; does not sing often. **DISTRIBUTION** Summer visitor to the Himalayan foothills; spreads in winter to plains; also breeds in many parts of peninsula. **HABITAT** Forests, orchards, gardens.

Black Drongo *Dicrurus macrocercus* 28cm 🔴

Glossy black plumage; long, deeply forked tail. Diagnostic white spot at bill-base. Sexes alike. Usually solitary; sometimes small parties. Keeps lookout from exposed perch. Drops to the ground to capture prey. Launches short aerial sallies. Rides on top of grazing cattle. Follows cattle, tractors, grass-cutters and fires; thus consumes vast numbers of insects. Bold and aggressive species. **VOICE** Harsh *tiu-tiu*; also *cheece cheece*. **DISTRIBUTION** Subcontinent, to about 1,800m in the outer Himalayas. **HABITAT** Open country, orchards, cultivation.

Ashy Drongo *Dicrurus leucophaeus* 30cm 🔴

Adult has ash-grey upperparts; slightly lighter underparts, paler towards belly; red or reddish-brown iris; black legs and bill; black chin. Juvenile more brown than adult, with white edge on underside of tail and brown iris. Sexes similar. Agile flier, executing remarkable twists and turns in the air with skill and speed. **VOICE** Noisy and varied; calls include *cha … ke wip … kit … whew*. **DISTRIBUTION** Fairly common breeding summer visitor to N foothills, east to Arunachal. Winters in plains and peninsula. **HABITAT** Forests and woodland.

White-bellied Drongo *Dicrurus caerulescens* 32cm 🔴

Adult has bluish-black upperparts; long, deeply forked tail; greyish-brown throat and breast; white belly and undertail-coverts; short legs. Sexes alike. Occurs in pairs, or small groups, sometimes with other birds. Noisy. Makes short flights. Often hunts until very late in the evening. Sits upright while perched prominently in shrike-like pose. **VOICE** Assortment of pleasant, whistling calls and some grating notes. **DISTRIBUTION** Most of S India and east of a line from SE Punjab to around Kutch; east to Bengal. **HABITAT** Open forests, well-wooded areas.

Bronzed Drongo *Dicrurus aeneus* 24cm 🔴

Small, glossy-black drongo with metallic bluish sheen. Similar to but distinguished from the Black Drongo (above) by smaller size, shorter tail with shallower, out-turned fork, slightly loose-feathered iridescent crown, nape, mantle and breast; face looks unglossed black by comparision. Solitary, in pairs; often joins mixed flocks. Vocal and active. Hunts in well-foliaged, shadier areas of forests. **VOICE** Various loud, harsh calls and mellower whistles. **DISTRIBUTION** Foothills of Punjab, eastwards and south, S Assam hills. **HABITAT** Breeding resident in forested areas.

Lesser Racket-tailed Drongo *Dicrurus remifer* 25cm 🔴

Distinctive, medium-sized drongo, with a seemingly flat head; similar to the Greater Racket-tailed Drongo (p. 154), but smaller, with shorter crest in form of tuft on forehead; flat, evenly shaped rackets at ends of long tail streamers (Greater has inwards facing, curved rackets). Square-ended tail when rackets are missing. Can be told by lack of crest. Solitary or in small groups. **VOICE** Good mimic; loud combination of musical and harsh notes. **DISTRIBUTION** East of Uttarakhand, NE India. **HABITAT** Dense, wet broadleaved evergreen and deciduous forests, forest edges.

Indian Golden Oriole

Garima Bhatia

Black Drongo

Ashy Drongo

Tejus Naik

White-bellied Drongo

Bronzed Drongo

Sumit Sen

Lesser Racket-tailed Drongo

Hair-crested Drongo *Dicrurus hottentottus* 32cm ⓡ

Glistening blue-black plumage; fine hair-like feathers on forehead; longish, downcurved, pointed bill; diagnostic square-cut and inwardly bent tail, (curling) towards outer ends. Sexes alike. Solitary or in scattered pairs. Strictly arboreal forest bird. Small numbers may gather on favourite flowering trees. Often seen in mixed hunting parties. Selects exposed branch and flies out to prey. **VOICE** Noisy; mix of whistling, metallic calls and harsh screams. **DISTRIBUTION** Lower Himalayan foothills, NE India, Eastern and Western Ghats. **HABITAT** Forests.

Greater Racket-tailed Drongo *Dicrurus paradiseus* 32cm ⓡ

Glossy blue-black plumage; prominent crest of longish feathers, curving backwards; elongated, wire-like outer-tail feathers ending in 'rackets', diagnostic. Sexes alike. Solitary or in pairs. Arboreal forest bird, moving a lot in forests, Confirmed exhibitionist; very noisy, bold and aggressive. The Lesser Racket-tailed Drongo (p. 152) is found in the lower Himalayas, east of Uttaranchal. **VOICE** Noisiest bird of forests; amazing mimic. **DISTRIBUTION** Forested parts of W, C, NE India and the Himalayan foothills. **HABITAT** Forests, forest edges, orchards.

White-throated Fantail *Rhipidura albicollis* 19cm ⓡ

Distinguished from other fantails by all-dark underparts. Himalayan and northeastern races have dark slate-grey upperparts and underparts rather than olive-brown; fine white supercilia, not extending to lores; white throat; black fantail tipped with white, except for central feathers. Solitary or in pairs. Confiding. Arboreal; actively flits about in vegetation. Constantly fans tail and droops wings. **VOICE** High *cheek*; harsh *chukrr*. **DISTRIBUTION** Fairly common breeding resident from Punjab, throughout NE India. **HABITAT** Shaded forests, scrub, gardens, wooded ravines.

Spot-breasted Fantail *Rhipidura albogularis* 19cm ⓔ

Adult has short white supercilium; slaty-grey crown, face and upperparts, including wing; slaty-grey tail; white-spotted grey breast; buff belly; white throat. Juvenile similar to adult, with rufous spots on wing-coverts. Characteristic fanning of tail as it moves through bushes. Intergrades with the White-throated Fantail (above) in peninsula. **VOICE** Male call distinctive. Calls include a scratcy *check* repeated irregularly. **DISTRIBUTION** Peninsular India, north to Rajasthan and Gangetic Plain. **HABITAT** Wooded areas, secondary forests.

White-browed Fantail *Rhipidura aureola* 17cm ⓡ

Characteristic habit of fanning black-and-white tail and flicking wings. Dark brown upperparts; black crown and face-sides; white forehead; broad nape-stripe; two rows of white spots form wing-bars; black centre of throat and breast-sides; white throat-sides; white underparts. Sexes alike, but female slightly duller than male. Solitary or in pairs. Tame and confiding. **VOICE** Call a lively whistle; grating *chuck ... chuck ... chuckrrr* note, usually when disturbed and agitated. **DISTRIBUTION** Most of India. **HABITAT** Forests, orchards, gardens, cultivation.

Black-naped Monarch *Hypothymis azurea* 16cm ⓡ

Male has lilac-blue plumage; black patch on nape; gorget on breast; slight black scaly markings on crown; sooty on wings and tail; white below breast. Female ash-blue; duller than male; lacks black on nape and breast. Solitary or in pairs in forests. Very active and fidgety, **VOICE** Common call a sharp, grating, high-pitched *chwich ... chweech* or *chwae ... chweech*, slightly interrogative in tone, the two notes quickly uttered. **DISTRIBUTION** India, south of the outer Himalayas, up to Arunachal; absent in arid NW and N India. **HABITAT** Forests, bamboo, gardens.

Hair-crested Drongo

Greater Racket-tailed Drongo

White-throated Fantail

Spot-breasted Fantail

White-browed Fantail

Black-naped Monarch

155

Indian Paradise Flycatcher *Terpsiphone paradisi* 21cm ⓡ

Glossy blue-black head, crest and throat; black in wings; silvery-white body, long tail-streamers. In rufous phase white parts replaced by rufous-chestnut. Female and young male 20cm; no tail-streamers; shorter crest; rufous above; ashy-grey throat and nuchal collar; whitish below. Solitary or in pairs. Makes short sallies, with tail-streamers floating. Strictly arboreal. **VOICE** Sharp, grating *chwae* or *chchwae* … call; melodious warbling song. **DISTRIBUTION** The Himalayan foothills; N India; widespread in peninsular India. **HABITAT** Light forests, gardens, open country.

Eurasian Jay *Garrulus glandarius* 33cm ⓡ

Pinkish-brown plumage; velvet-black malar stripe; closely black-barred blue wings; white rump contrasts with jet-black tail. Sexes alike. Occurs in small, noisy bands, often with other Himalayan birds. Common and familiar around Himalayan hill stations. Inquisitive and aggressive. Mostly keeps to trees, but also descends into bushes and on to the ground. Laboured flight. **VOICE** Noisy; guttural chuckles, screeching notes and whistles; good mimic. **DISTRIBUTION** Across the Himalayas; somewhat higher in east. **HABITAT** Mixed temperate forests.

Black-headed Jay *Garrulus lanceolatus* 33cm ⓡ

Similar to the Eurasian Jay (above), but range restricted to the W Himalayas. Adult has black head with crest; pinkish-buff body, washed grey on rump and mantle. Wings regularly patterned black, blue and white; tail black-barred blue. White-streaked throat contrasting with black head; yellow bill. Sexes alike. Less shy than Eurasian, and often around human habitation. **VOICE** Usually single, harsh *kraaa*. **DISTRIBUTION** Locally common breeding resident in N mountains. Some move lower in winter. **HABITAT** Mixed temperate forests, particularly oaks.

Red-billed Blue Magpie *Urocissa erythroryncha* 66cm ⓡ

Purple-blue plumage; black head and breast; white nape-patch and underbody; very long, white-tipped tail; yellow bill and orange legs. Sexes alike. Occurs in pairs or small bands. Arboreal, but also hunts low in bushes. Even descends to the ground, long tail cocked as it hops about. The similar **Yellow-billed Blue Magpie** *U. flavirostris* has yellow bill and orange legs; normally found at higher altitudes. **VOICE** Noisy. Calls include a great mix of metallic screams and loud whistles. **DISTRIBUTION** The Himalayas. **HABITAT** Forests, gardens, forest clearings.

Common Green Magpie *Cissa chinensis* 37–39cm ⓡ

Large green magpie with vivid red bill. Brilliant emerald-green upperparts; paler green underparts. Bold, broad black stripe extending from bill through eyes to short crest on to rear crown. Red legs. Wings black and white-tipped chestnut. Long, graduated, white-tipped tail. Sexes alike. Feeds low down in foliage in pairs or small groups. **VOICE** Very variable. Call a loud *kik … wee* note; also mimics. **DISTRIBUTION** Locally common breeding resident in N mountains up to Arunachal. **HABITAT** Dense broadleaved forests; particularly ravine sides.

Rufous Treepie *Dendrocitta vagabunda* 50cm ⓡ

Rufous above; sooty grey-brown head and neck; black, white and grey on wings, best seen in flight; black-tipped grey tail, long and graduated. Sexes alike. Occurs in pairs or small parties; often seen in mixed hunting parties. Feeds up in trees, but also descends low into bushes and on to the ground to pick up termites. Bold and noisy; rather tame and confiding in certain areas. **VOICE** Call a fluty, three-note *goo … ge … lay* or *ko … ki … la*; harsh, guttural notes often uttered. **DISTRIBUTION** Almost all India. **HABITAT** Forests, gardens, cultivation, human habitation.

Indian Paradise Flycatcher

Black-headed Jay

Common Green Magpie

Manoj Kejriwal

Eurasian Jay

Biswarup Satpati

Red-billed Blue Magpie

Biswarup Satpati

Yellow-billed Blue Magpie

Nitin Srinivasamurthy

Rufous Treepie

Grey Treepie *Dendrocitta formosae* 40cm **r**

Duller and less rufous than the Rufous Treepie (p. 156); long tail; grey-and-brown plumage; dusky-grey face; grey head, neck and underparts; rufous vent; radiated grey tail black-edged and tipped brownish-black; black wings with small white patch. Sexes alike. Less often near human habitation than Rufous. Arboreal. Often in groups or mixed hunting parties. **VOICE** Noisy and variable. Call a loud, clanking *klok … ti … klok … ti … ti*. **DISTRIBUTION** Locally common breeding resident in N hills of Arunachal; Eastern Ghats. **HABITAT** Forests, secondary growth.

White-bellied Treepie *Dendrocitta leucogastra* 48cm **e**

White, grey and chestnut crow with very long, black-tipped and pale grey-edged tail. Black face contrasts with white head and underparts. Chestnut mantle and black wings with white patches. Sexes alike. Sociable. Often with Greater Racket-tailed Drongos (p. 154), which it imitates freely. Feeds mainly on invertebrates at lower and middle levels. **VOICE** Noisy. Various loud, harsh and metallic notes, including *tikituk … tikituk*. **DISTRIBUTION** Local breeding endemic resident in S Western Ghats. **HABITAT** Evergreen hill forests, thick scrub, plantations.

Eurasian Magpie *Pica pica* 43–50cm **r**

Pied bird with glossy black head, neck, upper back and wings; tail glossed bronze-green and purple-blue; white scapulars, lower back (rump) and belly; black undertail. Sexes alike. Usually several in vicinity. Moves on the ground. Perches on fence-posts, trees and house tops. Frequents high-mountain villages. Typical crow, bold and aggressive, but also very alert; flicks tail often. **VOICE** Call a loud, grating *chak … chak*. **DISTRIBUTION** High NW Himalayas. **HABITAT** Open valleys, cultivation.

Spotted Nutcracker *Nucifraga caryocatactes* 32cm **r**

Chocolate-brown plumage, thickly speckled with white; dark central-tail feathers tipped white; white outertail- and undertail-coverts; heavy, pointed bill distinctive. Sexes alike. Several species based on size and abundance of white spots. Small parties. Keeps to tree tops, but readily descends to the ground. Rather wary. Flies short distances across glades. Noisy, attracting attention with its call. **VOICE** Loud; guttural *kharr … kharr … kharr*. **DISTRIBUTION** High Himalayas, sometimes decending in winter. **HABITAT** Coniferous, oak and rhododendron forests.

Red-billed Chough *Pyrrhocorax pyrrhocorax* 45cm **r**

Glossy black plumage; coral-red curved bill and legs. Sexes alike. The **Yellow-billed Chough** *P. graculus* is slightly smaller, with yellow bill and red legs. Highly gregarious. Feeds in cultivation, in and around human habitation. Probes the ground and dung for insects. Flocks often fly high into the sky, rising on thermals, and playing and dancing in air currents. Tame and confiding. **VOICE** Melodious, high-pitched and other squeaky notes. **DISTRIBUTION** High Himalayas; may descend in severe winters. **HABITAT** Cliff sides, alpine pastures, cultivation, human habitation.

House Crow *Corvus splendens* 40cm **r**

Sleek-looking crow with glossy black plumage; grey collar, upper back and breast; glossy black on forehead, crown and throat; long, prominent, arched bill; black feet; brown eyes. Sexes alike. Mobs other birds, even large raptors. Performs important scavenging services; occasionally flies very high into the sky when flying long distances. Roosts communally. **VOICE** Call a familiar *caw*; occasionally pleasant *kurrrr* note. **DISTRIBUTION** Subcontinent. **HABITAT** Rural and urban habitation, cultivation, edges of forests, wide range of habitats.

Grey Treepie

Clement M Francis

White-bellied Treepie

Eurasian Magpie

Biswarup Satpati

Spotted Nutcracker

Yellow-billed Chough

Red-billed Chough

Shiva Shankar

House Crow

Large-billed Crow *Corvus macrorhynchos* 48cm (r)

Glossy black plumage; heavy bill with noticeable culmen curve. Sexes alike. The **Carrion Crow** *C. corone* of NW mountains is confusingly similar, except for less curved culmen, although this characteristic is not easily visible in the field. Solitary or in groups of 2–6; most common around villages and only small numbers in urban areas; forested areas. **VOICE** Harsh *khaa … khaa* calls; several variations on this among the various races. **DISTRIBUTION** Subcontinent. **HABITAT** Forests, rural habitation, towns and cities.

Eurasian Jackdaw *Corvus monedula* 33cm (r)

Smallish black and grey crow with black crown and face; white iris, small, short beak and black legs. Very gregarious; large flocks often wheel around cliffs. Distinguished from the House Crow (p. 158) by smaller size and smaller bill. **VOICE** Noisy, with abrupt *jack* and repeated *kyaa*. **DISTRIBUTION** Locally common in Kashmir, sometimes occurring as far south and east as Uttarakhand. **HABITAT** Mountain cultivation and pastures, usually near cliffs. Also cultivation in winter in plains.

Common Raven *Corvus corax* 58–69cm (r)

Impressively sized, glossy black crow; long, decurved bill with distal culmen; prominent nasal bristles. Similar to the Large-billed Crow (above), but larger, with less domed head; beard-like throat feathers pale brownish-grey; less curved bill; distinct, wedge-shaped tail conspicuous in flight. Flight feathers and tail more brown. Powerful flight; soars on thermals. Aerial rolling displays. **VOICE** Call a deep, resounding *kraa … kraa … gunk … gunk … wock … wock*. **DISTRIBUTION** Thar Desert. **HABITAT** High-altitude deserts, alpine meadows, semi-deserts.

Grey Hypocolius *Hypocolius ampelinus* 25cm (m)

Long-tailed, short-winged bird with diagnostic black face-mask extending to hindneck. Overall bluish-grey. Slightly hooked bill. Often raises crown feathers, giving rise to crested appearance. In flight, shows black primaries with prominent white tips. Female and immature duller than male; brownish-grey and lacks black mask; well-defined creamy-white throat, less white in primaries and indistinct black tail-tip. **VOICE** Gives whistled notes, such as *wheew … whee … di … du …* **DISTRIBUTION** Scarce visitor to Gujarat. **HABITAT** Lowland wooded areas.

Yellow-bellied Fantail *Chelidorhynx hypoxanthus* 13cm (r)

Small, olive-green bird with broad black tail, tipped white. Upperparts mostly olive with fine white wing-bar; yellow head; olive rear crown; dark mask and eye-stripes. Underparts yellow. Very active. Forages for insects in foliage; frequently flycatches, returning to perch. **VOICE** Call a persistent *sip … sip … sip*; also musical *wee … too … wee too … wee*. **DISTRIBUTION** Common breeding resident in the Himalayas and NE India. **HABITAT** Mainly broadleaved forests, often near water.

Grey-headed Canary-flycatcher *Culicicapa ceylonensis* 13cm (r)

Ashy-grey head, throat and breast; darker crown; yellow-green back; yellow rump; yellow in browner wings and tail; yellow below breast. Sexes alike. Solitary or in pairs. Occasionally several in vicinity, especially in mixed parties. **VOICE** Vocal; high-pitched two- or three-syllable calls, *whi … chichee … whi … chichee*; longer, trilling song; also chattering notes. **DISTRIBUTION** Commonly breeds in the Himalayas; common in winter over much of

subcontinent. **HABITAT** Forests, gardens, orchards.

Large-billed Crow

Eurasian Jackdaw

Garima Bhatia

Carrion Crow

Grey Hypocolius

Nikhil Devasar

Common Raven

Yellow-bellied Fantail

Grey-headed Canary-flycatcher

Panchami Manoo Ukil

161

Fire-capped Tit *Cephalopyrus flammiceps* 9cm ⓡ

Small, rounded, yellow-and-green tit. Sharp-tipped, small, conical bill. Breeding male has bright scarlet-red crown and throat, golden-yellow lores and short yellow supercilium. Green upperparts; two thin white wing-bars; deep yellow underparts. Female has paler underparts than male. Beady black eyes and very short, pointed bill. Forest feeder. **VOICE** Call a soft *tsit* and *tsee … tsee … tsee*. **DISTRIBUTION** Local breeding summer visitor to N mountains up to Arunachal Pradesh. Winters in foothills, rarely in plains. **HABITAT** Alpine forests.

Yellow-browed Tit *Sylviparus modestus* 10cm ⓡ

Tiny tit with olive-grey upperparts and pale greyish-yellow underparts. Narrow yellowish eye-ring; thin, indistinct bright yellow supercilium; worn plumage duller grey-brown above; slight crest; olive-green, ill-defined wing-bar; pale bluish-grey legs. Sexes alike. Solitary or in pairs. Often overlooked. Arboreal. Mostly canopy feeder. Quiet and inconspicuous. Restless, with typical tit-like acrobatics. Raises crest when alarmed. **VOICE** Calls *psit … sisisi*. **DISTRIBUTION** N hills to Arunachal; S Assam hills. **HABITAT** Oak, broadleaved mixed forests, orchards, scrub.

Sultan Tit *Melanochlora sultanea* 20cm ⓡ

Male black above; yellow crown and crest; black throat and upper breast; yellow below. Female has deep olivish wash to black upper body and throat; crest as in male; some yellow also on throat. Occurs in small bands, in mixed hunting flocks. Active and inquisitive. Clings sideways and upside down. Checks foliage and bark crevices. Feeds in canopy but also descends to tall bushes. **VOICE** Noisy; loud, whistling *cheerie …* often mixed with harsh *churr* or *chrrchuk*. **DISTRIBUTION** C, E Himalayas, NE foothills. **HABITAT** Mixed forests, edges of forests.

Rufous-vented Tit *Periparus rubidiventris* 12cm ⓡ

Black-crowned bird with spiky crest and black bib. Western Himalayan race has olive-washed, dark grey upperparts, reddish-rufous underparts, pinkish-rufous belly, pale rufous-washed nuchal patch, white cheek-patch and greyish flanks. E Himalayan race *P. r. beavani* has whitish nuchal spot and blue-washed dark bib (instead of buff-grey bib). Sexes similar; male darker than female. **VOICE** Noisy. Rattling song. **DISTRIBUTION** Common breeding resident in N mountains east to Nagaland. **HABITAT** Open coniferous and broadleaved forests, particularly rhododendron.

Coal Tit *Periparus ater* 11cm ⓡ

Slender-billed, small tit with largish head and floppy crest. Black crown and upper mantle; large white nuchal and cheek-patches; extensive black bib continuing to black nape; underparts mainly buffy-white or grey with rufous breast-sides. Slaty-bluish-grey upperparts graduating to buffy-olive-brown towards rump; two distinct white-spotted wing-bars and white-tipped tertials. Sexes alike. Very active. Solitary or in pairs. **VOICE** Calls include thin *tsi … tsi …* and low-pitched, slow *wee … tsee …*, repeating. **DISTRIBUTION** The Himalayas. **HABITAT** Coniferous forests.

Grey-crested Tit *Lophophanes dichrous* 12cm ⓡ

Adult has dull brownish-grey upperparts; similarly coloured upright crest; dirty-whitish submoustachial stripe extending around neck to form collar; decurved eye-stripe; mottled grey cheeks; lighter grey-brown throat. Underparts washed pale cinnamon. Sexes alike. Rather quiet and inconspicuous. Acrobatic behaviour. **VOICE** Calls include thin *zai* and *ti … ti … ti … ti* and *chea … chea* alarm. Song *wee … wee tz … tz … tz*. **DISTRIBUTION** Locally common breeding resident in N mountains from E Kashmir to Bhutan. Most common in E. **HABITAT** Hill forests.

Fire-capped Tit

Yellow-browed Tit

Sultan Tit

Rufous-vented Tit

Coal Tit

Grey-crested Tit

163

Cinereous Tit *Parus cinereus* 13cm 🔴

Grey back; black crown continued along neck-sides to broad black band from chin along centre of underbody; white cheeks, nape-patch, wing-bar and outer feathers of black tail; ashy-white sides. Sexes alike. Occurs in pairs or small bands. Restless. The very rare and local **White-naped Tit** *Machlolopus nuchalis* has large white nuchal patch; male has glossy black mantle and wing-coverts, extensive white on wings and white cheeks. **VOICE** Loud, clear, whistling *whee ... chi ... chee ...*; other whistling and harsh notes. **DISTRIBUTION** Widespread in the Himalayas, Himalayan foothills, peninsular India. **HABITAT** Open forests, gardens, human habitation.

Green-backed Tit *Parus monticolus* 13cm 🔴

Yellow-green and black tit distinguished by two white wing-bars, bright green upperparts and blue leading edges on wing feathers. White cheeks. Sexes similar. **VOICE** Calls include loud *teacher ... teacher* note and repeated *whitee ... whittee*. **DISTRIBUTION** Locally common breeding resident to N mountains to Arunachal. May move lower down in foothills during winter. **HABITAT** Deciduous, coniferous mixed forests and tropical moist lowland forests.

Himalayan Black-lored Tit *Machlolophus xanthogenys* 14cm 🔴

Olive-green back; black crest (faintly tipped with yellow), stripe behind eye, broad central band from chin to vent; bright yellow nape-patch, supercilium and sides of underbody. Sexes alike. Occurs in pairs or small flocks, often with other small birds. Arboreal and active. Feeds in foliage; sometimes enters gardens. **VOICE** Cheerful, musical notes; loud, tailorbird-like *towit ... towit* calls near nest; whistling song; also harsh *charrr* and some chattering notes. **DISTRIBUTION** The Himalayas to E Nepal. **HABITAT** Forests, gardens.

Yellow-cheeked Tit *Machlolophus spilonotus* 14cm 🔴

Black-and-yellow tit with erect and pointed black crest, tipped yellow, and yellow forehead. Short black lines behind eye; heavily streaked greenish mantle; grey rump; white wing-bars. Sexes similar, but female duller than male. The similar **Indian Black-lored Tit** M. *aplonotus* is found in the E Himalayas and hills of NE India. **VOICE** Calls include *sit, si ... si ... si* and *chrrr*. Great Tit-like song *chee ... o ... chee ... pui*. **DISTRIBUTION** Locally common breeding resident in N mountains from E Nepal east to Arunachal. Moves lower down in winter. **HABITAT** Open forests.

Greater Hoopoe Lark *Alaemon alaudipes* 19cm 🔴

Overall sandy-brown lark with elongated body and long legs. Long, decurved bill; prominent white supercilium, black eye-stripe and moustachial stripe; faint black malar stripe. Creamy-white underparts with dark-spotted breast. Striking wing pattern, white at base and tips of black primaries and secondaries, showing as bands across wings, visible in flight. Sexes alike, but male smaller than female, with shorter bill. **VOICE** Song a series of flute-like whistles. **DISTRIBUTION** Rann of Kutch, Gujarat. **HABITAT** Arid deserts, low sand dunes, barren clay flats.

Black-crowned Sparrow Lark *Eremopterix nigriceps* 13cm 🔴

Small, short-tailed, broad-winged lark with short bill. Adult male has sandy-brown upperparts; large white patch on cheeks and forehead; black underwing-coverts distinct in flight. Unmistakable black throat, centre of crown and entire underparts; unstreaked belly. Female and juvenile indistinct sandy-brown with weak streaking on crown, nape and breast. Sociable in small flocks outside breeding. **VOICE** Song a short, warbled *dwee ... di ... ui ... twee*.

DISTRIBUTION NW India. **HABITAT** Arid regions, sandy deserts.

Cinereous Tit

Green-backed Tit

White-naped Tit

Yellow-cheeked Tit

Himalayan Black-lored Tit

Indian Black-lored Tit

Greater Hoopoe Lark

Black-crowned Sparrow Lark

165

Ashy-crowned Sparrow Lark *Eremopterix griseus* 13cm **r**

Thickish bill. Male sandy-brown above; white cheeks and breast-sides; dark chocolate-brown sides of face and most of underbody; dark brown tail with whitish outer feathers. Female sandy-brown overall; dull rufous sides of face and underbody. Mostly occurs in loose flocks, scattered over an area; pairs or small parties when breeding. Feeds on the ground. **VOICE** Pleasant, monotonous trilling song by male; sings on the wing and on the ground. **DISTRIBUTION** Almost entire India. **HABITAT** Open scrub, semi-cultivation, fallow river basins, tidal mudflats.

Bengal Bush Lark *Mirafra assamica* 15cm **r**

Adult has weakly streaked grey-brown crown and nape; pale indistinct supercilium; brownish ear-coverts; rufous-buff underparts with diffused streaking on breast. Often confused with **Jerdon's Bush Lark** (below). Solitary or in pairs. Nests on the ground; feeds on invertebrates and seeds on the ground. **VOICE** Call a thin, high *p … zee or tzee … tzee* delivered in high, circling song flight. **DISTRIBUTION** Locally common breeding resident in N Plains, Punjab to NE India. **HABITAT** Open grassland, irrigated cultivation.

Indian Bush Lark *Mirafra erythroptera* 14cm **r**

Yellowish-brown above, streaked black; rich chestnut-rufous on wings, easily seen in flight: pale white chin and throat, dull yellowish-brown below; blackish, triangular spots on breast. Sexes alike. Occurs in pairs or small flocks. Squats tight when approached. Spectacular display flight, accompanied by singing, when breeding; also indulges in display flights in the night. **VOICE** Faint *cheep chrep* call note; song a faint but lively twittering. **DISTRIBUTION** Almost all of N, NW and peninsular India. **HABITAT** Open cultivation, grass and scrub, fallow land.

Jerdon's Bush Lark *Mirafra affinis* 14cm **r**

Stocky lark with large bill, short tail and wings, and relatively long legs; narrow superciium; buffish-grey-brown crown and nape with dark streaking; distinct yellow nape-band; pale grey ear-coverts, streaked darker; rufous-buff underparts; heavily spotted breast; rufous patch on wings; rufous-buff outer webs to outer-tail feathers, and dark-centred coverts and tertials. **VOICE** Call a short, high-pitched trill; also dry, metallic trill, delivered from perch or during short song flight. **DISTRIBUTION** Peninsular India. **HABITAT** Dry, open areas with bushes and trees.

Oriental Skylark *Alauda gulgula* 16cm **r**

Brownish above, the feathers edged yellow-brown with black centres; short, indistinct crest not often visible; dark brown tail with pale buff outer feathers; dull buff below; more yellowish-brown on breast, faintly streaked and spotted darker. Sexes alike. Occurs in pairs or small parties on the ground, running in short spurts. Squats when approached. **VOICE** Longish, pleasant warble of male. Beautiful aerial song flight of male when breeding. **DISTRIBUTION** All India, with several races over subcontinent. **HABITAT** Grassland, cultivation, mudflats, fallow land.

Crested Lark *Galerida cristata* 18cm **r**

Sandy-brown above, streaked blackish; pointed, upstanding crest distinctive; brown tail has dull rufous outer feathers; whitish and dull yellowish-brown below, with breast streaked dark brown. Sexes alike. The **Malabar Lark** *G. malabarica* **e** and **Sykes's Lark** *G. deva* **e** are very similar, but both are birds of peninsular and S India. Occurs in small flocks. Runs briskly on the ground, with pointed crest carried upstanding. **VOICE** Call note a pleasant *tee … ur …* **DISTRIBUTION** N, NW, W India. **HABITAT** Semi-deserts, cultivation, dry, grassy areas.

Ashy-crowned Sparrow Lark

Bengal Bush Lark

Indian Bush Lark

Jerdon's Bush Lark

Oriental Skylark

Malabar Lark

Crested Lark

Sykes's Lark

Greater Short-toed Lark *Calandrella brachydactyla* 15cm 🔴

Medium-sized, heavily streaked lark without crest. Sandy-brown and sometimes brownish-black upperparts. Fine streaks on forehead; flattish head; dark cap; pale lores; short, pointed, pale pinkish bill; two black breast-patches. Whitish underparts; short dark tail. Sexes alike. Juvenile has dark brown feathers edged buff. Bold, undulating flight. **VOICE** Soft, dry, rippling *chirip* and *dyu* often combined. Flocks call constantly in flight. **DISTRIBUTION** Numerous; winter visitor to lowlands of N India. **HABITAT** Dry pasture, stubble, fallow land, semi-deserts, dry mudflats.

Crested Finchbill *Spizixos canifrons* 22cm 🔴

Medium to large bulbul with short, pale, conical bill. Dark grey head; pale grey forehead; dark chin, throat, mask and hindcrown; dark brown iris; pinkish feet; broad black terminal band on tail. Yellowish-green underparts. In flocks, in non-breeding season. Forages high in trees; also bushes and undergrowth. **VOICE** Call a long, dry, bubbling trill, *purr ... purr ... prruitprruit ... prruit*. Long, dry warble. **DISTRIBUTION** Hills of NE India. **HABITAT** Secondary growth, thickets, glades.

Grey-headed Bulbul *Brachypodius priocephalus* 19cm 🟢

Crestless, green-and-grey bulbul with thick yellowish bill and white irises. Unlike other bulbuls, has a thick-necked broadtailed appearance. Lime-green above, yellower below; forecrown and forehead bright yellow, rear crown and neck lavender-grey; rump and tail grey. Often perches with wings drooped and tail raised. Feeds in the canopy and in dense growth. Shy and unobtrusive. **VOICE** Calls *chalk*, a buzzing *dzee* and a high *tweep*. **DISTRIBUTION** Endemic to hills and forests of Western Ghats. **HABITAT** Forests with dense understorey and thickets.

Andaman Bulbul *Brachypodius fuscoflavescens* 17cm 🟢

Small bulbul distinguished by dark olive-green head, and dull black throat and forehead. Olive-yellow breast and belly; dull olive wings; yellow tip to tail with dark subterminal band. Male has brighter olive upperparts and brighter, yellower underparts than female. Usually in pairs and sometimes in mixed feeding parties; often inconspicuous. **VOICE** Penetrating *chek*; song a jolting series of unmelodious short, piping whistles. **DISTRIBUTION** Endemic to Andaman Islands. **HABITAT** Evergreen forests, light deciduous forests, forest edges and thick secondary growth.

Black-crested Bulbul *Rubigula flaviventris* 22cm 🔴

Glossy black head, tall, erect crest and black throat; olive-yellow nape and back, becoming brown on tail; yellow below throat. Sexes alike. Occurs in pairs or small bands, sometimes with other birds. Arboreal. Sits conspicuously on open perch and calls. Feeds mostly on local berries. **VOICE** Cheerful whistles; also a harsh *churr* call; 4–8-note song. **DISTRIBUTION** The Himalayas, from Himachal Pradesh eastwards; NE; foothills to about 2,000m. **HABITAT** Forests, bamboo, clearings, orchards.

Flame-throated Bulbul *Rubigula gularis* 19.5cm 🟢

Slim bulbul with very short, ragged crest and relatively short, very slightly rounded tail. Glossy black head and crest; olive-green upperparts; bright yellow breast and belly; bright ruby-red throat; indistinct white tips to outer tail. Juvenile similar to adults but has more brownish and yellow throat. Occurs in small flocks. Prefers dense cover. Nest made of dead leaves, held together with cobwebs. Feeds on *Ficus* and *Lantana* berries, other fruits and insects. **VOICE** Song sweet, hurried and rather high pitched. **DISTRIBUTION** Western Ghats. **HABITAT** Evergreen

foothill forests.

Greater Short-toed Lark

Crested Finchbill

Manjula Mathur

Grey-headed Bulbul

Andaman Bulbul

Anthony Grossy

Black-crested Bulbul

Flame-throated Bulbul

S Satisha

Red-whiskered Bulbul *Pycnonotus jocosus* 20cm **r**

Brown above, slightly darker on wings and tail; black perky crest distinctive; crimson 'whiskers' behind eyes; white underbody with broken breast-collar; crimson-scarlet vent. Sexes alike. Sociable, occurring in pairs or small flocks. VOICE Cheerful whistling notes; also harsh, grating alarm notes. DISTRIBUTION Uttarakhand east along Himalayan foothills. Most common south of Satpura mountains in peninsular India; disjunct population in hilly areas of S, SE Rajasthan and N Gujarat. HABITAT Forests, clearings, gardens, orchards, vicinity of human habitation.

Himalayan Bulbul *Pycnonotus leucogenis* 20cm **r**

Medium-sized bulbul with conspicuous curved crest. Brown head; short white superciliary stripe; black around eyes, chin and throat; white cheeks with black crescent-shaped patch below; white blaze on neck-sides. Upperparts greyish-brown; darker flight feathers; brownish-black tail. White underparts with grey-buff on breast and belly; bright sulphur-yellow undertail-coverts. Sexes alike. Small parties. VOICE Calls include pleasant whistling notes. DISTRIBUTION Himalayas from the lowlands upwards. HABITAT Open scrub, edges of forests. Breeds in wooded valleys.

White-eared Bulbul *Pycnonotus leucotis* 20cm **r**

Similar to the Himalayan Bubul (above), but smaller, no crest and larger white patch on cheek; pale, bare eye-ring. Black, slightly domed head; black chin. Brown above; pale buff below; orangish-yellow undertail-coverts; brown tail with white tip. Sexes alike. Feeds at all levels. Sociable, confiding, often perching openly. Mixes with other bulbuls. Powerful, undulating flight. VOICE Call a liquid *pip … pip*. Usually loud *whichyu … whichy*. DISTRIBUTION Locally common breeding resident in NW India. HABITAT Open woodland, scrub, gardens, parks.

Red-vented Bulbul *Pycnonotus cafer* 20cm **r**

Dark sooty-brown plumage; pale edges to feathers on back and breast give scaly appearance; darker head with slight crest; almost black on throat; white rump and red vent distinctive; dark tail tipped white. Sexes alike. Occurs in pairs or small flocks. Arboreal. Pleasantly noisy and cheerful. Indulges in dust-bathing. Hunts flycatcher style. VOICE Cheerful whistling calls; alarm calls on sighting snake, owl or some other intrusion, serving to alert other birds. DISTRIBUTION Subcontinent. HABITAT Light forests, gardens, human habitation.

Yellow-throated Bulbul *Pycnonotus xantholaemus* 20cm **e** **v**

One of India's rarest bulbuls, with limited distribution. No crest; greenish-grey upperparts; bright yellow throat, vent and tail-tip; yellowish-green head and wing edgings; dark greenish-grey tail; dirty-white breast washed grey; greyish belly and flanks. Sexes alike. Usually in pairs or small groups. Shy. Feeds on fruits and insects. Nest not well known. VOICE Lively *whichit woo … ichit woo … wee*. DISTRIBUTION Disjunct local breeding endemic restricted to a few hills in S Andhra Pradesh, E Karnataka and Tamil Nadu. HABITAT Rocky, scrub-covered hills.

White-browed Bulbul *Pycnonotus luteolus* 20cm **r**

Olive plumage, brighter above; whitish forehead and supercilium, and explosive calls confirm identity. Sexes alike. Occurs in pairs or small parties. Not an easy bird to see; skulks in dense, low growth, from where its chattering calls suddenly explode; seen only momentarily when it emerges on bush tops, or flies low from one bush patch to another. Usually does not associate with other birds. VOICE Loud, explosive chatter, whistling notes and chuckles. DISTRIBUTION Peninsular India. HABITAT Dry scrub, village habitation, light forests, clearings.

Red-whiskered Bulbul

Himalayan Bulbul

White-eared Bulbul

Red-vented Bulbul

Yellow-throated Bulbul

White-browed Bulbul

Yellow-browed Bulbul *Acritillas indica* 20cm 🅔 🅥

Overall bright olive-green and bright yellow bulbul. Black bill and eyes; yellow face and throat; slightly decurved bill; bright yellow orbital patch; upperparts bright olive-green; underparts bright yellow. Sexes alike. Juvenile duller than adults, with rufous in wings. Feeds on berries and invertebrates, usually at middle or lower levels. Lively and not shy. **VOICE** Noisy. Call a fluty *whit … wee* that is extended into song. Also harsh *churrs*. **DISTRIBUTION** Common endemic breeding resident in Western Ghats. **HABITAT** Forests and secondary cover.

Mountain Bulbul *Ixos mcclellandii* 23cm 🅡

Large but slim, olive-and-rufous bulbul with shaggy brown crown. Cheeks and breast pale rufous, streaked with buff; olive-green upperparts. Streaked white throat, often puffed out; buff belly and vent. Long, powerful bill. Sexes alike. Found in pairs or small groups. Nests high in trees. Feeds mostly on fruits in the canopy. **VOICE** Noisy, with a variety of calls. Most commonly, metallic *tsyi … tysi …* and *chep … har … lee*. **DISTRIBUTION** Breeding resident in N mountains from Uttarakhand east to Arunachal. Moves lower in winter. **HABITAT** Forests and secondary growth.

Ashy Bulbul *Hemixos flavala* 20cm 🅡

Grey bulbul with large, pale green patch on wing. Brownish-grey face and crown; black triangle-shaped patch on lores; brown cheeks; white throat. Dark grey outer wings and tail; whitish underparts washed grey. Sexes alike. Nests low down. Fly catches. **VOICE** Calls include liquid descending *tew … de … de … do … it* and variants. **DISTRIBUTION** Common breeding resident in N foothills from Uttarakhand east to Arunachal border. Winters lower down, sometimes in plains. **HABITAT** Submontane forests, plantations.

Black Bulbul *Hypsipetes leucocephalus* 23cm 🅡

Ashy-grey plumage; black, loose-looking crest; coral-red bill and legs diagnostic; whitish below abdomen. Sexes alike. Flocks in forests, often dozens together. Strictly arboreal; keeps to topmost branches of tall forest trees and rarely comes down. Noisy and restless, hardly staying on a tree for a few minutes. The **Square-tailed Bulbul** *H. ganeesa* is often considered a part of the fork-tailed variety. Southern race darker, with squarer tail. **VOICE** Assortment of whistles and screeches. **DISTRIBUTION** Several races; resident in the Himalayas and NE India. Southern race found in Western Ghats. **HABITAT** Forests, hill-station gardens.

Grey-throated Martin *Riparia chinensis* 12cm 🅡

Small, greyish-brown swallow. Pale white underparts; short, squarish tail; sometimes slight fork visible in tail; greyish-brown chin, throat and upper breast; does not show any kind of breast-band. Mostly seen in flight although sometimes seen perched during breeding. **VOICE** Rapid twittering. **DISTRIBUTION** N India. **HABITAT** Mostly near slow-flowing rivers, lakes, wet grassland and wetlands.

Sand Martin *Riparia riparia* 13cm 🅡

Small, dark brown swallow, almost always found near water. Underparts dark brown; wing edges slightly darker; white throat, half collar and belly contrast sharply with clearly marked dark brown breast-band; clear forktail; small black bill; blackish or dark brown legs and feet. Sexes similar. **VOICE** Cry a dry *truss*. **DISTRIBUTION** Assam and Arunachal Pradesh. **HABITAT** Vicinity of water.

Yellow-browed Bulbul

Mountain Bulbul

Black Bulbul

Ashy Bulbul

Square-tailed Bulbul

Grey-throated Martin

Sand Martin

Maanoj Kejriwal

Biswarup Satpati

Savio Fonseca

Deborshree Gogoi

Barn Swallow *Hirundo rustica* 18cm **r**

Bright blue-and-red, long-tailed swallow; upperparts deep glossy blue, with bluish-brown wings; chestnut-red forehead and throat, with blue-black breast-band below; underparts highly variable. Long, deeply forked tail, with rows of broad white subterminal spots and tail streamers; distinguished from other swallows by dark breast-band, in flight by unbroken dark upperparts, except for forehead. Gregarious. Communal rooster. Skilled flier. **VOICE** Soft *vhit vhit*; twittering song. **DISTRIBUTION** Throughout India. **HABITAT** Near cultivation, human habitation, water.

Wire-tailed Swallow *Hirundo smithii* 14cm **r**

Glistening steel-blue above; chestnut cap; unmarked, pure white underbody distinctive; two long, wire-like projections (tail-wires) from outer-tail feathers diagnostic. Sexes alike. Solitary or in small parties, either perched on overhead wires or hawking insects in graceful, acrobatic flight, swooping and banking. **VOICE** Soft, twittering note; pleasant song of breeding male. **DISTRIBUTION** Common breeding (summer) visitor to N India; breeds in many other parts of India. **HABITAT** Open areas, cultivation, human habitation, vicinity of canals, lakes and rivers.

Dusky Crag Martin *Ptyonoprogne concolor* 13cm **r**

Dark sooty-brown above; square-cut, short tail, with white spot on all but outermost and central feathers; paler underbody; faintly rufous chin and throat, with indistinct black streaking. Occurs in small parties; flies around ruins, crags and old buildings, hawking insects in flight. Acrobatic, swallow-like flight and appearance; rests during hot hours on rocky ledges. **VOICE** Faint *chip* …, uncommonly uttered. **DISTRIBUTION** Breeds in NW and W Himalayas and resident of peninsular India. **HABITAT** Vicinity of old forts, ruins and old stony buildings in towns.

Nepal House Martin *Delichon nipalense* 13cm **r**

Small, blue-and-white martin with blue cap, dark-streaked cheeks, chin and throat/upper-breast – depending on race; dark vent and undertail-coverts and dark underwing-coverts contrast with white belly and breast; dark, square-ended tail; distinguished from the similar **Asian House Martin** *D. dasypus* by no fork in tail; whitish underparts, darker chin, vent, undertail-coverts and underwing-coverts; smaller white rump with black markings. Gregarious. Communal rooster. Nests in cliff faces. Fast flier. **VOICE** Shrill *chee-ee*, short song. **DISTRIBUTION** Uttarakhand to Arunachal, S Assam hills. **HABITAT** Mountain cliffs, gorges, valleys, forests, cultivation.

Red-rumped Swallow *Cecropis daurica* 16–17cm **r**

Glossy steel-blue above; chestnut supercilium, head-sides, neck-collar and rump; dull rufous-white below, streaked brown; deeply forked tail diagnostic. Sexes alike. Small parties spend much of the day on the wing. Hawks insects. Flies with amazing agility, wheeling, banking and stooping with remarkable mastery. **VOICE** Mournful chirping note; pleasant twittering song of breeding male. **DISTRIBUTION** Subcontinent; resident and migratory. **HABITAT** Cultivation, vicinity of human habitation, town centres, rocky hilly areas.

Streak-throated Swallow *Petrochelidon fluvicola* 12cm **r**

Small, dusky swallow with notched, long, broad tail; blackish-blue mantle, brown wings, rump and tail, and deep chestnut crown. Heavily streaked blackish on face, throat and upper breast. Brown undertail. Often looks very dark. Juvenile browner than adults. Weak, martin-like flight. **VOICE** Calls *chrrp* and *trr … trr*. **DISTRIBUTION** Locally common breeding resident over W and C India. Mainly summer visitor to N India. **HABITAT** Open country and cultivation near water.

Barn Swallow

Dusky Crag Martin

Red-rumped Swallow

Savio Fonseca

Wire-tailed Swallow

Sunil Kini

Nepal House Martin

Wikipedia Commons

Asian House Martin

Kunan Naik

Streak-throated Swallow

Pygmy Wren Babbler *Pnoepyga pusilla* 9cm ®

Very small and overall brown babbler; extremely short tail. Upperparts dark brown with a few paler spots. Underparts beige-white with dark scaling. Unmarked throat; long legs; large grey bill. Sexes alike. Solitary or in pairs. Secretive. Flicks wings. Nests on mossy ground. The similar **Scaly-breasted Wren Babbler** *P. albiventer* is larger and rounder in shape, and occurs in both a rufous and white morph like Pygmy. **VOICE** Calls *tzook*. Song a repeated, drawn-out *tsee … tsu*. **DISTRIBUTION** Breeding resident in N mountains. Moves lower down in winter. **HABITAT** Ferny undergrowth.

Black-faced Warbler *Abroscopus schisticeps* 9cm ®

Small, brightly coloured warbler with distinct broad black mask. Prominent, broad brow; yellow supercilium, throat and vent; yellow-green lower mantle and wings; crown, nape, rear ear-coverts and upper mantle grey; upperparts mostly white; pinkish bill and pale legs. Similar to the Yellow-bellied Fantail (p. 160). Occurs in small bird waves. **VOICE** Call a buzzing alarm; trilling song. **DISTRIBUTION** Breeding resident from Uttarakhand to Arunachal Pradesh, S Assam hills. **HABITAT** Glades, thick undergrowth in moist broadleaved oak forests with mossy trees.

Brownish-flanked Bush Warbler *Horornis fortipes* 12cm ®

Small, nondescript dark warbler. Rounded crown; rufescent olive-brown above; buff eyebrow; dark through eyes; dull whitish below, tinged ashy-brown on throat; buff-brown flanks and undertail; relatively long tail; dark grey bill; pinkish-yellow lower mandible; pale pinkish-brown legs. Sexes alike. Loner; shy and secretive. Rarely seen. **VOICE** Loud, three-note call; single note *chak … or suck*. **DISTRIBUTION** Locally common breeding resident: the Himalayas, S Assam hills; winters lower down to foothills. **HABITAT** Undergrowth on hillsides, edges of forests.

Chestnut-headed Tesia *Cettia castaneocoronata* 8cm ®

Tiny bird with dumpy body, long legs and stubby tail; olive-green back and chestnut hood; bright lemon-yellow throat and underparts olive-washed yellow; breast-sides and flanks olive-green. Shy and elusive. Jerks body when calling. Keeps to the ground, hopping around in bushy undergrowth. **VOICE** Chattering *chirruk chirruk … or loud, piercing tzit…*, repeated when alarmed. **DISTRIBUTION** Resident in the Himalayas and NE Indian hills, to 3,900m. **HABITAT** Thick undergrowth in moist forests, dark ravines near streams.

Black-throated Tit *Aegithalos concinnus* 10.5cm ®

Distinctive tit; bright rufous-chestnut cap; prominent broad black mask, extending to back of neck; black throat; white irises; contrasting white rear supercilium, white chin and border around black throat and mask; tiny, deep-set black bill; grey mantle and upperparts. Several racial variations. Very gregarious; often in large flocks. Quite tame and confiding. **VOICE** Call a *ttrr-ttrr, tsip-tsip; chik-chik*. **DISTRIBUTION** Hills of Himachal to Arunachal; moves lower in winter. **HABITAT** Light broadleaved, moist deciduous and coniferous forests.

Buff-barred Warbler *Phylloscopus pulcher* 10cm ®

Small leaf warbler with two bright buff-orange wing-bars; yellow rump; yellowish supercilium; tail with white sides; looks mostly white from below; light crown-stripe, not always apparent; grey sides of crown; upperparts dark olive-green; underparts greyish with variable yellow wash; pale-based lower mandible on dark bill; in worn plumage wing-bars paler; upper wing-bar may be missing. Arboreal. **VOICE** Shrill, trilling song. **DISTRIBUTION** Himachal to Arunachal Pradesh, S Assam hills. **HABITAT** Temperate forests, subalpine shrubs, oak forests in winter.

Pygmy Wren Babbler

Scaly-breasted Wren Babbler

Brownish-flanked Bush Warbler

Black-throated Tit

Prateik Kulkarni CC

Black-faced Warbler

Nitin Srinivasamurthy

Chestnut-headed Tesia

Pranjal J Saikia

Buff-barred Warbler

177

Ashy-throated Warbler *Phylloscopus maculipennis* 9cm (r)

Tiny yellow, green and grey warbler. Similar to Buff-barred and Lemon-rumped Warblers (p. 176 and below). Dark olive-green upperparts; grey ear-coverts, throat and breast; brighter yellow belly distinctive; two yellowish wing-bars; greyish-white supercilium; greyish crown-stripe; dark grey sides of crown; black eye-stripe; bright yellow rump; white tertial spots; white in tail; small, mostly black bill. Arboreal. **VOICE** *Tzik; swit*; song: *chi-whee-cheew*. **DISTRIBUTION** The Himalayas, S Assam hills. **HABITAT** Deciduous and coniferous forests, broadleaved forests and secondary growth.

Hume's Warbler *Phylloscopus humei* 10–11cm (r)

Small warbler distinguished from the Lemon-rumped Warbler (below) by absence of yellow rump; faint, rather than distinct crown-stripe. Distinguished from the Buff-barred Warbler (p. 176) by no white in tail; paler buff or whitish wing-bars; fresh plumage grey-green above; buffy-white supercilium; wing-bars and underparts whiter, tinted grey in worn plumage; dark bill and legs. Mostly solitary. Forages actively in upper and mid-levels in forests. **VOICE** *Stzip* or *tiss-yip*. **DISTRIBUTION** Throughout region. **HABITAT** Mixed coniferous forests, open deciduous forests.

Lemon-rumped Warbler *Phylloscopus chloronotus* 9cm (r)

Small, brightly coloured warbler. Upperparts olive-green; strong patterning on head; dark lateral crown-stripe; distinct long pale yellow supercilium; broad grey-green eye-stripe and lores; underside whitish, sometimes with pale yellow wash; pale yellow rump and dark bill; two yellow wing-bars; short tail; pale legs. Sexes alike. **VOICE** Call a high *tsip*. Loud, trilling song. **DISTRIBUTION** Breeding resident in N hills of the Himalayas. Winters in NE hills; S Assam hills. **HABITAT** Hill forests, secondary growth.

Sulphur-bellied Warbler *Phylloscopus griseolus* 11cm (r)

Small, rather dark warbler with prominent, bright yellow-orange supercilia in front of eyes; dark brownish-grey above with no wing-bars; dull yellow below. Sexes alike. The similar **Tickell's Leaf Warbler** *P. affinis* has bright yellow supercilium and underparts, distinct dark eye-stripe and pale orange-yellow mandible on longish bill. Single or in pairs. Confiding but unobtrusive. **VOICE** Liquid *dip* or *pik*. **DISTRIBUTION** Locally common breeding summer visitor, mainly to N and C Indian plains. **HABITAT** Rocky areas with scrub and scattered trees.

Smoky Warbler *Phylloscopus fuligiventer* 10cm (m)

Upperparts, wings and tail dark grey-brown; underparts dusky-yellow to olive-green; dark eye-stripe; dull yellow lores; short yellowish or whitish supercilium; thin dark legs; dark brown tail; pale base to lower mandible; similar to Dusky Warbler (below); paler above and whiter below, with bolder supercilium and eye-stripe; pale legs. Confidently feeds on the ground near water. Sometimes flycatches over water. **VOICE** Calls include low *tsrik* and *chup*. **DISTRIBUTION** Rare breeding summer visitor to the Himalayas. **HABITAT** Montane scrub and boulder fields in summer.

Dusky Warbler *Phylloscopus fuscatus* 11cm (m)

Upperparts, wings and tail vary between dark and pale brownish-grey; whitish underparts with touches of buff on breast-sides and flanks; slender dark legs; broad dark eye-stripe; whitish-grey eye-ring; greyish lores. Notheastern wintering race darker above, and duskier below with touch of yellow on underparts in fresh plumage. Sulking; keeps low in undergrowth, often on the ground. Difficult to observe. **VOICE** Call a strong *chock … chock*. **DISTRIBUTION** Winter visitor to the Himalayan foothills and NE India. **HABITAT** Bushes, long grass.

Ashy-throated Warbler

Lemon-rumped Warbler

Smoky Warbler

Hume's Warbler

Mitash Biswas

Sulphur-bellied Warbler

Chinmay Rahane

Tickell's Leaf Warbler

Clement M Francis

Dusky Warbler

Devashish Deb

Common Chiffchaff *Phylloscopus collybita* 11cm ⓜ

Small, plain dull greyish-brown warbler often with olive wash. Creamish throat, breast and belly; dark eye-stripe; short whitish supercilium; short, rounded wings; long, square-ended tail; tail and flight feathers more brownish, edged olive-yellow; black bill and legs. Sexes alike. VOICE Song is a slightly jerky double-noted *chiff-chaff, chiff-chaff…* call a soft *wheep, zit* or *peeu*. DISTRIBUTION Common winter visitor throughout N plains. HABITAT Wooded country, reed beds, crops.

White-spectacled Warbler *Phylloscopus intermedius* 10cm ⓡ

Bright, with domed head, prominent eye-ring and crown-stripes; distinguished from Whistler's Warbler (below) by grey crown, white eye-ring, grey supercilium, grey neck-sides and more defined yellow wing-bar; from the **Grey-cheeked Warbler** *Seicercus poliogenys* by yellowish chin. Grey head, including lores; olive-green cheeks, paler grey crown-stripe and supercilium, darker lateral crown-stripes; pale lower mandible. Occurs in small groups. VOICE *Che-weet*; sweet song. DISTRIBUTION W Bengal to Arunachal Pradesh, S Assam hills. HABITAT Dense evergreen and pine forests.

Whistler's Warbler *Phylloscopus whistleri* 10cm ⓡ

Green upperparts, bright yellow underparts, domed head and deep olive crown; prominent pale eye-ring; diffused crown-stripe. Similar to the **Green-crowned Warbler** *Seicercus burkii*, but has broad, dark lateral crown-stripe, pale yellow lores and broader eye-ring, lower mandible pale; breast-sides and flanks have touches of green or brown, and usually more distinct wing-bar; more white in tail. Occurs in pairs. Secretive. VOICE Calls *titu*. Rich, warbling song. DISTRIBUTION Resident in the Himalayas. HABITAT Undergrowth in coniferous, deciduous, evergreen forests.

Greenish Warbler *Phylloscopus trochiloides* 11cm ⓜ

Medium-sized, slim, dull greenish-brown bird with cream underparts. Prominent long, sweeping supercilium; whitish eye-ring; broad eye-stripe; mottled ear-coverts; strong patterning on head; one wing-bar usually visible; brown legs. Sexes alike. Arboreal. Active and restless. Scattered parties or mixed hunting groups. Nests low down. The **Large-billed Leaf Warbler** *P. magnirostris* has brown-olive upperparts; greenish-grey wash on breast-sides and flanks. Dark eye-stripe distinctive. VOICE Call a loud *tis … lee*. DISTRIBUTION Winters widely in penisular lowlands. Common passage migrant elsewhere. HABITAT All types of wooded country.

Western Crowned Warbler *Phylloscopus occipitalis* 11cm ⓜ ⓡ

Stocky warbler with pale central crown-stripe, pale lower mandibles and dark legs. Underparts greyish-green, with more green on wings and tail; two yellowish wing-bars on each wing; striking yellowish supercilia; underparts white. Sexes alike. Seen in small parties and mixed hunting groups. Alternately flicks wings half open. Confiding. Nests low down. VOICE Rather quiet. Repeated *chit … weet*. DISTRIBUTION Summer breeding visitor to N hills; winters mainly in Western and Eastern Ghats; widespread in India on passage. HABITAT Well-wooded forests.

Blyth's Leaf Warbler *Phylloscopus reguloides* 11cm ⓡ

Medium-sized, green-and-yellow leaf warbler with marked crown-stripe, yellowish supercilium and dark sides to crown; two broad yellowish wing-bars, fairly bright green to olive upperparts, underparts washed yellow; white edges to outer-tail feathers. Habit of alternate flicking of wings distinguishes it from other leaf warblers. Solitary or in pairs. VOICE *Kee-kew-i; see-pit*; long, trilling song. DISTRIBUTION Summer visitor to the NW Himalayas; resident in E Uttarakhand

to S Assam hills. HABITAT Broadleaved evergreen forests, forest edges.

Common Chiffchaff

White-spectacled Warbler

Whistler's Warbler

Large-billed Leaf Warbler

Green-crowned Warbler

Greenish Warbler

Western Crowned Warbler

Blyth's Leaf Warbler

Grey-hooded Warbler *Phylloscopus xanthoschistos* 10cm **r**

Grey above; prominent, long white eyebrow; yellowish rump and wings; white in outer tail seen in flight; completely yellow below. Sexes alike. The **Grey-cheeked Warbler** *P. poliogenys* has dark slaty head, white eye-ring, and grey chin and cheeks. Occurs in pairs or small bands, often with mixed hunting parties. Actively hunts and flits in canopy foliage and tall bushes. Highly energetic. VOICE Quite vocal; familiar calls in Himalayan forests; loud, high-pitched, double-note call; pleasant, trilling song. DISTRIBUTION The Himalayas. HABITAT Forests, gardens.

Clamorous Reed Warbler *Acrocephalus stentoreus* 19cm **r**

Brown above; distinct pale supercilium; whitish throat, dull buffy-white below; at close range, or in the hand, salmon-coloured inside of mouth; calls diagnostic. Sexes alike. Solitary or in pairs. Difficult to see but easily heard. Elusive bird, keeping to dense low reeds, mangroves and low growth, always in and around water. Never associates with other species. Flies low. VOICE Highly vocal; loud *chack, chakrrr* and *khe* notes; distinctive, loud warbling; loud, lively song. DISTRIBUTION Kashmir valley, south through India. HABITAT Reed beds, mangroves.

Moustached Warbler *Acrocephalus melanopogon* 13cm **m**

Medium-sized, perky warbler with streaked crown. Overall dark, with whitish underparts with rufous-buff wash; short wings; bold, square-ended creamy supercilium; streaked crown has black border; dark eye-stripes and ear-coverts; greyish cheeks and white throat; unstreaked rusty rump. Sexes alike. Solitary or in pairs. Cocks tail when alarmed. Feeds in reed litter and on floating vegetation. Secretive and unobtrusive. VOICE Calls include a deep *truk* and short *trik*. Song an ascending rattling trill. DISTRIBUTION Scarce winter visitor to NW India. HABITAT Reed beds, waterside bushes.

Paddyfield Warbler *Acrocephalus agricola* 13cm **m**

Rufescent-brown above; brighter on rump; whitish throat, rich buffy below; short, rounded wings; darker tertials with darker centres and pale edges; short, stubby bill; long cream supercilium. Solitary, hopping amid low growth; rarely seen with other birds. Damp areas, especially reed growth and cultivation, are favourite haunts. Flies low, but soon vanishes into growth. VOICE Rather harsh *chrr … chuck* or *chack* note. DISTRIBUTION Winter visitor, common over most of India. HABITAT Damp areas, reed beds, tall cultivation.

Blyth's Reed Warbler *Acrocephalus dumetorum* 13cm **m**

Plain, olive or grey-brown warbler, with long, sloping forehead, short, diffused buff-brown supercilium, not very visible behind eye; fresh plumage olive-brown above; pale below with buff-washed flanks, breast and vent; worn plumage olive-grey above, whiter below with grey wash. Usually solitary. Moves inconspicuously. Often flicks and flares tail. VOICE Harsh *zuk*; *tcheeairr*; song: *chrek-chrek chuwee*. DISTRIBUTION Common winter visitor to plains of S and NE India. Common passage migrant in N India. HABITAT Well-wooded, often dry country.

Booted Warbler *Iduna caligata* 12cm **m**

Dull olive-brown above; short, pale white supercilium; pale buffy-white below. Sexes alike. Solitary or 2–4 birds; sometimes in mixed bands of small birds. Active and agile, hunting among leaves and upper branches. Calls diagnostic. The similar **Sykes's Warbler** *I. rama* differs in having longer tail, flatter crown, colder grey above, whiter below and less dark crown edges. VOICE Harsh but low *chak … chak … churrr*; soft, jingling song. DISTRIBUTION Winters over peninsular India. HABITAT Open country with acacias and scrub.

Grey-hooded Warbler

Clamorous Reed Warbler

Grey-cheeked Warbler

Paddyfield Warbler

Moustached Warbler

Booted Warbler

Blyth's Reed Warbler

Sykes's Warbler

Striated Grassbird *Megalurus palustris* 25cm 🔴

Long, graduated tail and upright posture. Mainly buff upperparts; blackish streaking from crown to rump; some rufous on crown; heavily streaked above; long whitish supercilium; whitish lores; light streaking on whitish-buff underparts; long, pale bill and pale legs. Sexes alike. Frequently seen perched on tall grasses or reeds. The **Bristled Grassbird** *Schoenicola striatus* is similar, but smaller and less streaked, with shorter, graduated tail with pale tips. **VOICE** Loud *weee ... choo*. **DISTRIBUTION** Floodplains of N and NE rivers. **HABITAT** Tall grass, scrub, reed beds near water.

Zitting Cisticola *Cisticola juncidis* 10cm 🔴

Rufous-brown above, prominently streaked darker; rufous-buff unstreaked rump; white tips to fan-shaped tail diagnostic; buffy-white underbody, more rufous on flanks; diagnostic calls. Sexes alike. Occurs in pairs or with several birds. Great skulker. Usually seen during short, jerky flights. Striking display of male, soaring, falling and rising. **VOICE** Sharp, clicking *zit ... zit* calls continuously during display in air. **DISTRIBUTION** All India, south of the Himalayan foothills; rare in NE. **HABITAT** Open country, grassland, cultivation, reed beds.

Striated Prinia *Prinia crinigera* 16cm 🔴

Large, drab-looking hill warbler with long, graduated, pointed tail. Breeding male greyish-brown with dark streaking; darker lores. Underparts dirty-white speckled dark. Non-breeding male has more rufous-brown with light streaking on head, breast and upperparts; buffish lores and eye-ring; indistinct dark ring to tail, dark strong bill and flesh-coloured legs. Sexes alike. Usually solitary or in pairs. Skulking. **VOICE** Calls include grating *chitzweet*, and hard *chuk*. **DISTRIBUTION** Common breeding resident from Punjab to Arunachal Pradesh. **HABITAT** Grassy and scrub-covered hillsides.

Grey-breasted Prinia *Prinia hodgsonii* 12cm 🔴

Grey-brown with some rufous above; long grey tail, tipped black and white; white underbody; when breeding, soft grey breast-band diagnostic. Sexes alike. The **Rufous-fronted Prinia** *P. buchanani* can be identified by rufous head and dark brown tail, tipped black and white. Keeps to low growth but often clambers into middle levels. **VOICE** Noisy when breeding; longish, squeaky song; contact calls almost continuous squeaking. **DISTRIBUTION** All India south of the Himalayan foothills **HABITAT** Edges of forests, cultivation, gardens, scrub.

Graceful Prinia *Prinia gracilis* 13cm 🔴

Dull grey-brown above, streaked darker; very pale around eyes; long, graduated tail, faintly cross-barred, tipped white; whitish underbody, buffy on belly. Plumage more rufous in winter. Sexes alike. Occurs in small parties. Solitary. Restless; flicks wings and tail often. Occasionally hunts like a flycatcher. **VOICE** *Szeep ... szip ...* Call note a longish warble when breeding. Wing snapping and jumping display of male. **DISTRIBUTION** The NW Himalayan foothills, terai, south to Gujarat, across Gangetic Plain. **HABITAT** Scrub, grass, canal banks, semi-deserts.

Jungle Prinia *Prinia sylvatica* 15cm 🔴

Medium to large, plain-looking prinia with long, graduated tail and long, stout bill. Short supecilium; red iris. Breeding adult has dark grey-brown upperparts and creamy-white underparts; prominent white tips and whitish outer feathers on tail; more rufous-brown in non-breeding plumage. Sexes similar. Occurs in pairs or small parties. Secretive. **VOICE** Song a loud, rhythmic *zee ... tu ... zee ... tu*. **DISTRIBUTION** Locally common breeding resident in lowlands and hills throughout India. Rare in NW India. **HABITAT** Dry scrub and grass, often in rocky areas.

Striated Grassbird

Zitting Cisticola

Niranjan Sant

Bristled Grassbird

Grey-breasted Prinia

Biswarup Satpati

Striated Prinia

Rufous-fronted Prinia

Nitin Srinivasamurthy

Graceful Prinia

Jungle Prinia

Clement M Francis

185

Yellow-bellied Prinia *Prinia flaviventris* 13cm **r**

Small to medium-sized warbler with short, rounded wings and long, graduated tail; upperparts olive-grey; grey crown; distinct white supercilium and eye-ring; creamy-white chin and breast; yellow belly and vent. Sexes alike. Usually solitary or in pairs. Active, inquisitive and confiding. Feeds on insects low in cover. Nests low down. **VOICE** Calls include *tzee* and *chink … chink*. Song a musical *twee … dulu … lu … lee*. **DISTRIBUTION** Locally common breeding resident in N river valleys, the NE. **HABITAT** Reed beds, tall grass and tamarisk scrub near water.

Ashy Prinia *Prinia socialis* 13cm **r**

Rich ashy-grey above, with rufous wings and long, white-tipped tail; whitish lores; dull buffy-rufous below. In winter less ashy, more rufous-brown; longer tail; common in some areas. Sexes alike. Actively moves in undergrowth. Often flicks and erects tail. Typical jerky flight when flying from bush to bush. Noisy and excited when breeding. **VOICE** Nasal *pee … pee … pee …*; song a loud and lively *jivee … jivee … jivee …* or *jimmy … jimmy …* **DISTRIBUTION** Subcontinent. **HABITAT** Cultivation, edges of forests, scrub, parks, vicinity of human habitation.

Plain Prinia *Prinia inornata* 13cm **r**

Pale brown above; whitish supercilium and lores; dark wings and tail; long, graduated tail, with buff tips and white outer feathers; buff-white underbody; tawny flanks and belly. In winter more rufous above. Sexes alike. Pairs or several move about in low growth. Skulker; difficult to see. Jerky, low flight, soon vanishing into bush. Tail often flicked. **VOICE** Plaintive *tee … tee*; also *krrik … krrik* sound; wheezy song. **DISTRIBUTION** Subcontinent, from terai and Gangetic Plain southwards. **HABITAT** Tall cultivation, grass, scrub; prefers damp areas.

Common Tailorbird *Orthotomus sutorius* 13cm **r**

Olive-green above; rust-red forecrown; buffy-white underbody; dark spot on throat-sides, best seen in calling male; long, pointed tail, often held erect. Sexes alike. Central-tail feathers about 5cm longer and pointed in breeding male. Usually in pairs together. Rather common amid human habitation; keeps to bushes. Tail often cocked. Makes nest of leaves sewn together. **VOICE** Very vocal; loud, familiar *towit … towit*; male sings on exposed perch. **DISTRIBUTION** Across subcontinent, to about 2,000m. **HABITAT** Forests, cultivation, human habitation.

Rusty-cheeked Scimitar Babbler *Erythrogenys erythrogenys* 25cm **r**

Olive-brown above; orangish-rufous (rusty) sides of face, head, thighs and flanks; remainder of underbody mostly pure white; long, curved 'scimitar' bill. Sexes alike. Small bands in forests. Bird of undergrowth, hopping on jungle floor; turns over leaves or digs with bill; sometimes hops into leafy branches, but more at ease on the ground. **VOICE** Noisy; mellow, fluty whistle, two-noted *cue … pe … cue … pe*, followed by single- (sometimes double-) note reply by mate. **DISTRIBUTION** Himalayan foothills. **HABITAT** Forest undergrowth, ravines, bamboo.

Indian Scimitar Babbler *Pomatorhinus horsfieldii* 22cm **e**

Sexes alike. Deep olive-brown above; long white supercilium; white throat, breast and belly-centre; long, curved yellow 'scimitar' beak. Occurs in pairs or small, loose bands in forest; keeps to undergrowth, more often heard than seen; hops on jungle floor; hops its way into leafy branches. The similar **White-browed Scimitar Babbler** *P. schisticeps* has a distribution mostly in the N hills from Punjab to Arunachal Pradesh, S Assam hills. **VOICE** Fluty, musical whistle, **DISTRIBUTION** Hilly forest regions of peninsular India. **HABITAT** Mixed forest, scrub, bamboo.

Yellow-bellied Prinia

Ashy Prinia

Savio Fonseca

Common Tailorbird

Savio Fonseca

Plain Prinia

Indian Scimitar Babbler

Clement M Francis

Rusty-cheeked Scimitar Babbler

White-browed Scimitar Babbler

JJ Harrison CC

Streak-breasted Scimitar Babbler *Pomatorhinus ruficollis* 19cm ⓡ

Fairly small scimitar babbler. Long, broad white supercilium merging above bill; black mask; decurved yellow bill; dark crown and olive-brown upperparts. Chestnut only around nape; olive-brown streaks on breast and belly, and plain olive-brown flanks; white only around chin and throat. Skulking and secretive. VOICE Off-and-on duets between males and females, *kwee … kwee*. DISTRIBUTION E Uttaranchal to Arunachal. HABITAT Forest undergrowth, hillside scrub.

Coral-billed Scimitar Babbler *Pomatorhinus ferruginosus* 22cm ⓡ

Distinctive scimitar babbler with bright coral-red bill. Long white supercilium. Black mask from bill to mantle; white upper throat. E Himalayan nominate race has black crown and nape. Bright chestnut-rufous throat, breast and belly; bristly rufous feathers on forehead and lores. Buff underparts. Often mistaken for the **Red-billed Scimitar Babbler** *P. ochraceiceps*, which has longer, more curved bill, and white breast and belly. Occurs in pairs when breeding or in small parties. VOICE Soft, fluty, oriole-like whistles. DISTRIBUTION Nepal to Arunachal Pradesh, S Assam hills. HABITAT Dense forest undergrowth; secondary growth, bamboo.

Slender-billed Scimitar Babbler *Pomatorhinus superciliaris* 20cm ⓡ

Very long, slender, sharply downcurved black bill; relatively small, dark grey head with long white supercilium; dark brown above and brighter rufous-brown below; whitish throat streaked with grey. Sexes alike. Skulking and secretive. Forages in bamboo or low undergrowth. Often in small flocks. VOICE Varied calls include series of repeated powerful, mellow hoots uttered rapidly. DISTRIBUTION Resident in the E Himalayas and NE India. HABITAT Moist broadleaved forests, bamboo thickets.

Rufous-throated Wren-babbler *Spelaeornis caudatus* 9cm ⓡ

Small, rotund babbler. Grey face and whitish chin; unmarked, bright orange-rufous throat, breast and flanks streaked and barred; black-and-white mottled belly; plain brown (with rufous tint) back and wings; almost no tail. Juvenile has more rufous upperparts than adults, and more diffused scaling. Difficult to see in dense ferns, undergrowth and mossy rocks. Territorial. VOICE Calls include chittering, churring, warbling and chirruping. DISTRIBUTION East of Nepal to W Arunachal Pradesh. HABITAT Undergrowth in most broadleaved evergreen forests.

Mishmi Wren-babbler *Spelaeornis badeigularis* 8.5cm ⓔ ⓥ

Sometimes referred to as the Rusty-throated Wren-babbler. Small, deep brown babbler with distinct rufous patch on throat; grey ear-coverts; darkly streaked lower throat; small whitish patch on chin. Black-and-white barred lower breast and belly; flanks and vent dark brown; small, short tail. Similar to the Rufous-throated Wren-babbler (above), but much darker and rufous restricted to throat. Largely terrestrial. VOICE Thought to be like that of Rufous-throated. DISTRIBUTION Resident of Mishmi hills in E Arunachal Pradesh. HABITAT Moist subtropical forests.

Sikkim Wedge-billed Babbler *Stachyris humei* 18cm ⓔ

Distinctly marked babbler. Underparts dark brown; dark pointed bill; blackish face-mask; dense spotting on neck-sides. Underparts dark; barred wings and tail; pale buff scales on belly; blackish legs and feet. The similar, but smaller **Cachar Wedge-billed Babbler** *S. roberti* ⓔ has bold white triangular scales on browner underparts and plain brownish cheeks; no supercilium and pale grey tips to mantle and tertials. VOICE Call and song mostly unknown. DISTRIBUTION Sikkim and Arunachal. Cachar found in S Assam hills. HABITAT Broadleaved and evergreen forests, bamboo.

Streak-breasted Scimitar Babbler

Coral-billed Scimitar Babbler

Slender-billed Scimitar Babbler

Red-billed Scimitar Babbler

Mishmi Wren-babbler

Rufous-throated Wren-babbler

Cachar Wedge-billed Babbler

Sikkim Wedge-billed Babbler

Dihyendu Ash CC

Ramki Sreenivasan

Amit Thakur

Ramki reenivasan

Black-chinned Babbler *Cyanoderma pyrrhops* 10cm ⓡ

Tiny, fulvous-brown babbler. Back of crown olive. Diagnostic black lores and chin; underparts orange-buff; head-sides more fulvous. Red iris; upper mandible brown; legs, feet and claws pale flesh-brown. Sexes alike. Feeds in pairs or small parties, often in mixed hunting groups. Active and not shy. Nests lower down. **VOICE** Calls include mellow *wit … wit … .wit … .wit*; also a soft, variable *chirr*. **DISTRIBUTION** Fairly common breeding resident in N mountains; moves lower in winter. **HABITAT** Edges of forests and secondary undergrowth; bamboo.

Golden Babbler *Cyanoderma chrysaeum* 10cm ⓡ

Small babbler with short, sharply pointed bill; gold head, with prominent black streaks from hindcrown to nape; partial black mask; black lores, thin brow line; black moustachial stripe; olive-green-gold upperparts; more golden underparts; dark red eye. In pairs when breeding. Moves constantly. **VOICE** Song typically 5–7 rather high-pitched, piping notes, *tu tu-tu-tu-tu-tu-tu*; introductory notes sometimes given singly. **DISTRIBUTION** Arunachal Pradesh, S Assam hills. **HABITAT** Undergrowth in moist broadleaved and evergreen forests, secondary growth.

Tawny-bellied Babbler *Dumetia hyperythra* 13cm ⓡ

Olivish-brown above; reddish-brown front part of crown; white throat in western and southern races; nominate race has underbody entirely fulvous. Sexes alike. Small, noisy parties in undergrowth. Rummages on the floor, hopping about. Always wary; hardly associates with other birds. Great skulker, difficult to see. **VOICE** Faint *cheep … cheep* contact notes; also mix of other whistling and chattering notes. **DISTRIBUTION** From SE Himachal Pradesh, east along foothills into peninsular India; absent in extreme NE India. **HABITAT** Scrub and bamboo, forests.

Dark-fronted Babbler *Rhopocichla atriceps* 13cm ⓡ

Smallish, rich rufous-brown babbler with black head. Creamy-white breast, throat and belly. Yellow eyes. Square-tipped tail. Top of head the same colour as back, and black confined to broad band through each eye joining across forehead. Strictly resident. **VOICE** Calls include unobtrusive *tup*, scolding *churr* and plaintive nasal mewing. **DISTRIBUTION** Endemic to subcontinent; Western Ghats, peninsular India. **HABITAT** Evergreen biotope in dense undergrowth, thickets near streams.

Pin-striped Tit-babbler *Mixornis gularis* 11cm ⓡ

Small brownish babbler; underparts yellow-brown, streaked finely with black; rusty-brown crown; pale yellow lores; plain rufous-brown wings and tail; mantle more olive; yellowish supercilium; pale iris; dark eye-stripe. Sexes alike. In pairs or small parties. Active but furtive, creeping on the ground. **VOICE** Very noisy. Call a loud *chunk … chunk … chunk*. **DISTRIBUTION** Common breeding resident in N foothills to Arunachal Pradesh, NE India and Eastern Ghats. **HABITAT** Forest undergrowth and bamboo, often feeding fairly high but also on the ground.

Chestnut-capped Babbler *Timalia pileata* 17cm ⓡ

Rather distinctive babbler, with bright chestnut cap contrasting with sturdy black bill; black mask, extending only up to eye; white supercilium, forehead, cheeks, chin, throat and breast; finely streaked lower throat and breast; grey neck-sides; drab olive-brown upperparts; mostly olive-buff below; relatively long, scruffy, typical babbler tail. In pairs when breeding. Secretive. **VOICE** *Tik, tik; chit, chit* and so on. **DISTRIBUTION** E Uttarakhand to Assam, Arunachal Pradesh. **HABITAT** Wetlands with tall grasses, reed beds, scrub and secondary growth.

Black-chinned Babbler

Golden Babbler

Tawny-bellied Babbler

Dark-fronted Babbler

Pin-striped Tit-babbler

Chestnut-capped Babbler

Avinash Khemka

Savio Fonseca

Kunan Naik

Yellow-throated Fulvetta *Schoeniparus cinereus* 10cm (r)

Small, mainly brown-and-yellow fulvetta; long, broad yellow supercilium, bordered by dark eye-stripe below and dark lateral crown-stripe above; greyish scaling and mottling on brownish crown; yellowish-brown upperparts. Brown wings; grey streaking on yellowish face; yellow throat and yellowish underparts; dusky flanks and breast-sides. Usually in small flocks. Active in forest understorey. **VOICE** Calls include *si … si … si … si … si … si*; *chrrp … prrp*. **DISTRIBUTION** Hills of NE India. **HABITAT** Understorey in dense, subtropical broadleaved and evergreen forests.

Brown-cheeked Fulvetta *Alcippe poioicephala* 15cm (r)

Olive-brown above; grey crown and nape distinctive; thin black stripe through eye; rufescent-brown wings and tail; dull fulvous underbody. Sexes alike. Occurs in pairs or small parties, often with other birds. Moves actively in undergrowth and leafy branches, clinging sideways or springing from perch. Rather shy in most areas, but occasionally emerges into open areas. **VOICE** Best-known call a 4–8-syllable song, harsh *churrr …* notes. **DISTRIBUTION** Peninsular India. **HABITAT** Forests, undergrowth, bamboo; hill-station gardens in Western Ghats.

Nepal Fulvetta *Alcippe nipalensis* 12cm (r)

Medium-sized, largely grey-and-brown fulvetta. Grey crown, nape and ear-coverts; black lateral crown-stripe; prominent white eye-ring; pale lower mandible; olive-brown upperparts and tail; whitish throat, centre of breast and belly; buffy-brown flanks, breast and undertail-coverts. Occurs in small, restless, vocal parties. Occasionally descends to the ground. Shy. **VOICE** Buzzes; trills; short song. **DISTRIBUTION** W Nepal to Arunachal Pradesh, S Assam hills. **HABITAT** Thick undergrowth in thick deciduous and evergreen forests, bamboo, secondary growth.

Abbott's Babbler *Malacocincla abbotti* 20cm (r)

Plain, drab brownish babbler with short tail, thick bill and stocky appearance; light grey supercilium and lores; greyish or greyish-white throat and breast; olive-brown above; unmarked throat and breast; rufous breast-sides; olive-brown flanks; rufous tail and uppertail-coverts; brighter rufous vent and undertail-coverts. Solitary or in pairs. Territorial and site loyal. Shy and secretive. **VOICE** Calls include trills, churrs and mews. Whistled song *tchwee … tchu … tchwee*. **DISTRIBUTION** Assam and Arunachal Pradesh. **HABITAT** Thick undergrowth, thickets.

Indian Grass Babbler *Graminicola bengalensis* 18cm (r)

Large grassbird with dark rufous-streaked crown, nape and mantle; whitish supercilium; darker rufous-brown streaking on back and lower mantle; rump and wings mostly rufous; long dark, graduated tail; whitish underparts with rufous-buff breast-sides and flanks; pale bill. Sexes similar. Skulks in dense grass and reed beds; dives back into cover when flushed. Noisy when breeding. **VOICE** Calls *er, wit, wit, wit*. Song a buzzing *wi wi wu wuoo … wuoo*. **DISTRIBUTION** Rarely seen resident in plains of India. **HABITAT** Grass and reed beds near water.

Puff-throated Babbler *Pellorneum ruficeps* 15cm (r)

Olivish-brown above; dark rufous cap; whitish-buff stripe over eye; white throat; dull fulvous-white underbody, boldly streaked blackish-brown on breast and sides. Sexes alike. Solitary or in pairs. Shy, secretive bird; mostly heard and very difficult to see. Rummages on the ground, amid leaf litter; hops about. **VOICE** Noisy; mellow whistle, interpreted as *he-will-beat-you*. **DISTRIBUTION** Hilly forest areas; the Himalayas, east of SE Himachal Pradesh; NE states; across C India, Eastern and Western Ghats. **HABITAT** Forest undergrowth, bamboo, overgrown ravines, nullahs.

Yellow-throated Fulvetta

Brown-cheeked Fulvetta

Savio Fonesca

Nepal Fulvetta

Abbot's Babbler

Bhanu Singh

ndian Grass Babbler

Puff-throated Babbler

Manjula Mathur

193

Striated Laughingthrush *Grammatoptila striata* 28cm **r**

Rich brown plumage, heavily white streaked, except on wings and rich rufous-brown tail; darkish, loose crest, streaked white towards front; heavy streaking on throat and head-sides, becoming less streaked from breast downwards. Sexes alike. Occurs in pairs or small, noisy parties. Feeds in both upper branches and low bushes; shows marked preference for certain sites in forest. **VOICE** Very vocal; clear, whistling call; loud, cackling chatter. **DISTRIBUTION** The Himalayas east of Kulu, parts of NE states. **HABITAT** Dense forests, scrub, wooded ravines.

Himalayan Cutia *Cutia nipalensis* 20cm **r**

Round and unmistakable babbler with slaty-blue head; male has broad, bluish-black mask; short, sturdy, slightly decurved bill; white underparts with diagnostic bold dark barring on buff-washed sides of breast and flanks; blue panels on bluish-black wings; rufous-chestnut mantle, back and long uppertail-coverts; long buff undertail-coverts, with just tip of black tail visible; orange legs. Seen in pairs and small groups. **VOICE** Calls include toots, squawks and *cheet ... cheet*. **DISTRIBUTION** C Nepal to Arunachal; S Assam hills. **HABITAT** Dense moist forests.

Scaly Laughingthrush *Trochalopteron subunicolor* 23cm **r**

Olive-brown laughingthrush with dense black scaling all over. Greyish crown; short dark bill; Diagnostic yellow in wings and tail feathers, tipped white; primaries show little blue-grey; underparts and vent olive-brown. Secretive. Keeps to dense vegetation. Occurs in pairs or small flocks. Feeds on berries and invertebrates. **VOICE** Normal song a two- or three-part wolf-whistle. **DISTRIBUTION** The Himalayas from Nepal east to Arunachal Pradesh. **HABITAT** Thick undergrowth in moist broadleaved and mixed broadleaved and coniferous forests.

Streaked Laughingthrush *Trochalopteron lineatum* 20cm **r**

Pale grey plumage, streaked dark brown on upper back, white on lower back; rufous ear-coverts and wings; rufous edges and grey-white tips to roundish tail; rufous streaking and white shafts on underbody. Sexes alike. Occurs in pairs or small bands; prefers low, bushy and grassy areas, only rarely going into upper branches. Hops, and bows; flicks wings and jerks tail often. Weak, short flight. **VOICE** Fairly noisy mix of whistling and squeaky notes; common call a whistle. **DISTRIBUTION** The Himalayas. **HABITAT** Bushy hill slopes, cultivation, forests.

Blue-winged Laughingthrush *Trochalopteron squamatum* 25cm **r**

Overall dark brown, finely scaled laughingthrush. Black supercilium; rusty-orange and sooty-grey wings; distinct wing-panel created by blue-grey outer webs on primaries; rufous wings with darker outer edges; chestnut-brown flanks and vent; chestnut undertail-coverts; black tail with rufous tip; striking white iris. Very shy, hiding in dense undergrowth. **VOICE** Alarm call a scratchy seek. Song a *cur ... white ... to ... go*. **DISTRIBUTION** The Himalayas; NE India. **HABITAT** Dense undergrowth in moist evergreen forests.

Variegated Laughingthrush *Trochalopteron variegatum* 24cm **r**

Olive-brown above; grey, black and white head and face; grey, black, white and rufous in wings and tail; black chin and throat, bordered with buffy-white; narrow white tip to tail, with grey subterminal band. Sexes alike. Occurs in small flocks of up to a dozen on steep, bushy hillsides. Keeps to undergrowth, but occasionally clambers into leafy branches. Wary and secretive. Weak flight. **VOICE** Noisy; clear, musical whistling notes; also harsh squeaking notes. **DISTRIBUTION** W and C Himalayas. **HABITAT** Forest undergrowth, bamboo, hill-station gardens.

Striated Laughingthrush

Himalayan Cutia

P Manjunath

Scaly Laughingthrush

Streaked Laughingthrush

Manjula Mathur

Blue-winged Laughingthrush

Variegated Laughingthrush

Manjula Mathur

Black-faced Laughingthrush *Trochalopteron affine* 25cm (r)

Diagnostic blackish face, throat and part of head, and contrasting white malar patches, neck-sides and part of eye-ring; rufous-brown above, finely scalloped on back; olivish-golden flight feathers tipped grey; rufous-brown below throat, marked grey. Sexes alike. Occurs in pairs or small bands. Moves on the ground and in low growth. Noisy when disturbed. **VOICE** Various high-pitched notes, chuckles; rolling *whirr* alarm call. **DISTRIBUTION** The Himalayas, from W Nepal eastwards. **HABITAT** Undergrowth in forests; dwarf vegetation in higher regions.

Chestnut-crowned Laughingthrush *Trochalopteron erythrocephalum* 28cm (r)

Variable laughingthrush with brilliant green-gold panel on wings and tail-sides; heavy black spots on upper mantle and scales on breast; chestnut forehead scales and fine black centres on ear-coverts; usually dark reddish eyes. Nominate racial group has entirely rufous crown and rufous cheek. In W Himalayas, nominate pale with bright rufous crown, greyish-olive mantle and pale, dull buff underparts. **VOICE** Song quite variable, sweet, clear, wiry and emphatic. **DISTRIBUTION** The entire Himalayas. **HABITAT** Dense vegetation in broadleaved forests.

Chestnut-tailed Minla *Actinodura strigula* 14cm (r)

Small, brightly coloured babbler with high-domed chestnut crown. Olive-brown above with black-, white- and chestnut-patterned wings and chestnut-centred black tail with yellow edgings. Dusky cheeks and finely black-barred white throat. Feeds actively on invertebrates and fruits in small parties or mixed hunting groups. **VOICE** Calls include whistling *tsee ... tsi ... tsay ... tsse* and *pseep*. **DISTRIBUTION** Locally common breeding resident in the Himalayas. Moves lower down in winter. **HABITAT** Lower canopy; high undergrowth of forests.

Rusty-fronted Barwing *Actinodura egertoni* 23cm (r)

Larger, slender barwing, with dark rufous-chestnut forehead, lores and chin; relatively long tail; feathery, unstreaked blue-grey crest, nape, upper mantle and neck-sides; unmarked, rufous-brown lower mantle; unbarred rufous-chestnut on greater coverts and bases of primaries; buff-barred primaries and secondaries; blue-grey edges to flight feathers; plain olive-brown below. Occurs in pairs or small parties. Arboreal. **VOICE** Song a sweet, whistled *tee ... tee ... ta*. **DISTRIBUTION** Nepal eastwards to W Arunachal Pradesh. **HABITAT** Thick undergrowth, broadleaved forests.

Blue-winged Minla *Actinodura cyanouroptera* 15cm (r)

Fairly small, slender, distinctive babbler, with blue crown, wings and tail; deep blue streaks and lateral stripes on blue-grey crown and nape; long white supercilium; pale greyish-white face; dark, beady eye; pale, flesh-coloured bill; mauve underparts; brown mantle; blue wings with grey-blue panel; blue-sided, square-ended tail. Usually in small groups. **VOICE** Calls *chip ...*; *chik*. Song a high-pitched, whistled *pee ... peeoo ...*; *si ... seeow*. **DISTRIBUTION** Hills of Uttaranchal to Arunachal. **HABITAT** Broadleaved evergreen forests, mixed broadleaved and coniferous forests.

Streak-throated Barwing *Actinodura waldeni* 22cm (r)

Two races. Greyish-white throat, breast and belly diffusely streaked with brownish-grey. Best distinguished by streaked underparts, lack of bold shaft streaking on crown and nape; weak moustachial stripe; even rufous-brown mantle. **VOICE** Contact calls rather nasal, grumbling *grrr ... ut ... grrr ... ut* and *grr ... grr ...* and so on. **DISTRIBUTION** Fairly common resident in hills of NE India (Arunachal Pradesh, Assam, Manipur, Nagaland). **HABITAT** Mossy broadleaved evergreen and mixed forests.

Black-faced Laughingthrush

Chestnut-crowned Laughingthrush

Chestnut-tailed Minla

Rusty-fronted Barwing

Blue-winged Minla

Streak-throated Barwing

197

Nilgiri Laughingthrush *Montecincla cachinnans* 20cm **e** **v**

Olive-brown above; deep slaty-brown crown; long white stripe over eye and much shorter streak below; black lores and stripe through and behind eye, chin and throat; rich rufous below throat. Sexes alike. Occurs in small parties of up to a dozen birds. The **Palani Laughingthrush** M. *fairbanki* has a dark eye-stripe and prominent white-eyebrow, grey bib and a rufous belly. **VOICE** Chattering 'laughter'; one of the most familiar bird calls of the Niigiris. **DISTRIBUTION** Restricted to the Nilgiris above 1,000m. **HABITAT** Dense evergreen forests, hill-station gardens.

Red-tailed Minla *Minla ignotincta* 14cm **r**

Black crown, prominent broad white supercilium and black mask extending to nape; brown mantle and back; pale yellowish underparts; light grey streaks sometimes visible on breast and flanks; white-edged black wing-coverts, secondaries and tertials. Male has red panel on flight feathers; male has chestnut cast to brown mantle; black tail, with red outer-tail and undertail feathers. Arboreal. **VOICE** Calls include *wi … wi … wi; chik … chik …* **DISTRIBUTION** E and NE India. **HABITAT** Moist broadleaved evergreen forests.

Red-billed Leiothrix *Leiothrix lutea* 13cm **r**

Male olive-grey above; dull buffy-yellow lores and eye-ring; yellow, orange, crimson and black in wings; forked tail with black tip and edges; yellow throat; orange-yellow breast diagnostic; scarlet bill. Occurs in small parties; often part of mixed hunting parties of small birds in forests. Rummages in undergrowth but frequently moves up into leafy branches. Lively, noisy bird. **VOICE** Quite vocal; often utters a wistful, piping *tee … tee … tee.* **DISTRIBUTION** The Himalayas. **HABITAT** Forest undergrowth, bushy hillsides, plantations.

Silver-eared Mesia *Leiothrix argentauris* 15cm **r**

Striking babbler, with bright yellow bill, forehead, chin and upper throat; orange-yellow lower throat, breast and upper mantle; black face and crown, partially encircling large, silver-grey ear-covert patch. Crimson wing-panel on greenish orange-yellow wings; grey on rest of mantle and back; greenish-yellow on rest of underparts; yellow-edged dark tail. Male has crimson uppertail- and undertail-coverts. **VOICE** Call a chattering *tiweet … cheweet … cheweet.* **DISTRIBUTION** Hills of Uttaranchal to Arunachal. **HABITAT** Bushes in evergreen forests, edges of forests.

Red-faced Liocichla *Liocichla phoenicea* 23cm **r**

Distinctive, mainly brown-and-crimson babbler; dark brown upperparts and underparts; streaked crown; black supercilium; bright red face, ear-coverts and neck-sides; large, crimson-and-orange patch on primaries; silver and black on secondaries; red undertail-coverts; extensive orange on wing-tips, underside and tips to black tail. Solitary; in pairs when breeding; shy and secretive; not easily seen. **VOICE** Calls include churrs, rattles and mews. **DISTRIBUTION** The E Himalayas and NE hills. **HABITAT** Thick undergrowth, deciduous and evergreen forests.

Bugun Liocichla *Liocichla bugunorum* 22cm **e** **v**

Olive-brown laughingthrush with black crown. Diagnostic orange-yellow lores; yellow postocular spot; grey cheeks; yellow, red and white patches in wings; black tail with reddish tip; scarlet-red undertail-coverts. **VOICE** Fluty calls on descending scale, slightly slurred and inflected at the end, *weee … keew, yu … weee … keew, wieuu … weei … tuui … tuuuw … tuoow.* **DISTRIBUTION** Globally threatened. Eaglenest Wildlife Sanctuary, Arunachal Pradesh. **HABITAT** Disturbed hillsides with dense shrubberies, small trees and bushes.

Nilgiri Laughingthrush

Palani Laughingthrush

Red-billed Leiothrix

Red-faced Liocichla

Red-tailed Minla

Silver-eared Mesia

Bugun Liocichla

Rufous Sibia *Heterophasia capistrata* 22cm **r**

Rich-rufous plumage; grey-brown centre of back (between wings); black crown; slightly bushy crest and head-sides; bluish-grey wings; black shoulder-patch; grey-tipped long tail; black subterminal tail-band. Sexes alike. Active gymnast. Moves amid moss-covered branches. The **Rufous-backed Sibia** *Leioptila annectens* has white streaks on black nape; rufous back, rump and uppertail-coverts; mainly black wings with white-edged tertials. **VOICE** Cheerful calls. Wide range of whistling and sharp notes. Rich song. **DISTRIBUTION** The Himalayas. **HABITAT** Forests.

Long-tailed Sibia *Heterophasia picaoides* 30cm **r**

Large, brown-grey babbler with long, white-tipped, graduated tail and distinct white wing-patch, graduated. Grey head and breast; red iris; slender, slightly downcurved bill; darkish lores; brownish back, wings and tail; underparts pale grey. Sexes alike. Arboreal. Very noisy. The medium-sized **Beautiful Sibia** *H. pulchella* has pale indigo-blue crown; black lores, ear-coverts and face; shorter blue, brown and grey tail. **VOICE** Call a ringing *tsip tsip tsip*. **DISTRIBUTION** Locally common breeding resident. E Nepal to Arunachal. **HABITAT** Evergreen forests; edges of forests.

Large Grey Babbler *Argya malcolmi* 28cm **r**

Grey-brown above; dark centres to feathers on back give streaked look; greyer forehead; long, graduated tail cross-rayed with white outer feathers, conspicuous in flight; fulvous-grey below. Sexes alike. Gregarious; flocks in open country. Weak flight, never for long; at any sign of danger, flock comes together. **VOICE** Very noisy; chorus of squeaking chatter; short alarm note. **DISTRIBUTION** From around Delhi environs, south through most of peninsula; east to Bihar; abundant in the Deccan. **HABITAT** Scrub, open country, gardens, vicinity of human habitation.

Common Babbler *Argya caudata* 23cm **r**

Dull brown above, profusely streaked; brown wings; olivish-brown tail, long and graduated, cross-rayed darker; dull white throat; pale fulvous underbody; streaked on breast-sides. Sexes alike. Pairs or small bands in open scrub. Skulker. Very wary. The **Striated Babbler** *A. earlei* is streaked darker; long, cross-barred tail; pale supercilium; pale yellow bill with dark tip. **VOICE** Noisy; pleasant, warbling whistles. **DISTRIBUTION** Most of N, NW, W and peninsular India, east to about W Bengal. **HABITAT** Thorn scrub, open cultivation, grass.

Jungle Babbler *Argya striata* 25cm **r**

Overall grey-brown babbler. Light brown head; whitish iris; stout yellow bill; short dark eyebrow; pale lores; dark brown tail. Underparts paler with some greyish streaking on breast. Feeds in groups. Confiding and inquisitive. The **Yellow-billed Babbler** *A. affinis* is drab looking with creamy-white crown; pale blue-grey eyes; yellowish-buff below breast. **VOICE** Very noisy. Calls include harsh *ke … ke … ke* and chattering and squeaking. **DISTRIBUTION** Common breeding resident throughout lowlands and foothills. **HABITAT** Open woodland, scrub, cultivation, gardens, villages.

White-crested Laughingthrush *Garrulax leucolophus* 28cm **r**

Olive-brown above; pure white head, crest, throat, breast and head-sides; broad black band through eye to ear-coverts; rich rufous nuchal collar, continuing around breast; olive-brown below breast. Sexes alike. Occurs in small parties in forests. Moves in undergrowth but readily ascends into upper leafy branches. Hops on the ground, rummaging in leaf litter. **VOICE** Very noisy; sudden explosive chatter or 'laughter'. **DISTRIBUTION** The Himalayas, east of N Himachal Pradesh; foothills. **HABITAT** Dense forest undergrowth, bamboo, wooded nullahs.

Rufous Sibia

Long-tailed Sibia

Manjula Mathur

Rufous-backed Sibia

Beautiful Sibia

Manjula Mathur

Large Grey Babbler

Common Babbler

Garima Bhatia

Jungle Babbler

Yellow-billed Babbler

White-crested Laughingthrush

Manjula Mathur

Spotted Laughingthrush *Ianthocincla ocellata* 32cm **r**

Very large, distinctive laughingthrush, with rufous face, chin and supercilium; dusky throat and ear-coverts; blackish cap; stark white iris; bold black-and-white spotting on rufous-chestnut upperparts. Dense, bold mottling, barring and spotting on buff breast and upper belly; grey-and-black edges to flight feathers; long, chestnut-grey, graduated tail with black-and-white edges. Solitary, in pairs or in small groups. **VOICE** Call a *tchu … wee, tchu … wee, tchu … witty.* **DISTRIBUTION** Uttaranchal to Arunachal Pradesh. **HABITAT** Undergrowth in mixed forests.

Rufous-chinned Laughingthrush *Ianthocincla rufogularis* 22cm **r**

Medium-sized, intricately patterned laughingthrush; variable rufous on chin, upper throat and ear-coverts; black crown; buff lores; black submoustachial area; black, scaly barring on mantle; black bands on wings; black spotting on variable grey or buff-white underparts; bright rufous-chestnut vent and tail edges; black subterminal band on tail. Solitary, in pairs or in small flocks. Quiet, shy and wary. **VOICE** Varied calls; squeals and chuckles. **DISTRIBUTION** Hills of Kashmir to Arunachal. **HABITAT** Forest undergrowth, scrub, forest edges, secondary growth.

Wayanad Laughingthrush *Pterorhinus delesserti* 23cm **e**

Large, ash-brown laughingthrush; crown and nape lighter grey; black mask; chestnut wing-coverts and back; white throat; greyish breast; blackish tail. Diagnostic yellowish-pink lower mandible. Breast light grey-brown and darker rufous vent. Moves in groups in dense forests. Hard to spot in the undergrowth. **VOICE** Calls include frenzied, discordant series of screeches. **DISTRIBUTION** Endemic to Western Ghats. **HABITAT** Humid broadleaved evergreen forests, cardamom sholas.

White-throated Laughingthrush *Pterorhinus albogularis* 28cm **r**

Greyish olive-brown above; fulvous forehead; black mark in front of eye; full, rounded tail with four outer pairs of feathers broadly tipped with white. Rufous below but with conspicuous pure white throat sharply demarcated by line of olive-brown. White gorget stands out in gloom of forest floor. Sexes alike. Seen in large flocks. **VOICE** Continual chattering; warning *twit-tzee* alarm. **DISTRIBUTION** Throughout the Himalayas, with distinct western race *whistleri*, to 3,000m in summer. **HABITAT** Dense forests, scrub, wooded ravines.

Greater Necklaced Laughingthrush *Pterorhinus pector* 29cm **r**

Large, stocky laughingthrush with striking black 'necklace'; olive-brown above; rufous flanks, sides of breast and neck; whitish centre to belly; long, graduated, white-tipped tail. Similar to the **Lesser Necklaced Laughingthrush** *Garrulax monileger*, but has bigger bill; necklace enclosing larger area on whitish breast; throat buff washed; variable ear-coverts completely enclosed by black moustachial stripe joining bill to necklace; grey legs. In pairs when breeding. Wary. **VOICE** Whistles; *week … week … week.* **DISTRIBUTION** W Nepal to Arunachal, S Assam hills. **HABITAT** Broadleaved forest undergrowth.

Fire-tailed Myzornis *Myzornis pyrrhoura* 12cm **r**

Bright, rich leaf-green above; slightly paler gold-green below; distinctive black spots on crown; black eye-mask; diffused greenish-gold outline around eye-mask, on bend of wing; thin black, downcurved bill; bright red throat and breast; orange-red vent; orange-red, white and black wing-panels; large white tips to primaries and secondaries; bright red sides to black-tipped tail. **VOICE** High pitched *tsi … tsir.* **DISTRIBUTION** E Himalayas. **HABITAT** Oaks, rhododendrons, bamboo.

Spotted Laughingthrush

Rufous-chinned Laughingthrush

Wayanad Laughingthrush

White-throated Laughingthrush

Greater Necklaced Laughingthrush

Lesser Necklaced Laughingthrush

Fire-tailed Myzornis

Lesser Whitethroat *Sylvia curruca* 12cm Ⓜ

Deep-grey above washed brownish on back and wings; dark, almost blackish ear-coverts give masked appearance; glistening white throat, white below; buff wash on breast and belly. Sexes alike. The **Eastern Orphean Warbler** *S. crassirostris* has large, dark grey head; underparts mostly grey; blackish crown; dark forehead, forecrown and ear-coverts. VOICE *Check* note, uttered as it moves in bushes. Song a mix of soft warbling. DISTRIBUTION Winter visitor over India. HABITAT Open bush country, groves, gardens.

Golden-breasted Fulvetta *Lioparus chrysotis* 11cm Ⓡ

Very small, striking golden-yellow, silver-grey and black babbler. Black face; greyish-black chin and throat; silver-grey cheeks; blackish-grey nape and mantle; golden to orangish-yellow breast and underparts; yellow-and-orange linear panels on black wings; yellow-sided black tail. Occurs in pairs or large mixed flocks. VOICE Call a twittering *quititit*. High-pitched, whistled song. DISTRIBUTION Hills of NE India. HABITAT Bamboo growth; temperate broadleaved evergreen forests.

White-browed Fulvetta *Fulvetta vinipectus* 11cm Ⓡ

Brown crown and nape; prominent white eyebrow with black or dark brown line above; blackish sides of face; olive-brown above, washed rufous on wings, rump and tail; some grey in wings; whitish throat and breast; olive-brown below. Sexes alike. Up to 20 birds occur in low growth or lower branches. Energetic, acrobatic birds, often seen in mixed hunting parties. VOICE Fairly sharp *tsuip* … or *tship* … call; also some harsh churring notes when agitated. DISTRIBUTION The Himalayas. NE regions. HABITAT Scrub in forests, ringal bamboo.

Yellow-eyed Babbler *Chrysomma sinense* 18cm Ⓡ

Rufous-brown above; whitish lores; short supercilium; yellow eye (iris) and orange-yellow eye-rim distinctive at close range; cinnamon wings; long, graduated tail; white below, tinged pale fulvous on flanks and abdomen. Sexes alike. Occurs in pairs or small bands. Noisy but skulking. Jerky flight. The similar **Jerdon's Babbler** *C. altirostre* has paler yellowish-brown bill, brown iris and dull yellowish-green orbital ring, no white lores and supercilium, and fleshy-brown legs and feet. VOICE Melodious, whistling notes; also mournful *cheep* … *cheep* call. DISTRIBUTION Subcontinent, from the Himalayan foothills south. HABITAT Scrub, tall grass, cultivation, edges of forests.

Brown Parrotbill *Cholornis unicolor* 21cm Ⓡ

Medium-sized, with small, bulbous, yellow or greyish bill; speckled, greyish-brown crown, sometimes raised in crest; long dark lateral crown-stripes; greyish supercilium, extending from behind eye to around ear-coverts; brown ear-coverts speckled with grey; pale eye-ring, broken into two crescents, above and below eye; more brown upperparts, with rich brown wing-panel on primaries; grey-tipped brown tertials. VOICE Calls include *chrrt* … *chrrt*; *wheeoo* … DISTRIBUTION Hills of E Nepal to Arunachal Pradesh. HABITAT Bamboo stands, shrubberies.

Black-throated Parrotbill *Suthora nipalensis* 10cm Ⓡ

Smallest parrotbill in subcontinent. Large head; tiny, mainly black bill; long, wavy black lateral crown-stripe to nape; variable triangular black throat-patch; variable white supercilium, face, malar stripe or patch; rufous wings; black primary covert-patch; silver-and-black wing-panels; grey to rufous underparts. Hyperactive and vocal, constantly twittering, and moving rapidly through bamboo. VOICE Calls include twitters and trills. DISTRIBUTION E Uttaranchal to Arunachal. HABITAT Bamboo, undergrowth in oak-rhododendron forests.

Lesser Whitethroat

Golden-breasted Fulvetta

Garima Bhatia

Eastern Orphean Warbler

Yellow-eyed Babbler

Gururaj Moorching

White-browed Fulvetta

Jerdon's Babbler

Garima Bhatia

Brown Parrotbill

Black-throated Parrotbill

Arpit Deomurari

White-breasted Parrotbill *Psittiparus ruficeps* 18cm **r**

Medium-sized, sturdy-looking parrotbill with large, rounded bill; distinctive, bright rufous-orange crown, nape, face and ear-coverts, sharply contrasting with paler underparts; bill has dark upper mandible, pale lower mandible; blue lores and orbital ring; brown upperparts and tail. Occurs in pairs or small groups; often joins mixed feeding flocks. Shy and skulking. Prefers to forage in lower forest storeys. **VOICE** Calls include *chitters* and *churrs*. **DISTRIBUTION** Arunachal Pradesh; S Assam hills. **HABITAT** Bamboo, undergrowth, broadleaved evergreen forests.

Black-breasted Parrotbill *Paradoxornis flavirostris* 19cm **e** **v**

Medium-sized, stocky parrotbill with rufous-brown head and olive-brown upperparts, black patch on ear-coverts and huge orange bill. Best distinguished by black breast and solid black chin (with black barring on white throat and malar area), rufous-buff underparts, and darker rufous-brown crown and nape. **VOICE** Call a striking, whistling *phew … phew … phew … phuit*. Also, bleating or mewing cry. **DISTRIBUTION** NE India. **HABITAT** Mixed grass and bamboo in hills, dense reed beds, elephant grass.

White-naped Yuhina *Yuhina bakeri* 13cm **r**

Distinctive rufous-crested yuhina. Prominent white nape, better seen when crest raised; short, dark, sturdy bill; rufous crest, face and upper mantle; dark lores and eye-ring; white streaks on ear-coverts; white throat with no moustachial stripe as in other yuhinas; olive-brown lower mantle with white shaft-streaks; buff-brown below, with pinkish cast and fine, faint dark streaks. In pairs. **VOICE** Calls *tsit … tsit; zhueh … zheuh*. **DISTRIBUTION** Hills from E Nepal to Arunachal, S Assam hills. **HABITAT** Subtropical moist, broadleaved evergreen forests, secondary growth.

Whiskered Yuhina *Yuhina flavicollis* 13cm **r**

Olive-brown above; chocolate-brown crown and crest; white eye-ring and black moustache seen from close up; rufous-yellow nuchal collar (less distinct in western race *albicollis*); white underbody, streaked rufous-olive on sides of breast and flanks. Sexes alike. Occurs in flocks. Active and restless, flitting about; moves between undergrowth and middle levels of forests. Keeps up a constant twitter. **VOICE** Quite vocal; mix of soft, twittering notes and fairly loud, titmice-like call, *chee … chi … chew*. **DISTRIBUTION** The Himalayas. **HABITAT** Forests.

Stripe-throated Yuhina *Yuhina gularis* 14cm **r**

Large yuhina, with long, upright and slightly forwards-drooping, greyish-olive crest, face and mantle; pale pink throat with black streaks; narrow white eye-ring; patchy rufous-and-buff underparts; more rufous on centre of belly and vent; bright rufous wing-patch on secondaries; white-edged black primaries; pale basal two-thirds of lower mandible. In pairs when breeding. **VOICE** Calls *kwee*. **DISTRIBUTION** Hills of Uttaranchal to Arunachal. **HABITAT** Temperate broadleaved, especially oak and rhododendron, forests; coniferous forests, secondary growth.

Black-chinned Yuhina *Yuhina nigrimenta* 11cm **r**

Small, distinctive mainly grey, brown and black yuhina, with relatively short tail. Grey head, ear-coverts, hindneck and upper mantle; black-streaked front to upright grey crest; black lores and chin; slightly curved dark bill, with red-based lower mandible; mostly greyish-brown upperparts; pale whitish-throat and upper breast; mostly buff belly and vent. **VOICE** Chattering; twittering; buzzing; whistled song. **DISTRIBUTION** Hills of Uttarakhand, east to Arunachal Pradesh, S Assam hills. **HABITAT** Subtropical broadleaved evergreen forests, secondary growth.

White-breasted Parrotbill

Black-breasted Parrotbill

Sunil Kini

White-naped Yuhina

Whiskered Yuhina

Manjula Mathur

Stripe-throated Yuhina

Black-chinned Yuhina

Biswarup Sarpati

Indian White-eye *Zosterops palpebrosus* 20cm 🔴

Olive-yellow above; dark lores; white eye-ring distinctive; bright yellow throat and undertail; whitish breast and belly. Sexes alike. Occurs in small parties, occasionally of up to 40 birds, either by themselves or in association with other small birds. Keeps to foliage and bushes. Actively moves among leafy branches, clinging sideways and upside down. Calls often, both when in branches and when flying in small bands from tree to tree. **VOICE** Soft, plaintive *tsee* … and *tseer* … notes. **DISTRIBUTION** All India. **HABITAT** Forests, gardens, groves.

Asian Fairy-bluebird *Irena puella* 25cm 🔴

Male glistening blue above; deep velvet-black sides of face, underbody and wings; blue undertail-coverts. Female has verditer-blue plumage; dull black lores and flight feathers. Occurs in pairs or small, loose bands. Spends the day in leafy tall branches; often descends into undergrowth to feed. Utters two-note calls while flitting among trees. **VOICE** Common call a double-noted *wit* … *weet* …; also *whi* … *chu* … **DISTRIBUTION** Disjunct distribution; Western Ghats; E Himalayas; Uttaranchal foothills; Andaman and Nicobar Islands. **HABITAT** Dense evergreen forests.

Goldcrest *Regulus regulus* 8cm 🔴

Male greyish-olive above; prominent golden-yellow median stripe on crown, bordered by black; two pale yellowish-white wing-bars; white ring around eye; yellowish in wings and tail; whitish below. Female similar to male but with yellow stripe on crown. In pairs or small flocks. Restless, moving energetically; occasionally hovers. **VOICE** High-pitched, squeaking *tsi* … *tsi* … call diagnostic. **DISTRIBUTION** The Himalayas; considerable altitudinal movement; breeds high in mountains, but descends low in winter. **HABITAT** Coniferous forests, orchards in winter.

Eurasian Wren *Troglodytes troglodytes* 9cm 🔴

Tiny, skulking Himalayan bird. Short, erect cocked tail distinctive; brown above, closely barred; paler below, whiter on belly, also closely barred. Sexes alike. Usually solitary. Very active, but also extremely secretive. Jerkily hops on boulders or moves mouse-like amid dense bush with tail cocked. Takes to dense cover if approached. **VOICE** Quite noisy, fairly loud *zirrr* … *tzi* … *izzt* alarm notes; shrill, rambling song. **DISTRIBUTION** The Himalayas; breeds high, but descends in winter. **HABITAT** Thickets, dense cover, mossy growth and rocky ground.

Chestnut-bellied Nuthatch *Sitta cinnamoventris* 12.5cm 🔴

Male blue-grey above; black stripe from lores to nape; whitish cheeks and upper throat; all but central-tail feathers black with white markings; chestnut below. Female duller chestnut below. Occurs in pairs or several together, often with other small birds. Restless climber; clings to bark and usually works up tree stem; also moves upside down and sideways. May visit the ground. **VOICE** Loud *tzsib* … call. **DISTRIBUTION** Lower Himalayas E of Uttaranchal; the recently split **Indian Nuthatch** *S. castanea* is found in the peninsula. **HABITAT** Forests, groves, trees.

White-tailed Nuthatch *Sitta himalayensis* 12cm 🔴

Smallish nuthatch with relatively short bill; bluish-grey upperparts, darker along edges of wing-coverts and tail; diagnostic white central patch at tail-base not always easy to see; pale chin; throat becomes increasingly deeper rufous-buff on breast, belly, flanks and undertail-coverts; bold black eye-stripe broadens and curves behind ear-coverts. Gregarious; often in pairs. Arboreal; usually in upper forest storey. **VOICE** Calls *tchip* … *tchip*. **DISTRIBUTION** Hills of Himachal Pradesh to Arunachal. **HABITAT** Mixed broadleaved and coniferous forests.

Indian White-eye

Asian Fairy-bluebird

Biswarup Sarpati

Goldcrest

Eurasian Wren

Sunil Kini

Chestnut-bellied Nuthatch

White-tailed Nuthatch

Sunil Kini

Velvet-fronted Nuthatch *Sitta frontalis* 10cm 🔴

Male violet-blue above; jet-black forehead; stripe through eye; white chin and throat, merging into vinous-grey below; coral-red bill. Pairs or several occur in mixed hunting parties. Creeps about on stems and branches; fond of moss-covered trees. Also clings upside down. Active and agile, quickly moving from tree to tree. **VOICE** Fairly loud, rapidly repeated, sharp, trilling *chweet ... chwit ... chwit* whistles. **DISTRIBUTION** From around W Uttaranchal east along the lower Himalayas; widespread over hilly, forested areas of C, S and E India. **HABITAT** Forests.

Beautiful Nuthatch *Sitta formosa* 15cm 🔴 🔵

Unmistakable but uncommon large nuthatch with striking bright blue-and-black pattern on upperparts; blue-and-white streaks down black crown and nape; broad blue scapular-band across black mantle; prominent bluish-white fringed edging on coverts and tertials; buff-white throat and long, straight supercilium; bright rufous below; paler on breast, vent and undertail-coverts. Gregarious; lives in pairs or small parties. Arboreal. **VOICE** Calls include chitters. **DISTRIBUTION** Patchy in Arunachal Pradesh. **HABITAT** Broadleaved evergreen forests.

Wallcreeper *Tichodroma muraria* 16cm 🔴

Striking bird with black, grey and crimson plumage; long, thin, pointed, downcurved bill; breeding male has slaty-grey crown and mantle; bright crimson patches on black wings; black throat and upper breast; smoky-grey underparts; non-breeding adult has white throat and upper breast; broad, rounded, crimson-and-black wings with short, broad black tail with white tips. Solitary. **VOICE** Calls *tu ... wee.* **DISTRIBUTION** Mountains of Kashmir to Arunachal. **HABITAT** Cliffs, gorges, boulders.

Bar-tailed Treecreeper *Certhia himalayana* 12cm 🔴

Streaked blackish-brown, fulvous and grey above; pale supercilium; broad fulvous wing-band; white chin and throat; dull ash-brown below; best recognized by dark brown barring on pointed tail. Sexes alike. Solitary. **VOICE** Long-drawn squeak, somewhat ventriloquial; loud but short, monotonous song; one of the earliest bird songs, heard much before other birds have begun to sing. **DISTRIBUTION** W Himalayas and Arunachal Pradesh (seen in Anjaw district, Arunachal). **HABITAT** Himalayan temperate forests.

Indian Spotted Creeper *Salpornis spilonota* 13cm 🟢

Plump, brown and buff bird with long, curved bill. Broad white supercilium; dark wings; short, squarish tail, broadly barred white. Upperparts streaked black and white; white throat; fulvous breast, barred and mottled brown. Sexes alike. Usually feeds singly, on invertebrates in bark. **VOICE** Calls include thin *see ... ee* and deep *kek ... kek ... kek.* Whistling song. **DISTRIBUTION** Rare and very local breeding resident in N peninsula. **HABITAT** Open woodland and groves, favouring trees with deep-fissured bark such as mangoes and babul.

Common Hill Myna *Gracula religiosa* 28cm 🔴

Black plumage with purple-green gloss; white in flight feathers; orange-red bill; orange-yellow legs, facial skin and fleshy wattles on nape and sides of face. Sexes alike. In the **Southern Hill Myna** G. *indica* nape-wattles extend up along sides of crown, and eye and nape wattles distinctly separated. In small flocks. Very noisy. Mostly arboreal. **VOICE** Amazing vocalist; wide variety of whistling, warbling, shrieking notes; excellent mimic. **DISTRIBUTION** The lower Himalayas and terai, from Uttarakhand eastwards. Southern is a bird of the Western Ghats. **HABITAT** Forest clearings.

Velvet-fronted Nuthatch

Beautiful Nuthatch

Wallcreeper

Bar-tailed Treecreeper

Indian Spotted Creeper

Common Hill Myna

Southern Hill Myna

Jungle Myna *Acridotheres fuscus* 23cm 🔴

Ash-brown myna with small crest at bill-base. Black head; no orbital patch; chin, throat and breast slaty-grey graduating to buffish-white belly; dark blue base to yellow-orange bill; yellow legs and bill; white wing-patch and white-tipped tail. Pale yellow eye. Gregarious; in pairs or small groups; larger flocks when not breeding. **VOICE** High, liquid note. **DISTRIBUTION** N hills to Arunachal Pradesh, Bengal to Odisha, Gujarat to Kerala in the west. **HABITAT** Edges of forests, wooded areas near cultivation and settlements, plantations, scrub.

Bank Myna *Acridotheres ginginianus* 23cm 🔴

Similar to the Common Myna (below) but smaller. Bluish-grey neck, mantle and underparts; black head with orange-red wattle around eye; orange-yellow bill; buff-orange tail-tips and wing-patch. Sexes alike. Usually seen in small, scattered groups around human habitation. Bold and confiding; often seen along roadside restaurants picking up scraps. **VOICE** Similar to Common Myna's but softer. **DISTRIBUTION** Widespread resident in N and C India. **HABITAT** Human habitation, cultivation, grassland.

Common Myna *Acridotheres tristis* 23cm 🔴

Rich vinous-brown plumage; black head, neck and upper breast; yellow bill, legs and naked wattle around eyes distinctive; large white spot in dark brown flight feathers, best seen in flight; blackish tail, with broad white tips to all but central feathers; whitish abdomen. Sexes alike. Solitary or in scattered pairs or small, loose bands. Hardly ever strays far from humans and their habitation. Aggressive and curious. **VOICE** Noisy; a great mix of chattering notes. **DISTRIBUTION** Subcontinent. **HABITAT** Human habitation, cultivation, light forests.

Asian Pied Starling *Gracupica contra* 23cm 🔴

Black-and-white (pied) plumage distinctive; orange-red bill and orbital skin in front of eyes confirm identity. Sexes alike. Sociable; occurs in small parties. **VOICE** Noisy; mix of pleasant whistling and screaming notes. **DISTRIBUTION** Bird of NC, C and E India, south and east of a line roughly from E Punjab, through E Rajasthan, W Madhya Pradesh to the Krishna delta. Escaped cage birds have established themselves in several areas out of original range, as in and around Mumbai. **HABITAT** Open cultivation, orchards, vicinity of human habitation.

Chestnut-tailed Starling *Sturnia malabarica* 21cm 🔴 🔵

Silvery-grey above, with faint brownish wash; dull rufous up to breast; brighter below; black and grey in wings. Sexes alike. Sociable; noisy parties occur in upper branches of trees, often with other birds. Descends to the ground to pick up insects. **VOICE** Noisy; metallic, whistling call. **DISTRIBUTION** Widespread in winter. India, east and south from S Rajasthan to around W Uttaranchal; in Himalayan foothills. **Malabar Starling** *S. m. blythii* breeds in SW India, Karnataka and Kerala, spreading north in winter. **HABITAT** Light forests, open country, gardens.

Brahminy Starling *Sturnia pagodarum* 20cm 🔴

Grey, black and rufous myna; black crown, head and crest; grey back; rich buff sides of head, neck and underbody; black wings with brown tail, with white sides and tip distinctive in flight. Sexes alike; female has slightly smaller crest than male. Small parties. Walks in typical myna style, with head held straight up. Communal roosting sites. **VOICE** Quite noisy; pleasant mix of chirping notes and whistles; warbling song; good mimic. **DISTRIBUTION** Subcontinent, to about 2,000m in W and C Himalayas. **HABITAT** Light forests, cultivation, vicinity of human habitation.

Jungle Myna

Bank Myna

Common Myna

Asian Pied Starling

Malabar Starling

Chestnut-tailed Starling

Brahminy Starling

213

Rosy Starling *Pastor roseus* 21cm ⓜ

Rose-pink and black plumage; glossy black head, crest, neck, throat, upper breast, wings and tail; rest of plumage rose-pink, brighter with approach of spring migration. Sexes alike. Gregarious; flocks often contain young birds (crestless, dull brown and sooty). Overall aggressive, very noisy bird. Huge roosting colonies. **VOICE** Very noisy; mix of guttural screams, chattering sounds and melodious whistles. **DISTRIBUTION** Winter visitor to India; absent or uncommon east of Bihar. **HABITAT** Open areas, cultivation, orchards, flowering trees.

Common Starling *Sturnus vulgaris* 20cm ⓜ

Glossy black plumage with iridescent purple and green; plumage spotted with buff and white; hackled feathers on head, neck and breast; yellowish bill and red-brown legs. Summer (breeding) plumage mostly blackish. Gregarious, restless birds. Feeds on the ground, moving hurriedly, digging with bill in soil. Entire flock may often take off from the ground. Flies around erratically or in circles. **VOICE** Mix of squeaking, clicking notes. **DISTRIBUTION** Summer visitor to Kashmir and winters in N and NW India. **HABITAT** Meadows, orchards, open fallow land.

Orange-headed Thrush *Geokichla citrina* 21cm ⓡ

Blue-grey above; orangish-rufous head, nape and underbody; white ear-coverts with two dark brown vertical stripes; white throat and shoulder-patch. Orange-headed nominate race has entirely rufous-orange head. Usually in pairs. Feeds on the ground, rummaging in leaf litter. **VOICE** Vocal when breeding. Loud, rich song; noisy in the early mornings and late evenings; also a shrill, screechy *kreeee … * call. **DISTRIBUTION** Peninsular India; nominate race breeds in the Himalayas, NE; winters in foothills. **HABITAT** Shaded forests, bamboo groves, gardens.

Alpine Thrush *Zoothera mollissima* 27cm ⓡ

Largish, warm brown thrush with prominent black patch on cheek. Dark face and lores; heavy barring and streaks on creamish underparts; large spots on upper throat; broad white bands on underwings visible in flight. Sexes alike. Terrestrial. Shy. The **Long-tailed Thrush** *Z. dixoni* has two dull buffy wing-bars and larger wing-patch, visible in flight. **VOICE** Usually silent; song has short, mellow descending phrases. **DISTRIBUTION** Local breeding resident in N mountains from Kashmir to NE India, above treeline. **HABITAT** Open woodland, grassy, fallow, bushy country.

Himalayan Thrush *Zoothera salimalii* 26cm ⓡ

Recently split from the Alpine Thrush (above), and found below treeline. Stocky-looking thrush with shorter legs, tail and wings, and longer, heavier bill. Uniform caramel-brown upperparts; densely black-scaled underparts; white eye-ring. Arboreal. Scientific name honours the Indian ornithologist Salim Ali. **VOICE** Song much more musical than Alpine's; ringing, melodious thrush song. **DISTRIBUTION** Breeding resident of the E mid-Himalayas; moves lower in winter. **HABITAT** Forests, well-wooded country.

Nilgiri Thrush *Zoothera neilgherriensis* 26cm ⓔ

Medium-sized, heavily scaled thrush. Underparts scaled from belly vent; dark mottled cheeks, with dark patch behind ear; dark, indistinct malar stripe; two narrow yellowish-buff wing-bars. Similar to the **Scaly Thrush** *Z. dauma*, but has darker brown and more even upperparts, mantle and scapulars; bill larger and face plainer. Scaly distinguished from other thrushes by prominent black or buff-tipped feathers, and olive-buff upperparts. Skulking. Terrestrial. **VOICE** Apparently unrecorded. **DISTRIBUTION** Western Ghats. **HABITAT** Dense evergreen forests, sholas.

Rosy Starling

Common Starling

Orange-headed Thrush

Alpine Thrush

Himalayan Thrush

Long-tailed Thrush

Scaly Thrush

Nilgiri Thrush

Ami Sharma

Wikipedia Commons

Manjula Mathur

Clement M Francis

Tickell's Thrush *Turdus unicolor* 22cm (r)

Male has light ashy-grey plumage; duller breast and whiter on belly; rufous underwing-coverts in flight. Female olive-brown above; white throat, streaked on sides; tawny flanks and white belly. Occurs in small flocks on the ground, sometimes with other thrushes. Hops fast on the ground. Digs worms from under soil. Flies into trees when approached. **VOICE** Rich song; double-note alarm call; also some chattering calls. **DISTRIBUTION** Breeds in the Himalayas east to Sikkim; winters along foothills and parts of C and E peninsular India. **HABITAT** Open forests, groves.

White-collared Blackbird *Turdus albocinctus* 27cm (r)

Large, distinctive thrush with pale collar. Adult male black, with white collar extending around throat, upper breast, nape and upper mantle; yellow bill, eye-ring and legs; longish tail. Female brown with pale, faintly streaked collar. Solitary or in pairs; sometimes in winter flocks. Shy. Forages on forest floor, grassy slopes and trees. **VOICE** Deep *chuck … chuck*; song a whistled *tchew … tchew … tchew*. **DISTRIBUTION** Hills of Uttarakhand to Arunachal Pradesh. **HABITAT** Mixed broadleaved coniferous forests, forest edges, pastures, clearings.

Grey-winged Blackbird *Turdus boulboul* 28cm (r)

Large dark thrush with longish tail. Adult male black, with contrasting light grey wing-panel; bright orange bill; yellowish eye-ring; yellow legs. Female brown, with less distinct, paler brown wing-panel; yellow bill. Solitary or in pairs; sometimes in small winter flocks. Fairly shy. Arboreal and terrestrial. Forages on shrubs, trees and forest floor. **VOICE** Call a deep *chuck … chuck*. Melodious song. **DISTRIBUTION** Hills from Kashmir to Arunachal. **HABITAT** Mixed broadleaved oak and coniferous forests, edges of forests.

Indian Blackbird *Turdus simillimus* 25cm (r)

Male lead-grey above, more ashy-brown below; blackish cap distinctive; darker wings and tail; reddish-orange bill and yellowish eye-rim distinctive. Female dark ashy-brown above, browner below, with grey wash; streaked dark brown on chin and throat. Male **Tibetan Blackbird** *T. maximus* entirely black with yellow bill; female dark brown. Solitary or in pairs. Rather confiding, especially breeding males. **VOICE** Loud, melodious song; great mimic; screechy *kreeee* during winter. **DISTRIBUTION** Western Ghats and hills of C India. **HABITAT** Forest, ravines, gardens.

Mistle Thrush *Turdus viscivorus* 27cm (r)

Large, pale grey-brown thrush. Brownish rump and yellow-brown lower flanks; dark patch on ear-coverts and breast-sides. Round spots prominent on otherwise evenly pale underparts. Pale underwings and axillaries. Longish brown tail with white tips often visible on outer-tail feathers. Sexes alike. Solitary. Wary. **VOICE** Call a harsh rattle, usually in flight; song mellow and haunting. **DISTRIBUTION** Breeding resident in N mountains. **HABITAT** Open mountain forests, grassland, scrub.

Green Cochoa *Cochoa viridis* 28cm (r)

Overall green with blue crown and nape. Black eyebrows and lores; dark blue ear-coverts; mantle has faint black scaling; wing has pale blue pane; pale blue tail with black tip; emerald-green underparts with blue wash on throat and belly. The similar-sized **Purple Cochoa** *C. purpurea* is overall greyish-purple; black mask; silvery-blue crown; prominent wing-patch; tail silvery-blue with black terminal band. **VOICE** Call a pure, drawn-out, monotone whistle. **DISTRIBUTION** The Himalayas, hills of NE India. **HABITAT** Dense, moist, broadleaved evergreen forests.

Tickell's Thrush

Grey-winged Blackbird

Mistle Thrush

White-collared Blackbird

Swati Sidhu CC

Indian Blackbird

Garima Bhatia

Green Cochoa

Biswapriya Rabut

Purple Cochoa

Pema Bhuta

217

Indian Robin *Copsychus fulicatus* 16cm **r**

Male has dark brown, blackish-brown or glossy blue-black upperbody; white wing-patch; glossy blue-black below; chestnut vent and undertail. Female lacks white in wings; duller grey-brown below. Solitary or in pairs in open country, and often in and around human habitation. Several races in India. **VOICE** Call a long-drawn *sweeeech* or *weeeech*. Warbling song when breeding; also guttural *charrr* … note. **DISTRIBUTION** Subcontinent; absent in extreme NE India. **HABITAT** Open country, edges of forests, vicinity of human habitation, scrub.

Oriental Magpie-robin *Copsychus saularis* 20cm **r**

Familiar bird of India. Male glossy blue-black and white; white wing-patch and white in outer tail distinctive; glossy blue-black throat and breast; white below. Female rich slaty-grey; male black. Solitary or in pairs, sometimes with other birds in mixed parties. Hops on the ground. Prefers shaded areas. Common around human habitation. When perched often cocks tail; flicks tail often, especially when making short sallies. Active at dusk. **VOICE** Common call a plaintive *sweee* … **DISTRIBUTION** Subcontinent. **HABITAT** Forests, parks, towns.

White-rumped Shama *Copsychus malabaricus* 25cm **r**

Male has glossy-black head and back; white rump and sides of graduated tail distinctive; black throat and breast; orange-rufous below. Female grey where male is black; slightly shorter tail and duller rufous below breast. Usually in pairs. Arboreal bird of forests and hill-station gardens. Keeps to shaded areas and foliage. Launches short sallies and hunts until late in the evening. **VOICE** Rich songster; 3–4 melodious whistling notes very characteristic; variety of call notes. **DISTRIBUTION** Himalayan foothills. **HABITAT** Forests, bamboo, hill-station gardens.

Dark-sided Flycatcher *Muscicapa sibirica* 14cm **r**

Small flycatcher with dark greyish-brown upperparts; streaked across breast and flanks; white throat and centre of belly; large dark eyes with white eye-ring. Similar to the Asian Brown Flycatcher (below), but has smaller, dark bill, and less contrasting eye-ring and lores; darker upperparts and breast-bands and flanks; wings and primary projections longer; head and body slimmer. **VOICE** Calls *tsee … tsee … tsee*. **DISTRIBUTION** Kashmir to Arunachal Pradesh. **HABITAT** Edges of temperate or subalpine mixed broadleaved coniferous forests.

Asian Brown Flycatcher *Muscicapa dauurica* 13cm **r**

Ashy-brown; greyish wash on dirty-white breast; short tail; large head with huge eye and prominent eye-ring; basal half of lower mandible pale and fleshy; black legs. Sexes alike. The **Brown-breasted Flycatcher** M. *muttui* is similar but has pronounced brown breast-band, and larger bill with entirely pale lower mandible. Usually solitary. **VOICE** Call a thin *tzee*; whistling song. **DISTRIBUTION** Breeding resident of the Himalayan foothills. Resident in hills of C and peninsular India; winter visitor in peninsula. **HABITAT** Open forests, groves, gardens.

White-bellied Blue Flycatcher *Cyornis pallidipes* 15cm **e**

Male indigo-blue above; black lores; bright blue forehead and supercilium; indigo-blue throat and breast; white lower breast. Female deep olive-brown above; greyish on head; chestnut tail; rufous-orange to breast; whiter below. Solitary and rarely in pairs; sometimes in mixed parties. Unobtrusive. Hunts in low growth. Often flicks tail. **VOICE** Soft, two-note call; longish, squeaky song when breeding; silent for rest of the year. **DISTRIBUTION** Western Ghats, south of C

Maharasthra, around latitude of Pune. **HABITAT** Dense forests, undergrowth.

Indian Robin

Oriental Magpie-robin

Garim Bhatia

White-rumped Shama

Dark-sided Flycatcher

Ramki Sreenivasan

Asian Brown Flycatcher

White-bellied Blue Flycatcher

Savio Fonseca

Tickell's Blue Flycatcher *Cyornis tickelliae* 14cm 🔴

Male dark indigo-blue above; bright blue on forehead and supercilium; darker, almost appearing black, on sides of face; rufous-orange throat and breast; whitish below. Female duller overall. Usually in pairs in shaded areas; often in mixed hunting parties. Vicinity of wooded streams a favoured haunt. **VOICE** Clear, metallic song of six notes, sometimes extending to nine or ten; often uttered in winter. **DISTRIBUTION** All India; absent in extreme N, NW India. **HABITAT** Shaded forests, bamboo, gardens.

Blue-throated Blue Flycatcher *Cyornis rubeculoides* 14cm 🔴 Ⓜ

Small flycatcher with blue throat. Male bright blue; glossy blue forehead; orange upper breast; white belly to vent. Distinguished from Tickell's Blue Flycatcher (above) by blue throat. Female brown above; more rufous on rump and tail, with pale orange throat and upper breast. Lores, belly and vent white. **VOICE** Calls include harsh *chrr* and hard *tak … tak*. Rapidly delivered, warbling song. **DISTRIBUTION** Locally breeding summer visitor to N hills from Arunachal. Winters in foothills. **HABITAT** Damp forests, particularly overgrown ravines.

Rufous-bellied Niltava *Niltava sundara* 18cm 🔴

Blue patch on neck-sides. Male has deep purple-blue back and throat; dark blue mask; black forehead; brilliant blue crown, shoulders and rump; chestnut-rufous underbody. Female olivish-brown overall; rufescent tail; white on lower throat diagnostic. The **Large Niltava** *N. grandis* male is dark blue with tufted forehead. Mostly solitary. Keeps to undergrowth. Highly unobtrusive. **VOICE** Squeaky churring note. **DISTRIBUTION** The Himalayas, NE; winters in foothills and adjoining plains. **HABITAT** Dense forest undergrowth, bushes.

Small Niltava *Niltava macgrigoriae* 13cm 🔴

Very small flycatcher, similar to the **Large Niltava** *N. grandis*, but almost half its size. Male has greyish-blue underparts; very dark blue-black head-sides; glistening pale blue forehead and neck-patch; white vent. Female brown with orangish-brown wings and tail; small glossy blue-black neck-patch. Partly crepuscular. Large has a dark bill and legs; male dark blue with black face; female rich brown above. **VOICE** Call a high-pitched *see … see*; *chrr*. **DISTRIBUTION** Uttaranchal to Arunachal. **HABITAT** Bushes, undergrowth, paths, forest clearings, lowland reeds, jungles.

Verditer Flycatcher *Eumyias thalassinus* 15cm 🔴

Male has verditer-blue plumage, darker in wings and tail; black lores. Female duller; more grey overall. **Pale Blue Flycatcher** *Cyornis unicolor* male uniform blue, with white on belly; female olive-brown. Solitary or in pairs in winter. Rather more noticeable than other flycatchers because of its continuous movement and habit of perching in open exposed positions. **VOICE** Silent in winter, save for rare, faint *chwe …* **DISTRIBUTION** Breeds in the Himalayas; winters in Indian plains and hill forests of C, E and S India. **HABITAT** Open forests.

Nilgiri Flycatcher *Eumyias albicaudatus* 15cm ⓔ

Small to medium-sized, long-tailed flycatcher. Male has slaty-indigo upperparts; forehead and supercilium have faint reddish-purple cast; greyer on belly, with white scaling on vent; small white basal spots on tail. Female dark greenish-grey. Both much darker than similar species. Occurs in pairs. **VOICE** Call *tsik … tsik*, *… chip … chip*. Song a slow, hesitant warble. **DISTRIBUTION** Globally near threatened but fairly common endemic breeding resident restricted to Western Ghats. **HABITAT** Evergreen forests and forest edges; also plantations.

Tickell's Blue Flycatcher

Blue-throated Blue Flycatcher

Panchami Manoo Ukil

Rufous-bellied Niltava

Small Niltava

Niranjan Sant

Verditer Flycatcher

Large Niltava

Manjula Mathur

Pale Blue Flycatcher

Nilgiri Flycatcher

Gururaj Moorching

Gould's Shortwing *Heteroxenicus stellatus* 13cm 🔴

Small, round, strikingly coloured bird with short tail. Adult has black face; bright chestnut upperparts and tail; finely barred, dark slaty-blue-grey underparts with distinctive triangular white spots on belly, flanks and rump. Juvenile duller than adults, streaked rufous above and on breast. Not very shy; often seen in the open and on low, exposed perches. **VOICE** Alarm call *tik … tik*. Loud, shrill song consists of *tsi … tsi* notes accelerating into continuous chitter. **DISTRIBUTION** Uttaranchal to Arunachal Pradesh. **HABITAT** Rocky montane forests above treeline.

Rusty-bellied Shortwing *Brachypteryx hyperythra* 13cm 🔴 🟣

Plump bird with short tail and short wings. Male has rich orange-chestnut underparts that extend up to throat; upperparts very dark blue, except for conspicuous, short white eyebrow; male's pale bill turns black when breeding; long, pale pink legs. Female lacks rusty belly; slaty-brown above; dark brown face; pale rufous throat; pale belly. Skulking and inconspicuous. Mainly terrestrial. **VOICE** Fast, long and musical high-speed warble consisting of rather slurred series of notes. **DISTRIBUTION** N Bengal hills, Sikkim, Assam and Arunachal Pradesh. **HABITAT** Undergrowth in forests, thick secondary scrub, dense thickets of bamboo.

Lesser Shortwing *Brachypteryx leucophris* 13cm 🔴

In Himalayan race *nipalensis* male grey-blue above; in race *carolinae* of S Assam hills, brown above. Both races have prominent white supercilia. Pink legs and very short tail. Rare in the Himalayas, but quite easily found in Nagaland and adjoining hills. Often near water. **VOICE** Calls include hard *tock … tock* and plaintive whistle. **DISTRIBUTION** The Himalayas; S Assam hills. **HABITAT** Thick undergrowth in damp broadleaved forests and secondary growth.

Indian Blue Robin *Larvivora brunnea* 15cm 🔴 🌕

Male deep slaty-blue above; white supercilium; blackish lores and cheeks; rich chestnut throat, breast and flanks; white belly centre and undertail. Female brown above; white throat and belly; buffy-rufous breast and flanks. The **White-browed Bush Robin** *Tarsiger indicus* male has conspicuous supercilium, and rufous-orange underbody; resident in the Himalayas. Solitary. **VOICE** High-pitched *churr* and harsh *tack …* in winter; trilling song in breeding male. **DISTRIBUTION** Breeds in the Himalayas. Winters in Western Ghats. **HABITAT** Dense rhododendron, bamboo undergrowth in summer; evergreen forest undergrowth and coffee estates in winter.

Bluethroat *Luscinia svecica* 15cm 🌕

Male is pale brown above; whitish eyebrow; rufous in tail; bright blue chin, throat, with chestnut spot, black and rufous bands below blue; whitish-buff below. Female lacks blue; blackish malar stripe continues to broken gorget of brown spots across breast. Solitary, skulker; cocks tail; difficult to observe, though rather tame and confiding. **VOICE** Harsh *tack*. **DISTRIBUTION** Breeds in Ladakh and Kashmir; winters across subcontinent. **HABITAT** Damp ground, culivation.

Himalayan Rubythroat *Calliope pectoralis* 15cm 🔴

Male slaty above; white supercilium; white in tail; scarlet chin and throat; jet-black sides of throat, continuing into broad breast-band; white below, greyer on sides. Female grey-brown above; white chin and throat; greyish breast; winters in NE and E India. Solitary. The closely related **Chinese Rubythroat** *C. tschebaiewi* is differentiated by white submoustachial stripe. **VOICE** Short, metallic call note. **DISTRIBUTION** Breeds in the Himalayas; winters in N, NE India; winter range not properly known. **HABITAT** Dwarf vegetation, rocky hills in summer.

Gould's Shortwing

Indian Blue Robin

Khushboo Sharma

Rusty-bellied Shortwing

White-browed Bush Robin

Arpit Deomurari

Lesser Shortwing

Himalayan Rubythroat

Kintoo Dhawan

Bluethroat

Chinese Rubythroat

Kintoo Dhawan

223

Siberian Rubythroat *Calliope calliope* 15cm Ⓜ

Plumpish, heavy-bodied bird. Breeding male overall olive-brown. Bold white supercilium and submoustachial stripe, edged black; black lores and malar stripe; plain brown rump and tail; ruby-red throat, bordered by thin black band; varying amounts of grey on breast; greyish-brown underparts; short, unmarked tail. Skulks in dense vegetation. Mainly terrestrial. Feeds on the ground. Cocks tail. Feeds singly. **VOICE** Call a *shuk; ee … lu*, and so on. **DISTRIBUTION** Uttaranchal to Arunachal. **HABITAT** Dense undergrowth, tall grass, edges of cultivation.

Nilgiri Sholakili *Sholicola major* 15cm Ⓔ Ⓥ

Male has bright blue-grey underparts, head, neck and throat; dusky lores. Rufous tinge on white lower breast to vent in nominate race; red iris; long legs and short tail. Female brown. The **White-bellied Sholakili** *S. albiventris* has dark slaty-blue upperparts, black mask and short white supercilium meeting above bill; slaty-blue breast graduates to pale grey belly; short tail and wings; centre of belly and vent white. **VOICE** Call a piercing whistle; song a varied series of loud whistles. **DISTRIBUTION** Globally threatened. Rare endemic; breeding resident in the Nilgiris and S Karnataka hills. **HABITAT** Shady evergreen forests, ravines, sholas.

Himalayan Bush Robin *Tarsiger rufilatus* 15cm Ⓡ

Longer-tailed chat with diagnostic orange flanks and white throat. Male deep blue above and on breast-sides; brighter, glistening blue forehead, supercilium, shoulder and rump; pale grey-blue underparts; blue tail. Hunts and forages aerially and on the ground. Flares tail and flicks wings. Closely related to the **Red-flanked Bush Robin** *T. cyanurus*. **VOICE** Call a deep *tok … tok; weet*. Short, soft song. **DISTRIBUTION** Kashmir to Arunachal Pradesh. **HABITAT** Damp undergrowth in oak, rhododendron, coniferous and evergreen forests.

Golden Bush Robin *Tarsiger chrysaeus* 15cm Ⓡ

Golden-coloured chat. Male has olive-brown crown; distinct bright yellow supercilium; black stripe running through eye to form cheek-patch; golden-yellow scapulars, sides of back and rump; golden-yellow underparts; black and golden-yellow tail. Shy. Forages on the ground and in low undergrowth, with quick aerial forays. **VOICE** Calls *tchek … tchek; … trrrr*. High, thin song. **DISTRIBUTION** Hills from Kashmir to Arunachal. **HABITAT** High-altitude scrub, edges of coniferous forests, dense forest undergrowth, bushes, scrub.

Little Forktail *Enicurus scouleri* 12cm Ⓡ

Black-and-white plumage. Black above, with white forehead; white band in wings extends across lower back; small black rump-patch; slightly forked, short tail with white in outer feathers; black throat, white below. Sexes alike. Solitary or in pairs. Bird of mountain streams, waterfalls and small, shaded forest puddles. Constantly wags and flicks tail. Occasionally launches short sallies, but also plunges underwater, dipper style. **VOICE** Rather silent. **DISTRIBUTION** The Himalayas, west to east. **HABITAT** Rocky mountain streams, waterfalls.

Slaty-backed Forktail *Enicurus schistaceus* 25cm Ⓡ

Medium-sized forktail with slaty-grey crown and mantle; long, deeply forked black-and-white tail; black throat and wing-coverts; broad white wing-bars; white rump; narrow white band across forehead extending behind eye; flesh-pink legs; slaty with dark streaking on breast. Solitary or in pairs. Shy. **VOICE** Calls include high-pitched *tsee*; soft *cheet*; metallic *teenk*.

DISTRIBUTION Mountains from Uttaranchal east. **HABITAT** Rocky forested streams.

Siberian Rubythroat

Himalayan Bush Robin

Little Forktail

Nilgiri Sholakili

White-bellied Sholakili

Golden Bush Robin

Slaty-backed Forktail

Blue Whistling Thrush *Myophonus caeruleus* 33cm **r**

Large, bulky, purple-blue ground thrush with mainly yellow bill. Whole body spotted with spangles of brighter blue. Forehead, shoulders, wings and tail edges bright blue. Sexes alike. Juvenile duller than adults, with dusky bill. Noisy, bold and usually approachable. Often close to human habitation; even enters buildings. Usually solitary or in pairs. The **Malabar Whistling Thrush** M. *horsfieldii*, **e** of the Western Ghats is darker with no spotting. **VOICE** Piercing *tzeet* and *zee … zeee*. Rambling, whistling song. **DISTRIBUTION** Common breeding resident in N mountains to Arunachal. **HABITAT** Damp forests and wooded areas near water.

Rufous-gorgeted Flycatcher *Ficedula strophiata* 14cm **r**

Male has dark olive-brown upperparts; blackish face and throat; conspicuous white forehead and eyebrow; diagnostic rufous-orange gorget that is not always visible; grey breast; white sides to black tail. Female similar but duller, with less distinct eyebrow and gorget. Often seen perched quietly in shaded areas or dense canopy. Like all flycatchers, hawks insects but sometimes feeds on the ground. **VOICE** Metallic *pink*, harsh *trrt*. **DISTRIBUTION** Uncommon resident in the Himalayas and NE Indian hills. **HABITAT** Forest clearings and edges.

Red-breasted Flycatcher *Ficedula parva* 13cm **m**

Male dull brown above with greyish-brown head; bright rufous-orange bib; whitish below. Bold white basal patches to black tail diagnostic. Female has pale cinnamon upperparts; white throat; pale buff breast; narrow white eye-ring; no bib. In the similar looking **Taiga Flycatcher** F. *albicilla* red patch restricted to throat and sometimes separated by grey band from cream breast. Shy when breeding. Solitary or in scattered pairs. **VOICE** Sharp clicking sound. Call a double *tick … tick*. **DISTRIBUTION** Winter visitor, all India. **HABITAT** Forests, gardens.

Ultramarine Flycatcher *Ficedula superciliaris* 12cm **r**

Male deep blue above and on sides of head, neck and breast, forming broken breast-band; long white eyebrow; white in tail; white below. Female dull slaty above; grey-white below. Eastern race *aestigma* lacks white over eye and in tail. Solitary or in pairs; seen in mixed parties during winter. Active, hunting in characteristic flycatcher style. **VOICE** Faint *tick … tick …* in winter; *chrrr* alarm note; three-syllable song in the Himalayas. **DISTRIBUTION** Breeds in the Himalayas; winters in N and C India. **HABITAT** Forests, groves, orchards, gardens.

Slaty-blue Flycatcher *Ficedula tricolor* 13cm **r**

Slim, long-tailed flycatcher. Male slaty-blue above; greyish-white (Himalayas) or buff (S Assam hills) below; black mask; white patch at base of black tail. Female has brown upperparts; warm brownish-buff flanks; rufescent rump and tail. Usually solitary or in pairs. Feeds near the ground with tail cocked. **VOICE** Faint *tick tick* call. **DISTRIBUTION** Breeds in the Himalayas at 1,800–2,600m; winters in foothills. **HABITAT** Forest undergrowth, reeds, bushes, grass.

Black-and-orange Flycatcher *Ficedula nigrorufa* 11cm **e** **v**

Male has rich orange-rufous plumage; blackish crown, nape, sides of face and wings. Female like male, but deep olive-brown head; pale eye-ring. Usually solitary, but pairs often close by. Keeps to dense, shaded undergrowth, either hopping low or making short, flycatcher-like sallies from low perch. In its restricted range, quite tame and confiding once spotted. **VOICE** Soft, gloomy *pee …* call note; sharp *zit … zit* alarm call. **DISTRIBUTION** Very local; restricted to Nilgiris and associated hills in S Western Ghats. **HABITAT** Dense forest, undergrowth, bamboo.

Blue Whistling Thrush

Malabar Whistling Thrush

Biswarup Sarpati

Rufous-gorgeted Flycatcher

Red-breasted Flycatcher

Clement M Francis

Ultramarine Flycatcher

Taiga Flycatcher

Savio Fonseca

Slaty-blue Flycatcher

Black-and-orange Flycatcher

Khushboo Sharma

Pygmy Blue Flycatcher *Ficedula hodgsoni* 10cm 🔴

Male has cobalt-blue upperparts and more vivid glossy-blue crown; bluish-black lores; dark greyish-blue wings and tail; pale orange underparts. Female has olive-brown upperparts; bright orange rump and uppertail; white underparts washed with orange on throat, breast and belly. Distinguished from other flycatchers by tiny size, small, fine bill and short tail. Arboreal. Solitary or in pairs. **VOICE** Calls include *tchurr* … and weak *tseep* …; song soft, very high pitched. **DISTRIBUTION** Nepal to Arunachal Pradesh. **HABITAT** Dense, moist broadleaved forests, thick secondary growth.

Blue-capped Redstart *Phoenicurus coeruleocephala* 15cm 🔴

Adult male has black back, tail, head and breast; white belly and speculum on wings; greyish-blue crown. Non-breeding male more grey-brown. Female greyish-brown with two buff wing-bars; dark brown tail and chestnut uppertail. Often near water. . Shivers and slowly wags tail. Often confiding. Nests on the ground. **VOICE** Call a soft *tik* … *tik* … *tik*. **DISTRIBUTION** Locally common breeding resident in N hills from Kashmir to Bhutan; more common in west; winters lower down. **HABITAT** Open forests and scrub, rocky slopes, secondary cover.

Black Redstart *Phoenicurus ochruros* 15cm 🔵

Male black above (marked with grey in winter); grey crown and lower back; rufous rump and tail-sides; black throat and breast; rufous below. Female dull brown above; tail as in male; dull tawny-brown below. Mostly solitary in winter, when common all over India. Characteristic shivering of tail and jerky body movements. Makes short dashes to the ground, soon returning to perch with catch. **VOICE** Squeaking *tictititic* … call. **DISTRIBUTION** Breeds in the Himalayas; winters over much of subcontinent. **HABITAT** Open country, cultivation.

White-winged Redstart *Phoenicurus erythrogastrus* 18cm 🔴

Big black, white and orange chat with unmarked orange tail. Male has black throat and upperparts with large white wing-patches and crown; orange underparts, rump and tail. Female brown above and warm buff below, with orange rump and tail. Feeds on invertebrates on the ground and through aerial sallies. Perches low. Nests among rocks. **VOICE** Calls include soft *lik* and hard *teek* … *teek*. **DISTRIBUTION** Locally common breeding resident in N mountains from Kashmir east to Arunachal Pradesh. **HABITAT** Stony hillsides, pastures, riverbeds.

Blue-fronted Redstart *Phoenicurus frontalis* 15cm 🔴

Male has bright blue forehead with darker blue crown and back; orange-chestnut underparts; rufous rump; orange tail with broad blackish terminal band and central feathers. Female dark olive-brown; yellowish-orange below; rump and tail as in male; tail pattern diagnostic, to separate it from other female redstarts. Mostly solitary. Perches on rocks or bushes. Drops to the ground to feed. Pumps tail. **VOICE** Squeaking *tik* or *prik*. **DISTRIBUTION** Altitudinal migrant; breeds in the Himalayas; winters in the Himalayan foothills. **HABITAT** Cultivation, open country.

Plumbeous Water Redstart *Phoenicurus fuliginosus* 12cm 🔴

Male has slaty-blue plumage; chestnut tail diagnostic; rufous on lower belly. Female darkish blue-grey-brown above; two spotted wing-bars; white in tail; whitish below, profusely mottled slaty. Pairs occur at mountain rivers. Active birds, making short dashes from boulders. **VOICE** Sharp *kreee* … call; also a snapping *tzit* … *tzit*. **DISTRIBUTION** The Himalayas; also breeds south of Brahmaputra river; in winter may descend into foothills and terai. **HABITAT** Mountain

streams, rivers, rushing torrents.

Pygmy Blue Flycatcher

Blue-capped Redstart

Nikhil Devasar

Black Redstart

White-winged Redstart

Garima Bhatia

Blue-fronted Redstart

Plumbeous Water Redstart

Garima Bhatia

White-capped Redstart *Phoenicurus leucocephalus* 19cm (r)

Black back, head-sides, wings and breast; white crown diagnostic; chestnut rump and tail; black terminal tail-band; chestnut below breast. Sexes alike. Solitary or pairs on Himalayan torrents. Rests on rocks amid gushing waters. Flies very low over water to catch insects. Jerks and wags tail, and dips body; restless bird. Interesting display in courting male. **VOICE** Loud, plaintive *tseeee* call; also a *psit … psit …* call. **DISTRIBUTION** The Himalayas; descends into foothills in winter. **HABITAT** Rocky streams; also canals in winter.

Blue Rock Thrush *Monticola solitarius* 20cm (m)

Male has blue plumage; brown wings and tail; pale fulvous and black scales more conspicuous in winter; belly whiter in winter. Female duller than male, grey-brown above; dark shaft-streaks; black barring on rump; dull white below, barred brown. Solitary. Perches on rocks, stumps and roof tops. Rather upright posture. Flies on to the ground to feed. **VOICE** Silent in winter; short, whistling song in breeding male. **DISTRIBUTION** Breeds in the Himalayas; winters from NE foothills, south throughout peninsula. **HABITAT** Open rocky country, cliffs, ravines, ruins, human habitation.

Chestnut-bellied Rock Thrush *Monticola rufiventris* 23cm (r)

Male has cobalt-blue head and upperparts; blackish mask; rich chestnut belly. Female olive-brown with buff throat and lores; heavy scaling on underparts; distinctive face pattern with eye-ring, dark malar stripe and neck-patch. Mostly solitary or seen in pairs. Perches upright. **VOICE** Harsh rattle; fluty song. **DISTRIBUTION** Himalayan forests to 3,500m. **HABITAT** Open country, forest edges, groves on rocky hillsides.

Blue-capped Rock Thrush *Monticola cinclorhyncha* 17cm (r) (m)

Male has blue crown and nape; black back; broad stripe through eyes to ear-coverts; blue throat and shoulder-patch; white wing-patch and chestnut rump distinctive; chestnut below throat; back feathers edged fulvous in winter. Female unmarked olive-brown above; buffy-white below, thickly speckled with dark brown. Solitary or in pairs. **VOICE** Mostly silent in winter, save for occasional harsh single or double-note call. **DISTRIBUTION** Breeds in the Himalayas; winters in Western Ghats. **HABITAT** Shaded forests, groves.

Stoliczka's Bushchat *Saxicola macrorhynchus* 17cm (v)

Male has blackish ear-coverts; creamy-white supercilium; white wing-patches; white throat. Dark blackish-brown upperparts, paler and more streaked in winter. White in outer-tail feathers. Creamy-white underparts, washed peachy-pink on breast. Long legs and long bill. Unique 'puff and roll' display on the ground. **VOICE** Very quiet. Call a soft *prupp … prupp*. **DISTRIBUTION** Globally threatened. Very local. Breeding areas and nest unknown. **HABITAT** Dry semi-deserts with grass clumps in Rajasthan and Gujarat.

Siberian Stonechat *Saxicola maurus* 13cm (r)

Male black above; white rump, wing-patch and sides of neck/breast (collar); black throat; orange-rufous breast. In winter, black feathers broadly edged buff-rufous-brown. Female rufous-brown above, streaked darker; unmarked yellowish-brown below; white wing-patch and rufous rump. Solitary or in pairs in open country. Restless. **VOICE** Double-note *wheet chat* call; soft, trilling song in breeding male in the Himalayas. **DISTRIBUTION** Breeds in the Himalayas; winters all India except Kerala and much of Tamil Nadu. **HABITAT** Dry areas, cultivation, tidal creeks.

White-capped Redstart

Blue Rock Thrush

Garima Bhatia

Arpit Deomurari

♀

♀

Chestnut-bellied Rock Thrush

Blue-capped Rock Thrush

Garima Bhatia

Stoliczka's Bushchat

Siberian Stonechat

Biswarup Satpati

Pied Bushchat *Saxicola caprata* 13cm 🔴

Breeding male has glossy metallic black plumage; white in wing, rump and belly. Female brown above, paler on lores; darker tail; dull yellow-brown below with rusty wash on breast and belly. Solitary or in pairs. Makes short sallies to prey on the ground or carries it to perch. Active. Flicks and spreads wings. **VOICE** Harsh, two-note call serves as contact and alarm. Short, trilling song in breeding male. **DISTRIBUTION** Subcontinent, from the outer Himalayas to about 1,500m. **HABITAT** Open country, scrub, cultivation, ravines.

Grey Bushchat *Saxicola ferreus* 15cm 🔴

Male dark grey above, streaked black; black mask; white supercilium, wing-patch and outer tail; white throat and belly; dull grey breast. Female rufous-brown, streaked; rusty rump and outer tail; white throat; yellow-brown below. Solitary or in pairs. Keeps to open country and forest edges. Flits tail often. Regularly seen in an area. Flies to the ground on spotting insects. Slow and languid. **VOICE** Double-note call; also a grating *traee* …; trilling song of male. **DISTRIBUTION** Mid-Himalayas, descending lower in winter. **HABITAT** Open scrub, forest edges, cultivation.

Isabelline Wheatear *Oenanthe isabellina* 17cm 🔴

'Isabelline' refers to this bird's pale greyish-yellow or pale fawn overall colouration. Wings slightly darker than body; long, strong, slightly hooked bill; relatively short tail; long body usually held upright; black-and-white tail. Sexes similar. White basal patches on black tail. Looks long legged because of very upright stance. Solitary and territorial. Shy. **VOICE** Calls include *chak … chak* and *tew*. **DISTRIBUTION** Locally common breeding summer visitor. Fairly common winter visitor to NW India. **HABITAT** Sandy semi-deserts and overgrazed pasture.

Desert Wheatear *Oenanthe deserti* 15cm Ⓜ

Male sandy above, with whitish rump and black tail; black wings; white in coverts; black throat and head-sides; creamy-white below. Female has brown wings and tail; lacks black throat. In winter male throat feathers fringed white. Male **Northern Wheatear** *O. oenanthe* grey above, with white rump and tail-sides, black tail-centre and tip like an inverted 'T'; black ear-coverts and wings. **VOICE** Occasional *ch … chett* alarm note in winter. **DISTRIBUTION** Winter visitor over N, C and W India. **HABITAT** Open rocky, barren country; sandy areas.

Brown Rock Chat *Oenanthe fusca* 17cm 🟢

Brown above, more rufous below; dark brown wings; almost blackish tail. Overall appearance like that of female Indian Robin (p. 218). Usually in pairs, around ruins, dusty villages and rocky hillsides. Often approaches close; tame and confiding. Captures insects on the ground. Rather aggressive when breeding. **VOICE** Harsh *chaeck* note; also whistling *chee* call; melodious song in breeding male; good mimic. **DISTRIBUTION** Confined to parts of N and C India. **HABITAT** Dry, open country, rocky hills, ravines, ruins, human habitation.

Variable Wheatear *Oenanthe picata* 14.5cm Ⓜ

Male black with white vent, white breast to vent, or white crown and breast to vent. Female also varies, but usually grey above and whitish below. Both sexes have extensive white rump, black central tail-bar and black tail-tip. Usually solitary. Often perches on low bushes or walls, from which it flies to feed on invertebrates on the ground or in the air. Nests in holes in the ground. **VOICE** Calls include hard *chek … chek* and low whistle. **DISTRIBUTION** Winters in NW Indian plains. **HABITAT** Dry, open country.

Pied Bushchat

Grey Bushchat

Arpit Deomurari

Isabelline Wheatear

Desert Wheatear

Savio Fonseca

Brown Rock Chat

Variable Wheatear

Savio Fonseca

233

White-throated Dipper *Cinclus cinclus* 20cm **r**

Similar to the Brown Dipper (below), but has large patch of pristine white from chin to breast, diagnostic. Brown head, mantle and belly; rest of upperparts blackish-brown; short tail, often cocked. Stubby legs. Sexes alike. Walks on stream beds. Flies fast and low. Bobs and sways on boulders. **VOICE** Call a loud *dzitz*, mainly in flight and audible above the sound of running water. **DISTRIBUTION** Locally common breeding resident in N mountains from Kashmir to Arunachal Pradesh; scarce in S Himalayan ranges. **HABITAT** High-altitude, fast-flowing streams.

Brown Dipper *Cinclus pallasii* 20cm **r**

Largely uniform dark brown dipper. Small, stocky body; grey-brown mantle, wings and tail; short, stubby tail, often cocked; brown iris. Sexes alike. Juvenile has some pale spotting on upperparts and underparts. Solitary, or in pairs or small groups. Commonly seen at mountain streams; perches on mid-stream boulders, bobbing up and down. Flies low over the water; dives and swims underwater, often walking on riverbeds; floats downstream briefly on emerging from the water. Whirrs wings in display. **VOICE** Calls *dzit, dzit*; rich song. **DISTRIBUTION** Mountain streams in N, NE India. **HABITAT** Shallow, fast-flowing, high-altitude rocky streams and mountain lakes.

Jerdon's Leafbird *Chloropsis jerdoni* 20cm **r**

Distinguished immediately from the Golden-fronted Leafbird (below) by lack of orange-gold crown. Male has black throat-patch that continues to eye; black cheeks; blue moustache; greenish-yellow forehead. Bluish-green lesser wing-coverts. Underparts softer green. Female has greenish-blue throat and cheeks; blue moustache. Prefers canopy; well-camouflaged in foliage. **VOICE** Noisy; wide assortment of whistling notes. **DISTRIBUTION** Peninsular India. **HABITAT** Forests.

Golden-fronted Leafbird *Chloropsis aurifrons* 19cm **r**

Leaf-green plumage; golden-orange forehead; blue shoulder-patches; dark blue chin and cheeks; black lores and ear-coverts, continuing as loop around blue throat. Pairs in leafy canopy; lively bird, actively hunting in foliage. Voice immediately attracts attention. **VOICE** Noisy; wide assortment of whistling notes, including imitations of several species; most common call a drongo- or shikra-like *che … chwe*. **DISTRIBUTION** Uttaranchal Himalayas; east to Bihar, Orissa, south along Eastern Ghats and up Western Ghats. **HABITAT** Forests.

Orange-bellied Leafbird *Chloropsis hardwickii* 20cm **r**

Dramatically coloured leafbird with bright orange lower breast and belly. Bright leaf-green back; yellowish-green forehead, crown and nape; broad, iridescent blue moustachial band; blue patch over throat and chest; blue edges to outer wing-coverts, primaries and tail-sides; blue shoulder-patches. Solitary, in pairs or in mixed parties. Arboreal; usually in canopy or upper forest storeys. **VOICE** Wide variety of harsh and whistling notes. **DISTRIBUTION** Himachal to entire NE India. **HABITAT** Broadleaved evergreen deciduous forests, secondary growth.

Thick-billed Flowerpecker *Dicaeum agile* 10cm **r**

Olive-grey above, greener on rump; white-tipped tail; dull whitish-grey below, streaked brown, more on breast; orange-red eyes and thick blue-grey bill seen at close range. Sexes alike. Solitary or in pairs in canopy foliage. Arboreal. Restless; flicks tail often as it hunts under leaves or along branches. Frequents parasitic clumps of *Loranthus* and *Viscum*. **VOICE** Loud, sharp *chik … chik*. **DISTRIBUTION** India south of and including the Himalayan foothills; absent from arid parts of NW India. **HABITAT** Forests, orchards, gardens.

White-throated Dipper

Brown Dipper

Jerdon's Leafbird

Golden-fronted Leafbird

Orange-bellied Leafbird

Thick-billed Flowerpecker

Pale-billed Flowerpecker *Dicaeum erythrorhynchos* 8cm ⓡ

Olive-brown above; unmarked grey-white below; pinkish-flesh and yellow-brown bill seen only at close range or in good light. Sexes alike. The **Nilgiri Flowerpecker** *D. concolor* has dark bill and pale supercilium. Solitary or 2–3 birds in canopy. Arboreal. Restless and territorial. Frequents parasitic *Loranthus* and *Viscum*. Flits from clump to clump. VOICE Sharp, loud *chik … chik*. DISTRIBUTION From Kangra east along foothills to NE India; peninsular India south of a line from W Gujarat to S Bihar. HABITAT Light forests, groves.

Fire-breasted Flowerpecker *Dicaeum ignipectus* 9cm ⓡ

Male metallic blue-green-black above; buffy below, with scarlet breast-patch and black stripe down centre of lower breast and belly. Female olive-green above, yellowish on rump; bright buff below; flanks and sides tinged olive. Mostly solitary. Arboreal and active; flits about in foliage canopy, attending to *Loranthus* clumps. May be seen in restless mixed hunting bands. VOICE Sharp, metallic *chip … chip* note; high-pitched, clicking song. DISTRIBUTION Himalayas, Kashmir to extreme east; winters lower. HABITAT Forests, orchards.

Scarlet-backed Flowerpecker *Dicaeum cruentatum* 9cm ⓡ

Small, distinctive flowerpecker. Male has scarlet forehead, crown, nape, centre of mantle, back and uppertail-coverts; black face and ear-coverts, sides of neck, throat and breast; blue-black wings; black tail; buff underparts. Female dull brownish above with scarlet rump and uppertail-coverts; pale buff below. Solitary; in pairs when breeding. Usually in canopy. Makes short aerial sallies. VOICE *Chik; tissit, tissit, tissit.* DISTRIBUTION E Nepal to Arunachal Pradesh, S Assam hills. HABITAT Occurs where *Loranthus* or mistletoe is found; open broadleaved forests.

Purple-rumped Sunbird *Leptocoma zeylonica* 10cm ⓡ

Male has deep chestnut-crimson back; metallic green crown and shoulder-patch; metallic purple rump and throat; maroon collar below throat; yellow below. Female ashy-brown above with rufous in wings; whitish throat; yellow below. Usually in pairs. Very active. Flits from flower to flower; occasionally descends into flowering garden bushes. VOICE Utters *tsiswee … tsiswee …* calls; sharp, twittering song in breeding male, much lower in tone and volume than that of the Purple Sunbird (below). DISTRIBUTION Peninsular India. HABITAT Open forests, gardens, orchards.

Purple Sunbird *Cinnyris asiaticus* 10cm ⓡ

Breeding male metallic purple-blue above, and on throat and breast; dark purplish-black belly; narrow chestnut-maroon band between breast and belly; yellow-and-scarlet pectoral tufts, normally hidden under wings. Female olive-brown above; pale yellow below (*zeylonica* female has whitish throat). Non-breeding male much like female but with broad purple-black stripe down throat-centre to belly. Solitary or in pairs. The common breeding resident of peninsular India, **Loten's Sunbird** *C. lotenius* is a large dark sunbird with diagnostic long, steeply curved bill. VOICE Loud *chweet …* notes. DISTRIBUTION Subcontinent. HABITAT Open forests, gardens, groves.

Mrs Gould's Sunbird *Aethopyga gouldiae* 10cm ⓡ

One of India's most iconic sunbirds. Male strikingly coloured with rich red mantle and back; bright yellow underparts; purplish-blue crown and throat; metallic blue tail; yellow rump. Female olive-brown with yellow belly, vent and rump-band; grey crown and throat. Mostly solitary. VOICE Sharp *tzit-tzit.* DISTRIBUTION Resident in the Himalayas and NE Indian hills. HABITAT Rhododendrons, forests, gardens, scrub.

Pale-billed Flowerpecker

Fire-breasted Flowerpecker

Nilgiri Flowerpecker

Scarlet-backed Flowerpecker

Purple-rumped Sunbird

Purple Sunbird

Mrs Gould's Sunbird

Loten's Sunbird

Green-tailed Sunbird *Aethopyga nipalensis* 11cm **r**

Male has dark metallic blue-green head and nape, bordered by maroon mantle; olive-green back and wings; metallic blue-green tail (appears dark); underparts bright yellow with red-streaked breast; yellow rump not always visible. NW Himalayan race *horsfieldi* has less maroon on mantle. Female olive-green with greyish-olive throat; yellowish-olive on belly; rump slightly yellower than upperparts; pale tips to tail. **VOICE** Sharp *zig-zig*. **DISTRIBUTION** Resident in the Himalayas. **HABITAT** Oak and rhododendron forests, scrub, gardens.

Black-throated Sunbird *Aethopyga saturata* 11cm **r**

Very dark, mainly black, crimson and greyish-olive sunbird. Distinctive male looks mostly black, with dark, iridescent purple crown, nape, malar stripe and long tail; black throat, breast, face and wings; crimson mantle and sides of neck and throat; underparts greyish-olive. Smaller female has yellow band across back, and no yellow on plain greyish-olive-green underparts; whitish flanks; ill-defined pale supercilium around eye. Solitary or in pairs. **VOICE** Calls *tzit ... tswi ... ti ... ti ... ti ... ti*. **DISTRIBUTION** Uttaranchal to Arunachal. **HABITAT** Forests, scattered bushes.

Crimson Sunbird *Aethopyga siparaja* 11cm **r**

Male has long tail; metallic green crown and tail; deep crimson back and neck-sides; yellow rump not commonly seen; bright scarlet chin and breast; olive-yellow belly. Female has olive plumage, yellower below. In Western Ghats **Vigor's Sunbird** *A. s. vigorsii* **e** male's breast streaked yellow. Solitary or in pairs. Active gymnast, hanging upside down and sideways as it probes flowers; also hovers. Moves a lot in forests, between tall bushes and canopy. **VOICE** Sharp, clicking call notes. **DISTRIBUTION** The Himalayas, hills of NE India. **HABITAT** Forests, gardens.

Fire-tailed Sunbird *Aethopyga ignicauda* 11cm **r**

Very long red tail-streamers and uppertail-coverts of male distinctive. Male has dark purple cap, face, chin and throat; bright red nape, sides of head, neck and mantle; yellow band on back; yellow breast and belly have orange wash; paler yellow to greyish flanks and vent; brown wings. Smaller female has olive upperparts with more brown wings; olive-yellow on rump; olive underparts; orange-yellow on centre of belly. **VOICE** Calls *zizi ... zizizi*. **DISTRIBUTION** Himachal Pradesh to Arunachal. **HABITAT** Summers in conifer forests; winters in broadleaved or mixed forests.

Little Spiderhunter *Arachnothera longirostra* 16cm **r**

Olive-green above; dark tail, tipped white; grey-white throat, merging into yellow-white below; orangish pectoral tufts. Very long, curved bill diagnostic. Sexes alike. Usually solitary. Active, moving considerably between bushes and canopy. Wild banana blossoms a favourite food; birds clinging upside down on bracts. Long, curved bill specially adapted to nectar diet. **VOICE** High-pitched *chee ... chee* call. **DISTRIBUTION** Disjunct: Western and Eastern Ghats, Nepal eastwards, E Himalayas and much of NE states. **HABITAT** Forests, secondary growth, nullahs.

Streaked Spiderhunter *Arachnothera magna* 18cm **r**

Fairly unmistakable spiderhunter. Distinguished from the Little Spiderhunter (above) by large size, exceptionally long bill and streaking; dusky-olive above with fine dark streaking on face and head, and broader streaking on mantle; pale, diffused eye-ring; yellowish-white underparts with bold dark streaking; yellower vent; prominent sturdy, pinkish-orange legs. Solitary or in pairs. **VOICE** Calls include harsh chirruping; short *chik* notes. **DISTRIBUTION** E Nepal to Arunachal Pradesh, and Assam. **HABITAT** Wild bananas and dense undergrowth.

Green-tailed Sunbird

Biswarup Sarpati

♀

Crimson Sunbird

♀

Garima Bhatia

Fire-tailed Sunbird

Black-throated Sunbird

Savio Fonseca

Vigor's Sunbird

Little Spiderhunter

Ramki Sreenivasan

Streaked Spiderhunter

House Sparrow *Passer domesticus* 15cm r

Breeding male has grey crown, black lores, chin, throat and variable patch on upper breast; chestnut stripe behind eye and on nape; whitish ear-coverts; black streaking on chestnut-and-buff mantle and wings; one broad and one less distinct wing-bar; grey lower back and rump; greyish-white underparts; black bill. Female has brown-streaked, buff-brown mantle; two wing-bars; darkish eye-stripe, pale buff supercilium; pale bill; greyish-white underparts. **VOICE** Chips, chirrips, cheeps. **DISTRIBUTION** All India. **HABITAT** Around human habitation.

Russet Sparrow *Passer cinnamomeus* 15cm r

Male has rufous-chestnut upperparts streaked black on back; whitish wing-bars; black chin and centre of throat, bordered with dull yellow. Female brown above, streaked darker; pale supercilium and wing-bars; dull ash-yellow below. Often perches on dry branches and overhead wires. Male of the **Eurasian Tree Sparrow** *P. montanus* has black patch on white ear-coverts and lacks yellow on throat-sides. **VOICE** Chirping notes, *swee …* **DISTRIBUTION** The Himalayas; NE India; descends in winter. **HABITAT** Cultivation, forest edges, mountain habitation.

Yellow-throated Sparrow *Gymnoris xanthocollis* 14cm r

Uniformly grey bird with bold chestnut shoulder-patches. Prominent yellow patch on chin and throat; broad white tips to median coverts; narrower white tips on greater coverts. Underparts pale buff-grey. Breeding male has yellow bill, black in non-breeding male. Short, notched tail. Long, slender bill. Difficult to spot in foliage. **VOICE** Noisy. Calls include *cheellup* and *cheep.* **DISTRIBUTION** Common resident and local migrant in Indian plains and hills except extreme NW and NE India. **HABITAT** Open woodland, forests, thorn scrub, cultivation.

Black-winged Snowfinch *Montifringilla adamsi* 17cm r

Dull grey-brown above with some streaking on back (less pronounced in juveniles and fresh plumage); blackish wing with white panel in wing-coverts; male has greyish-black bib (not usually seen in female); breeding male has black bill; in flight shows obvious white wing-patch; white tail with central black feathers and narrow black terminal band. Gregarious. **VOICE** Calls include a hard *pink pink* and soft mewing. **DISTRIBUTION** Breeding resident in the high N Himalayas. **HABITAT** High-altitude scrub, meadows, rocky bushy slopes, hillsides.

Streaked Weaver *Ploceus manyar* 15cm r

Breeding male has yellow crown; blackish head-sides; fulvous streaks on dark brown back; heavily streaked lower throat and breast. Female and non-breeding male streaked above; yellow stripe over eye continues to behind ear-coverts; very pale below, boldly streaked on throat and breast. The **Black-breasted Weaver** *P. benghalensis* male has dark breast-band. Gregarious. Prefers tall grass and reed beds. **VOICE** High-pitched chirping, wheezy notes and chatter. **DISTRIBUTION** Most of India. **HABITAT** Reed beds, tall grass in well-watered areas, marshes.

Baya Weaver *Ploceus philippinus* 15cm r

Breeding male has bright yellow crown; dark brown above, streaked yellow; dark brown ear-coverts and throat; yellow breast. Female buffy-yellow above, streaked darker; pale supercilium and throat, turning buffy-yellow on breast, streaked on sides. Non-breeding male bolder streaking than female. Gregarious. Best known for its nest. Feeds on the ground and in standing crops. **VOICE** Chirping and high-pitched, wheezy notes in breeding male; very noisy at nest colony.
DISTRIBUTION Most of India. **HABITAT** Open country, tree- and palm-dotted cultivation.

House Sparrow

Panchami Manoo Ukil

Russet Sparrow

Yellow-throated Sparrow

Nitin Srinivasamurthy

Eurasian Tree Sparrow

Streaked Weaver

Manjula Mathur

Black-winged Snowfinch

Black-breasted Weaver

Manjula Mathur

Baya Weaver

241

Finn's Weaver *Ploceus megarhynchus* 17cm ⓡ ⓥ

Unlike other weavers, breeding male has bright yellow head with dark brown ear-coverts; golden-yellow underparts; yellow rump and uppertail-coverts; streaked mantle and back; dark patches on breast; yellow in breeding female and first-year male paler; mantle has dark streaking. No yellow on non-breeding adult and immature, but plumage similar to the Baya Weaver's (p. 240). Roosts in tall grass aand sugar-cane stands. **VOICE** Call a harsh *twit … twit*. **DISTRIBUTION** Mostly NE India with a few pockets in N India. **HABITAT** Open country, tree- and palm-dotted cultivation.

Red Munia *Amandava amandava* 10cm ⓡ

Breeding male crimson and brown, spotted white on wings and flanks; white-tipped tail. Female brown above, spotted on wings; crimson rump; dull white throat; buffy-grey breast, yellow brown below. Non-breeding male like female, but greyer throat; upper breast distinctive. Occurs in small flocks. Partial to tall grass and scrub. The tiny **Green Munia** *A. formosa*, ⓔ with distinct striped flanks, green upperparts, and black-and-red tail, is a globally threatened endemic, known from only a few breeding sites. **VOICE** Shrill and high-pitched notes. **DISTRIBUTION** Subcontinent, south of the Himalayan foothills. **HABITAT** Tall grass, reeds, sugar cane, scrub.

Indian Silverbill *Euodice malabarica* 10cm ⓡ

Dull brown above with white rump; very dark, almost black wings; pointed tail; pale buffy-white below, with some brown on flanks; thick, grey-blue or slaty bill striking. Sexes alike. Gregarious. Mostly keeps to scrub in open country. **VOICE** Faint *tee … tee …* notes; sometimes also a whistling note. **DISTRIBUTION** Subcontinent to about 1,500m in the Himalayas, chiefly in outer ranges. **HABITAT** Prefers dry areas; cultivation, scrub and grass; sometimes light, open forests.

White-rumped Munia *Lonchura striata* 10–11cm ⓡ

Slim dark brown and whitish munia with short, thick conical bill; dark brown head, throat and upper breast, mantle, wings, tail and vent with sharp streaking; white patch on lower back; white belly; short, wedge-shaped tail. Occurs in small family parties when breeding, otherwise large flocks. Communal rooster, usually associated with other munias and weavers. **VOICE** Weak up and down twittering. **DISTRIBUTION** Foothills of Uttarakhand to Arunachal Pradesh. **HABITAT** Light wooded areas, scrub, fields, grassland.

Scaly-breasted Munia *Lonchura punctulata* 10cm ⓡ

Chocolate-brown above; olive-yellow, pointed tail; white bars on rump; chestnut sides of face, chin and throat; white below, thickly speckled with very dark brown on breast, flanks and parts of belly (speckles may be absent during winter and much of summer). Sexes alike. Sociable, moving in flocks of six to several dozen birds. Feeds on the ground and low bushes, but rests in trees. **VOICE** Common call a double-noted *ki.tee … ki.tee*. **DISTRIBUTION** Most of India; absent in much of Punjab NW regions and W Rajasthan. **HABITAT** Open scrub, cultivation with trees, gardens.

Black-throated Munia *Lonchura kelaarti* 10cm ⓔ

Male has black head, throat, breast, belly-centre and thighs; rufous-chestnut back, deeper chestnut on rump; white upper belly and sides of underbody. Female similar to male, but has deep brown undertail-coverts. Gregarious, except when breeding. Prefers reed beds and cultivation, especially where flooded. During breeding season (rains), often seen with the Streaked Weaver (p. 240). Feeds on the ground. **VOICE** Faint *pee … pee …* **DISTRIBUTION** Hills and forests of Western Ghats. **HABITAT** Reed beds, paddy, grass, scrub.

Finn's Weaver

Red Munia

Indian Silverbill

Green Munia

White-rumped Munia

Scaly-breasted Munia

Black-throated Munia

Tricoloured Munia *Lonchura malacca* 10cm **r**

Male has black head, throat, breast, belly-centre and thighs; rufous-chestnut back, deeper chestnut on rump; white upper belly and sides of underbody. Female similar to male, but has deep brown undertail-coverts. The **Chestnut Munia** *L. atricapilla* has black head, nape, crown, throat and upper breast; striking silver-blue bill; chestnut upperparts; rusty-orange rump and tail. Gregarious. Prefers reed beds and cultivation. **VOICE** Faint *pee … pee*. **DISTRIBUTION** Foothills of terai east to NE India, N Odisha, peninsular India, S of Mumbai. **HABITAT** Reed beds, paddy, grass, scrub.

Alpine Accentor *Prunella collaris* 17cm **r**

Unmarked grey head, nape, upper mantle, sides of neck, and throat, breast and centre of belly; white throat-patch with fine black barring; thin pale supercilium mark; buff-and-brown streaked mantle; black wing-covert panel with white tips; diffused rufous-chestnut streaking on flanks and wings; rufous-chestnut uppertail-coverts; darkly streaked undertail-coverts. The **Altai Accentor** *P. himalayasna* resembles the House Sparrow (p. 240), with back streaked brown, but adult has grey head and reddish-brown spotting on underparts. **VOICE** Calls *chirrirrip*. Mellow song. **DISTRIBUTION** Kashmir to Arunachal Pradesh. **HABITAT** Alpine pastures.

Robin Accentor *Prunella rubeculoides* 17cm **r**

Pale brown above, streaked darker on back; grey head and throat; two whitish wing-bars; rufous breast and creamy-white belly; streaks on flanks. Sexes alike. Flocks in winter. Rather tame and confiding. Hops on the ground; flies into bushes if intruded upon beyond a point. **VOICE** Sharp trilling note; also *tszi … tszi …*; short, chirping song. **DISTRIBUTION** High Himalayas; descends in winter. **HABITAT** Damp grass, scrub, high-altitude human habitation.

Rufous-breasted Accentor *Prunella strophiata* 15cm **r**

Small chestnut-and-brown accentor; heavily streaked throat; brown-streaked crown and upperparts; orange supercilium with white in front of eyes and buffy-white moustache. Sexes alike. Nests in low bushes on hillsides. **VOICE** Sharp, trilling note; also *twitt … twitt …*; short, chirping song. **DISTRIBUTION** The Himalayas: breeds at 2,700–5,000m; descends to about 1,200m in summer, rarely below 600m. **HABITAT** Montane scrub, high-altitude human habitation; descends lower in winter to bushy and fallow fields.

Maroon-backed Accentor *Prunella immaculata* 15cm **r**

Small and dark, uniquely coloured accentor with white iris. Grey head, breast and wing-panel; white scaling on crown. Maroon-brown upperparts and belly, darker on wings and tail. Pale legs. Sexes alike. Feeds on invertebrates and seeds on the ground. Difficult to see. Usually in small parties. **VOICE** Calls *zeh … dzit*. **DISTRIBUTION** Scarce; presumed breeding resident in N mountains from C Nepal east to Arunachal Pradesh. Moves lower in winter. **HABITAT** Ground beneath rhododendrons, coniferous forest undergrowth, forest edges, nearby cultivation.

Forest Wagtail *Dendronanthus indicus* 18cm **m**

Distinctive wagtail with relatively short tail; olive or grey-brown upperparts; whitish throat and underparts; two broad black 'half-necklace' breast-bands; white supercilium, and patch below ear-coverts. Broad white median coverts, barred greater wing-coverts; white patches on primaries and secondaries; white-edged, grey-brown tail; pale pinkish legs. Solitary or in pairs. Walks and runs along openings and paths in forests. **VOICE** Calls *pink; zi … fi* or *zi … chu zi … chu*. **DISTRIBUTION** C Nepal to entire NE India; Western Ghats. **HABITAT** Paths, clearings in forests.

Tricoloured Munia

Alpine Accentor

Nitin Srinivasamurthy

Chestnut Munia

Altai Accentor

Vaidehi Gunjal

Robin Accentor

Rufous-breasted Accentor

Kintoo Dhawan

Maroon-backed Accentor

Forest Wagtail

Panchami Manoo Ukil

Western Yellow Wagtail *Motacilla flava* 17cm (m)

Very variable, mainly greenish-and-yellow wagtail; many races and hybrids occur. Only wagtail with olive-green or brownish mantle, back and rump. Relatively short tail; yellow underparts and vent; two wing-bars. Breeding male has greenish-yellow to dark grey crown and ear-coverts. Gregarious. Female and nonbreeding male duller and drabber. The very variable **Eastern Yellow Wagtail** M. *tschutschensis* is bright yellow below with paler throat and greyish-olive back. VOICE Calls include *swee … ip; zhrreep*. DISTRIBUTION Lowlands throughout region. HABITAT Marshy pastures, flooded fields, waterbodies.

Citrine Wagtail *Motacilla citreola* 19cm (r) (m)

Grey back; diagnostic yellow head, sides of face and complete underbody; white in dark wings. Race *calcarata* has deep black back and rump; yellow of head may be paler in female; plumage of races often confusing. Sociable; often with other wagtails. Sometimes moves on floating vegetation. Makes short dashes. VOICE Ordinary call note a wheezy *tzzeep*. DISTRIBUTION Breeds in the Himalayas; winter visitor to most of India. HABITAT Marshes, wet cultivation, jheels.

Grey Wagtail *Motacilla cinerea* 17cm (r) (m)

Breeding male grey above; white supercilium; brownish wings with yellow-white band; yellow-green at tail-base; blackish tail with white outer feathers and white malar stripe; yellow below. Mostly solitary or in pairs. Typical wagtail, feeding on the ground and incessantly wagging tail. VOICE Sharp *tzitsi … calls*, uttered on the wing; pleasant song and display flight in breeding male. DISTRIBUTION Breeds in the Himalayas; winters from foothills south throughout India. HABITAT Rocky mountain streams in summer; open areas, forest clearings, watersides.

White Wagtail *Motacilla alba* 19cm (r)

Very variable black, white and/or grey wagtail. For purposes of identification, races characterized as black-backed or grey-backed; several races have white foreheads. Breeding birds have extensive black on throat and/or breast; non-breeding birds generally have white throats. Variable wing patterns. Solitary, or in pairs. Sometimes in large flocks. Sits prominently on exposed perches. VOICE *chee-cheep; cheezik*. DISTRIBUTION Throughout India. HABITAT Upland meadows or open areas near streams in summer; wet fields, often near water in winter.

White-browed Wagtail *Motacilla maderaspatensis* 21cm (r)

Large wagtail with black above; prominent white supercilium, large wing-band and outer-tail feathers; black throat and breast; white below. Female usually browner where male is black. Mostly in pairs or small parties feeding together. Feeds at edge of water, wagging tail frequently. VOICE Sharp *tzizit* or *cheezit … call*; pleasant whistling song in breeding male. DISTRIBUTION Most of India south of the Himalayan foothills; only resident wagtail in Indian plains, breeding in peninsular mountains. HABITAT Rocky streams, rivers, ponds; may enter wet cultivation.

Paddyfield Pipit *Anthus rufulus* 15cm (r)

Fulvous-brown above, with dark brown centres of feathers, dark brown tail with white outer feathers, easily seen in flight; dull fulvous below, streaked dark brown on sides of throat, neck and entire breast. Sexes alike. **Blyth's Pipit** A. *godlewskii* similar to Richard's, but has shorter bill, tail, legs and hind-claws; also more buff below with a harsher call note. **Richard's Pipit** A. *richardi* streaked, with strong thrush-like bill. VOICE Thin *tsip, tseep* and *tsip … tseep …* calls. DISTRIBUTION South of Himalayas. HABITAT Grassland, marshy ground, cultivation.

Western Yellow Wagtail

Eastern Yellow Wagtail

Grey Wagtail

White-browed Wagtail

Citrine Wagtail

White Wagtail

Paddyfield Pipit

Blyth's Pipit

Richard's Pipit

Tawny Pipit *Anthus campestris* 16cm Ⓜ

Plain, medium-sized, sandy pipit with dark lores. Adult plain sandy-brown above with streaking only on crown and breast-sides. Long pale supercilium and indistinct moustache. Obvious white-edged black median coverts. Outer-tail feathers buff. Horizontal, wagtail-like carriage. The **Long-billed Pipit** A. *similis* is the largest of all Indian pipits and occurs in both northern and southern races, differing in streaking. **VOICE** Calls *tseep* or *chulp*. **DISTRIBUTION** Common winter visitor to Kashmir and NW India. **HABITAT** Dry open country including semi-deserts, fallow land.

Olive-backed Pipit *Anthus hodgsoni* 15cm Ⓜ

Olive-brown above, streaked dark brown; dull white supercilium, two wing-bars and in outer-tail feathers; pale buff-white below, profusely streaked dark brown on entire breast and flanks. Distinctive facial pattern: broad, pale lines around eye and dark ear patch. Sexes alike. The **Tree Pipit** A. *trivialis* is brown above, without olive wash. Gregarious in winter. **VOICE** Faint *tseep* … call; lark-like song in breeding male. **DISTRIBUTION** Breeds in the Himalayas; winters in foothills and almost all India. **HABITAT** Forests, grassy slopes.

Rosy Pipit *Anthus roseatus* 15cm Ⓜ

In non-breeding plumage has heavy black streaks on greyish-olive upperparts and heavily streaked breast. Prominent buff supercilium, white eye-ring, and black eye-stripe and moustache. Greenish-olive wash to wing-feather edges; light pinkish wash on underparts when breeding. **VOICE** Short, thin *ceep … ceep*. **DISTRIBUTION** Common breeding summer visitor to N mountains from Kashmir east to Arunachal Pradesh; winters in N plains, south to Rajasthan and Odisha. **HABITAT** Breeds in high-altitude meadows; winters in marshes and damp cultivation.

Black-and-yellow Grosbeak *Mycerobas icterioides* 22cm Ⓡ

Male has black head, throat, wings, tail and thighs; yellow collar, back and underbody below breast; thick finch bill. Female grey above; buffy rump and belly. Very similar **Collared Grosbeak** M. *affinis* brighter yellow (often with orangish wash), with yellow thighs. Rather noisy. **VOICE** Loud 2–3-note whistle a familiar bird call of the W Himalayas; loud *chuk … chuk* note when feeding; rich song in male. **DISTRIBUTION** High Himalayas from Punjab to C Nepal; winters lower. **HABITAT** Mountain forests.

Spot-winged Grosbeak *Mycerobas melanozanthos* 22cm Ⓡ

Large finch with very large, stout bill, and relatively short tail; white spots on greater wing-coverts, secondaries and tertials; male has greyish-black hood, mantle, tail, rump, nape and throat; breast, belly and vent bright yellow; black on flanks. Female heavily streaked on yellow upperparts and underparts, with dark eye and malar stripe; yellow supercilium; white-spotted dark wings. Occurs in pairs or fairly large groups. **VOICE** A *teew … teew, kirrk*. **DISTRIBUTION** Punjab hills to Arunachal Pradesh. **HABITAT** Mixed broadleaved and coniferous forests.

Brown Bullfinch *Pyrrhula nipalensis* 17cm Ⓡ

Smallish bullfinch with ashy-brown back, head, nape and breast, mottled darker. Forehead, lores and edge of chin edged grey-black; dark patch surrounding eye; white cheeks. Thick, short dark grey bill; centre of belly and undertail-coverts white; black wings with ashy-brown bars; deeply notched black tail; white rump seen in flight. Female has small whitish wing edgings. In pairs or small flocks. Confiding. **VOICE** Call a mellow *per … lee*. **DISTRIBUTION** Resident in the Himalayas. **HABITAT** Moist forests; dense undergrowth in thick oak, fir and rhododendron forests.

Tawny Pipit

Olive-backed Pipit

Nikhil Devasar

Long-billed Pipit

Tree Pipit

Savio Fonseca

Rosy Pipit

Black-and-yellow Grosbeak

Megh Roy Choudhury

Spot-winged Grosbeak

Brown Bullfinch

Biswarup Satpati

Red-headed Bullfinch *Pyrrhula erythrocephala* 17cm ⓡ

Male has black around bill-base; brick-red crown; grey back; white rump; glossy purple wings; forked tail; black shins; rusty-red below; ashy-white belly. Female like male, but olive-yellow on crown; grey-brown back and underbody. The male **Orange Bullfinch** *P. aurantiaca* of the W Himalayas has orange-yellow back and underbody; female yellowish-brown. In small parties, occasionally with other birds. Quiet and secretive. VOICE Single- or double-noted *pheu … pheu* call. DISTRIBUTION Himalayas, Kashmir to extreme Arunachal Pradesh. HABITAT Forest bushes.

Dark-breasted Rosefinch *Procarduelis nipalensis* 16cm ⓡ

Dark rosefinch with brown upperparts washed with crimson; slender bill; dark brownish-maroon mantle, wings, flanks, breast-band and rump; broad eye-stripe; rose-pink forehead, forecrown, supercilium, throat and belly; diffusely streaked mantle; pale scaling on undertail-coverts. Occurs in pairs or small flocks. Feeds on the ground, bushes and trees. Wary. VOICE Twittering, churring, monotonous chipping song. DISTRIBUTION Kashmir to Arunachal Pradesh. HABITAT Oak, rhododendron and fir forests; alpine pastures, shrubberies, grassy slopes.

Common Rosefinch *Carpodacus erythrinus* 15cm ⓡ

Male crimson above, tinged brown; dark eye-stripe; crimson rump and underbody, fading into dull rose-white belly. Female buff-brown above, streaked dark; two pale wing-bars; dull buff below, streaked, except on belly. Occurs in small flocks. Feeds on bushes and crops. Often descends to the ground. Associates with other birds. VOICE Rather quiet in winter; pleasant song of up to eight notes; also double-note, questioning *twee … ee* call. DISTRIBUTION Breeds in the Himalayas; winters in most of India. HABITAT Cultivation, open forests, gardens, bushes.

Plain Mountain Finch *Leucosticte nemoricola* 15cm ⓡ

Grey-brown above, streaked dark brown; greyer on rump; pale buffy bar and markings in dark brown wings; dull grey-brown below, streaked browner on breast-sides and flanks. Sexes alike. Gregarious; good-sized flocks on the ground, amid stones. Calls often when feeding. **Brandt's Mountain Finch** *L. brandti* darker above with rosy-pink rump and white in outer tail. VOICE Twittering and chattering notes, rather sparrow-like in tone; calls frequently. DISTRIBUTION High Himalayas; descends in winter. HABITAT Open meadows, dwarf scrub, cultivation.

Scarlet Finch *Carpodacus sipahi* 18cm ⓡ

Bright scarlet bird from head to uppertail. Slightly brown from lower forehead to lores; dark wings and tail edged scarlet; short, square-ended tail edged dark red. Large, strong bill with upper and lower mandible curving towards tip. Female has olive-green upperparts with dark scaling on crown, nape and mantle, and finer scaling on throat and breast; greyish underparts; rump bright yellow. Solitary or in pairs. VOICE Call a pleasant *tu … wee*; *quee … i … eu*. DISTRIBUTION Uttaranchal to Arunachal Pradesh. HABITAT Coniferous and oak forests; streamsides, ravines.

Great Rosefinch *Carpodacus rubicilla* 20cm ⓡ

Large-billed rosefinch. Male has crimson-red forehead, crown, lores, cheeks, nape and ear-coverts, streaked or spotted white and pale pink; pale brown tinged with crimson back and mantle with mild streaking; deep pink rump; notched tail darker brown. Chin and throat crimson; rest of underparts pale with crimson wash and spotted. Female pale brown-grey, finely streaked brown. VOICE Drawn-out *weeep* and *twink*. DISTRIBUTION Scarce breeding resident in N mountains. HABITAT Dry, rocky and mountainous country.

Red-headed Bullfinch

Dark-breasted Rosefinch

Pranjal J Saikia

Orange Bullfinch

Plain Mountain Finch

Manjula Mathur

Common Rosefinch

Brandt's Mountain Finch

Biswapriya Rahut

Scarlet Finch

Great Rosefinch

Manjula Mathur

Pink-browed Rosefinch *Carpodacus rodochroa* 15cm

Bright pink rosefinch with distinct broad, pink supercilium. Male has dark-streaked, pinkish-brown upperparts; unstreaked, reddish-brown crown with pink wing-bars. Dark crimson-brown eye-stripe; pink rump. Underparts uniformly dark pink with indistinct streaking. Occurs in small flocks in non-breeding season. **VOICE** Calls include *swe … eet perle* and *chew … eee.* **DISTRIBUTION** Locally common breeding resident in N mountains, moves lower down in winter. **HABITAT** Open forests and scrub. Winters in oak forests and scrub, near villages.

Himalayan White-browed Rosefinch *Carpodacus thura* 17cm

Male brown above, streaked blackish; pink-and-white forehead and supercilium; dark eye-stripe; rose-pink rump and double wing-bar. Female streaked brown; broad, whitish supercilium and single wing-bar; yellow rump; buffy below, streaked. White in supercilium easily identifies this species. Occurs in small flocks. Mostly feeds on the ground. **VOICE** Calls often when feeding on the ground, a fairly loud *pupuepipi …* **DISTRIBUTION** The Himalayas; winters lower. **HABITAT** Tree-lined forests with firs, juniper and rhododendrons; open mountainsides and bushes in winter.

Yellow-breasted Greenfinch *Chloris spinoides* 14cm

Medium-sized finch with bright yellow forehead and lores, and stout pink bill; yellow supercilium extends below eye and around cheeks; greenish-black submoustachial stripe. Upperparts blackish-brown with olive-brown mantle. Yellow bars on wings, rump and tail-base. Female duller than male. Prefers trees. Occurs in small flocks. Undulating flight. Nests in trees. **VOICE** Noisy. Calls include *tzweee …* and *weeee … chu.* **DISTRIBUTION** Locally common breeding resident in N mountains and NE. **HABITAT** Edges of forests, cultivation, meadows.

Red Crossbill *Loxia curvirostra* 15cm

Male dull red above, lightly marked brown; dark stripe through eye; blackish wings; short, forked tail; unmarked dull red below. Female olivish above, lightly marked brown, and yellower on rump; dark brown wings and tail; olive-yellow below. Crossed mandibles seen at close range. Occurs in small, active parties. **VOICE** Fairly loud *chip … chip … chip* call, both when feeding and during flight; creaking, trilling song. **DISTRIBUTION** High Himalayas from Himachal eastwards; may descend in winter. **HABITAT** Coniferous forests.

European Goldfinch *Carduelis carduelis* 14cm

Crimson forehead; greyish-brown above, with large white rump-patch; black-and-yellow wings striking, at rest and in flight. Sexes alike. Sociable; flock size ranges from four to several dozen birds, sometimes with other finches. Forages on the ground; also attends to flowerheads. Undulating, somewhat dancing flight. **VOICE** Ordinary call note a somewhat liquid *witwit … witwit …* **DISTRIBUTION** The Himalayas, extreme W to around C Nepal; descends into foothills in winter. **HABITAT** Open coniferous forests, orchards, cultivation, scrub.

Fire-fronted Serin *Serinus pusillus* 12cm

Scarlet-orange forehead; blackish-grey crown; buffy back, streaked dark; yellow-orange rump and shoulders; yellow wing-edges and whitish wing-bars; sooty-brown below, with grey and buff; dull yellow-buff belly and flanks, streaked brown. Sexes alike. Gregarious. Quite active and constantly on the move. **VOICE** Pleasant twittering *chrr … chrr …*; faint *tree … tree …* call note. **DISTRIBUTION** W Himalayas, extreme W to Uttarakhand; 750–4,500m; breeds mostly at 2,400–4,000m. **HABITAT** Rocky, bush-covered mountainsides.

Pink-browed Rosefinch

Himalayan White-browed Rosefinch

Garima Bhatia

Yellow-breasted Greenfinch

Red Crossbill

Ramki Sreenivasan

European Goldfinch

Fire-fronted Serin

Khushboo Sharma

Crested Bunting *Emberiza lathami* 17cm ⓡ

Male has striking glossy black plumage, with long, pointed crest and chestnut wings and tail. Female crested; olive-brown above, streaked darker; rufous in wings distinctive; buffy-yellow below, streaked dark on breast; darkish moustachial stripe. In small flocks. VOICE Faint *chip* … call; pleasant, although somewhat monotonous, song in breeding male. DISTRIBUTION Resident over wide part of India. HABITAT Open, bush- and rock-covered mountainsides.

Rock Bunting *Emberiza cia* 15cm ⓡ

Male has bluish-grey head with black coronal stripe, eye-stripe and malar stripe, the latter curled and meeting eye-stripe diagnostic; whitish supercilium and cheeks; pale chestnut-brown back, streaked dark; unmarked rump; white outer sides of dark tail distinctive; blue-grey throat and breast; rufous-chestnut below. Female slightly duller. Solitary or in small parties. Active and restless. Flicks tail often. VOICE Squeaky *tsip* … *tsip* … note; calls often. Squeaky song of several notes. DISTRIBUTION The Himalayas. HABITAT Grassy, rocky hillsides in open forests.

White-capped Bunting *Emberiza stewarti* 15cm ⓡ ⓜ

Male has grey-white top of head; black eye-stripe, whitish cheeks, black chin and upper throat distinctive; chestnut back and rump; white outer tail; white breast with chestnut gorget below; dull fulvous below, chestnut flanks; brown above, streaked; rufous-chestnut rump; fulvous-buff below, with rufous breast. Male **Striolated Bunting** *E. striolata* has grey-white head, and completely streaked back. VOICE Faint *tsit* … or *chit* … note. DISTRIBUTION Breeds in the W Himalayas; winters in W and C India. HABITAT Open, grass-covered, rocky hillsides, scrub.

Grey-necked Bunting *Emberiza buchanani* 15cm ⓜ

Male has grey head with white eye-ring; brown back with faint rufous wash and dark streaks; white edges to dark tail; whitish throat, mottled rufous; dark moustachial stripe, not easily visible; pale rufous-chestnut below. Female somewhat duller; more prominent moustachial stripe. Winter visitor; small flocks. VOICE Faint single note. DISTRIBUTION Winter visitor; quite common over W and C India-Gujarat, S and W Rajasthan, SW Uttar Pradesh, W and C Madhya Pradesh, Maharashtra and Karnataka. HABITAT Open, rocky grassy country, scrub.

Chestnut-eared Bunting *Emberiza fucata* 16cm ⓡ

Large bunting with distinctive chestnut cheeks and lower breast. Grey-mottled crown and nape; creamy-white throat and upper breast; black moustache extends to upper breast, forming broad gorget of spots; buffish flanks and belly. Upperparts buff, heavily streaked russet; rufous rump; white outer-tail feathers. Never seen in large flocks. VOICE Calls include loud *pzik* …, *zii* and *chutt*. DISTRIBUTION Uncommon breeding resident in N hills from Kashmir east to C Nepal. Winters in nearby foothills and plains. HABITAT Rocky, grassy and bushy hillsides.

Little Bunting *Emberiza pusilla* 13cm ⓡ

Smallest of the buntings, with small, pointed bill and rufous-chestnut face. Breeding male has rufous-chestnut crown-stripe; dark blackish-brown lateral crown-stripes; rufous-chestnut face; pale eye-ring; dark brown rear surround to ear-coverts; broad buffish-white submoustachial stripe curving around behind ear-covert stripe; dark brown malar stripe; buffish-white chin and throat; dark streaking on rufescent brown upperparts; two pale wing-bars; whitish underparts with prominent streaking on breast and flanks. Occurs in small parties. VOICE *Zik*. DISTRIBUTION Nepal to Arunachal Pradesh. S Assam hills. HABITAT Grass, stubble, fields, orchards, gardens.

Crested Bunting

Rock Bunting

Garima Bhatia

White-capped Bunting

Grey-necked Bunting

Manjula Mathur

Striolated Bunting

Chestnut-eared Bunting

Little Bunting

Nikhil Devasar

Western Hoolock Gibbon *Hoolock hoolock* 🔴 🔵

Body colour entirely black, with continuous white brow with curved ends. Distinctive dark brown genital tuft. Female lighter brown than male, with whitish ring around eyes. Males weigh about 6–8kg; females around 5–7kg. **DIET** Fruits, figs, leaves, insects and spiders. **DISTRIBUTION** Assam, Garo Hills in Meghalaya, Brahmaputra and Dibang. The similar **Eastern Hoolock Gibbon** *H. leuconedys* is found in the Lohit Valley. **HABITAT** Lowland and hill forests, tropical and subtropical wet evergreen forests.

Bengal Slow Loris *Nycticebus bengalensis* 🔴 🔵

Body weight about 2kg; length around 25–35cm. Large eyes with brown circles around them. Stout body with silvery coat; head and shoulders greyish-cream. Distinctive brown stripe runs along back to crown. **DIET** Omnivorous, feeding on fruits and animal matter like birds' eggs, small birds, larvae of insects and similar. **DISTRIBUTION** E India in Assam and parts of NE. **HABITAT** Tropical and subtropical evergreen and semi-evergreen forests.

Slender Loris *Loris lydekkerianus* 🔴 🔵

Body weight variable, 85–350g; body length about 18–26cm. Second digits on hands and feet reduced. Body colour dark grey to brown, with silverish hairs in between. Underside paler than upperside. Dark spinal stripe less prominent than in the Bengal Slow Loris (above). Eyes encircled with black, and white muzzle. **DIET** Omnivorous, feeding on berries and insects, lizards, small birds and frogs. **DISTRIBUTION** S India. **HABITAT** Dry deciduous and moist deciduous forests.

Rhesus Macaque *Macaca mulatta* 🔴

Common macaque of N India. Squat and sturdy with sandy-brown or tawny-red coat. Face essentially naked and pink. Differentiated from other macaques by orange-red fur on loins and rump. Short tail, about 30cm in length. High variation in size and amount of fur. Well habituated to human settlements. Vocal, squeaky, raucous alarm call. **DIET** Steals food from houses and raids crops and fields. **DISTRIBUTION** The Himalayas, N India, NE India and peninsula. **HABITAT** Human habitation, agricultural fields, open woodland.

Bonnet Macaque *Macaca radiata* 🟢

The common macaque in S India. Similar in general body structure to the Rhesus Macaque (above), differing primarily in two key features. Head has distinctive parting of hair shown by no other macaque in region; long tail unlike short tail of Rhesus. Face naked and pink. Similar in behaviour to Rhesus. Vocal, with a squeaky, raucous alarm call. **DIET** Similar to that of Rhesus. **DISTRIBUTION** S India south of Tapi and Godavari rivers. **HABITAT** Similar to that of Rhesus.

Assamese Macaque *Macaca assamensis* 🔴 🔵

Similar in build and appearance to the Rhesus Macaque (above), with the same heavy and thickset build, but Assamese can be told apart by absence of orange-red patch on loins and rump. Coat generally darker than that of Rhesus, with greyer rather than redder tones. Also often more woolly than Rhesus's and occasionally bearded. In most localities, not as habituated to humans as Rhesus. Keeps to forests in close-knit troops. **DIET** Primarily insects and fruits. **DISTRIBUTION** N Bengal, Sikkim and NE India. **HABITAT** Low-lying

forests.

Western Hoolock Gibbon

Bengal Slow Loris

Roon Bhuyan

Slender Loris

Rhesus Macaque

Karthikeyan Srinivasan

Bonnet Macaque

Assamese Macaque

Clement M Francis

Northern Pig-tailed Macaque *Macaca leonina*

Large, forest-dwelling primate, easily separated from other macaques in its range by squarish head and distinctive cap of short black hair. Tail moderate in size and thin, very similar to that of a pig. Tail held erect while walking. Fur usually light brown and small mane around face. **DIET** Insects and fruits, as well as human-mediated food in places where habituated. **DISTRIBUTION** Vulnerable species. NE India south of Brahmaputra. **HABITAT** Moist lowland and montane broadleaved forests, forest edges.

Stump-tailed Macaque *Macaca arctoides*

Large, stocky monkey with distinctly bright and bald red face. Coat thick and furry; bearded face. Tail, as name suggests, reduced to stump and often invisible. Infants bright golden at first, gradually changing to white and finally brown, which is the adult pelage. **DIET** Insects and fruits. **DISTRIBUTION** Vulnerable species; shy and commonly seen only in certain pockets. NE India south of Brahmaputra. **HABITAT** Moist lowland and montane broadleaved forests, forest edges.

Lion-tailed Macaque *Macaca silenus*

Medium-sized macaque; rather stocky in build with distinctive appearance. Immediately identifiable by dark, shaggy jet-black coat and ash-grey to white mane. Tail moderate in size and slightly bulbous at tip, like that of a lion. Mainly arboreal, seldom descending. Calls like a pigeon. **DIET** Fruits and insects. **DISTRIBUTION** Endangered primate. Scattered and isolated locations in Western Ghats of Kerala, Tamil Nadu and S Karnataka. **HABITAT** Dense and moist evergreen forests with continuous canopy cover.

Nilgiri Langur *Semnopithecus johnii*

Large black langur with greyish or yellowish-white mane. Fur shaggy and black. Rump and tail-base often grizzled. Female identified by white patch on inner sides of thighs. Young reddish for first two months of their lives, then turn darker. Strictly arboreal, living high up in trees. Vocal; booming *hoo* can be heard at dawn and dusk. **DIET** Herbivorous. **DISTRIBUTION** Scattered locations in Western Ghats, south of Kodagu. **HABITAT** Dense and moist evergreen forests with good canopy cover.

Northern Plains Langur *Semnopithecus entellus*

Until recently this familiar langur was described as a single species, the Common Langur *S. entellus* composed of several subspecies. Recent studies have elevated most of the subspecies to species level. Medium in size; greyish-white coat and black face. Long, whip-like tail forwards looped while walking. Mostly seen in troops. Adapted to living in human settlements. **DIET** Leaves, fruits, flowers and buds; also human-mediated food. **DISTRIBUTION** All India. **HABITAT** Dry and open forests.

Capped Langur *Trachypithecus pileatus*

The most colourful primate in region. Name derives from cap of black hair that is 'combed' backwards. Coat variable in colour; four subspecies recognized. In some underparts are bright orange in colour, in others they have a yellowish or grey wash. Hairs on cheeks long, giving rise to creamish-red 'whiskers'. Strictly arboreal. Shy and takes flight as soon as it senses human presence. **DIET** Leaves, fruits, flowers and buds. **DISTRIBUTION** NE India. **HABITAT** Dense, moist broadleaved forests, bamboo and evergreen forests.

Northern Pig-tailed Macaque

Stump-tailed Macaque

Lion-tailed Macaque

Nilgiri Langur

Northern Plains Langur

Capped Langur

Gee's Golden Langur *Trachypithecus geei* 🟠 🔵

Easily the most striking primate in India. Deep cream-coloured coat that turns to bright golden during breeding season in winter. Face, palm and soles contrasting black. Face has long, spiky hair that forms whiskers from cheeks. Tail very long; much longer than head-to-body length. Strictly arboreal. Forms small troops of up to 10 individuals. **DIET** Leaves, fruits, flowers and buds. **DISTRIBUTION** Highly range restricted and endemic. Found between Sankosh and Manas rivers in Assam. **HABITAT** Subtropical moist deciduous forests, montane forests.

Asian Elephant *Elephas maximus* 🟠

Head anterio-posteriorly compressed. Eyes small compared with size of head. Back convex. Dorsal borders of large ears folded. Distinctive trunk used for feeding, smelling and dusting. Tip of trunk has one finger-like process. Adult male can weigh to 5,000kg, and measure above 3m at shoulder. Body colour varies from grey to greyish-black. **DIET** Both browser and grazer, feeding on grasses, bamboo, shrubs and bark. **DISTRIBUTION** Most of India, where thick forests are found. **HABITAT** Variety of vegetation types.

Indian Wild Ass *Equus hemionus* 🟠 🔵

Male weighs about 240kg; female around 200kg; shoulder height about 110–127cm. Summer coat dark greyish to reddish-grey, becoming greyish to chestnut during winter. Dark brown band extends from mane, fading midway. Underparts white, which extends halfway to flanks. **DIET** Generalist herbivore, consuming coarse plants and grasses. **DISTRIBUTION** Deserts in NW India around Dhrangadhra Wild Ass Sanctuary in the Little Rann of Kachchh in Gujarat. **HABITAT** Hot salt deserts below sea level.

Tibetan Wild Ass *Equus kiang* 🟠 🔵

Body weight about 250–300kg; measures 140cm at shoulder. Thick, blunt muzzle and thick neck with short, upright mane. Coat chestnut, becoming dark brown in winter and reddish-brown in summer. Dark brown band extends on dorsal side from mane to end of tail. **DIET** Generalist herbivore, consuming coarse plants and grasses. **DISTRIBUTION** Indo-Tibet borders of Ladakh, Jammu and Kashmir, N Sikkim and Himachal Pradesh. **HABITAT** Broad valleys and riverine tracts, around high-altitude lakes and basins with grasses and sedges.

Indian Rhinoceros *Rhinoceros unicornis* 🟠 🔵

Huge and prehistoric looking, with strong build. Measures about 182cm at shoulder. Grey body skin is in form of shields with heavy folds. Shoulders, hindquarters and flanks dotted with tubercle-like structures. Single horn above snout. Hunted mercilessly for its horn. **DIET** Grazer, feeding mostly on grasses. Mostly solitary but feeds occasionally in loose groups. **DISTRIBUTION** Dooars in W Bengal, Assam and Terai Arc Landscape. **HABITAT** Floodplains, riverine forests, swamps, grassland.

Indian Spotted Chevrotain *Moschiola indica* 🟢 🔵

One of the smallest ruminants, with unusual three-chambered stomach, shoulder height of 25–30cm and rather short limbs. Coat colour reddish-brown with small white spot coming together as stripes along flanks; three prominent white stripes along throat. Crown, forehead and region between eyes dark brown or blackish. **DIET** Mainly forages on shrubs and herbs. **DISTRIBUTION** Western Ghats, Eastern Ghats to Odisha and forests of C India. **HABITAT** Tropical deciduous, moist evergreen and semi-evergreen forests.

Gee's Golden Langur

Asian Elephant

Indian Wild Ass

Tibetan Wild Ass

Indian Rhinoceros

Indian Spotted Chevrotain

261

Himalayan Musk Deer *Moschus leucogaster* (r) (v)

Stocky deer about 50cm at shoulder height, with small head and bounding gait. Hindlegs longer than forelegs by about 5cm. Coat colour reddish, with golden underside, inner surfaces of limbs and mid-line of throat. White stripes on throat and orange eye-ring. Limbs dark brown on upperside, becoming light towards lower end. **DIET** Primary browser that feeds on leaves of woody plants, lichen, moss, ferns and grasses. **DISTRIBUTION** Mountains of NE India, the Himalayas. **HABITAT** Alpine scrub, oak-fir-maple habitat, birch-rhododendron forests.

Indian Muntjac *Muntiacus muntjak* (r) (v)

Muntjacs are commonly known as barking deer, and are small, solitary forest deer species. They have uniform reddish coats without any conspicuous markings; underside and inner sides of legs slightly paler. Forelimbs longer than hindlimbs. Male has two black lines running along antler pedicles, extending down face. **DIET** Nibbler, feeding mainly on fruits, buds, seeds and fresh leaves. **DISTRIBUTION** Throughout peninsular India, Terai region, NE India and lower reaches of the Himalayas. **HABITAT** Dense forest areas, thick deciduous and evergreen forests.

Sambar *Rusa unicolor* (r)

Adults have a shoulder height of 140–150cm. Summer coat brown to chestnut-brown. Underside, rump and inner parts of legs light brown. Winter coat grey-brown; rutting male almost black. Tip of tail black. Conspicuous ruff of hair around neck in both stags and hinds. Fawns have chestnut-brown coats without any spots. Only male has antlers. **DIET** Mainly grass and shoots. **DISTRIBUTION** Throughout India, except arid regions of W India. **HABITAT** Dry deciduous, moist deciduous, semi-evergreen and evergreen forests.

Hangul *Cervus elaphus* (r) (v)

Large brownish deer with black tail. Small orange-white rump-patch bordered by black band. Underside inner ears whitish. Antlers have five tines. Highly endangered due to loss of habitat; population of less than 300. Competes with domestic sheep for grazing grounds. **DIET** Main diet consists of leaves, twigs and grasses. **DISTRIBUTION** Dachigam National Park, Gurez, Waragat-Naranag and Chandaji Nullah in Jammu and Kashmir. **HABITAT** Moist broadleaved and coniferous forests and alpine meadows.

Brow-antlered Deer *Recervus eldii* (r) (v)

Moderately built deer with shoulder length of 80–90cm in both sexes. Male heavier than female. Summer coat reddish-brown in both sexes, becoming greyish-brown during winter. Prominent preorbital scent gland below each eye, and subcaudal scent glands at tail-base in both sexes. **DIET** Mainly grazer and additionally feeds on fruits, cultivated crops (rice), ferns and similar plants. **DISTRIBUTION** Restricted to Keibul Lamjao National Park in Manipur, India. **HABITAT** Dry deciduous forests and open, grassy areas.

Swamp Deer *Recervus duvaucelii* (r) (v)

Large-bodied deer with shoulder height of 110–125cm. Summer coat reddish-brown, with white spots along spine in both sexes. Underside and inner parts of legs whitish. Winter pelage greyish-brown, and a lot darker during rut. Ears roundish with tufts of thick hair. Twelve-point antler pattern. **DIET** Feeds mostly on grasses. **DISTRIBUTION** Patchy distribution in Dudhwa National Park, in Manas and Kaziranga National Parks. Also recorded in Kanha National Park in Madhya Pradesh. **HABITAT** Lowland swampy grassland.

Himalayan Musk Deer

Indian Muntjac

Sambar

Hangul

Brow-antlered Deer

Swamp Deer

263

Indian Hog Deer *Axis porcinus* 🅡 🆅

Small solitary deer considered to be one of the primitive deer species. Summer coat light brown to reddish-brown. Dark dorsal stripe with parallel white spots along both sides; not apparent during winter as coat colour changes to darker brown. Upper portions of forelegs dark in stags. Underside, throat and insides of legs paler than body. Stags heavily built with three-tined antlers. **DIET** Mainly grazer of short grass. **DISTRIBUTION** N India. **HABITAT** Moist, tall grassland and riverine forests. Prefers low-lying areas.

Indian Spotted Deer (Chital) *Axis axis* 🅡

Distinctive deer with white spots sprinkled on rufous coat. Coat provides good camouflage in forest undergrowth. Stag has pair of antlers attached to pedicels. Adult male has antlers more than 60cm long. **DIET** Primary grazer as well as browser. Favours grass sprouts, blade tips and flowering heads of tall grasses. Also consumes leaves, flowers and fruits, mainly during dry season. **DISTRIBUTION** Throughout India. **HABITAT** Widespread in forests and grassland in flat terrains and on hill slopes.

Gaur *Bos gaurus* 🅡

One of the heaviest land mammals. Muscular ridge on shoulders is one of the most striking morphological features. Both sexes have crescent-shaped horns with sharp, tapering ends. Forelegs and hindlegs white or yellowish to knees – an identifying feature of this species. **DIET** Grazer and browser on leaves, shrubs, herbs and bamboo shoots. **DISTRIBUTION** Forested tracts of India in isolated pockets in Western Ghats, Central Indian Highlands and NE Himalayas. **HABITAT** Tropical moist deciduous and dry deciduous forests.

Mithun *Bos frontalis* 🅡 🆅

Smaller than the Gaur (above) but with white 'stockings'. Body colour varies from reddish-brown to blackish-brown. Can weigh 650–1,000kg. Both sexes have pairs of horns. Muscular ridge on shoulders. Mostly used as domestic cattle, where it counts as wealth among the tribal community. **DIET** Browser and grazer, feeding on grasses, forbs and leaves. **DISTRIBUTION** NE India in hills of Tripura, Mizoram, Arunachal Pradesh, Mizoram and Nagaland. **HABITAT** Hill forests and grassy clearings.

Wild Buffalo *Bubalus arnee* 🅡 🆅

Bigger and heavier than domestic buffalo. Can weigh to 700–1200kg, with shoulder height of 150–190cm. Body colour grey to black. Both sexes have horns with wide bases, which spread to about 2m. Forehead covered with tuft of hair. **DIET** Grazer, feeding mainly on grasses and sedges. Also consumes fruits and bark, and browses on shrubs. **DISTRIBUTION** Distributed in small pockets in Assam, Arunachal Pradesh, Meghalaya, Chhattisgarh, Madhya Pradesh and Odisha. **HABITAT** Wet grassland, swamps and densely vegetated riversides.

Nilgai *Boselaphus tragocamelus* 🅡

Adult male steel-grey or blue-grey; female light brown. Dark and white markings on head, underparts and tail in both sexes. Inner sides of ear white. Tuft of hair on ventral side of neck. **DIET** Feeds on variable proportions of grass and herbs. Sometimes feeds on fallen leaves, fruits and flowers. **DISTRIBUTION** From foothills of the Himalayas through C India, to southern districts of Andhra Pradesh. Found in 16 protected areas. **HABITAT** Open areas with undulating or flat terrain.

Indian Hog Deer

Indian Spotted Deer (Chital)

Gopinath Kollur

Gaur

Mithun

Bikram Grewal

Wild Buffalo

Nilgai

Gopinath Kollur

Four-horned Antelope *Tetracerus quadricornis* r v

The only ungulate with four horns. Front pair shorter than rear pair. Small antelope weighing about 20kg; shoulder height 55–60cm. No sexual dimorphism. Coat golden-brown with coarse hair, becoming darker during monsoon and winter. Neck and underparts paler than rest of body. Rounded ears with whitish tufts towards inner edges. The only forest antelope found in India. **DIET** Nibbler and browser, feeding on fruits, flowers and pods. **DISTRIBUTION** Widespread in C and S India. **HABITAT** Favours deciduous habitat with open areas.

Chinkara *Gazella bennettii* e v

Small, graceful gazelle weighing about 23kg; 65cm high at shoulder. Male has cylindrical, slender black horns with rings, measuring about 25–30cm in length. Female does not have horns, only stubs. Coat chestnut with white underside and black tail. Dark brown line extends from eyes to mouth. Knees have tuft of hair. **DIET** Mostly browser. **DISTRIBUTION** Found in Rajasthan and N plains with Karnataka-Andhra Pradesh in southern limit. **HABITAT** Open scrubland, plain broken terrain, riverbeds, sandy areas.

Blackbuck *Antilope cervicapra* r

Male strikingly coloured in black and white, with pair of spiralling horns that are about 70cm in length and ringed. Female has brown coat and white underside. White eye-patch in both sexes. **DIET** Primarily grazer, feeding on fresh grass shoots. In winter sometimes feeds on seed pods of *Prosopis cineraria* and *P. juliflora*. **DISTRIBUTION** A few scattered populations in W through C to S India. **HABITAT** Known to favour open plain areas, but found in semi-arid grassland, open scrub, grassy clearings and open forests.

Tibetan Antelope *Panthalops hodgsonii* r v

Male about 80cm at shoulder. Muzzle characteristically swollen in male – understood to be a high-altitude adaptation. Gland under eyes. Body covered in thick fawn wool coat; underside white. Dark brown face and stripe down each leg. Lyre-shaped long horns in male only. **DIET** Grazer of sprouting grass. **DISTRIBUTION** Chang Chen Mo Valley in N Ladakh in India, which is continued to the great desert in N Tibet. **HABITAT** Cold desert areas, grassy flats, ravines.

Tibetan Gazelle *Procapra picticaudata* r v

Male and female 50–60cm at shoulder; weight 10–15kg. Male has long, tapering horns with ridges, reaching lengths of 30cm. Female has no horns. Body coat greyish-brown; summer coat greyer than winter coat. Short tail in white rump-patch. Thin, long legs for running in order to escape from predators. **DIET** Feeds on grasses, forbs and sedges. **DISTRIBUTION** Rare and seldom seen in Sikkim and Ladakh. **HABITAT** High-elevation steppe and alpine regions.

Asiatic Ibex *Capra sibirica* r v

Sturdy goat-like animal. Face short with longer beard in male than female. Stocky legs that help it to climb rocks. Legs, thighs and underparts whitish in some males. During summer, coat becomes a lot paler. Horns backwardly arched or scimitar shaped, with prominent ridges. **DIET** Feeds on grasses, sedges, forbs and sometimes shrubs. **DISTRIBUTION** Shyok Valley in Ladakh to Sutlej Gorge in Himachal Pradesh. **HABITAT** Rugged mountains of cold, arid regions. Mostly alpine scrub and dry alpine steppe vegetation.

Four-horned Antelope

Chinkara

Blackbuck

Tibetan Antelope

Tibetan Gazelle

Asiatic Ibex

Ladakh Urial *Ovis orientalis* 🔴 🆅

Smaller than wild sheep, measuring about 90cm at shoulder. Summer coat rufous-grey, turning to brownish-grey in winter. Adult ram has ruff growing from either side of chin and extending down throat region. Horns curvy and wrinkled. **DIET** Mainly feeds on grasses and leaves; sometimes shrubs. **DISTRIBUTION** Ladakh, eastwards to N Tibet, Punjab, Sind and Baluchistan. **HABITAT** Steep, grassy hill slopes, open, grassy mountain slopes, rocky, scrub-covered hills.

Bharal *Pseudois nayaur* 🔴

Stockily built, with strong but short legs to survive in rugged terrain. Contains characteristics of both sheep and goats. Male has massive horns that curve outwards and have distinct annual rings; female has smaller horns with less distinct annual rings. Body coat greyish-buff on dorsal side; white underside and legs; often horizontal black stripe on flank. **DIET** Mixed feeder, consuming grasses, herbs and shrubs. **DISTRIBUTION** Throughout the Himalayas. **HABITAT** Mountain pastures, steppe vegetation and subalpine slopes, close to cliffs.

Himalayan Tahr *Hemitragus jemlahicus* 🔴 🆅

Heavy-bodied, with robust limbs for climbing rocky mountains. Body covered with tangled coarse hair. Prominent ruff and hair; rump covered with long mantle of hair. Body coat deep reddish-brown; adult male darker than female. Insides of legs white. Both sexes have horns that grow to about 40cm and are curved backwards. **DIET** Primary grazer, feeding on grasses, sedges, herbs, ferns and mosses. **DISTRIBUTION** Patchy distribution in S Greater Himalayas, N India to Nepal and Sikkim. **HABITAT** Mountainous habitat.

Nilgiri Tahr *Nilgiritragus hylocrius* 🅴 🆅

Shoulder height about 110cm; weight about 100kg. Adult male has dark brown to black coat. Female paler grey or tan, blending with the gneiss cliffs in its habitat. Both sexes have horns; those of male heavier and longer than those of female. **DIET** Primary grazer, but also feeds on forbs and shrubs. **DISTRIBUTION** States of Kerala and Tamil Nadu along narrow stretch in Western Ghats. **HABITAT** Grassland areas close to rock faces and sheer cliffs at 1,200–2,700m.

Himalayan Goral *Nemorhaedus goral* 🔴

Goat-like species with short, stumpy legs adapted for jumping and climbing. Weighs about 20–30kg; shoulder height 58–70cm. Both sexes have backwards-curved, pointed horns. Horns in male thicker at base than those of female, and up to 23cm in length. **DIET** Primary grazer, feeding on lichens, grasses, tender stems and leaves. **DISTRIBUTION** NW to NE India. **HABITAT** Tropical moist deciduous forests, subtropical pine forests, montane wet evergreen forests, up to alpine pastures and birch forests.

Himalayan Serow *Capricornis thar* 🔴 🆅

Rarely seen medium-sized species with large head, broad thick neck, mule like ears, short limbs and a coat of dark hair. It looks like a cross between a cow, pig donkey and goat. Adult weighs 90 kg. Limbs chestnut at top and whitish below; shoulders and flanks reddish; head and mane black. **DIET** Browser, feeding on shrubs. **DISTRIBUTION** At 200–3,600m in the W Himalayas and NE India. **HABITAT** Moist, forested gorges and mountain habitats. Hilly evergreen montane forests.

Ladakh Urial

Bharal

Gopinath Kollur

Himalayan Tahr

Nilgiri Tahr

Rohit Chakravarty

Himalayan Goral

Himalayan Serow

Dushyant Parashar

Mishmi Takin *Budorcas taxicolor* 🔴 🔵

Large and heavy bodied; very strong, thick legs. Characteristic convex face; stout, broad neck. Body coat yellowish-grey with a shaggy appearance. Flanks dark brown or black. Male has more prominent horns than female. **DIET** Generalist browser. Feeds on steep hillside scrub and subalpine patches. **DISTRIBUTION** Sikkim, Arunachal Pradesh. **HABITAT** Steep mountain forests above 1,300m. Dense, forested habitats near coniferous forests, broadleaved forests and sometimes evergreen forests.

Pygmy Hog *Porcula salvania* 🟢 🔵

Male weighs about 8–10kg, female 6–8kg; measures 20–22cm at shoulder. Hindlimbs longer than forelimbs; short ears. Pelage blackish-brown along mid-dorsal line. Dark facial band. Coarse hair behind shoulders. Underside and inner legs much paler, with sparse hairs. **DIET** Omnivorous, feeding on roots and tubers, grasses, leaves, shoots, fruits, seeds, insects and similar. **DISTRIBUTION** Small pockets in foothills of the Himalayas, Manas National Park, Assam. **HABITAT** Flat terrain with sal riverine forests and tall grassland.

Wild Boar *Sus scrofa* 🔴

Bulky pig with relatively thin legs. Weighs 60–80kg. Head adapted for digging, with elongated nose and strong neck muscles. Body coat dark greyish with long, coarse hair. Male has mane running down back, particularly noticeable in autumn and winter. Canine teeth much more prominent in male than in female, and grow throughout life. Piglets have stripes on back. **DIET** Fruits, seeds, roots and tubers; wide range of other foods including some animal matter. **DISTRIBUTION** Throughout India. **HABITAT** Deciduous and mixed forests.

Tiger *Panthera tigris* 🔴 🔵

Largest of all extant cats. Adult about 300cm in length; weight around 250kg. Coat colour ochre to orangish-yellow. White underside, inner limbs and cheeks. Black stripes all over body, used for identifying individuals. Stripes aid Tigers in ambush and camouflage. **DIET** Strict carnivore, mainly feeding on ungulates, cervids and livestock. **DISTRIBUTION** Patchy distribution in S, C and NE India, as well as the Terai Arc Landscape and Sunderbans. **HABITAT** Grassland, hill forests, and deciduous and evergreen forests.

Asiatic Lion *Panthera leo* 🔴 🔵

The only cat with mane and tufted tail. Mane colour and growth vary according to age. Longitudinal belly skin-folds distinguish it from the African Lion. Body colour yellow-ochre. Whisker patterns used to identify individuals. Population of around 500 individuals. Highly endangered due to restricted range. **DIET** Strict carnivore, mainly feeding on ungulates, cervids and livestock. **DISTRIBUTION** Restricted to the Gir forests in Gujarat. **HABITAT** Tropical dry deciduous forests interspersed with thorn forests.

Indian Leopard *Panthera pardus* 🔴

Weight about a quarter of that of Tigers and Asiatic Lions (above). Agile and built for speed; useful for hunting. Coat colour ranges from pale yellow to ochre. White underside of body and tail. Black rosettes all over body help in individual identification. **DIET** Strict carnivore, mainly feeding on ungulates, cervids and livestock. **DISTRIBUTION** Throughout India; may be found in human habitation. **HABITAT** Tropical grassland, woodland, and dry deciduous, moist deciduous and evergreen forests. Conifer and broadleaved forests in the Himalayas to 3,000m.

Mishmi Takin

Sujan Chatterjee

Pygmy Hog

Wild Boar

Tripta Sood

Tiger

Asiatic Lion

Tripta Sood

Indian Leopard

Snow Leopard *Uncia uncia* 🅡 🅥

Medium to small cat. Pelage smoky-grey, patterned with dark grey rosettes and spots. Forelimbs short as adaptation to rocky mountainous habitat. Thick, long tail acts as balancer when climbing up mountain cliffs. **DIET** Hunts for small animals like marmots, Bharal, Goral and livestock. **DISTRIBUTION** The Himalayas in states of Jammu and Kashmir, Himachal Pradesh, Sikkim, Uttrarakhand and Arunachal Pradesh, at 1,800–5,800m. **HABITAT** Subalpine and alpine zones.

Asian Golden Cat *Catopuma temminckii* 🅡 🅥

Largest of the small cats in India. Coat golden-brown and unmarked. Two distinctive moustache-like white stripes on face, and forehead has longitudinal markings. Melanistic forms are also known, which can be identified by distinctive white moustachial stripes. Tail long and not bushy. **DIET** Hunts for birds, small animals and reptiles. **DISTRIBUTION** Uncommon. NE India. **HABITAT** Tropical and subtropical evergreen and moist deciduous forests to 3,000m.

Marbled Cat *Pardofelis marmorata* 🅡 🅥

Miniature version of the Clouded Leopard (below), with long, furry tail. Coat greyish-brown or reddish, replete with blotches and irregular rosettes that give it a marbled appearance. Blotches have pale borders. Face has stripes running from eyes through cheeks, and longitudinal stripes on forehead. Legs strongly spotted. Nocturnal and mainly arboreal. Habits largely unknown. **DIET** Mainly birds, but also takes rodents and small mammals. **DISTRIBUTION** Rare. NE India. **HABITAT** Tropical and subtropical evergreen and moist deciduous forests.

Clouded Leopard *Neofelis nebulosa* 🅡 🅥

Very elegant cat with warm ochre coat with cloud-like grey markings. 'Clouds' turn into oval black spots along hindquarters, reducing further to black spots in very long tail. Stripes on cheeks, and two bold longitudinal stripes on forehead. Nose prominently pink. Has the largest canine teeth among all living cats. Nocturnal and very secretive. Mainly arboreal. **DIET** Probably monkeys, lorises and flying squirrels; also birds. **DISTRIBUTION** NE India. **HABITAT** Tropical and subtropical evergreen and moist deciduous forests.

Caracal *Caracal caracal* 🅡 🅥

Tall and sleek cat known for its agility and quick pace. Coat tawny or rufous in colour. Fur short, thick and soft. Distinctive feature is long tuft of hair at tip of ear, which is black on the back. Tail not very long and tall legs unmarked. Mainly nocturnal. Not much known of its habits. **DIET** Birds, hares, rodents and reptiles; can also hunt small deer or gazelle. **DISTRIBUTION** Rare. Arid NW extending east into Madhya Pradesh. **HABITAT** Arid and semi-arid scrub forests and open, rocky areas.

Pallas's Cat *Octocolobus manul* 🅡 🅥

Unusual cat, with distinctive broad head, low forehead, short, widely separated ears, furry mane and long whiskers. Eyes have white borders, giving it a spectacled appearance. Coat grey with thick, long fur. Probably shelters among rocks or in fox and marmot burrows. Very secretive and little is known of its behaviour in the wild. **DIET** Rodents and birds. **DISTRIBUTION** Rare. Trans-Himalayas of Jammu and Kashmir, and Sikkim. **HABITAT** Scrub and rocky outcrops in cold deserts.

Snow Leopard

Asian Golden Cat

Marbled Cat

Clouded Leopard

Caracal

Pallas's Cat

Jungle Cat *Felis chaus* 🇷

The most common wild cat in India. Distinctive appearance with rather long legs making it appear tall, and relatively short tail. Coat generally uniform sandy-grey to fawn in colour. Legs faintly banded with black; tail also ringed, ending in black tip. Short tuft of hair at ear-tip. Largely nocturnal. **DIET** Lizards, mice, birds and frogs. **DISTRIBUTION** Common. Widespread throughout mainland India. **HABITAT** Wide variety of habitats – arid and semi-arid scrub forests, dry and moist deciduous forests, montane evergreen forests.

Desert Cat *Felis sylvestris* 🇷 🇻

Small cat, much like domestic cat in size and appearance. Fur pale yellowish infused with grey, with black spots throughout. Terminal half of tail ringed with black; legs have black stripes. Horizontal stripes on cheeks and longitudinal stripes on forehead. Lives in network of burrows by day. Nocturnal and not well studied. **DIET** Gerbils and jirds, and birds and reptiles. **DISTRIBUTION** Uncommon. Arid parts of NW, particularly in Rann of Kutch, and Desert National Park. **HABITAT** Scrub forests, deserts and cultivated tracts.

Fishing Cat *Prionailurus viverrinus* 🇷 🇻

Large and robust cat. Fur olive-grey with spots neatly arranged in rows. Tail short, stubby and ringed. Stripes on cheeks and longitudinal stripes on forehead. Short ears with white spot on back. Partly webbed feet. Nocturnal. **DIET** Primarily fish and molluscs, but also hunts rodents and even domestic goats. **DISTRIBUTION** Rare. Terai floodplains, NE India, mangroves and wetlands, S Bengal and Andra Pradesh, S Western Ghats. **HABITAT** Undisturbed wetlands with tall grass, mangroves and freshwater pools.

Leopard Cat *Prionailurus bengalensis* 🇷 🇻

Small, forest-dwelling cat with yellowish fur; strongly marked with black spots and blotches. Tail has combination of rings and spots, and legs spotted. Face has typical horizontal stripes on cheeks and longitudinal stripes on forehead. White spot on back of ear. Nocturnal and semi-arboreal. Known to live in tree hollows by day. **DIET** Birds, rodents, frogs and lizards. **DISTRIBUTION** Throughout the Himalayas, NE India and S Western Ghats. **HABITAT** Moist deciduous and evergreen forests, grassland and mangroves.

Rusty-spotted Cat *Prionailurus rubiginosus* 🇷 🇻

Smallest wild cat in the world; half the size of a domestic cat and easily confused with kitten of a Jungle Cat (above). Fawn coat with rusty-brown spots (which often become faint and diffuse) arranged neatly. Eyes faintly ringed with white. Two longitudinal stripes on forehead. Nocturnal and fairly tolerant of human presence, yet an uncommon species. **DIET** Mainly small birds and rodents. **DISTRIBUTION** Peninsular India up to Rajasthan and Madhya Pradesh in north. **HABITAT** Dry scrub, rocky outcrops and dry deciduous forests, often near human habitation.

Himalayan Palm Civet *Paguma larvata* 🇷 🇻

No spots on body and distinctive white whiskers. Body coat grey or tawny, and white underside. Markings on face vary, with white mark on forehead and below ears. Round black blotch under eye. Thick, unmarked black tail; black chin and throat. Habits not well known. **DIET** Fruits, vegetables, small birds, rodents and similar. Also known to take domestic poultry. **DISTRIBUTION** Assam, Jammu, Kashmir, and C and E Himalayas. **HABITAT** Hill forests and mountains to 2,500m.

Jungle Cat

Desert Cat

Fishing Cat

Leopard Cat

Rusty-spotted Cat

Himalayan Palm Civet

Common Palm Civet *Paradoxurus hermaphroditus* 🔴 🔵

Body colour black or brownish-black. Broad faint stripes on either side of body. Black limbs and variable facial markings. Whitish patch below eye and either side of nose. Solitary except for brief mating sessions. Both terrestrial and arboreal. **DIET** Mostly fruits, and sometimes vegetables, small birds, rodents and similar. **DISTRIBUTION** Throughout India, except the Himalayas and arid region. **HABITAT** Deciduous, evergreen and scrub forests. Found around human habitation.

Brown Palm Civet *Paradoxurus jerdoni* 🟢 🔵

Very similar to the Common Palm Civet (above) but without any facial markings. Coat uniform chocolate-brown in colour, and grey flanks. Tail, limbs and head region dark blackish. Solitary and nocturnal. Known to rest in holes in dense foliage by day. Often killed for meat by tribal communities. **DIET** Mostly fruits, and sometimes vegetables, small birds, rodents and similar. **DISTRIBUTION** Western Ghats in Goa, Tamil Nadu, Nilgiris and Anamalais. **HABITAT** Wet evergreen forests.

Small Indian Civet *Viverricula indica* 🔴 🔵

Base body colour greyish-brown, with black spots arranged in rows in flank region; black lines and streaks on back; tail has black rings; underside whitish up to throat region. Terrestrial and nocturnal. Digs its own burrows; also uses old burrows. In suburban areas, known to live in drains. **DIET** Mostly fruits, and sometimes vegetables, small birds, rodents and similar. **DISTRIBUTION** Throughout India except high mountains. **HABITAT** Grass or scrubland, semi-evergreen, deciduous and bamboo forests, riverine areas.

Large Indian Civet *Viverra zibetha* 🔴 🔵

Long, compressed body; short legs. Distinctive black crest of long hair along back. Base body colour greyish-brown, with black bands and rosettes; black-ringed tail and dark limbs. Nocturnal and purely terrestrial, spending most of its time on the ground. Little is known about its breeding habits, although it is thought to breed twice a year. **DIET** Small birds, rodents, insects and sometimes fruits. **DISTRIBUTION** Sikkim, upper Bengal and Assam. **HABITAT** Hills, moist deciduous and evergreen forests, scrubland.

Binturong *Actitis binturong* 🔴 🔵

Bear-like civet species, often called Bearcat, despite being neither bear nor cat. Shaggy body coat; tail thicker than body. Grizzled black-and-white coat; white whiskers. Tail often used as fifth limb. Mostly arboreal; favours trees with strangler fig creepers. Noisy, with a range of vocal calls, squeaks and growls. Mostly solitary but often seen in small groups, where female is dominant. **DIET** Small birds, rodents, insects and sometimes fruits. **DISTRIBUTION** NE India. **HABITAT** Dense forests.

Indian Grey Mongoose *Herpestes edwardsii* 🔴

Tawny to grey-coloured mongoose; body densely furred, with salt-pepper appearance; tail long with white or pale tip; ruddy face and limbs. Shy species, but a bold and fierce hunter. Generally seen individually or in groups of 3–4. Lives in hedgerows, thickets, tree holes, burrows and termite mounds, and is mostly diurnal. **DIET** Omnivorous, eating anything that it can procure. **DISTRIBUTION** Throughout India, except the High Himalayas. **HABITAT** Cosmopolitan; open scrub and bushes, jungles, cultivation, vicinity of human habitation.

Common Palm Civet

Brown Palm Civet

Small Indian Civet

Large Indian Civet

Binturong

Indian Grey Mongoose

Ruddy Mongoose *Herpestes smithii* 🔴

Similar to Indian Grey Mongoose (p. 276). Tawny to grey in colour but generally more fawn coloured than Indian Grey; underparts have reddish-brown infusions. Easily distinguished by tail, which has a bushy black tip, curved upwards. Legs dark rufous tending to black. Shy and generally solitary. Lives in hedgerows, thickets, tree holes, burrows and termite mounds. Mostly diurnal. **DIET** Omnivorous, but mainly feeds on small mammals, reptiles, birds, insects and arachnids. **DISTRIBUTION** Peninsular India. **HABITAT** Dry deciduous forests.

Small Indian Mongoose *Herpestes auropunctatus* 🔴

Nearly half the size of the Indian Grey Mongoose (p. 276), with golden-tawny coat. Muzzle black with pink nose. Tail relatively short and tip either dark or concolourous to rest of tail. Very active and moves around swiftly. Generally solitarily or in group of mother with her pups. Lives within bushes and burrows. **DIET** Highly varied; omnivorous but feeds mostly on small mammals, reptiles, birds, insects and arachnids. **DISTRIBUTION** Northern plains. Also plains of NE India. **HABITAT** Open scrub and hedges, deserts, human habitation.

Marsh Mongoose *Herpestes palustris* 🔴 🔵

Considered by some as a subspecies of the Small Indian Mongoose (above) and similar in appearance. Lives in burrows dug by itself and also by other animals. Mainly diurnal. Mostly solitary, but occasionally becomes gregarious. **DIET** Probably feeds mainly on small crustaceans, molluscs and amphibians. **DISTRIBUTION** Endangered and highly restricted; currently known only from East Kolkata Wetlands and Hooghly, West Bengal. Endemic species. **HABITAT** Wetlands with tall grass and reed beds.

Crab-eating Mongoose *Herpestes urva* 🔴 🔵

Large, stocky mongoose with bushy tail. Coat light grey-brown with broad white stripe on back and white stripes on cheeks and neck. Feet black and partly webbed. Partly aquatic, adeptly hunting for crabs, snails, fish and frogs. Cracks open hard shells of crustaceans and molluscs by throwing them at stones. Largely crepuscular and nocturnal. **DIET** Crustaceans, molluscs, fish and amphibians. **DISTRIBUTION** Rare. From Dooars of N Bengal to plains of NE India (rarely in hills). **HABITAT** Streams, shaded rivers, tea gardens.

Stripe-necked Mongoose *Herpestes vitticollis* 🔴

Largest mongoose in India. Large and stocky; fur varies from grey (N Western Ghats) to ruddy (S Western Ghats). Characteristic black stripes on neck. Head rather greyish; tail bushy, black and slightly upturned. Diurnal. Seen scampering along the forest floor and on trails in pursuit of prey. **DIET** Opportunistic feeder, eating anything it can find. **DISTRIBUTION** Western Ghats south of Goa. **HABITAT** Dry and moist evergreen forests, plantations and swampy areas; found in partly hilly country.

Striped Hyena *Hyaena hyaena* 🔴 🔵

Shaggy with dog-like build, and shorter and weaker hindlegs than forelegs. Muzzle broad; ears triangular and erect. Crest of long hair all along back, ending in bushy tail; crest erected when animal is alert. Grey fur with uneven stripes. Clumsy gait due to weak hindquarters and sloping body. Vocal, chattering conspicuously. **DIET** Primarily adapted to feeding on carrion. **DISTRIBUTION** Throughout dry tracts of peninsular India. **HABITAT** Semi-arid scrub, dry grassland, rocky outcrops, open forests. Not found in dense forests.

Ruddy Mongoose

Small Indian Mongoose

Marsh Mongoose

Crab-eating Mongoose

Stripe-necked Mongoose

Striped Hyena

Indian Wolf *Canis lupus* 🔴 🟢

Largest canid in India. Tall and sleek, resembling slim German Shepherd dog. Long legs, sandy-brown coat of short hair, and thin, long tail with black tip. Lives in small packs of up to 10 individuals, and shelters pups in burrows. Packs known to follow pastoral nomadic tribes to hunt injured or diseased goats and sheep. **DIET** Gazelle, antelope, hares, domestic goats and sheep. **DISTRIBUTION** Throughout peninsular India in dry regions. **HABITAT** Dry, open country and grassland; also occasionally dry forests.

Jackal *Canis aureus* 🔴

'Meek'-looking animal of medium size, with short limbs. Coat buffy in colour, heavily grizzled with grey-and-black hair. Distinguished from a wolf by small size, shorter ears and bushy tail; face also more pointed and acute than long face of wolf. Largely crepuscular and nocturnal; roams the countryside using a quick and 'sly' gait. Vocal, giving out a long-drawn howl. **DIET** Rodents, birds and other small game; carrion. **DISTRIBUTION** Throughout mainland India. **HABITAT** Dry to semi-arid grassland, scrub forests.

Asiatic Wild Dog (Dhole) *Cuon alpinus* 🔴 🟢

Nearly the size of a wolf. Endangered forest-dwelling canid. Handsome brick-red fur with varying amounts of white. Extensive white on throat and belly in C Indian individuals. Does not bark or howl, communicating hunting activity using infrasonic whistles. Sociable; almost always seen in packs. Vicious hunter. **DIET** Deer and other large game. **DISTRIBUTION** Discontinuous range in C India, Eastern Ghats and NE India and the High Himalayas. **HABITAT** Dry and moist forests; also temperate subalpine forests.

Indian Fox *Vulpes bengalensis* 🔴

'Meek'-looking mammal, asymmetrically built, with slim body and long, bushy tail. Coat generally greyish with extensive grizzling of black and grey. Legs short and slim; individuals in arid north-west often have rufous-coloured legs. Ears large; prominent smudge of black on muzzle. Spends the day in burrows and active mainly at night. **DIET** Mainly rodents, birds and insects. **DISTRIBUTION** Throughout peninsular India in dry regions. **HABITAT** Dry, open grassland and semi-arid scrub, often near human habitation.

Red Fox *Vulpes vulpes* 🔴 🟢

Beautiful fox, richly coloured with silky, red or orange fur. Thick coat makes it seem rather heavily built, unlike its desert cousin, the Desert Fox *V. v. pusilla*, which is thin and sleek. Tail-tip prominently white in both subspecies. Large ears. **DIET** Rodents, birds, lizards, carrion and insects. **DISTRIBUTION** Throughout the Himalayas. **HABITAT** In the Himalayas, Red lives among bushes in coniferous forests or rocks above treeline. Desert lives in network of interconnected burrows.

Asiatic Black Bear *Ursus thibetanus* 🔴 🟢

Large, forest-dwelling bear with short, smooth coat and less clumsy gait than other large bears. Bold white crescent on breast; black claws. Nocturnal. Spends the day in dens and searches for food at night. May climb trees in search of food. **DIET** Broad diet, including insects, grubs, honey, nuts, plums and apricots. **DISTRIBUTION** Throughout the Himalayas and NE India. **HABITAT** Subalpine meadows, forested hill slopes, broadleaved and coniferous forests; also moist deciduous forests in NE India.

Indian Wolf

Tripta Sood

Jackal

Ashwini H P

Indian Fox

Asiatic Wild Dog (Dhole)

Red Fox

Wikimedia CC

Asiatic Black Bear

281

Himalayan Brown Bear *Ursus arctos* 🄡 🅅

Very large bear; the world's largest terrestrial carnivore. Coat thick; reddish-brown with silvery tinge, turning to rich wood-brown in summer. Prominent hump; white claws. Due to its size (and also its habitat), it is terrestrial and spends a lot of time turning over stones in search of food. Hibernates in winter. **DIET** Wide variety of foods, including fresh alpine grass, insects and grubs, voles, marmots and fruits. **DISTRIBUTION** W Himalayas from Jammu and Kashmir to Uttarakhand. **HABITAT** Alpine meadows above treeline; avoids forests.

Sloth Bear *Melursus ursinus* 🄡

Widespread and familiar species with shaggy coat of unkempt, long black hair. Long, broad muzzle tan in colour. Claws conspicuously white and long. Most individuals have 'V'-shaped white crescent on chest. Poor vision, and relies mainly on sense of smell to find its way. Clumsy gait but an adept climber. Mostly nocturnal. **DIET** Insects and grubs, and partial to termites; also honey and fallen flowers. **DISTRIBUTION** Peninsular India, NE India and foothills of the Himalayas. **HABITAT** Dry deciduous forests, scrubland and rocky outcrops.

Red Panda *Ailurus fulgens* 🄡 🅅

One of the most striking and elegant animals found in India. Rounded head, triangular, erect ears; white markings around nose, eyes and ears on chestnut face; body chestnut; tail ringed with white. Generally solitary and primarily nocturnal. Mainly arboreal but often descends to the ground in search of food. Spends most of the day sleeping in tall trees, wrapping itself in its long and bushy tail. **DIET** Eggs, insects and fruits. **DISTRIBUTION** N Bengal, Sikkim and Arunachal Pradesh.

Hog Badger *Arctonyx collaris* 🄡 🅅

Odd in appearance; squat and bear-like in habits and gait; has body of a pig, but face and claws of a badger; snout like that of a pig. Coat thick, dense and woolly; grey or tawny-grey in colour grizzled with black. Face has bold white markings running up nose and down cheeks. Rare and elusive, with very little known about its behaviour. **DIET** Omnivorous, hunting rodents, birds and small mammals; also eats fruits and tubers. **DISTRIBUTION** NE India. **HABITAT** Dense and moist deciduous and evergreen forests.

Honey Badger *Mellivora capensis* 🄡

Unmistakable and unique appearance. Bear-like in build and habits; badger-like in ferocity and nature. Colour unusual – silvery-grey on dorsal half of body, and black on ventral half. Tail short and stubby, and same in colour as body. Reputation for being among the boldest animals on Earth. Although widespread, shy, elusive and rarely seen. **DIET** Small mammals, birds, reptiles and termites. **DISTRIBUTION** Peninsular India in dry regions. **HABITAT** Dry deciduous forests, riverine tracts, rocky outcrops.

Yellow-throated Marten *Martes flavigula* 🄡

Body length about 50–60cm; weight around 2–3kg. Elongated body with short legs. Body coat variegated brown, black and yellow, with dark bands along nape; throat region yellow with dark bands. Aggressive and fights with other males during courtship. Patrols its territory, often covering 20km in a day. Mostly terrestrial, but can climb trees with agility. **DIET** Birds, small animals and insects. **DISTRIBUTION** The Himalayas and Assam hill ranges. **HABITAT**

Temperate forests at 1,200–3,000m.

Himalayan Brown Bear

Tripta Sood

Sloth Bear

Aditya Singh

Hog Badger

Red Panda

SarwanDeep Singh

Honey Badger

Yellow-throated Marten

Nilgiri Marten *Martes gwatkinsi* (e) (v)

One of the rarest and most seldom seen mammals in India. Body length about 50–60cm; weight around 2–3kg. Elongated body with short legs suited to arboreal nature. Entire body brown to dark brown, with characteristic yellow patch on throat. Said to be mostly diurnal; feeds in the mornings and afternoons. Mostly solitary. **DIET** Birds, small mammals and insects. **DISTRIBUTION** Nilgiri Hills and parts of Western Ghats. **HABITAT** Moist tropical rainforests, and moist deciduous and montane evergreen forests away from human habitation.

Smooth-coated Otter *Lutrogale perspicillata* (r)

Largest of S Asian otters. Weighs around 7kg. Body coat can be blackish-brown, light brown, rufous or tawny-brown; underside paler than dorsal side; whitish chin and throat regions. Webbed and large front and hind paws. Tail-end flat and tapering. **DIET** Fish eater, but also feeds on shrimps, crayfish, crabs, frogs, insects, mudskippers, birds and rats. **DISTRIBUTION** Throughout India. **HABITAT** Mostly plains. Rocky stretches along rivers, swamp forests, mangroves, estuaries and even semi-arid regions.

Asian Small-clawed Otter *Aonyx cinerea* (r)

Smallest of otter species. Distinguished from other species by narrow and shallow feet, minute claws and emarginated webs. Typical dark brown body coat; ventral side paler than dorsal side, with greyish tinge. Grey or nearly white chin, cheeks, upper lip, sides of neck and throat. **DIET** Feeds on invertebrates like crabs, molluscs, insects and small fish. Sometimes takes rodents, snakes and amphibians. **DISTRIBUTION** Kerala coast, E and NE region. **HABITAT** Hill streams, mangroves, freshwater swamps, meandering rivers, tidal pools.

Mountain Weasel *Mustela altaica* (r) (v)

Probably the most common weasel in India. Mainly brownish above and creamy-yellow below; greyish above instead of brown in summer. Lips and cheeks have white patches; legs conspicuously white. Tail uniformly coloured and concolourous to dorsal pelage. Very active and constantly on the move. Lives in holes in walls and burrows in the ground. Efficient hunter. Partly diurnal and also active at night. **DIET** Varied; mostly small mammals and birds. **DISTRIBUTION** Throughout the High Himalayas. **HABITAT** Dry, sandy valleys above treeline.

Stoat (Ermine) *Mustela erminea* (r) (v)

Smallest weasel in India. Chestnut-brown, chocolate-brown or olive above, and bright white below. Moults before winter to pure white plumage. Tail short and has diagnostic brown or black bushy tip that distinguishes it from all other weasels. Active by day and hunts efficiently. **DIET** Same as that of other weasels. **DISTRIBUTION** High altitudes (3,000–4,000m) in the W Himalayas and Sikkim. **HABITAT** Alpine and temperate forests, and open, rock-strewn rivers and valleys above treeline.

Indian Hare *Lepus nigricollis* (r)

Common, medium-sized grey to brown hare with large, ovate ears. Upperparts variable in colour depending on geography: pale rufous or grey in northern areas, pale yellowish or sandy-grey in desert areas, and with dark brown or black patch on nape and shoulder in south. Roosts in burrows by day and active at night. Fast runner. **DIET** Herbivorous, feeding on dry grasses and seeds. **DISTRIBUTION** Throughout mainland India except the High Himalayas and dense forests of NE India. **HABITAT** Open scrub, grassy patches and dry forests.

Nilgiri Marten

Asian Small-clawed Otter

Stoat (Ermine)

Smooth-coated Otter

Roon Bhuyan

Mountain Weasel

Biswapriya Rahut

Indian Hare

Tripta Sood

285

Woolly Hare *Lepus oiostolus* 🅡 🅥

Plump and stocky hare with thick, woolly fur. Coat curly, pale overall and grizzled dark brown or black above – ideal for concealment in its snowy or rocky habitat. Ears long with black patches at tips; white eye-ring. Roosts in burrows of marmots. Solitary and mostly nocturnal, resting in secluded spots. Repeatedly returns to same spot for foraging. **DIET** High-altitude herbs and grass. **DISTRIBUTION** Trans-Himalayas of Jammu, and Kashmir and Sikkim (above 3,000m). **HABITAT** Alpine meadows and open, rocky terrain.

Royle's Pika *Ochotona roylei* 🅡

The most common pika in India. Rich russet or chestnut in colour, with some mottling of grey on head, shoulders and back. Juvenile extensively mottled. Snout slightly arched. Shows very high geographic variation in pelage colour, hence requires further study. Frequents grassy meadows and seeks cover under stones and boulders, darting in among them on sensing danger. **DIET** Grass and alpine herbs. **DISTRIBUTION** The Himalayas. Probably the only pika found at altitudes below 3,000m. **HABITAT** Subalpine and alpine meadows strewn with rocks.

Large-eared Pika *Ochotona macrotis* 🅡

Similar in appearance to Royle's Pika (above) but less russet and more grey-brown in colour. Ears broad and made conspicuous by long hair emerging from them. Feet pale. Moults before winter to adopt straw-coloured coat. Behaviour similar to that of other pikas. Territorial, with an adult pair occupying an exclusive patch. Does not make a burrow, but occupies crevices in shattered rocks. **DIET** Similar to that of other pikas. **DISTRIBUTION** Throughout the Himalayas in alpine regions at 3,000–6,000m. **HABITAT** Alpine meadows and cold deserts strewn with rocks.

Ladakh Pika *Ochotona ladacensis* 🅡

Large pika with sandy-brown fur and dirty-white underparts. Ears large and broad, and generally held backwards. Lives in scattered family groups and digs large holes into which it darts on sensing danger. Alert and agile and darts at sign of danger. Defends its territory vigorously. Commonly seen. Diurnal. Moves around in the mornings and afternoons and takes a sun bath at midday. **DIET** Grass and alpine herbs. **DISTRIBUTION** Ladakh in Jammu and Kashmir at altitudes above 4,500m. **HABITAT** Cold deserts and barren plateaus.

Indian Pangolin *Manis crassicaudata* 🅡 🅥

Unique mammal with large yellow scales covering body. Long snout and longer sticky tongue to help it catch ants and termites. Eyes small and ears like slits in skin, without any ear-flap. Three long claws help it break open termite mounds. Adept climber. Rolls into a ball in self-defence. **DIET** Small insects like ants and termites. **DISTRIBUTION** Throughout mainland India except the Himalayas, NE India and deserts. Now highly endangered and increasingly rare due to rampant poaching. **HABITAT** Dry deciduous forests, scrub.

Madras Tree Shrew *Ananthana ellioti* 🅡

'Meek', squirrel-like animal. Chocolate-brown with pale eye-ring and characteristic white shoulder-stripe. Snout acutely pointed. Shows slight geographic variation in pelage – C Indian forms more reddish; those from dry forests of S India more sandy-grey. Moves about actively. Despite its name, spends a fair amount of time scampering on rocky terrain looking for food. **DIET** Insects. **DISTRIBUTION** Peninsular India up to Jharkhand. **HABITAT** Dry deciduous forests; often in rocky areas.

Woolly Hare

Royle's Pika

Manjula Mathur

Large-eared Pika

Ladakh Pika

SarvanDeep Singh

Indian Pangolin

Madras Tree Shrew

Giri Cawale

Indian Hedgehog (Pale Hedgehog) *Paraechinus micropus* ⓡ

Masked face with greyish-white hairs on cheeks and forehead. Spine pale sandy-brown in colour, with grizzled appearance. Smaller ears and limbs, hence more compact than the sympatric Collared Hedgehog (below). Roosts in burrows or under *Zizyphus* clumps. Becomes torpid in unfavourable conditions. When threatened, rolls itself into a ball. **DIET** Insects, worms, lizards, mice and birds' eggs; plant tubers. **DISTRIBUTION** Arid NW India from Rajasthan to W Madhya Pradesh and Uttar Pradesh. **HABITAT** Arid and rocky areas, thorn forests.

Collared Hedgehog *Hemiechinus collaris* ⓡ

Distinguished from the sympatric Indian Hedgehog (above) by its dark spines, black belly and tail, and long ears. Roosts in burrows or dens; becomes torpid during unfavourable conditions. When threatened, rolls itself into a ball. **DIET** Insects, worms, lizards, mice and birds' eggs; also *Zizyphus* berries and tubers of other plants. **DISTRIBUTION** Arid NW from Rajasthan to W Madhya Pradesh and Uttar Pradesh. **HABITAT** Arid and rocky areas, thorn forests.

Indian Porcupine *Hystrix indica* ⓡ

Large and robust rodent, armed profusely with long, black-and-white quills and under-armature of black bristles. Roosts in dens and caves, or makes network of interconnected burrows. Roost often strewn with bones, which it gnaws at (also doing the same with fallen deer antlers) to strengthen its quills. Leaves behind tell-tale cigar-shaped droppings. Nocturnal. **DIET** Vegetables, grains, fruits, roots and tubers. **DISTRIBUTION** Throughout mainland NE India. **HABITAT** Rocky hillsides, dry and moist forests, dry scrub.

Himalayan Crestless Porcupine *Hystrix brachyura* ⓡ

Smaller than the Indian Porcupine (above), with shorter quills that are double banded with black and white. Also distinguished from Indian by very short or absent crest. Ranges generally do not overlap. Like Indian, lives in caves, dens and burrows. Due to its short quills, does not produce strong rattling sound when provoked. Nocturnal. **DIET** Vegetables, grains, fruits, roots and tubers. **DISTRIBUTION** N Bengal, Sikkim and NE India. **HABITAT** Moist forests and edges with rocky outcrops.

Brush-tailed Porcupine *Atherurus macrourus* ⓡ ⓥ

Unusual, rare and little-known porcupine. Smallest porcupine in India, with very short, grey-brown, spiny quills all over body similar to fur. Tip of tail brush-like with tangle of long quills. Roosts in underground burrows by day. Nocturnal. **DIET** Vegetables, grains, fruits, roots and tubers; also an effective seed predator. **DISTRIBUTION** NE India; currently known only from Assam, Arunachal Pradesh and Meghalaya. **HABITAT** Dense rainforests with thick growth of bamboo and rattans.

Himalayan Marmot *Marmota himalayana* ⓡ

Large, stocky and robust rodent that lives in the Trans-Himalayas. Coat short but coarse, and uniform tawny-brown in colour, often with black blotches but never a dark saddle-like patch like that of the **Long-tailed Marmot** M. *caudata*. Lives in large groups that excavate deep interconnected burrows. A sentry may stand guard on its haunches and shriek in alarm when danger threatens. Hibernates in winter. **DIET** Grasses, herbs, grains, roots and tubers. **DISTRIBUTION** Throughout the Himalayas. **HABITAT** Alpine meadows, grassland, cold deserts.

Indian Hedgehog (Pale Hedgehog)

Collared Hedgehog

Taksh Sangwan

Indian Porcupine

Himalayan Crestless Porcupine

Rohan Pandit

Brush-tailed Porcupine

Himalayan Marmot

Amit Sharma

Indian Giant Squirrel *Ratufa indica* (e)

Large and robust squirrel. Fur generally reddish above and buffy below. Shows high geographic variation in pelage colour. Individuals from N Western Ghats purely chestnut above; those from C and S Western Ghats generally black with maroon on back. Arboreal. Makes loud alarm calls. Builds nest during breeding season. **DIET** Flowers, fruits and foliage of a variety of forest trees. **DISTRIBUTION** Western and Eastern Ghats. **HABITAT** Forest dependent; dry and moist deciduous forests.

Malayan Giant Squirrel *Ratufa bicolor* (r)

Slightly smaller than the Indian Giant Squirrel (above). Elegant species, dark brown or black above and buffy-yellow below. Ears large and black, with tufts. Arboreal. Fairly vocal and similar in behaviour to Indian. Sometimes descends to the ground to feed. Rarely enters plantations and human habitation. **DIET** Flowers, fruits and foliage of a variety of forest trees. **DISTRIBUTION** N Bengal and NE India. **HABITAT** Low-lying and montane moist deciduous and semi-evergreen forests.

Grizzled Giant Squirrel *Ratufa macroura* (r)

Smallest giant squirrel in India. Pelage varies from grey to dark brown above and pale below. Dorsal pelage interspersed with pale and dark hairs, giving grizzled appearance. Characteristic black crown and snout-tip; pale pink lips and nose. Vocal. Makes nest during breeding season. **DIET** Flowers and fruits of dry-scrub forest plant species. **DISTRIBUTION** Isolated pockets of S India between dry rain shadow of Western Ghats and Eastern Ghats. **HABITAT** Riverine patches in dry-scrub forests of rain-shadow regions of Western Ghats.

Red Giant Flying Squirrel *Petaurista petaurista* (r)

Large flying squirrel with red coat. Male chestnut-red; female rufous-brown. Very high geographic variation. Climbs high up on one tree, then glides from tree to tree, covering distances of up to 100m in a glide. Nasal call produced frequently at dusk. **DIET** Fruits and flowers; also gnaws on bark. **DISTRIBUTION** Throughout the Himalayas and NE India. **HABITAT** Oak, pine and deodar forests in the W Himalayas, and tropical broadleaved forests in the E Himalayas and NE India.

Indian Giant Flying Squirrel *Petaurista philippensis* (r)

The most common flying squirrel on the peninsula. Coat varies from rufous to grey grizzled with white. Pale grey underparts and rufous patagium. High geographic variation; individuals from south darkest, and often have rufous upperparts. Head concolourous to body. Most active at dusk. **DIET** Fruits and flowers; also gnaws on bark. **DISTRIBUTION** Scattered localities in undisturbed forests all over peninsula. **HABITAT** Undisturbed, dry and moist deciduous forests with tall stands of trees.

Hoary-bellied Squirrel (Irrawady Squirrel) *Callosciurus pygerythrus* (r) (e)

Handsome but drab brown squirrel, larger in size than the familiar striped squirrels of cities. Pale underparts and distinctive rufous tinge at bases of limbs. Pale patches may be present on the hips. Long tail about as large as rest of body. Vocal, producing harsh chuckles. Diurnal. **DIET** Fruits, flowers and foliage. **DISTRIBUTION** Sikkim, N Bengal and plains of NE India. Threatened by habitat loss. **HABITAT** Montane forests in the Himalayas, and lightly wooded areas and human habitation in NE India.

Indian Giant Squirrel

Malayan Giant Squirrel

Grizzled Giant Squirrel

Red Giant Flying Squirrel

Indian Giant Flying Squirrel

Hoary-bellied Squirrel (Irrawady Squirrel)

Orange-bellied Himalayan Squirrel *Dremomys lokriah* 🔴

Drab squirrel, superficially like a small Hoary-bellied Squirrel (p. 290); face small and 'meeker', often with some rufous at snout. Belly faint rufous or orange, and never bright enough to be conspicuous. Unlike the suggestion in its name, orange belly barely visible. Shy species, moving about actively. **DIET** Fruits, flowers and foliage. **DISTRIBUTION** Sikkim, N Bengal and hills of NE India. **HABITAT** Montane forests and foothills.

Three-striped Palm Squirrel *Funambulus palmarum* 🔴

Familiar squirrel, commensal of humans in peninsular India. Sooty-brown to black above, with three bold, parallel white stripes on back. Two broken and faint stripes visible on flanks. Tail as long as rest of body, and bushy with soft hair. Highly vocal, uttering shrill, bird-like *tee ... tee ... tee* call, repeated endlessly. **DIET** Berries and other fruits, flowers and small insects; also known to raid birds' nests. **DISTRIBUTION** Peninsular India south of Madhya Pradesh and Jharkhand. **HABITAT** Gardens, groves, human habitation, lightly wooded areas.

Five-striped Palm Squirrel *Funambulus pennantii* 🔴

Familiar, commensal species on Northern Plains. Generally paler than the Three-striped Palm Squirrel (above), but as dark in some parts of its range. Light sandy-brown above with three bold parallel white stripes on back and two on flanks. Where ranges overlap with those of Three-striped, best separated by its trilling, bird-like call, given out with frenzied jerking of tail. **DIET** Berries and other fruits, flowers and small insects. **DISTRIBUTION** N India. **HABITAT** Gardens, groves, human habitation, lightly wooded areas.

Jungle Striped Squirrel *Funambulus tristriatus* 🟢

Larger and slightly bulkier than previous striped squirrels, with ruddy colouration. Dorsal fur dark, like that of the Three-striped Palm Squirrel (above), but face, rump and hindquarters are rufous. Similar in behaviour to other striped squirrels. Often considered a pest for its habit of raiding fruit plantations. Studies show that more males are born than females. **DIET** Similar to that of other striped squirrels. **DISTRIBUTION** Endemic to Western Ghats from Dangs in Gujarat to Kerala. **HABITAT** Moist deciduous hill forests.

Indian Gerbil *Tatera indica* 🔴

Gerbils and jirds have large hindlimbs and move about in a series of leaps and bounds. They are distinguishable from mice and rats by a long, hairy tail that ends in a tassel. The Indian Gerbil is biscuit coloured, with a long tail that is half cream and half black. Feet pale and holds erect posture. Lives in networks of interconnected burrows. Mainly nocturnal, but also active by day. **DIET** Grains, roots and grasses. **DISTRIBUTION** Throughout mainland India. **HABITAT** Deserts, open semi-deserts, fields, fallow land.

Indian Desert Jird *Meriones hurrinae* 🔴

Smaller than the Indian Gerbil (above), with shorter tail that is uniformly brown in colour and ends in tassel of black hair. Grey-brown above and paler below. Incisors orange. Much more gregarious than the Indian Gerbil, and lives in wider interconnected burrows. When alarmed, produces drumming sound by stamping hindlimbs. Mainly diurnal. **DIET** Seeds, tubers, grasses, leaves, flowers and nuts of *Salvadora*. **DISTRIBUTION** Arid deserts of W Gujarat and Rajasthan.

HABITAT Barren, fallow land, semi-deserts.

Orange-bellied Himalayan Squirrel

Three-striped Palm Squirrel

Five-striped Palm Squirrel

Jungle Striped Squirrel

Indian Gerbil

Indian Desert Jird

293

Indian Star Tortoise *Geochelone elegans* 38cm 🔴 🔵

Carapace elongated in adults, rounded in juveniles, domed dorsally; weak bicuspid or tricuspid upper jaw; several distinct conical tubercles on thigh; carapace and plastron star marked with pattern of dark brown or black on yellow or beige; superimposed dark colour especially prominent in juveniles. **DIET** Largely herbivorous. **DISTRIBUTION** NW, SE and S India. **HABITAT AND HABITS** Found in scrub forests and edges of deserts, agricultural fields, teak forests, grassland and thorn scrub.

Asian Giant Tortoise *Manouria emys* 50cm 🔴 🔵

Carapace relatively low and rounded; vertebral region depressed; distinct growth rings on scutes of carapace; outer surfaces of forelimbs have large scales; paired tuberculate scales on thighs; carapace blackish-brown; plastron lighter; limbs dark brown to greyish-brown. **DIET** Largely herbivorous, although insects and frogs also eaten. **DISTRIBUTION** NE India. **HABITAT AND HABITS** Found in evergreen forests, especially with hill streams and dense leaf litter. Constructs mound nest by sweeping leaf litter, and lays 23–51 hard-shelled eggs.

River Terrapin *Batagur baska* 59cm 🔴

Carapace domed, heavily buttressed; long plastron; head small with narrow, upturned snout; forehead covered with small scales; jaws serrated; four claws on each forelimb, which has wide webbing; carapace olive-grey or brown, and head similarly coloured but lighter on sides; breeding males develop black forehead and back of neck; front portion of neck bright red. **DIET** Molluscs, crustaceans and fish. **DISTRIBUTION** Estuaries such as the Sunderbans, Bhitarkanika. **HABITAT AND HABITS** Occurs in mouths of large rivers with mangroves.

Indian Black Turtle *Melanochelys trijuga* 38.3cm 🔴 🔵

Carapace elongated, tricarinate, fairly high in adults, depressed in juveniles; head moderate with short snout; upper jaw notched; toes fully webbed; carapace typically brown; plastron usually dark with pale yellow border that may be lost in old individuals; head colour variable, and forms basis of subspecific differentiation. **DIET** Omnivorous, eats prawns, grass, water hyacinth and fallen fruits. **DISTRIBUTION** N, peninsular and NE India. **HABITAT AND HABITS** Found in still waters with aquatic vegetation, and may also occur in small rivers.

Indian Roofed Turtle *Pangshura tecta* 23cm 🔴

Carapace elevated, oval, with distinct keel on third vertebral shield; that is spike-like, especially in juveniles; head small with projecting snout; upper jaw unnotched, serrated; digits entirely webbed; first vertebral as long as wide or longer than wide; fourth vertebral longer than wide, flask shaped; head has orange or red crescentic postocular markings from below eyes to forehead; neck dark grey with thin yellow or cream stripes. **DISTRIBUTION** N India. **HABITAT AND HABITS** Found in standing waters. Basks communally.

Indian Flapshell Turtle *Lissemys punctata* 37cm 🔴

Carapace oval, with seven callosities on plastron; skin-clad, hinged anterior lobe of plastron closes completely; paired plastral flaps; carapace olive-green with dark yellow blotches in northern subspecies *andersoni*, unpatterned in southern *punctata*; plastron cream or pale yellow. **DIET** Frogs, tadpoles, fish, crustaceans, snails, earthworms, insects and carrion. **DISTRIBUTION** All India. **HABITAT AND HABITS** Found in salt marshes, rivers, ponds, oxbow lakes, streams, rice fields and canals in cities. Active by day and night, feeding at dusk.

Indian Star Tortoise

River Terrapin

Indian Roofed Turtle

Abhijit Das

Asian Giant Tortoise

Abhijit Das

Indian Black Turtle

Abhijit Das

Indian Flapshell Turtle

Indian Softshell Turtle *Nilssonia gangeticus* 94cm **r** **v**

Carapace low and oval; snout slightly downturned; upper jaw without ridges; carapace has longitudinal series of warts in juvenile, smooth in adults; carapace greyish-black, grey or green, with darker reticulation; forehead green, with oblique black stripes on top and sides. **DIET** Water plants, invertebrates and vertebrates. **DISTRIBUTION** N to NE India. **HABITAT AND HABITS** Inhabits rivers, ponds, lakes and reservoirs. During droughts, buries itself in mud at bottoms of ponds and lakes. Seen basking on sand banks. Clutches comprise 13–35 eggs.

Hawksbill Sea Turtle *Eretmochelys imbricata* 1m **m** **v**

Carapace heart shaped; four pairs of overlapping costal scutes; two pairs of prefrontal scales; upper jaw relatively narrow and elongated, and forwards projecting, to form bird-like bill; carapace olive-brown; juvenile has darker blotches than adults. **DIET** Mainly consists of sponges; algae, corals and shellfish also eaten. **DISTRIBUTION** India, including Andaman Islands. **HABITAT AND HABITS** Associated with coral reefs, bays, estuaries and lagoons. Nesting varies with locality: mainland. Clutches comprise 96–177 eggs.

Olive Ridley Sea Turtle *Lepidochelys olivacea* 80cm **m** **v**

Carapace broad, heart shaped, posterior marginals serrated, with juxtaposed costal scutes; 5–9 pairs of costals; adult shell smooth; hatchling shell tricarinate, lateral and with vertebral keels that disappear with growth; upper jaw hooked, but lacks ridge; carapace olive-green or greyish-olive; plastron greenish-yellow; juvenile grey-black dorsally; cream coloured ventrally. **DISTRIBUTION** India, including Andaman Islands. **HABITAT AND HABITS** Nesting takes place in large aggregations (referred to as 'arribadas') of up to several thousands.

Green Forest Lizard *Calotes calotes* 130mm **r**

Body robust; head large; cheeks swollen in adult male; crest on head and body distinct; oblique fold in front of shoulder; throat sac not well developed; dorsal scales smooth or weakly keeled, pointing backwards and upwards; tail long and rounded; dorsum bright green, with 4–5 bluish-white or green cross-bars; belly pale green. **DIET** Insects. **DISTRIBUTION** S peninsular India. **HABITAT AND HABITS** Found in moist deciduous and evergreen forests in mid-hills and plains. Arboreal; associated with shrubs and tree trunks. Clutches comprise 6–12 eggs.

Garden Lizard *Calotes versicolor* 140mm **r**

Body stout; head rather large; scales on body point backwards and upwards; no fold or pit in front of shoulders; two separated spines above tympanum; colouration variable and changeable, head becoming bright red, and black patch on throat appearing in displaying male, fading to dull grey at other times; female may become yellow, changing to dull greyish-olive after mating. **DIET** Insects and other invertebrates. **DISTRIBUTION** All India. **HABITAT AND HABITS** Found in forests as well as shrubs and hedges. Clutches comprise 6–23 eggs.

South Indian Rock Agama *Psammophilus dorsalis* 135mm **e**

Body robust, depressed; dorsal crest or gular sac absent; head large; limbs small; scales uniform, keeled; deep fold in front of shoulder; dorsum of adult male brown, with dark brown or black stripe along flanks; belly yellow; juvenile and adult female olive-brown, with dark brown spots and speckles and white areas on neck-sides; upper body of adult male bright red or orange in breeding season. **DIET** Includes insects. **DISTRIBUTION** Peninsular India. **HABITAT AND HABITS** Found in rocky biotopes in scrub country. Clutches comprise 7–8 eggs.

Indian Softshell Turtle

Hawksbill Sea Turtle

Olive Ridley Sea Turtle

Green Forest Lizard

Garden Lizard

South Indian Rock Agama

Indian Chameleon *Chamaeleo zeylanicus* 183mm **r**

Body laterally compressed; head has helmet-like, bony projection; orbit of eye large; eyeball covered with skin, leaving tiny aperture; low, serrated dorsal crest extending to prehensile tail; fingers and toes opposable; dorsum green to yellow, with spots or bands. **DIET** Includes insects. **DISTRIBUTION** Peninsular and W India. **HABITAT AND HABITS** Difficult to see. Found in dry forests and scrubland. Arboreal, inhabiting shrubs and trees. Clutches comprise 10–31 eggs.

Indian Golden Gecko *Calodactylodes aureus* 89mm **e**

Body robust; head wider than body; body covered with small, flat scales, with scattered rounded tubercles; undersurfaces of fingers and toes have plate-like, expanded scansors; adult males have two preanal pores; 1–6 femoral pores; dorsum of adult male bright yellow, especially on throat; female and juvenile olive-yellow, reddish-brown or blackish-brown. **DIET** Grasshoppers, beetles, butterflies and their larvae, spiders, ants and lizard eggs. **DISTRIBUTION** Peninsular India. **HABITAT AND HABITS** Rocky landscapes and scrubland. Clutches comprise two eggs.

Indian Day Gecko *Cnemaspis indica* 38mm **e**

Body slender; head distinct from neck; snout elongated; eyes large, with rounded pupils; dorsal scales keeled; spines on sides of body absent; tubercles on dorsum of body absent; smooth scales on belly; 4–5 femoral pores; tail segmented, with flattened scales forming whorls; dorsum light brown, with red or orange spots and mottling; belly brownish-cream; throat dark brown. **DIET** Insects. **DISTRIBUTION** Western Ghats, particulary Nilgiris. **HABITAT AND HABITS** Found in evergreen forests. Associated with tree trunks and rocks.

Bengal Monitor *Varanus bengalensis* 1.7m **r**

Body slender; snout somewhat elongated; nostrils nearer eye than snout-tip; nostril an oblique slit; nuchal scales rounded; crown scales larger than nuchal scales; midventral scales smooth; tail flattened; snout unpatterned; belly cream or yellow, lacking dark vertical 'V'-shaped marks extending to sides of belly. **DIET** Insects, spiders, snails, crabs, frogs, mammals, birds, lizards and snakes, as well as carrion. **DISTRIBUTION** All India. **HABITAT AND HABITS** Found in semi-deserts and scrub, to evergreen forests and plantations. Clutches comprise 12 eggs.

Yellow Monitor *Varanus flavescens* 83cm **r**

Body stout; snout short and convex; nostril an oblique slit, closer to snout-tip than to orbit; nuchal scales strongly keeled; crown scales smaller than nuchals; midventral scales smooth; tail strongly compressed; juvenile has transverse rows of fused yellow spots on dark background; dorsum light to dark brown, with brownish-red areas between yellow transverse bands. **DIET** Insects, earthworms, amphibian and reptile eggs. **DISTRIBUTION** All India. **HABITAT AND HABITS** Found in wetlands such as marshes, and flooded fields of rice paddy. Clutches comprise 4–30 eggs.

Water Monitor *Varanus salvator* 3.2m **r**

Body stout; snout depressed; nostril rounded or oval, twice as far from orbit as from snout-tip; nuchal scales strongly keeled; crown scales larger than nuchal scales; midventral scales feebly keeled; tail strongly compressed with double-toothed crest above; juvenile dark dorsally, yellow spotted or occelli in transverse series; snout black barred. **DIET** Insects, fish, crabs and turtles. **DISTRIBUTION** E and NE India; Andaman and Nicobar Islands. **HABITAT AND HABITS** Found in wetlands, rivers and canals in cities, mangroves and streams. Clutches comprise 7–30 eggs.

Indian Chameleon

Indian Golden Gecko

Indraneil Das

Indian Day Gecko

Bengal Monitor

Indraneil Das

Yellow Monitor

Water Monitor

Indraneil Das

Reticulated Python *Malayopython reticulatus* 9.8m 🔴 🟣

Body long and relatively slender; sensory pits in rostral and first four supralabials and some infralabials present; dorsum yellow or light brown, with series of dark brown spots, each edged with black; dark streak along forehead and another on each side of head. **DIET** Birds and mammals. **DISTRIBUTION** Nicobar Islands, India. **HABITAT AND HABITS** Found in lowland forests in region. Oviparous, producing clutches of 15–100 eggs, which are incubated by the mother and hatch in 65–105 days.

Burmese Rock Python *Python bivittatus* 7m 🔴 🟣

Body stout; head lance shaped; sensory pits in rostral and first two supralabials and some infralabials present; spurs small; dorsum dark brownish-grey above, with series of large, squarish dark grey or brown marks; rounded or irregular-shaped blotches on flanks lack light centres; dorsal and lateral spots are darker; dark subocular stripe. **DIET** Includes warm-blooded prey. **DISTRIBUTION** E and NE India. **HABITAT AND HABITS** Evergreen and deciduous forests, grassland and mangroves. Clutches comprise up to 100 eggs.

Indian Rock Python *Python molurus* 7.6m 🔴 🟣

Body stout; head lance shaped; sensory pits in rostral and first two supralabials and some infralabials present; sixth or seventh supralabial contacts eye; spurs small; dorsum yellowish-grey to mid-brown above, with series of large, squarish dark grey or brown marks; flanks have rounded or irregular-shaped blotches with light centres. **DISTRIBUTION** Peninsular India. **HABITAT AND HABITS** Forests and scrubland. Emerges from burrows of porcupines, bears and rodents to ambush warm-blooded prey and monitor lizards. Oviparous, producing clutches of 8–107 eggs.

Common Sand Boa *Eryx conicus* 100cm 🔴

Body short, stout, cylindrical; dorsals keeled, head indistinct from neck; mental groove absent; snout rounded; nostrils and eyes small; pair of spurs on each side of vent; tail short, tapering to acute point; tail scales strongly keeled; dorsum brownish-grey, with series of large, irregular dark brown or reddish-brown blotches, sometimes fused or forming zigzag pattern. **DIET** Small mammals and birds. **DISTRIBUTION** Peninsular and W India. **HABITAT AND HABITS** Arid regions with loose, sometimes sandy soil. Active at dusk. Ovoviviparous, producing 3–16 young.

Red Sand Boa *Eryx johnii* 125cm 🔴

Body short, stout, cylindrical; dorsals smooth; head indistinct from neck; snout broad, depressed; chin with mental groove; nostrils slit-like; eyes small; head scales small, only slightly larger than dorsals, slightly keeled; spur on each side of vent; tail short, blunt; dorsum of adult grey, brownish-red or dark brown, uniformly coloured or with indistinct black spots, especially towards and on tail. **DIET** Small mammals. **DISTRIBUTION** Peninsular and W India. **HABITAT AND HABITS** Dry countryside. Crepuscular and nocturnal. Ovoviviparous, producing 6–8 young.

Common Vine Snake *Ahaetulla nasuta* 200cm 🔴

Body long, slender; snout pointed with dermal appendage; distinct middorsal groove on snout; pupils form horizontal slits; dorsum usually bright green, with longitudinal yellowish line along outer margin of ventrals. **DIET** Includes tadpoles, lizards, birds, small mammals and even leeches. **DISTRIBUTION** India, Bangladesh, Bhutan, Nepal and Sri Lanka; also SE Asia. **HABITAT AND HABITS** Found in lightly forested areas, including gardens, in lowlands as well as mid-hills. Ovoviviparous, producing 3–23 young.

Reticulated Python

Indian Rock Python

Red Sand Boa

Burmese Rock Python

Common Sand Boa

Common Vine Snake

301

Oriental Vine Snake *Ahaetulla prasina* 185cm 🔴

Body long, slender; snout not as long as Common Vine Snake's (p. 324); eyes have horizontal pupils; distinct groove in front of eyes; dorsum usually green, sometimes brown and yellow; yellow stripe along flanks of body; belly light green. **DISTRIBUTION** NE India, Bangladesh and Bhutan; also SE Asia. **HABITAT AND HABITS** Found in forests, and associated with shrubs and saplings; also enters parks and gardens in search of lizards and birds. Ovoviviparous, producing 4–6 young.

Green Cat Snake *Boiga cyanea* 187cm 🔴

Body slender, compressed; head large, distinct from neck; eyes large, pupils vertical; centre of back has low ridge; vertebral scale row has enlarged scales; dorsals smooth; dorsum green; interstitial skin black; lower lips and chin pale blue; belly greenish-white or greenish-yellow, unpatterned or spotted with dark green; juvenile bright reddish-brown or olive, with green forehead and black postocular streak. **DISTRIBUTION** E and NE India, Nicobar. **HABITAT AND HABITS** Found in forest edges and disturbed habitats. Nocturnal. Clutches comprise 3–10 eggs.

Common Indian Cat Snake *Boiga trigonata* 125cm 🔴

Body slender, compressed; head distinct from neck; eyes large, pupils vertical; dorsals smooth; vertebral scales feebly enlarged; dorsum yellow to greyish-brown, with light grey, black-edged, arrowhead-shaped markings that may form vertebral stripe; light grey, black-edged, 'Y'-shaped mark on forehead; narrow dark streak, bordered above with light grey, from behind eye to mouth; belly white or grey, speckled with dark grey or black spots. **DISTRIBUTION** Peninsular India. **HABITAT AND HABITS** Forests, parks and gardens. Nocturnal and arboreal. Clutches comprise 3–11 eggs.

Common Bronzeback Tree Snake *Dendrelaphis tristis* 150cm 🔴

Body slender; head distinct from neck; eyes large, pupils rounded; tail long, third of total length; dorsals smooth; dorsum purplish- or bronze-brown; vertebral scales on neck and forebody yellow; buff flank-stripe from neck to vent; light blue on neck between scales revealed during display; belly pale grey, green or yellow. **DIET** Frogs and lizards, and insects. **DISTRIBUTION** India, Bangladesh, Nepal, Pakistan and Sri Lanka. **HABITAT AND HABITS** Secondary forests and forest clearings. Diurnal and arboreal. Makes long jumps between trees. Clutches comprise 5–7 eggs.

Red-tailed Trinket Snake *Gonyosoma oxycephalum* 240cm 🔴

Body thick-set in adults, more slender in juvenile; head elongated, coffin shaped, slightly wider than neck; dorsals feebly keeled or smooth; dorsum emerald-green, with pale green throat; black stripe along sides of head, across eyes; belly yellow; tail russet-brown; juvenile olive-brown with narrow white bars towards back of body. **DIET** Includes rats, squirrels and birds. **DISTRIBUTION** Andaman Islands, India; also SE Asia. **HABITAT AND HABITS** Found in lowland rainforests. Arboreal as well as terrestrial. Clutches comprise 5–12 eggs.

Common Wolf Snake *Lycodon aulicus* 80cm 🔴

Body slender; head distinctly flattened; snout projects beyond lower jaw; dorsals smooth; dorsum dark brown or greyish-brown, with 12–19 white or pale yellow cross-bars, sometimes speckled with brown, which expand laterally; bands disappear posteriorly; upper lip cream coloured; belly cream or yellowish-white. **DIET** Geckos, snakes and rodents. **DISTRIBUTION** India, Bangladesh, Nepal, Pakistan and Sri Lanka; also Myanmar. **HABITAT AND HABITS** Found in parks and within human habitation, occupying roofs and cracks on walls. Clutches comprise 3–11 eggs.

Oriental Vine Snake

Green Cat Snake

Common Indian Cat Snake

Common Bronzeback Tree Snake

Red-tailed Trinket Snake

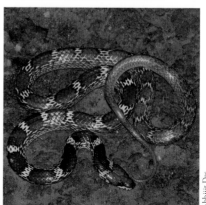

Common Wolf Snake

Banded Wolf Snake *Lycodon fasciatus* 85cm (r)

Body slender, subcylindrical; head flattened; two enlarged posterior maxillary teeth; eyes small, pupils vertical; tail long; dorsals weakly keeled; keels more pronounced at back; dorsum glossy black, with 22–48 irregular cross-bars on body and tail, or reticulated or spotted pattern; belly blotched. **DIET** Includes snakes, geckos and skinks. **DISTRIBUTION** E Himalayas and NE India. **HABITAT AND HABITS** Found in evergreen forests at about 914–2,300m. Clutches comprise 4–14 eggs.

Banded Kukri Snake *Oligodon arnensis* 64cm (r)

Body stout, cylindrical; snout short and blunt; dorsals smooth; dorsum brown, usually with red or purple markings, lighter on flanks, with 32–41 black cross-bars or spots that break up on flanks into streaks, sometimes edged with cream; bars 1–5 scales wide; head has three arrow-shaped dark marks; belly cream with indistinct lateral spots. **DISTRIBUTION** Peninsular India. **HABITAT AND HABITS** Found in forests, as well as parks and gardens. **DIET** Includes rats, lizards and reptile eggs; also known to scavenge. Clutches comprise 3–9 eggs.

Himalayan Trinket Snake *Orthriophis hodgsonii* 210cm (r)

Body slender; snout rounded; ventral keels developed; dorsum olive-brown; some scales bordered with black and white, resulting in reticulated pattern; large dark blotch on mid-forehead; belly yellow with dark spots. **DIET** Includes rats, toads and skinks. **DISTRIBUTION** The Himalayas of N and E India. **HABITAT AND HABITS** Found in moist forests at 1,000–3,200m, in addition to edges of agricultural fields in vicinity of water. Oviparous.

Indian Rat Snake *Ptyas mucosa* 370cm (r)

Body slender; head elongated, distinct from neck; eyes large, pupils rounded; dorsals smooth; dorsum yellowish-brown, olivaceous-brown to black; posterior of body has dark bands or reticulated pattern; lip and flank scales dark edged; belly greyish-white or yellow. **DIET** Includes frogs, rats, bats, birds, lizards, turtles and snakes. **DISTRIBUTION** Throughout India. **HABITAT AND HABITS** Found in forests, scrubland, agricultural fields, parks and cities. Clutches comprise 5–18 eggs.

Olive Keelback Water Snake *Atretium schistosum* 100cm (r)

Body slender; snout short; nostrils slit-like, placed on top of snout; scales distinctly keeled, and strongest on posterior part of body and tail; dorsum olive-brown or greenish-grey, unpatterned or with two series of small black spots; occasionally, dark lateral streak; some individuals have red lateral line; outer row of scales and belly yellow, cream or red. **DIET** Includes frogs, tadpoles, fish, crustaceans and crabs. **DISTRIBUTION** India, Bangladesh, Nepal and Sri Lanka. **HABITAT AND HABITS** Found in lowlands associated with wetlands, to about 1,000m. Clutches comprise 10–32 eggs.

Himalayan Keelback *Rhabdophis himalayanus* 125cm (e)

Body stout; head distinct from neck; eyes large, pupils rounded; dorsals keeled; dorsum olive, olive-brown or dark brown, with two dorsolateral rows of orange-yellow spots, more numerous anteriorly; anterior body checkered; neck has yellow or orange collar, edged with black; black postocular stripe; lips yellow, edged with black; belly yellowish-white, darker towards tip. **DIET** Frogs, lizards and fish. **DISTRIBUTION** E and NE India. **HABITAT AND HABITS** Inhabits forests, particularly on rocky slopes. Oviparous.

Banded Wolf Snake

Banded Kukri Snake

Himalayan Trinket Snake

Indian Rat Snake

Olive Keelback Water Snake

Himalayan Keelback

Checkered Keelback Water Snake *Xenochrophis piscator* 150cm 🔴

Body stout; eyes have rounded pupils; nostrils directed slightly upwards; dorsal scales strongly keeled; dorsum olive-brown, with black spots arranged in 5–6 rows; head brown with black stripe from eye to upper lip, and from postoculars to edge of mouth. **DIET** Includes fish and frogs. **DISTRIBUTION** India; range extends from Afghanistan to S China and SE Asia. **HABITAT AND HABITS** Found in wetlands in plains, including flooded rice fields, ponds, marshes and rivers. Aquatic and active by day and night. Clutches comprise 30–80 eggs.

Indian Krait *Bungarus caeruleus* 175cm 🔴 🔵

Body slender, triangular in cross-section, with raised vertebral region; head indistinct from neck; eyes small, pupils rounded; dorsals smooth; vertebral scales enlarged, hexagonal; dorsum steely-blue, black or dark brown; upper lips cream; belly unpatterned cream. **DIET** Includes snakes, lizards, frogs and rodents. **DISTRIBUTION** India (except NE). **HABITAT AND HABITS** Found in plains, thinly wooded forests and agricultural fields. Nocturnal. Clutches comprise 6–15 eggs. Venom highly neurotoxic and causes respiratory failure.

Banded Krait *Bungarus fasciatus* 225cm 🔴 🔵

Body slender, triangular in cross-section, with raised vertebral region; tail short and stumpy; subcaudal scales undivided; forehead has 'V'-shaped mark; dorsum has alternating black-and-yellow bands that are subequal. **DIET** Water snakes, rat snakes, pythons, vine snakes, lizards, frogs and fish. **DISTRIBUTION** India (except extreme north, west and south). **HABITAT AND HABITS** Found in lowlands, including forests, swamps and vicinity of villages. Clutches comprise 4–14 eggs.

Monocled Cobra *Naja kaouthia* 230cm 🔴

Body stout; head indistinct from body; neck capable of dilating into hood; dorsals smooth; dorsum brown, greyish-brown, blackish-brown or black; some individuals have darker bands; hood marking light circle with dark centre; pale throat colour extends less far backwards than in the Spectacled Cobra (below). **DIET** Rodents, frogs, fish and snakes. **DISTRIBUTION** E to NE India. **HABITAT AND HABITS** Found in forests and often encountered in agricultural fields and plantations. Clutches comprise 12–33 eggs.

Spectacled Cobra *Naja naja* 220cm 🔴

Body stout; head indistinct from body; neck capable of dilating into hood; dorsals smooth; dorsum greyish-brown, brown-black or jet-black, without markings or with dark or light bands; hood marking light spectacle, which may occasionally be absent; pale throat colour extends further backwards than in the Monocled Cobra (above). **DIET** Rodents, frogs, birds, lizards, fish and snakes. **DISTRIBUTION** Peninsular, N and E India. **HABITAT AND HABITS** Dry forests and plantations, occasionally entering human habitation. Clutches comprise 12–30 eggs.

King Cobra *Ophiophagus hannah* 5.5m 🔴 🔵

Body stout in adults, slender in juvenile; head distinct from neck, which is capable of dilating into elongated hood; dorsals smooth; large pair of occipital scales; dorsum dark brown, olive-brown or grey-black, with pale yellow or orange bands in young that may or may not persist in adults. **DIET** Includes snakes and occasionally monitor lizards. **DISTRIBUTION** India. **HABITAT AND HABITS** Terrestrial as well as arboreal; sometimes found on branches of tall trees. Female constructs mound nest of leaves, where 24 eggs are produced.

Checkered Keelback Water Snake

Indian Krait

Banded Krait

Monocled Cobra

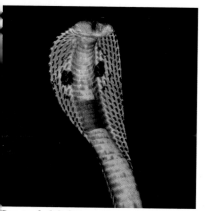

Spectacled Cobra

King Cobra

White-lipped Pit Viper *Cryptelytrops albolabris* 104cm 🅡

Body slender; head long, distinct from neck; small scales on forehead; dorsals keeled; tail prehensile; iris yellow; head and dorsum green; male has white stripe on first row of dorsals, which is indistinct or absent in female; belly green or yellowish-cream. DIET Mice, birds, lizards and frogs. DISTRIBUTION NE India and Bangladesh; also S China and SE Asia. HABITAT AND HABITS Found in forests, near streams. Ovoviviparous, producing 7–16 young.

Red-tailed Pit Viper *Cryptelytrops erythrurus* 105cm 🅡

Body slender; head long, narrow, distinct from neck; body stout; small scales on forehead; forehead scales keeled; dorsals strongly keeled; tail prehensile; iris yellow; dorsum bright green; belly pale green or yellow; tip of tail spotted or mottled with brown. DIET Rodents and birds. DISTRIBUTION NE India, Bangladesh, Bhutan and Nepal; also SE Asia. HABITAT AND HABITS Found in forests, generally in vicinity of streams. Reproductive habits unknown.

Northern Pit Viper *Cryptelytrops septentrionalis* 60cm 🅡

Body slender; head relatively long, narrower than neck; small scales on forehead; dorsals strongly keeled; tail prehensile; eyes yellow; dorsum green; belly pale green or yellow; upper lips pale green; pale yellow stripe runs from below loreal pit to back of head; tail-tip brown. DIET Rodents, lizards and birds. DISTRIBUTION NW India and Nepal. HABITAT AND HABITS Found in submontane forests, generally in vicinity of streams. Reproductive habits unknown.

Russell's Viper *Daboia russelii* 185cm 🅡 🅥

Body stout; head large, neck thin; tail short; pupils vertical; forehead with small scales; nostrils large; dorsals keeled; dorsum brown, with three rows of spots along body, a dark brown one along mid-line, and a blackish-brown or black one on each side; belly cream coloured, with numerous small, crescentic marks on belly scales. DIET Rodents, crabs, frogs, lizards and birds. DISTRIBUTION India. HABITAT AND HABITS Inhabits grassland, scrub forests and other open forests, entering agricultural fields with tall grass. Ovoviviparous, producing 6–40 young.

Saw-scaled Viper *Echis carinatus* 80cm 🅡

Body moderately stout; head oval, slightly distinct from neck; dorsals with sharp keels; eyes large; dorsum brown to greyish-brown, with series of pale, dark-edged blotches that are fused on each side to chevron-like marks; belly cream coloured. DIET Mice, squirrels, lizards, snakes, frogs, locusts and centipedes. DISTRIBUTION India (except wet zone of south and north-east). HABITAT AND HABITS Found in arid plains and deserts of peninsula and areas to its west. Clutches comprise 3–19 live young.

Himalayan Pit Viper *Gloydius himalayanus* 86cm 🅡

Body relatively stout; head somewhat flattened, distinct from neck, with enlarged scales; deep sensory pits between eye and nostril; dorsum brown, with darker patterns, typically with 23–45 cross-bars demarcated by their darker edges. DIET Rodents, skinks and centipedes. DISTRIBUTION N India, Bhutan, Nepal and Pakistan; also China and possibly Afghanistan. HABITAT AND HABITS Found in low to middle elevations of the Himalayas at 1,524–4,877m.

Ovoviviparous, producing 3–7 young.

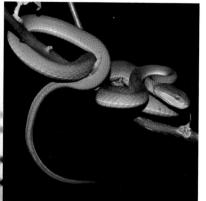

White-lipped Pit Viper

Red-tailed Pit Viper

Abhijit Das

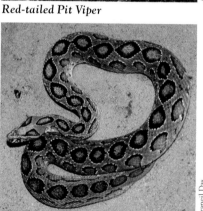

Northern Pit Viper

Russell's Viper

Indraneil Das

Saw-scaled Viper

Himalayan Pit Viper

Indraneil Das

Hump-nosed Pit Viper *Hypnale hypnale* 55cm **r**

Body stout; head distinct from neck; snout upturned; pupils vertical; dorsum light brown to blackish-brown, stippled with grey and brown; series of 20–33 oval or triangular marks on flanks, meeting at vertebral region; dark stripe from eye to jaws; dark cross-bands on tail. **DIET** Includes geckos and rodents. **DISTRIBUTION** Western Ghats of India. **HABITAT AND HABITS** Found in lowland forests and associated with leaf litter, tree buttresses, rocks and low vegetation, at elevations of 30–1,500m. Ovoviviparous, producing 4–17 young.

Brown-spotted Pit Viper *Protobothrops mucrosquamatus* 116cm **r**

Body slender; head relatively elongated; forehead scales reduced; dorsals strongly keeled; dorsum greyish-olive or brown, with series of large brown spots with dark edges; head sometimes has dark streak on sides; tail light brown with black spots; belly cream with light brown speckles. **DIET** Frogs, lizards, bats, rats and birds. **DISTRIBUTION** NE India. **HABITAT AND HABITS** Found in montane evergreen forests. Oviparous, producing clutches of 5–13 eggs.

Bamboo Pit Viper *Trimeresurus gramineus* 80cm **e**

Body slender; head long, narrow, distinct from neck; forehead scales small; dorsals weakly keeled; tail prehensile; eyes yellow; dorsum green or greenish-yellow, sometimes with dark brown blotches; upper lips cream coloured; dark postocular stripe; belly pale green or yellowish-cream. **DIET** Lizards and birds. **DISTRIBUTION** Peninsular India. **HABITAT AND HABITS** Found in forested habitats, including bamboo groves. Arboreal. Ovoviviparous, producing 6–20 young.

Mugger Crocodile *Crocodylus palustris* 5m **r** **v**

Snout relatively broad and heavy; forehead concave; ridges in front of eyes absent; dorsal scales in 16–17 rows on trunk; postoccipital scutes absent; juvenile light tan or brown with dark cross-bands on body and tail; adults grey to brown, usually without dark bands. **DIET** Mammals as large as deer and goats, small mammals, waterbirds, fish, snakes, lizards and turtles. **DISTRIBUTION** India. **HABITAT AND HABITS** Found in fresh water, including rivers, lakes, dams and reservoirs, generally away from tidal influence. Nest is a hole in the ground, where 10–50 eggs are laid.

Saltwater Crocodile *Crocodylus porosus* 6.2m **r** **v**

Head large; snout heavy; paired ridges from orbit to centre of snout; oval scales on back; juvenile brightly coloured, black spotted or blotched on pale yellow or grey background; colouration less bright in adults. **DIET** Includes turtles, birds and mammals. **DISTRIBUTION** Mangroves on east coast, as well as Andaman and Nicobar Islands. **HABITAT AND HABITS** Associated with mangrove forests, estuaries and sea coasts. Occasionally attacks humans. Constructs a mound nest, in which 60–80 eggs are deposited, and female guards nest.

Indian Gharial *Gavialis gangeticus* 7m **r** **v**

Body relatively slender, elongated; snout slender, parallel sided, with distinctive knob in adult male; about 100 sharp, interlocking teeth; dorsum olive to tan, with dark blotches or bands; belly pale. **DIET** Specialized fish eater. **DISTRIBUTION** Rivers Indus, Ganga, Brahmaputra and Mahanadi of N and E India. **HABITAT AND HABITS** Inhabits large rivers with sand banks. Congregates to mate and make nests during the dry season, when female lays 7–60 eggs in sandbanks along slow-moving sections of water.

Hump-nosed Pit Viper

Brown-spotted Pit Viper

Bamboo Pit Viper

Mugger Crocodile

Saltwater Crocodile

Indian Gharial

311

Crimson Rose *Pachliopta hector* 9–11cm **e**

Black butterfly with two white bands on forewing and two rows of bright crimson patches on hindwing, abdomen, thorax and head. Serrated outer margins. Sexes similar, but female larger and duller than male, with smaller crimson patches. Mimicked by *romulus* form of the Common Mormon (below), which is distinguished by its black thorax and abdomen. **DISTRIBUTION** Endemic to India. **HABITAT AND HABITS** Inhabits low-elevation forests and scrubland. Flight slow and fluttering. Roosts in large numbers. Distasteful to birds. Fond of *Lantana* flowers.

Common Mormon *Papilio polytes* 9–10cm **r**

Black butterfly with row of white spots along middle of hindwing. Male sometimes has yellow marks on hindwing instead of red. One male and three female forms. Known for the mimicry displayed by females. Form *cyrus* looks like male; *stichius* resembles the Common Rose *Pachliopta aristolochiae*; *romulus* resembles the Crimson Rose (above). All forms distinguished by black abdomen. **DISTRIBUTION** Throughout India. **HABITAT AND HABITS** Flies rapidly and close to the ground. Not eaten by birds. Males often congregate by the hundreds on wet sand.

Blue Mormon *Papilio polymnestor* 12–15cm **e**

Distinguished by velvety black wings dotted with bright blue spots. Black forewings and underside; yellowish band divided by black veins or strips at margin; light blue hindwings. Female bluish and grey, often with red patch at base of upperside forewing. **DISTRIBUTION** Found only in subcontinent. **HABITAT AND HABITS** Common at low elevation in gardens and forests. Flies low and fast along forest edges and paths, stopping briefly to visit *Lantana* and other flowers. Males come to wet sand.

Common Crow *Euploea core* 8.5–9.5cm **e**

Dark brown upperside, paler along terminal margins; forewing and hindwing with subterminal and terminal series of white spots. Underside similar, but colour more uniform; cell, costal and discal spots on both forewing and hindwing nearly always present. Sexes similar. **DISTRIBUTION** Throughout India. **HABITAT AND HABITS** Ascends to more than 2,000m. Migrant in parts of India. Flight slow and leisurely, but sustained over long distances. Both sexes fond of flowers. In evergreen forests in S India, thousands may congregate under shady banks by roadsides. Poisonous.

Striped Tiger *Danaus genutia* 7.5–9.5cm **r**

Tawny-orange with venation forming broad black bands; black wing borders dotted with two rows of white spots. Male has pouch on each of the secondary wings and distinct black-and-white spot on ventral side of secondary wing. Underside similar, but paler. **DISTRIBUTION** Throughout India. **HABITAT AND HABITS** Migrant species, with large congregations overwintering in some S Indian valleys. Flight weak, a few metres above the ground. Males congregate around plants containing pyrrolizidine alkaloids, such as *Crotalaria* spp. Poisonous. Both sexes fond of flowers.

Plain Tiger *Danaus chrysippus* 7–8cm **r**

Sexes similar, but male has additional black spot on hindwing. Hindwing margin not crenulate. Form *dorippus* lacks white band on forewing, and in form *alcippoides* all or most of hindwing is white. **DISTRIBUTION** Throughout India and Sri Lanka; Africa to southern Europe and Australia. **HABITAT AND HABITS** Flight slow, in keeping with its reputation for being highly poisonous. Both sexes fond of flowers. Plain Tiger is mimicked by several butterflies edible by birds, one of which – the **Danaid Eggfly** *Hypolimnas missipus* female – even copies the forms of this species.

Crimson Rose

Peter Smetacek

Common Mormon

Blue Mormon

Peter Smetacek

Common Crow

Striped Tiger

Peter Smetacek

Plain Tiger

Tawny Coster *Acraea violae* 5–6.5cm (r)

Male deep orange; female more yellowish-orange. Narrow wings with row of white spots on black hindwing border; head and thorax spotted black with pale yellow and white. Costal margin and termen black. **DISTRIBUTION** Throughout India. **HABITAT AND HABITS** Flight weak and fluttering, generally in vicinity of its food plant, but occasionally stragglers ascend to 2,400m in the Himalayas in dispersal flights. Fond of flowers. Poisonous; rarely attacked by predators. Mated female has tip of abdomen plugged by mate to prevent mating with other males.

Commander *Moduza procris* 6–7.5cm (r)

Sexes similar. Red-brown upperside; cells of wings and forewing have red bar edged black. Broad white band breaks into patches towards upper margin; diffused red and brown band along exterior of white band. Underside similar, but lacks red bar. **DISTRIBUTION** Peninsular India; the Himalayas from Uttarakhand eastwards to NE India. **HABITAT AND HABITS** Found around forests. Flight powerful, comprising a flap and glide interspersed with rapid series of flaps. Males visit wet sand; sometimes territorial, usually at level of bushes or small trees.

Great Eggfly *Hypolimnas bolina* 7–11cm (r)

Dorsal wing of male black with three pairs of white spots surrounded by iridescent bluish-purple (female paler and edged with white spots, with blue patch on each forewing). Ventral wing black, edged with white spots; diagonal white band runs across both wings. Male never has light rufous-brown ground colour on underside, which is characteristic of the **Danaid Eggfly** *H. missipus* male. **DISTRIBUTION** Throughout India. **HABITAT AND HABITS** Flight powerful and butterfly is capable of rapid progress. Both sexes fond of flowers.

Black Rajah *Charaxes solon* 7–8cm (r)

Sexes similar. Upperside dark brownish-black with yellow discal band stretching from forewings to hindwings. Band broken into spots towards apex of forewing. Hindwing has two similar-sized tails at veins, longer and more pointed in females. **DISTRIBUTION** Throughout plains of India, except arid regions and at low elevation along the Himalayas from Himachal Pradesh to NE India. **HABITAT AND HABITS** Males come to wet sand. Both sexes perch on high trees and descend readily to feed on over-ripe fruits, dung, carrion and tree sap.

Common Wanderer *Pareronia hippia* 6.5–8cm (r)

Pale blue upperside with well-defined black veins. Both sexes have four pale spots on black margin below forewing apex. Female white with thicker black marking on veins. Round white spots on black margin below forewing apex. **DISTRIBUTION** Throughout India, except arid parts of Indo-Gangetic Plain. **HABITAT AND HABITS** Prefers open forests at low elevation, but also ventures into semi-urban gardens. Male's flight hurried, usually within forest. Female's flight slow, mimicking that of the **Glassy Tiger** *Parantiga aglea*. Both sexes visit flowers occasionally.

Common Jay *Graphium doson* 7–8cm (r)

Upperwings black with broad bluish-green band running from sub-apical area of forewing to basal area of hindwing. On forewing, black border has row of blue spots. Underside has similar spotting against dark brown base, with spots larger and more silvery green. Sexes similar. **DISTRIBUTION** Most of India. Has recently colonized Delhi. **HABITAT AND HABITS** In its range, common in forested areas of moderate to heavy rainfall, and confined to low elevations.

Flight rapid and jerky. Males visit wet mud. Both sexes fond of flowers.

Tawny Coster

Commander

Great Eggfly

Black Rajah

Common Wanderer

Common Jay

315

Tailed Jay *Graphium agamemnon* 8.5–10cm **r**

Hindwing has tail. Bright green spots on wings on black base. Underside has similar green spots on purplish-brown base; antennae, head, thorax and abdomen black; thorax above and abdomen sides streaked greenish-grey; lacks hindwing tails. Sexes similar. **DISTRIBUTION** All India. **HABITAT AND HABITS** In its range, occurs in humid forests and rural landscapes. Common at low elevations. Flight swift and skipping, and butterfly rarely settles. Females ascend the Himalayas to more than 2,000m in search of host plants. Both sexes fond of flowers.

Common Baron *Euthalia aconthea* 5.5–8cm **r**

Ground colour varies from plain brown to greenish with a broad obscure post-discal band on both wings. Female larger than male and pale buff brown, with larger white spots on forewing. Underside paler with submarginal series of black spots on forewings and hindwings. Subspecies *anagama* is from N Western Ghats and peninsular India, *garuda* from NE India. **DISTRIBUTION** Throughout India. **HABITAT AND HABITS** Males territorial and females found in immediate vicinity of host plant, the Mango tree. Flight powerful. Both sexes fond of over-ripe fruits.

Gaudy Baron *Euthalia lubentina* 6–8cm **r**

Male has dark greenish-brown upperside. Bar across middle of forewing and bar beyond apex of the cell crimson bordered with black. Crescent-shaped black loop on hindwing. Underside dark purplish-brown; markings larger and more clearly defined. Head, thorax and abdomen dark greenish-brown. Female similar, but paler. **DISTRIBUTION** Peninsular India; the Himalayas from Himachal Pradesh eastwards. **HABITAT AND HABITS** Flight powerful, usually high around tree tops in forests. Both sexes fond of over-ripe fruits and tree sap.

Common Jezebel *Delias eucharis* 6.6–8.3cm **r**

Female brighter coloured than male with more black areas along veins in both wings. Male has more white, and no black on basal parts of hindwing. Underside pattern distinctive in both sexes. Forewing marked in white patches, amid black veins. Red marks along bottom edge of under hindwing heart shaped on black background. Sexes similar. **DISTRIBUTION** Throughout India. **HABITAT AND HABITS** Flies high around trees in search of its larval host plants. Distasteful to predators. Both sexes fond of flowers.

Painted Jezebel *Delias hyparete* 7–8cm **r**

White wings on upperside with veins black dusted towards outer margins. Female more heavily black dusted on veins. Inner edge of red hindwing-band not bordered with black. Underneath, wings are white with black-dusted veins. In hindwing, basal half is bright yellow with bright orange-red marginal border. **DISTRIBUTION** Eastern Ghats from Tamil Nadu to W Bengal; low elevations in the Himalayas. **HABITAT AND HABITS** Flight slow, usually high among trees. Distasteful to predators. Male visits wet sand. Both sexes fond of flowers.

Yellow Pansy *Junonia hierta* 4.5–6cm **r**

Upperside black, yellow and orange, with blue, circular patch on forewings. Underside of wing is greyish-brown. Hindwing greyish-yellow. Sexes similar, but female duller than male with more defined eye-spots. Underside differs from that of the **Blue Pansy** *J. orithya* in forewing being yellow, without white band and reddish bars. **DISTRIBUTION** Throughout India. **HABITAT AND HABITS** Found in the Himalayas to more than 2,000m, but it is unlikely that it breeds there. Common in sunny, open places. Flight rapid, near the ground. Both sexes fond of flowers.

Tailed Jay

Gaudy Baron

Painted Jezebel

Common Baron

Peter Smetacek

Common Jezebel

Milind Bhakare

Yellow Pansy

Mohit Patel

Peacock Pansy *Junonia almana* 6–6.5cm **r**

Upperside rich yellowish-brown with darker brown edges. Four distinct costal bars on forewings. Prominent 'peacock' eye-spot near tornal area. Underneath, wings are duller and costal bars are paler. Wet-season form underside has eye-spots; dry-season form has angular wings, and underside resembles a dry leaf. Sexes similar. **DISTRIBUTION** Throughout India. **HABITAT AND HABITS** Open, sunny places near forests at low elevations. Flight swift, flap and glide. Usually occurs singly, although males do not appear to be strongly territorial. Both sexes fond of flowers.

Common Emigrant *Catopsilia pomona* 5.5–8cm **r**

All three forms have no mottling on underside. Sexes dissimilar. Male and female *crocale* have plain, unmarked underside. Male and female *pomona* have red-ringed silver spots in centre of wings on underside. Female *catilla* has large purple blotches on underside of hindwings. Male upperside chalky-white with narrow black border to forewing. Female *crocale* upperside white with broad black markings on forewing that are very variable. Female *pomona* and *catilla* uppersides identical, lemon-yellow with dark border and dark spot on forewing. **DISTRIBUTION** Throughout India. **HABITAT AND HABITS** Flight powerful. Descends to flowers and wet sand.

Mottled Emigrant *Catopsilia pyranthe* 5–7cm **r**

Underside pale greenish, mottled with dark lines. Form *pyranthe* has small dark speck in centre of wings on underside and black antennae; form *gnoma* has red ring and red antennae and upperside black forewing border in form of separate dark marks. Sexes dissimilar. Female has indistinct series of 3–4 dark specks below apex of upperside forewing. **DISTRIBUTION** Throughout India. **HABITAT AND HABITS** Both sexes visit flowers and are fond of wet sand.

Common Grass Yellow *Eurema hecabe* 4–5cm **r**

Sexes similar, although female often has broader black margins to wings than male. Very variable. Dry-season form often has rust-coloured patch near apex of underside forewing. Underside forewing has two dark marks in cell, one or both of which may be absent. Black border on upper forewing variable, with or without an excavation in middle. **DISTRIBUTION** Common all India. **HABITAT AND HABITS** Favours open areas, stream edges and hedgerows, where it flies near the ground. Fond of wet sand, where hundreds of males congregate.

Large Cabbage White *Pieris brassicae* 6.5–7.5cm **r**

Large; forewing apex sharply angled. Male's upper forewing has no black spots; female has two black spots and black mark along dorsum. **DISTRIBUTION** Throughout the Himalayas; winter visitor to Gangetic Plain as far south as Delhi. **HABITAT AND HABITS** One of the few butterflies of economic importance, because its larvae feed on cabbages. Flight strong, jerky and generally a few metres above the ground. One of the most common butterflies in temperate Himalayan forests in spring. Rarely visits wet sand. Fond of flowers.

Indian Cabbage White *Pieris canidia* 4.5–5.5cm **r**

Female has two black spots on upper forewing; in male lower spot is almost obsolete. Forewing apex not as sharply angular as in the Large Cabbage White (above). **Small Cabbage White** *P. rapae* smaller, with reduced black apex to forewing. **DISTRIBUTION** In India, on southern slopes of the Himalayas, generally above 1,000m, venturing on to Gangetic Plain as far south as Delhi and upper reaches of Nilgiris, Palani and Anamalai hills in S India. **HABITAT AND HABITS** Flight jerky and erratic, with butterflies settling often to bask.

Peacock Pansy

Mottled Emigrant

Large Cabbage White

Peter Smetacek

Common Emigrant

Peter Smetacek

Common Grass Yellow

Muhammad Ackram

Small Cabbage White

Butterflies & Other Insects

319

Golden Birdwing *Troides aeacus* 15–17cm **r**

Male has black forewings, with whitish-bordered veins. Bright yellow hindwings. Underside of wings similar. Female larger with dark brown or black wings. Head, thorax and abdomen mainly black, with small red patches on thorax and yellow underside of abdomen. **DISTRIBUTION** The Himalayas, at 1,200–2,750m in W Himalayas, descending to plains in Assam. **HABITAT AND HABITS** Fond of flowers of *Lantana*, thistles and horse chestnuts. Males can be seen settled on damp grass early in the morning. Distasteful to birds.

Southern Birdwing *Troides minos* 14–19cm **r**

Male has plain yellow hindwings with broad black border. Female has row of large dark spots across hindwing. In both sexes hindwing on upperside has soft, silky, long brownish-black hairs from base along dorsal area. Females are the largest butterflies on the subcontinent. **DISTRIBUTION** Western Ghats from Maharashtra southwards. **HABITAT AND HABITS** Common at low elevations in humid forests. Visits flowers early in the morning, and soars about tree tops during daytime. Powerful flight. Distasteful to birds.

White Orange-tip *Ixias marianne* 5–5.5cm **r**

White upperside with large orange patch on forewing bordered with thick black line. Female has four black spots in orange area on upper forewing. Underside yellow, mottled darker, with pale orange area on forewing. White patches on distal band sometimes greatly reduced. Similar orange-tips are distinguished by smaller size and different undersides. **DISTRIBUTION** Endemic to Indian subcontinent. **HABITAT AND HABITS** Open, semi-arid country. Flight rapid, near the ground. Males occasionally visit wet sand. Both sexes fond of flowers.

Common Gem *Poritia hewitsoni* 3.1–3.8cm **r**

Male has dark iridescent blue upperside, with submarginal and apical spots. Underside brown with variable pale lineation. Female brown above, with a few blue spots. Upper forewing has yellow discal patch above a blue area. Black markings on upperside variable. **DISTRIBUTION** Uttarakhand to Arunachal Pradesh. **HABITAT AND HABITS** Occurs at low elevations, ascending the Himalayas to 1,500m. Flight rapid and powerful. Usually in the forest canopy but descends to water. No other known attractants. Males territorial.

Common Copper *Lycaena phlaeas* 2.6–3.4cm **r**

Unmistakable, with its bright copper-coloured forewings. Hindwings dark with orange border. Row of blue spots may be present on hindwing. Sexes similar, but female generally has brighter orange on upperside forewing than male. **DISTRIBUTION** Throughout India along the Himalayas. **HABITAT AND HABITS** Occurs on sunny, open hillsides. Flight brisk and not sustained. Both sexes visit flowers and generally found in vicinity of their larval host plant, *Rumex.*

Constable *Dichorragia nesimachus* 6.5–8.5cm **r**

Ground colour dark olive-green with bluish sheen on upper half of hindwing. Both wings with black markings and white zigzagging lines on outer margins. Dark olive-brown underside with more prominent white forewing markings. Sexes similar. **DISTRIBUTION** Along the Himalayas from Himachal Pradesh to NE India. **HABITAT AND HABITS** In west, ascends to 1,800m, but most common at low elevations in NE India. Butterfly of dense forests that ventures into clearings. Flight fast, using a flap-and-glide technique. Males often territorial. Males visit wet sand. Both sexes fond of over-ripe fruits and tree sap.

Golden Birdwing

Southern Birdwing

Susanth Kumar

White Orange-tip

Common Gem

Parixit Kafley

Common Copper

Constable

Ngangom Aomoa

Kaiser-i-Hind *Teinopalpus imperialis* 9–12cm r

Mainly metallic green with yellow patch and single tail to hindwing. Male has prominent yellow-tipped green tail on hindwing as well as four tooth-like projections. Underside forewing mainly orange-brown. Female larger with two prominent tails, and lacks yellow patch on hindwing. **DISTRIBUTION** Nepal to Arunachal Pradesh. **HABITAT AND HABITS** Montane butterfly, usually at about 2,000m. Males fond of hill-topping, spending the morning circling a prominent tree. Females less often seen and seem to prefer forests. Both sexes attracted to over-ripe fruits.

Bhutan Glory *Bhutanitis lidderdalii* 9–11cm r

Sexes similar. Upperside black with thin whitish striations running across wings. Long rounded forewings and many-tailed hindwings. Hindwing has prominent, yellow-orange patch. Underside duller and greyer, with pronounced striations. **DISTRIBUTION** Sikkim eastwards. **HABITAT AND HABITS** Restricted to elevation above 1,800m in the Himalayas, where its larval host plant grows. Found in dense forests, where it sails about above the tree tops with a weak, fluttering flight. Both sexes rarely visit flowers.

Large Salmon Arab *Colotis fausta* 4–5cm r

Upperside salmon-buff, underside pale yellow. Male has small brown patch on base of forewing. Black spot on forewing and dark markings on margins. Sexes similar in N Indian subspecies *fausta*. S Indian female subspecies *fulvia* white. In S India, dark area on upperside forewing margin has three orange or white spots. **DISTRIBUTION** Punjab as far east as Madhya Pradesh, southwards to drier parts of peninsular India. **HABITAT AND HABITS** Flight low and rapid; settles often to bask. Neither sex visits wet sand. Both sexes visit flowers.

Small Salmon Arab *Colotis amata* 3.5–5cm r

Salmon-pink butterfly with broad black borders on outer and upper margins of upperside of forewing. Black patch at base of forewing touching upper border. Sexes similar, but on upperside entire hindwing of male is bordered with black; in female, dark border begins at apex. On underside, female has series of discal brown spots across both wings. In female form *pallida*, ground colour is white. **DISTRIBUTION** Punjab to W Bengal; peninsular India. **HABITAT AND HABITS** Scrubland. Active during hottest part of summer days. Visits flowers.

White Arab *Colotis phisadia* 4–5cm r

Sexes similar. White ground colour and large pale spot in middle of dark forewing border distinguish this species. The **Blue-spotted Arab** C. *protractus* (deserts of W India) has plain underside, pink upperside ground colour, and distinctive blue spots and blue suffusion on upperside. **DISTRIBUTION** Drier parts of N India as far east as Uttar Pradesh, south to Gujarat and Maharashtra. **HABITAT AND HABITS** Hot, arid zones. Flight rapid, low among bushes and scrub; active on hot, sunny days.

Common Peacock *Papilio polyctor* 9–13cm r

Upper hindwing blue patch may or may not be connected to inner margin, but never by sharply defined, thin green line. Female lacks two woolly black streaks across lower half of diffuse green band on upper forewing. On underside, inner half of forewing is plain, with no markings in cell. The **Krishna Peacock** P. *krishna* has green band across forewing on upperside, represented as similar yellow band on underside of forewing. **DISTRIBUTION** Along the Himalayas. **HABITAT**
AND HABITS Swarms at wet mud; visits *Lantana* and marigold flowers.

Kaiser-i-Hind

Bhutan Glory

Large Salmon Arab

Small Salmon Arab

Blue-Spotted Arab

Common Peacock

Common Banded Peacock *Papilio crino* 9–10cm (e)

Narrow, sharply defined peacock-green bands across uppersides of both wings. Some males have woolly streaks across green band on forewing. Hindwing has bluish-green band. Underside pale brown to blackish brown with scattered yellowish scales. Antennae, head, thorax and abdomen dark brownish-black, with a sprinkling of glittering green scales. Sexes similar. **DISTRIBUTION** Drier parts of peninsula India south of Orissa and Karnataka. **HABITAT AND HABITS** Butterfly of hot, dry regions. Flight swift, near the ground. Not attracted to wet sand.

Tamil Yeoman *Cirrochroa thais* 6–7cm (r)

Male has rich bright fulvous upperside, with dark brown outer margin on forewing. Hindwing has thin dark brown outer margin, with two subsequent bands of wavy markings and another band of spot markings. Underside is shades of reddish-ochre washed with pale grey. Sexes similar; female more heavily marked on upperside than male. **DISTRIBUTION** Endemic to Western Ghats and hills of S India. **HABITAT AND HABITS** Dense forests at low elevations. Flight moderately powerful. Females usually seen within forests. Males attracted to wet sand and perspiration.

Malabar Tree Nymph *Idea malabarica* 11–16cm (e)

Primarily white butterfly with black markings. Forewing has narrow black margins on both sides of veins, a dusky streak along dorsum and large sub-basal spots. Antennae black; head and thorax streaked and spotted with black. Sexes similar, but female has broader wings than male. **DISTRIBUTION** Western Ghats. **HABITAT AND HABITS** Dense evergreen forests with heavy rainfall, where males take up a beat in clearings. Flight very slow, almost floating while patrolling or courting, but can be powerful when travelling. Both sexes visit flowers.

Malabar Raven *Papilio dravidarum* 8–10cm (e)

Sexes similar and mimic the Common Crow (p. 294). Distinguished from the Common Crow by arrowhead-shaped white marks on hindwing. Upper forewing has small white spot (in some individuals) and row of marginal white spots decreasing in size towards apex. Outer halves of wings have dusting of yellowish-brown scales. **DISTRIBUTION** Evergreen forests along seaward face of Western Ghats from Goa to Kerala. **HABITAT AND HABITS** Ascends to shola forest in Anamalai hills. Males attracted to wet sand. Both sexes fond of flowers.

Great Nawab *Polyura eudamippus* 10–12cm (r)

Sexes similar, although female considerably larger than male. Upperside black forewing border has two rows of pale spots. On underside, two vertical brown bands across forewing are never connected to form an 'H'. **DISTRIBUTION** Uttarakhand to NE India. **HABITAT AND HABITS** Inhabitant of forested hills at low elevation. Flight swift and powerful. Males are avid mud puddlers. Settles with wings closed. Both sexes fond of over-ripe fruits, tree sap, dung and animal carcasses. Males visit damp sand. They often settle in damp grass.

Indian Red Admiral *Vanessa indica* 5.5–6.5cm (r)

Upper forewing dark brown in colour. Upper hindwing brown with black-spotted red border. Antennae black, tipped with pale ochre; head, thorax and abdomen with dark olive-brown pubescence. Sexes similar. **DISTRIBUTION** Hills of Karnataka and Kerala, and along the Himalayas to NE India; Sri Lanka. **HABITAT AND HABITS** Occurs from 400m to over 2,500m. Forest insect that also ventures into gardens. Flight powerful and swift. Highly territorial and always found singly at the level of bushes in sunny glades.

Common Banded Peacock

Tamil Yeoman

Chinmayi S.K

Malabar Tree Nymph

Malabar Raven

C. Susanth Kumar

Great Nawab

Indian Red Admiral

Peter Smetacek

Blue Admiral *Kaniska canace* 6–7.5cm 🔴

The only butterfly with non-iridescent blue band across wings. Upperside black with bluish sheen; jagged outer margins on all wings. Blue band in distal area larger in female than in male. Underside is shades of black, grey and brown. Sexes similar. Himalayan subspecies *canace* has moderate blue band; S Indian subspecies *viridis* has narrow greeenish-blue band on forewing. **DISTRIBUTION** Hills of S India; Himalayan NE India. **HABITAT AND HABITS** Forest insect. Males come occasionally to wet sand; strongly territorial. Fond of over-ripe fruits and tree sap.

Orange Oakleaf *Kallima inachus* 8.5–11cm 🔴

Wings shaped and marked with veins to resemble dead leaf when closed. Orange band and deep blue base across upperside forewing distinctive. Two white ocelli, along margin of apical black band, and bordering orange and deep blue areas. Underside highly variable, individually and seasonally. Sexes similar, but female larger than male. **DISTRIBUTION** The Himalayas to NE India; C Indian hills to Gujarat; Maharashtra. **HABITAT AND HABITS** Himalayas to nearly 3,000m. Forest insect, never in open country. Both sexes fond of fruits and tree sap.

Common Pierrot *Castalius rosimon* 2.4–3.2cm 🔴

Sexes similar; female often more heavily marked than male, with smaller blue area at wing bases on upperside. Outer margins marked black on upperside with row of white lines on hindwing. Forewing has black basal line extending to thorax. Underside singular. Wet-season form more heavily marked than dry-season form. **DISTRIBUTION** N and E India. **HABITAT AND HABITS** Found in forests and open woodland. Flight weak and fluttering. Males congregate in large numbers on wet sand. Both sexes fond of flowers.

Red Pierrot *Talicada nyseus* 3–3.6cm 🔴

Upperside black with broad red band on outer margin of hindwing, underside with white patches on red marginal band. Forewing has two rows of white patches on black outer margin. Patches on underside highly variable. Sexes similar. Male distinguished by smaller orange area on upperside hindwing. **DISTRIBUTION** Throughout India except eastern coast and Bihar. **HABITAT AND HABITS** Flight weak and fluttering. Generally found in vicinity of its succulent host plants, within whose leaves the butterfly spends its early stages.

Owl Moth *Brahmaea wallichii* 16cm 🔴

Moth with well-developed eye-spots on front wings and characteristic pattern of black-brown stripes; light-brown margins of back wings display small, triangular white spots; robust body also black and brown, with characteristic orange-brown stripes. Eye-spots and stripes give it appearance of an owl. **DISTRIBUTION** N India. **HABITAT AND HABITS** Found in tropical and temperate forests. Larvae feed on *Fraxinus excelsior*, *Ligustrum* and common lilac. They are able to neutralize plant toxins produced by *Ligustrum*. Active at night; rests with outspread wings on tree trunks or on the ground by day. When disturbed, does not fly away, but shakes fiercely.

Harlequin Tiger Moth *Campylotes histrionicus* 16cm 🔴

Day-flying moth with multicoloured wings. Forewings have two long red streaks below upper margin; one red and yellow streak in cell; three yellow streaks below cell; red spot between veins; six white spots beyond cell and two on wing-tip; hindwing red streak below outer margin; two red streaks in cell; four below; red-and-yellow spot between veins. **DISTRIBUTION** The Himalayas.
HABITATS AND HABITS Trees; larvae feed on *Lyonia ovalifolia* and rhododendron species.

Blue Admiral

Ngangom Aomoa

Orange Oakleaf

Common Pierrot

Sarab Seth

Red Pierrot

Owl Moth

L Shyamlal CC

Harlequin Tiger Moth

Luna Moth *Actias selene* 16cm **r**

Male has white head, thorax and abdomen; pink palpi; prothorax with dark pink band; pink legs. Forewing very pale green, white at base; dark pink costal fascia; pale yellow ante-medial line; two slightly curved submarginal lines; pale yellow marginal band; dark red-brown lunule at end of cell with pinkish centre. Hindwing similar to forewing. Outer margin less excised and waved in female; yellow markings less developed. **DISTRIBUTION** Throughout India. **HABITAT AND HABITS** Found in tropical and montane forests. Host plants are sweetgum, rhododendrons, *Prunus*, *Malus*, *Coriaria*, *Pieris*, *Hibiscus*, *Salim*, *Crataegus*, *Photinia*, *Juglans regia* and *Musa*.

Tropical Tiger Moth *Asota caricae* 5.5–5.8cm **r**

Palpi with black spots on first and second joints. Forewings brownish-fuscous. Basal orange patch with two sub-basal black spots and series of three spots on its outer edge. Veins streaked with white. White spot at lower angle of cell. Hindwings orange-yellow. Black spot at end of cell, one beyond, one below vein two and submarginal irregular series, which sometimes becomes nearly complete marginal band. Veins crossing band yellowish. **DISTRIBUTION** Throughout India. **HABITAT AND HABITS** Found in forest and agricultural areas. Larvae recorded on *Ficus*, *Broussonetia*, *Mesua*, *Tectona* and *Shorea* species. Pupation occurs in slight cocoon, fixed to leaf.

Ruddy Marsh Skimmer *Crocothemis sevilia* 3.8–4cm **r**

Medium-sized red dragonfly. Male has blood-red eyes; abdomen and thorax; female's eyes brownish-green. Abdomen yellowish-brown with black stripe down middle and brownish-green thorax. Transparent wings with amber-yellow base. Brown wing-spot. **DISTRIBUTION** E India. **HABITAT AND HABITS** Adults seen near ponds, tanks, wells and paddy fields. Breeds in same locales. Adults found through the year.

Kodagu Club Tail *Gomphidia kodaguensis* 4–4.4cm **V**

Large dragonfly with bottle-green eyes, black thorax with yellow markings, yellow stripes on sides and black abdomen; most segments marked with dorsal yellow spots. Female has more yellow markings and stouter abdomen than male. Clear, transparent wings; female has longer wingspan than male. **DISTRIBUTION** Restricted to Western Ghats. Near Threatened in status. **HABITAT AND HABITS** Adults found in and near ponds, lakes and streams in hilly areas.

Blue-tailed Green Darner *Anax guttatus* 5–5.5cm **r**

Dragonfly with bluish-yellow eyes that meet at back, and light green thorax. First two abdominal segments green with blue-and-orange spots. Third segment has two triangular turquoise-blue spots. Segments 4–7 have several spots. Number of spots reduces from segment eight; male has amber-yellow patch on hindwing; red wing-spot. Female lacks amber-yellow patch. **DISTRIBUTION** Throughout India. **HABITAT AND HABITS** Diurnal. Adults found in May–November, near wells, marshes and ponds. Breeds in marshes. Voracious and agile predator.

Pied Paddy Skimmer *Neurothemis tullia* 2–2.5cm **r**

In male, base of wings opaque black bordered by white patch and end transparent; blackish-brown eyes; black thorax with cream midline; black abdomen with cream midline. In female, tips of all wings black; front edge of wing has sickle-shaped black spot; paler brown eyes; yellowish abdomen with black border. **DISTRIBUTION** Throughout India in plains. **HABITAT AND HABITS** Adults seen throughout the year; more in July–September. Found and breeds near ponds, marshes and paddy fields. Perches close to the ground. Slow, weak flier.

Luna Moth

Tropical Tiger Moth

Ruddy Marsh Skimmer

Kodagu Club Tail

Blue-tailed Green Darner

Pied Paddy Skimmer

329

Stream Glory *Neurobasis chinensis* 4.4–5cm 🅮

Abdomen of male damselfly iridescent green with black underside; transparent forewings; broader hindwings; rounded tips, opaque with basal side iridescent peacock-green. Underside of hindwing black with gold specks; blackish-brown eyes. Female has dull iridescent-green abdomen; amber coloured with opaque white wing-spot; brown eyes. **DISTRIBUTION** Western Ghats. **HABITAT AND HABITS** Male flashes wings to attract female. Common in hill streams at to 2,000m. Lays eggs on submerged stones and logs in mountain streams. Seen in May–November.

Stream Ruby *Heliocypha bisignata* 3.5–3.8cm 🅮

Male damselfly has black abdomen with yellow markings on underside; black thorax with red stripes; transparent forewings; hindwings with two iridescent red streaks; blackish-brown eyes. Female similar to male, but with duller abdomen and transparent, amber-coloured forewings and hindwings. **DISTRIBUTION** Forested streams in Western Ghats. **HABITAT AND HABITS** Common in hill streams at higher altitudes, where it also breeds. Seen throughout the year.

Malabar Torrent Dart *Euphaea fraseri* 2.9–3.4cm 🅮

Medium-sized damselfly. Abdomen in male bright red with black end. Thorax black above, brown below; stripes above and along sides. Wings transparent with black wing-spot; brown tips to forewings, iridescent copper above, blue below on hindwings. Female's abdomen yellow up to sixth segment; seventh tipped black, rest all black. Thorax yellow above, brown below. **DISTRIBUTION** Endemic to Western Ghats. **HABITAT AND HABITS** Common in hill streams where it breeds. Adults found in May–December. Flits near water; eats small insects caught in flight.

Travancore Bambootail *Esme mudiensis* 3–3.5cm 🅮

Abdomen black, marked with azure-blue on segments one and two. Segments 3–6 have very narrow baso-dorsal annules. Segments 8–10 blue. Narrow black basal annule on segment eight. Ventral borders of all segments broadly black; velvet-black on dorsum with azure-blue on sides of thorax; wings have diamond-shaped pterostigma; wings transparent. Black anal appendages; black-capped blue eyes. Female similar to male, but more robustly built. **DISTRIBUTION** Endemic to Western Ghats. **HABITAT AND HABITS** Occurs around hill streams; riparian vegetation.

Black Torrent Dart *Dysphaea ethela* 3.2–4cm 🅮

Abdomen black, marked with yellow apical annules up to segment eight; yellow lateral stripes up to segment six. Anal appendages black; thorax black, marked with narrow greenish-yellow stripes; yellow stripe on base of lateral sides. Wings transparent, but evenly coloured brown; eyes brown, capped pale grey. Female short and robust; yellow marks more broad and vivid; yellow lateral stripes continued to segment seven. **DISTRIBUTION** Western Ghats. **HABITAT AND HABITS** Streams and breeds in evergreen forests.

Antlion *Palpares pardus* 6cm 🆁

Adult brown; long antennae with long hairs at bases; pronotum broader than long, hairy, with median and narrow lateral black stripes; forewing has several quadrate brown spots; brown dots at base and along hind margin besides a few large brown spots; legs brown to blackish. Larvae found in shallow funnels in sand; pincer-like mandibles held in front of head. **DISTRIBUTION** Peninsular and Himalayan India. **HABITAT AND HABITS** Feed on ants and other insects that fall into their pits. Larvae found in sandy areas.

Stream Glory

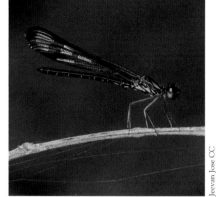

Stream Ruby

Malabar Torrent Dart

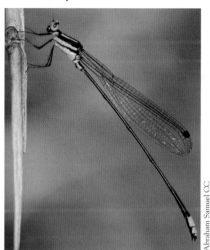

Travancore Bambootail

Black Torrent Dart

Antlion

Jeevan Jose CC

Abraham Samuel CC

Alandmanson CC

Water Strider *Gerridae* spp. 1cm ⓡ

Black head, brownish-black elongated body and no wings. Legs held outwards with second and third pairs as long as body; first pair of legs short and used to capture prey. **DISTRIBUTION** Throughout India. **HABITAT AND HABITS** Found in freshwater ponds and other freshwater habitats. Feeds by piercing and sucking. Predates on small insects in the water. Able to use the surface of water for movement, creating hemispherical vortices on the water's surface that propel the insect forwards by as much as 1.5m/s. Leg surface coated with waxy secretion.

Oleander Aphid *Aphis nerii* 0.2cm ⓡ

Usually minute, pear-shaped, soft-bodied insects, yellowish-brown in colour. Two long, tail-like structures at rear end called cornicles produce the sugary waste substance called honeydew. **DISTRIBUTION** Throughout India. **HABITAT AND HABITS** Winged males and females appear together towards autumn. Aphids also have endosymbiotic bacteria called *Buchnera* that are present in their digestive tracts. These provide essential amino acids for the processing of phloem.

Cicada *Platypleura* spp. 2.1–2.2cm ⓡ

Large insects with head as wide as body. Antennae present between eyes. Wings membranous and transparent. Forewings larger than hindwings. Greenish-brown markings on dark brown-black body. **DISTRIBUTION** Throughout India. **HABITAT AND HABITS** Adults found in trees, while juveniles usually burrow into the ground. Seldom seen but heard in any wooded area. Male has tympanum, or drum, on abdomen that produces the cicada song to attract mates; this sounds like a loud buzz. Cicada lifecycle up to three years.

Painted Grasshopper *Poekilocerus pictus* 5–9cm ⓡ

Bright yellow grasshopper with blue-and-green spots and markings; short antennae; pronotum does not cover most of thorax; pale red hindwings; spear-shaped head; wings very well developed. Male smaller than female. **DISTRIBUTION** Throughout India. **HABITAT AND HABITS** Found on *Calatropis gigantea* or *C. procera*; uses compounds found in these plants to make itself distasteful to predators. Lays 70–200 eggs in pods; these hatch in September. Used to be commonly found in most parts of S India, even in cities.

Hooded Grasshopper *Crytacanthacris tatarica* 3.8–4cm ⓡ

Small to medium, leaf-green grasshopper. Pronotum expands into large, sharp 'hood' structure edged with yellow-orange, giving insect the general appearance of a leaf. Wings short and do not cover abdomen; antennae ensiform, green at bases, tinged with red-and-yellow tip; small eyes with oval yellow band around them; hind femur elongated, with teeth on both femur and tibia. **DISTRIBUTION** Throughout India. **HABITAT AND HABITS** Found on small shrubs; very well camouflaged. Severe pest of Teak and Sandalwood.

Mulberry Locust *Terratodes monticollis* 1.8–2.2cm ⓡ

Small locust with bright green body; black band arising from eye-base extending over pronotum to middle of metasoma, bordered on lower side by white streak on thorax; pronotum has red line beneath black band and above black band on metathorax; legs green; ventral side yellowish-green. Elongated head, as long as pronotum; antennae stout, filiform, and longer than head and pronotum together. **DISTRIBUTION** Peninsular India. **HABITAT AND HABITS** Found on mulberry plants.

Water Strider

Oleander Aphid

J. Poorani

Cicada

Painted Grasshopper

TNA Perumal

Hooded Grasshopper

Mulberry Locust

Rison Thumboor CC

Giant Ground Beetle (Domino Beetle) *Anthia sexguttata* 4cm 🔴

Blackish-grey eyes; upper side of thorax black with two white spots along sides; black elytra with four white spots along sides; prominent antennae, held straight ahead. Long legs held out at sides, built for rapid running; also keep body off the ground, especially in desert and other hot areas. Elytra or hardened forewings soldered together. Flightless. **DISTRIBUTION** S India. **HABITAT AND HABITS** Adults found in undergrowth; mostly in arid or scrub regions. Of economical importance: natural predator of caterpillars of some moths, primarily *Pyrausta machaeralis* Walker and *Hyblaea puera* Cramer, which are defoliators of Teak and other timber trees in S India.

Elephant Dung Beetle *Heliocopris bucephalus* 3–5cm 🔴

Blackish-grey eyes; upper side of thorax black with two white spots along sides; black elytra with four white spots along sides, two in front and two on rear; prominent antennae, held straight ahead. Long legs held out at sides; also keep body off the ground, especially in hot areas. Elytra or hardened forewings soldered together. Flightless. **DISTRIBUTION** S India. **HABITAT AND HABITS** Adults found in undergrowth; mostly in arid or scrub regions. Natural predator of caterpillars of some moths, which are defoliators of Teak and other timber trees in S India.

Green Jewel Bug Scutelleridae 0.5–2cm 🔴

Oval-shaped bug with triangular head. Antennae have 3–5 segments. Iridescent green with black spot and variable orange markings. End part of thorax forms a shield-like structure that completely covers abdomen and wings. Jewel bugs have four membranous wings underneath their scutellum or shield. **DISTRIBUTION** Bengal to Maharashtra, to Karnataka and Kerala. **HABITAT AND HABITS** Easily seen on flowers, leaves and branches.

Oriental Hornet *Vespa orientalis* 2.5–3.5cm 🔴

Adult has two pairs of wings. Drones and workers smaller than queen. Reddish-brown with distinctive thick yellow bands on abdomen and yellow patches on head between eyes; very strong jaws and will bite if provoked. Females (workers and the queen) have ovipositor; extends from end of abdomen and also used as stinger. Males (drones) distinguished from workers by number of segments on antennae. **DISTRIBUTION** Peninsular India. **HABITAT AND HABITS** Lives in nest that it digs underground. Paper nests sometimes constructed in protective hollows such as insides of hollow trees. Captures other insects. Adults eat nectar, honeydew and fruits.

Yellow Ichneumon Wasp *Xanthopimpla punctata* 1.8cm 🔴

Wasp with narrow body and even narrower waist. Female has long, yellow ovipositor; three dark ocelli on top of head and compound eyes; long antennae; mesothorax has three dark spots; abdomen has four black spots. **DISTRIBUTION** Kerala, Maharashtra. **HABITAT AND HABITS** Plays important role as biocontrol agent by parasitizing lepidopteran larvae or eggs. Ovipositor used to probe and lay eggs within host. Larvae develop and eat it from within, emerging as adults.

Indian Rose Mantis *Gongylus gongylodes* 5cm–11cm 🔴

Bizarre-looking mantis with large appendages attached to very narrow limbs. Particularly known for swaying body back and forth to imitate a stick moving in the wind. Predominantly brown, but green forms also seen. Male capable of flight. **DISTRIBUTION** S India. **HABITAT AND HABITS** Found in shrubbery. Feeds on flying insects. Not particularly aggressive; communal species living and breeding in large groups without unnecessary cannibalism.

Giant Ground Beetle (Domino Beetle)

Elephant Dung Beetle

Green Jewel Bug

Oriental Hornet

Yellow Ichneumon Wasp

Indian Rose Mantis

Banjh Oak *Quercus leucotrichophora* up to 30m 🔘

Evergreen tree that grows tall and is known to live for a very long time. Lance-shaped leaves have serrated edges; silver-grey underneath and arranged alternately. Flowers minute, appearing in spikes. Male catkins borne on branch tips; female flowers grow on bases of leaves. Fruits oval-shaped nuts, called acorns. **HABITAT** Grows at high altitudes in the Himalayan range. **USES** Wood used in building construction and for making agricultural tools. Wood pulp used to make hardboards. Acorns possess medicinal properties.

Chamrod *Ehretia laevis* 5–9m 🔘

Small tree of delicate proportions – light-coloured bark and knotted trunk are distinctive features. Leaves simple, oval with sharp tip, and arranged alternately. Small white flowers appear in clusters in spring. Blossoms open in the evening and fall by dawn, covering the ground beneath the tree in a carpet of fine white flowers. Fruits are small berries that turn yellow when ripe in loose, drooping clusters. **HABITAT** Occurs in dry deciduous forests of India. Drought and frost tolerant. **USES** Root and bark known to be medicinal.

Freshwater Mangrove *Barringtonia racemosa* 10–15m 🔘

Coastal tree with straight-growing trunk and dense, rounded crown. Large leathery leaves simple, oval in shape, with blunt-pointed tip. Flowers fragrant, similar to powder-puffs, comprising numerous white stamens that are pink at the ends; night blooming. Fruits curiously shaped, almost conical but angular. **HABITAT** Tree of moist tropical regions, growing near riverbanks and swamps; associated with mangroves in less saline conditions. **USES** Quick growing, and used as avenue tree along city roads.

Ber *Zyzyphus mauritiana* 5–8m 🔘

Deciduous with low, spreading crown. Dark green leaves simple, with silvery underleaves covered in fine hair. Flowers minute and whitish-green, appearing in clusters a couple of times a year. Oval fruits fleshy and edible; green ripening to yellow-orange in colour. **HABITAT** Native to India and most parts of Asia, and cultivated widely for its fruits. **USES** Fruits rich in vitamins, and eaten fresh, dried or preserved. Local communities use wood as firewood and leaves as fodder. Leaves, fruits and bark used in medicinal remedies.

Barna *Crataeva nurvala* 10–12m 🔘

Small tree often with crooked branches and light crown. Leaves compound and comprise three oval leaflets with acute pointed tips. Deciduous and sheds its leaves in winter. Dramatic blossoms eye-catching; white flowers turn yellow with time and have long, antennae-like stamens. Fruits globular, with seeds encased in a pulp. **HABITAT** Occurs naturally in dry deciduous forests in large parts of India. Prefers moist growing conditions alongside rivers and streams. **USES** Bark and roots are medicinal.

Mango *Mangifera indica* 20–30m 🔘

Evergreen tree with dense, rounded crown, grown for its celebrated fruits. Simple leaves long with pointed tips shaped like lances. Emits aromatic smell when crushed. Flowers minute, greenish-white and arranged in clusters. Oval-shaped fruits green, ripening to yellow-orange. Size and shape of fruits differ according to variety of Mango. **HABITAT** Native to India. Found wild in forests; cultivated widely throughout India. **USES** Wood considered an inferior-quality timber.

Banjh Oak

Freshwater Mangrove

Barna

Chamrod

Ber

Mango

Pradeep Sachdeva/ Vidya Tongbram

Pradeep Sachdeva/ Vidya Tongbram

Pradeep Sachdeva/ Vidya Tongbram

Amla *Phyllanthus emblica* 10–15m ⓝ

Medium-sized deciduous tree with drooping branches. Simple leaves small and oblong, and arranged in opposite pairs. Minute flowers produced in clusters. Fleshy, rounded fruits with segments grow around hard nut, in large clusters. **HABITAT** Found in deciduous forests of India and cultivated throughout subcontinent. **USES** Cultivated for fruits, a rich source of vitamins and minerals. Most parts of tree, including flowers, fruits, roots and bark, are medicinal. Fruits contain rejuvenating properties.

Indian Quince *Aegle marmelos* 10–15m ⓝ

Medium-sized tree with deciduous crown. Leaves compound, comprising three leaflets, and oval shaped with acute pointed tip. Flowers white and fragrant, similar to others in citrus family. Woody fruits round and large, and contain numerous seeds in yellow-orange pulp. Fruits take many months to ripen on the tree, hence the large hanging fruits are its characteristic feature. **HABITAT** Native to India; distributed in rainforests. **USES** Ripe orange pulp of fruits edible and eaten fresh or made into a summer drink.

Kaim *Mitragyna parvifolia* up to 20m ⓝ

Deciduous tree with rounded crown. Simple leaves vary in size and shape, and arranged in opposite pairs. Minute fragrant flowers appear in May–June, clustered spherically on long stalks to form a globe. Fruits are tiny pods clustered around sphere. Leaves and flowers resemble those of *Anthocephalus cadamba*, commonly known as the Kadamb. **HABITAT** Native to India, occurring in deciduous forests. Favours moist conditions. **USES** Wood medium hard and durable; used in light interior construction and carpentry work. Leaves used as fodder.

Arjun *Terminalia arjuna* up to 24m ⓝ

Evergreen tree often planted along roads. Leaves simple, oblong, with pointed tips, and arranged in opposite pairs. Minute flowers inconspicuous, appearing on spikes. Fruits an interesting star shape, prominently drooping in clusters. **HABITAT** Native to India. Grows naturally along waterbodies and streams; also cultivated. **USES** Leaves used as food for silkworms. Bark and gum have medicinal applications due to their astringent properties. Brown dye from bark used for tanning. Grown in parks and as avenue tree.

Indian Almond *Terminalia catappa* 15–25m ⓝ

Large tree of distinct form, with branches growing horizontally in defined tiers. Large leaves oval with rounded tips, and clustered at tips of branches; semi-deciduous, turning yellow and red before shedding. Small, whitish-green flowers clustered along curved spikes. Fruit large, almond shaped and green. **HABITAT** Coastal tree of moist tropical climates, growing in sandy, loamy soil. Naturalized in India. **USES** Fast growing; often planted along avenues and in parks as shade tree.

Queen's Crape Myrtle *Lagerstroemia speciosa* 10–15m ⓝ

Medium-sized deciduous tree celebrated for its profuse flowering. Simple large leaves with prominent veins, arranged in opposite pairs. Leaves turn red before they are shed. Attractive mauve-purple flowers with crinkled petals grow in clusters, and cover tree's crown. Spherical fruits growing in clusters turn woody when ripe. **HABITAT** Native to tropical Asian countries. Occurs in forests. Cultivated widely throughout subcontinent. Favours moist, damp climate.

USES Wood strong and durable.

Amla

Indian Quince

Kaim

Arjun

Indian Almond

Queen's Crape Myrtle

339

Elephant Apple Tree *Dillenia indica* 10–15m 🅝

Robust evergreen tree with low, spreading crown. Dark green leaves large and simple, with prominent veins and serrated edges; distinguishing feature of tree. Flowers white with yellow centres; faintly fragrant, and attract bees and other insects. Large, round fruits edible and known to be favourites among elephants in forests. **HABITAT** Native to evergreen forests of E and S of Indian peninsula. Grows into very large tree in its natural habitat. **USES** Fruits eaten and preserved for use in pickles.

Sal *Shorea robusta* 20–30m 🅝

Tall forest tree with straight-growing trunk. Large leaves simple and deciduous; oval in shape with pointed tips. Produces dramatic clusters of fragrant, cream-white flowers. Oval fruits with wings are a true characteristic of the dipterocarp family. **HABITAT** Native to India. Found in dry to moist deciduous forests, as well as in evergreen forests. Favours moist, sandy soil with good drainage. **USES** Important timber tree used in construction and – popularly – for railway sleepers. Heartwood durable and resistant to termites. Leaves used as fodder.

Banyan *Ficus benghalensis* 15–20m 🅝

Large evergreen tree with spreading canopy that sometimes covers acres of land. Strangler with aerial roots, spreading by means of roots that lower to the ground and develop into trunks, thus forming colony of trunks. Large, oval-shaped leaves simple with leathery texture. Fruits formed from cluster of flowers, with each flower in cluster producing a fruit; flowers mature into a single mass. Each fig thus forms an enclosure with numerous fruits within it. **HABITAT** Grows widely throughout India. **USES** Figs edible by humans.

Peepal *Ficus religiosa* 18–20m 🅝

Deciduous tree with rounded crown. Leaves simple, shaped like hearts and with acutely pointed tips. New leaves a flush of red and show prominent veins. Flowers and fruits typical of fig family and are borne directly on branches. **HABITAT** Grows widely throughout India. **USES** Of religious significance to both Hindu and Buddhist religions. Venerated tree best known as the Bodhi Tree under which Gautama Buddha attained enlightenment, in Bodhgaya.

Rubber Tree *Ficus elastica* 20–30m 🅝

Tree of gigantic proportions with aerial roots that snake down to form buttresses to support the large form. Leaves large, oval in shape, with thick, leathery texture. New leaves appear with red sheaths wrapped around them, rendering tree visually distinct. Figs similar to others in family and oval in shape. **HABITAT** Native habitat is foothills of the E Himalayas in NE India. **USES** White latex is drawn from tree to manufacture rubber; therefore it was widely cultivated.

Pilkhan Tree *Ficus virens* 20–25m 🅝

Large tree with dense, spreading crown. Trunk short, topped by overbearing crown of lush foliage. Network of aerial roots wraps around trunk. Leaves simple, elliptical in shape and taper to pointed tips. Leaves shed at end of winter; new leaves appear in spring in various shades of copper, maturing to fresh green. **HABITAT** Found in the Sub-Himalayan range of NW India and parts of C India. **USES** Fast-growing shade tree, often planted as avenue tree along roads and in parks. Common tree for landscapes due to it's unique exotic appearance,evergreen with tolerance to both sun and shade and is a good air purifier. Both the leaves and fruits are edible

and are often use in cooking.

Elephant Apple Tree

Banyan

Rubber Tree

Sal

Peepal

Pilkhan Tree

341

Iron Wood *Messua ferrea* 20–25m ⓷

Slender evergreen tree with beautiful foliage. Leaves simple, shaped like lances and arranged in opposite pairs. New leaves tender red and drooping. Mature leaves have silver-grey underleaf. Showy, fragrant flowers with white petals and yellow centres appear in February–June, depending on the part of the country. Oval fruits have pointed tips. **HABITAT** Native to India and parts of SE Asia. Distributed in tropical rainforests of E and S India, and in Western Ghats. USES Hard and durable wood is referred to as ironwood.

Drumstick *Moringa oleifera* 10–15m ⓷

Common deciduous tree with uneven form and light crown. Compound leaves complex, comprising leaflets that are further divided into leaflets in opposite pairs. Small white flowers appear in clusters 2–3 times a year. Fruits are long pods, like beans, commonly known as drumsticks. **HABITAT** Native to India. Tolerates wide range of climates and soil types, and cultivated in most of India. USES Drumsticks an essential ingredient of S Indian cooking.

Golden Champak *Michelia champaca* 25–30m ⓷

Large-leaved evergreen tree. Simple leaves acutely pointed and arranged in spirals. Fragrant flowers appear in April–May; colours range from creamy-white to orange. Fruits oval shaped and clustered along a spike. **HABITAT** Native to India, and distributed along foothills of the NE Himalayas and Western Ghats. Popularly cultivated in south for its flowers. USES Fine-grained wood used in furniture making. Bark, leaves and flowers used in medicinal remedies. Flowers often worn in the hair as an adornment.

Neem *Azadirachta indica* 10–15m ⓷

Medium-sized tree with nearly evergreen crown; one of the most common trees planted in India. Feathery leaves compound in nature; leaflets lance shaped with serrated edges, and arranged in near-opposite pairs. Flowers small and white. Oblong fruits berry-like; turn yellow when ripe. **HABITAT** Widely cultivated and naturalized in most parts of India; occurs wild in dry forest of Deccan Peninsula, Myanmar. USES Wood very durable. Leaves contain compound called azadirachtin that repels insects.

Persian Lilac *Melia azedarach* up to 15m ⓷

Medium-sized tree with light deciduous crown. Leaves compound with leaflets arranged in opposite pairs; similar to Neem (above) leaves but have sharply serrated edges. Minute flowers faintly fragrant; white petals tinged with hint of mauve; purple centres. Green berries turn yellow when ripe, and droop in bunches – a characteristic of this tree. **HABITAT** Native to large part of SE Asia, including India. Can adapt to various soil and climatic conditions. USES Wood used to manufacture agricultural tools and tool handles.

Silk Cotton Tree *Bombax ceiba* 20–30m ⓷

Large tree with spiky trunk supported by buttressed roots. Branches arranged in tiers, with light crown of leaves. Compound leaves palmate – a common characteristic of the mallow family. Flowers large and showy, with thick, waxy petals whose colours range from yellow to scarlet; bloom in February–March and are rich in nectar, attracting a variety of birds and bees. Fruits angular, woody pods containing seeds attached to silky floss. **HABITAT** Native to tropical Asia, and widely distributed. USES Planted in city parks and gardens. Important medicinal plant used in many ailments. Fibres from the fruit are woven into thread and used for stuffing pillows and mattresses.

Iron Wood

Drumstick

Golden Champak

Neem

Persian Lilac

Silk Cotton Tree

White Silk Cotton *Ceiba pentandra* 20–25m ⓘ

Large deciduous tree with distinctive spiky green trunk, developing large buttressed roots with age. Compound leaves comprising 5–8 leaflets arranged palmately, and shed in winter. Creamy-yellow flowers small and inconspicuous, blooming at night. Fruits are long pods, tapered at both ends; they open when ripe to release seeds that are attached to silky floss. **HABITAT** Tropical tree from South America and South Africa. Planted widely in India. **USES** Silky floss used to stuff bedding and cushions.

Kanak Champa *Pterospermum acerifolium* 15–25m ⓝ

Tall tree with dense crown of large leaves that are deciduous. Rounded leaves simple with wavy edges, and covered with silvery fine hair. Large and longish flowers creamy-white and fragrant; they bloom at night and fall during the day. Their characteristics are typical of flowers pollinated by bats. Large woody pods open up into neat segments to release papery thin seeds. **HABITAT** Occurs in foothills of the Himalayas. Favours moist situations like banks of rivers and waterbodies. **USES** Moderately hard wood used in interior construction.

Jamun *Syzygium cumini* 15–20m ⓝ

Tall evergreen, fast-growing tree with dense foliage. Glossy green leaves simple and are shed in dry climates; oblong with pointed tips, and arranged in opposite pairs. Whitish-green flowers appear in clusters in March–May. Fleshy berries deep purple when ripe and delicious. **HABITAT** Native to India and parts of SE Asia. Thrives in moist situations and does not survive arid conditions. **USES** Wood used for making oars and boats; also for agricultural tools. Tree mostly cultivated for its fruits.

Harsingar *Nyctanthes arbor-tristis* 4–6m ⓝ

Small tree with drooping branches. Its most attractive feature is its fragrant flowers. Oval leaves simple, with acute pointed tips, and arranged in opposite pairs; rough, sandpaper-like texture and serrated edges. Flowers small and produced in loose clusters in July–October; they have white petals and orange-coloured throats. Fruit a round, flat pod. **HABITAT** Occurs in foothills of the Himalayas and in deciduous forests. Widely cultivated in India. **USES** Fragrant flowers used as votive offerings.

Orchid Tree *Bauhinia purpurea, B. variegata* 8–12m ⓝ

Attractive flowering plant that grows to a medium-sized tree. The two species that are the most commonly seen in India are *B. purpurea* and *B. variegata*, which are deciduous or semi-deciduous trees. **HABITAT** Both species indigenous to India and parts of SE Asia, occurring in lower altitudes of the Himalayan Range in dry deciduous forests. **USES** Wood used to make agricultural tools. Root and bark used medicinally. Leaves used as fodder. A natural hybrid, *B. blackeana*, with deep purple flowers, is also commonly planted in Indian gardens.

Laburnum *Cassia fistula* 10–15m ⓝ

Tree of modest size and form transforming into highly ornamental one when in full bloom. Compound leaves deciduous, oval in shape, with pointed ends. Showy flowers saturated yellow and borne in drooping clusters when tree is leafless, in April–July. Fruits long, dangling pods, containing many seeds in pulp. **HABITAT** Indigenous tree of India, occurring in deciduous forests. Hardy and drought resistant. **USES** Bark used in tanning. Valuable plant medicinally, with fruit pulp, root, bark and leaves being used as purgative.

White Silk Cotton

Kanak Champa

Jamun

Harsingar

Orchid Tree

Laburnum

Anjan *Hardwickia binata* 25–30m 🅝

Tall tree with straight trunk and drooping branches. Open crown light and covered in fine foliage of deciduous leaves. Small leaves compound and comprise two leaflets joined at bases. Greenish-white flowers minute and inconspicuous. Fruits long, flat pods each containing single seed, which is carried by the wind. **HABITAT** Native to India, occurring in dry deciduous forests of C India. Thrives in dry climate and can grow in difficult soil conditions with rocky ground. **USES** Used in heavy construction for structures.

Sita Ashok *Saraca asoca* 7–10m 🅝

Evergreen tree with dense, rounded crown. Leaves compound, and arranged in opposite pairs; young leaves red and drooping. Orange flowers turn red with time; borne in clusters directly from branches. **HABITAT** Native to India; occurs naturally in moist evergreen forests. **USES** Ornamental tree often seen in parks. In certain parts of India wood used for building and furniture making. All parts of plant have medicinal properties; widely used in the Ayurveda, Unani and Siddha systems of medicine.

Tamarind *Tamarindus indica* 20–25m ℹ️

Large tree with straight dark trunk and rounded crown of feather-like leaves. Leaves compound, with small, oblong leaflets arranged in opposite pairs; they fold up and close at sunset. Flowers small, on long stalks, and droop in loose clusters; petals yellow with maroon stripes. Fruits long and curved pods containing seeds in acidic pulp. On ripening they turn brown and brittle. **HABITAT** Common tree cultivated throughout India. **USES** Pulp best used after storing for a year when sweetly sour; used in Indian cooking.

Catechu *Acacia catechu* up to 9m 🅝

Small tree with dark, often crooked trunk. Deciduous with compound leaves. Leaves twice pinnate and comprise numerous small, oblong leaflets. Pale yellow flowers minute, densely arranged on long spike, and appear in May–June. Fruits flattish long pods that turn dark brown when mature. **HABITAT** Native Indian tree, distributed widely in plains. **USES** Cultivated for product called *Cutch* or *Catechu*, which is popularly used to flavour an Indian delicacy called *Paan* and referred to as *Kattha*.

Siris *Albizia lebbeck* up to 15m 🅝

Medium-sized tree with deciduous crown. Most distinct in form when leafless and covered with clusters of loosely rattling seed pods. Compound leaves, like others of pea family, twice pinnate, comprising small, oval leaflets. Creamy-white, powder-puff flowers fragrant and rich in nectar, appearing in April–May. Fruit pods long and tapered at both ends; they remain on tree for many months. **HABITAT** Widely distributed in Indian landscape. **USES** Cultivated throughout India as a shade tree.

Flame of the Forest *Butea monosperma* 9–15m 🅝

Deciduous tree taking interesting forms, often with crooked trunk. Large, rounded leaves compound, and comprise three leaflets. Underleaf covered with fine hair, giving silvery-grey hue. Flowers showy, and clustered along spike; petals beak shaped, varying in colour from yellow to deep orange. Fruits flat pods containing single seed, as suggested by the species name monosperma. **HABITAT** Native to India and parts of SE Asia. Widely distributed in dry areas and grassland. **USES** Round leaves stitched together to make plates.

Anjan

Sita Ashok

Pradeep Sachdeva/Vidya Tongbram

Tamarind

Catechu

Pradeep Sachdeva/Vidya Tongbram

Siris

Flame of the Forest

Pradeep Sachdeva/Vidya Tongbram

347

Indian Beech *Pongamia pinnata* up to 15m 🄝

Low, spreading tree with drooping branches also commonly known as Karanj. At most times can be identified by mottled leaves that have been damaged by leaf-mining worms. Leaves compound, broadly oval in shape and have pointed tips. Flowers pink and purple. **HABITAT** Versatile tree that can adapt to varying conditions; can tolerate saline and fresh water in dry inland regions. **USES** Often planted along roads as avenue tree in N India. Pongam oil extracted from seeds is flammable and is used to light lamps.

Chir Pine *Pinus roxburghii* 20–30m 🄝

Tall evergreen tree with tapering crown; becomes semi-deciduous in dry climate. Long, needle-like leaves grow in bunches of threes. Male and female flowers borne separately with females in cones, in February–April. Woody cones take more than two years to mature and release seeds. **HABITAT** Thrives at up to 2,000m in the Himalayan range. Also grows in plains. **USES** Wood is of inferior timber quality, and is used in carpentry works. Tapped for resin commercially. Suited to being shaped and altered to bonsai plants.

Deodar *Cedrus deodara* up to 60m 🄝

Tall tree with tapering crown of dense, dark green foliage. Needle-like leaves arranged alternately in clusters on drooping branches. Male and female flowers borne separately on different trees. Female cones appear in August and take about a year to ripen. **HABITAT** Tree of high altitudes of the W Himalayas, at about 1,200–3,000m. **USES** Wood durable, with characteristic scent, and used structurally in buildings, for doors and windows, and for railway sleepers. Oil extract used as antiseptic.

Oriental Plane (Chinar) *Platanus orientalis* up to 30m 🄝

Tree of large proportions with dense, spreading crown, known for its longevity. Leaves sharply lobed, and divided into three, five or seven parts; they are deciduous, turning bright red before they are shed in autumn. Minute flowers clustered to form sphere. Fruits a spiky globe containing a single seed. **HABITAT** Native to SE parts of Europe and SW Asia. **USES** Wood used to make furniture and small objects. Grown in parks and gardens as ornamental shade tree.

Camphor *Cinnamomum camphora* 10–12m 🄘

Semi-evergreen tree with dense, rounded crown. Aromatic leaves simple, arranged alternately and smell of camphor when crushed. Creamy-white flowers minute and inconspicuous. Fruits round berries that turn purple-black when ripe and contain a single seed. **HABITAT** Tree of SE Asia originating in China and Japan. In India, cultivated in the Nilgiris in south and the Himalayan foothills in north. **USES** Camphor is extracted from stems and roots of plant.

Tree of Heaven *Ailanthus excelsa* up to 20m 🄝

Large tree with distinct branching pattern forming rounded canopy. Yellowish-white flowers small and inconspicuous. Fruits are flat pods containing a single seed, hanging in large clusters. **HABITAT** In India, distributed in parts of Indian peninsula and C India. Hardy plant that does well in dry, difficult conditions; popular in cultivation along roadsides and parks in N India. **USES** Quick-growing, hardy species, grown as a shade tree. Light-coloured wood used in making packing cases. Bitter bark and leaves are used in folk medicine as a tonic and cure for fever, bronchitis and dyspepsia. Fruit is, prominently veined, oblong, copper red, twisted at the base. The bark is rough, with branchlets with permanent leaf scars.

Indian Beech

Chir Pine

Deodar

Oriental Plane (Chinar)

Camphor

Tree of Heaven

Lac Tree (Kusum) *Schleichera oleosa* 15–20m (n)

Large deciduous tree with straight, short trunk topped by large, dense crown. Compound leaves oval shaped, with pointed tips and arranged in opposite pairs. Tree conspicuous when new leaves appear in flush of red in March. Yellowish flowers minute and appear in clusters; followed by berry-like, fleshy fruits. **HABITAT** Mostly found in mixed deciduous forests, foothills of the Himalayas, and C and S India. **USES** Wood used to make agricultural tools. Shellac found on bark used commercially.

Himalayan Horse Chestnut *Aesculus indica* 20–30m (n)

Handsome tree of temperate climates with large, rounded crown. Deciduous, with compound leaves that are arranged palmately and comprise 5–9 leaflets. Flowers showy white tinged with pink, on tall spikes, and appear in summer around June. Fruits rounded and spineless, unlike those of other chestnuts, and contain shiny seed. **HABITAT** Indigenous to the NW Himalayas. **USES** Popularly grown as ornamental in parks and large gardens for its beautiful foliage and flowers. Seed oil used in traditional medicine.

Mahua *Madhuca longifolia* up to 20m (n)

Large, handsome deciduous tree that is dramatic in new leaf. Large, oval-shaped leaves simple, with pointed tips, and arranged at ends of branches. Minute, creamy-white flowers, produced in February–April, fragrant and borne in clusters; bloom at night and fall by dawn. Fruit a berry-like green that turns orange-red on ripening. **HABITAT** Native to India, occurring in dry deciduous forests of the Himalayan foothills and C India. **USES** Flowers consumed in different forms – fresh, dried or fermented as country liquor.

Maulsari *Mimusops elengi* 10–15m (n)

Straight-trunked evergreen tree with dense, rounded crown. Simple leaves elliptical in shape, with pointed tips and wavy edges. Small, creamy-white flowers bloom at night, and are subtly fragrant. Fruit an edible, oval green berry that turns deep orange when ripe. **HABITAT** Native to W peninsula of India. Cultivated in most parts of India. **USES** Wood strong and durable; used in heavy constructions. Oil from seeds used in cooking. Fruits can be preserved and pickled. Tree has religious significance to Hindus.

Sandalwood *Santalum album* 5–10m (n)

Small, slender tree with drooping branches, valued for scented heartwood and also known as Chandan in India. Smallish leaves simple, of varying shapes and arranged in opposite pairs. Flowers minute and inconspicuous, and borne in clusters in February–April. Small, fleshy, spherical fruits, each containing one seed, eaten by birds. **HABITAT** Occurs in dry tropical areas and coastal sand dunes. **USES** Heartwood scented and yields an essential oil. Sandalwood oil used in cosmetics, perfumes, incense sticks and medicines.

Teak *Tectona grandis* 20–30m (n)

Tall tree with straight trunk, but often buttressed stem and a spreading crown. Mainly cultivated for its timber. Large leaves deciduous and simple, oval shaped and arranged in opposite pairs. Flowers showy white, and minute in size, arranged in frothy clusters. **HABITAT** Native to India and parts of SE Asia. **USES** High-quality timber valued in construction due to its durability, resistance to pests and beautiful grain. Mostly used for furniture, doors and windows. Seeds and

flowers used in local medicinal remedies.

Lac Tree (Kusum)

Himalayan Horse Chestnut

Mahua

Maulsari

Sandalwood

Teak

Pradeep Sachdeva/ Vidya Tongbram

Pradeep Sachdeva/ Vidya Tongbram

Pradeep Sachdeva/ Vidya Tongbram

Milkweed *Calotropis gigantea* up to 4m 🔵

Erect shrub with large, oval succulent leaves with pointed ends. Greyish-green in colour. White flowers appear in loose clusters, on and off throughout the year. *C. procera* varies from *C. gigantea* in colour of flowers, which have purple tinge. Swollen, dry pod fruits have numerous seeds covered with silky fibres. **HABITAT** Found across India and from Iran to S China, growing in wasteland and in cultivation. **USES** Host plant of butterflies. Valued for medicinal properties, and latex, flowers and leaves are used in Ayurvedic remedies.

Indian Crocus *Kaempferia rotunda* 0.3m 🔵

Herbal deciduous shrub of the ginger family that remains dormant in winter. White-purple flowers appear when shrub is leafless, directly from the ground – hence the plant's other name Bhumi-champa, or Flower of the Earth. Broad green leaves variegated with purple undersides. **HABITAT** Found in E and NE India, and many parts of SE Asia. **USES** Rhizome has many medicinal properties; used to treat stomach disorders. Young leaves and rhizomes used for culinary purpose.

Phalsa *Grewia asiatica* up to 4m 🔵

Straggling shrub that can grow to be a small tree. Dwarf variety popular in cultivation. Leaves simple and deciduous, broad and with coarse texture. Small yellow flowers clustered in groups of 2–5. Fruits small round berries, ripening to deep purple or red. **HABITAT** Native to tropical and subtropical India and Pakistan. Does well in habitats with distinct summer and winter seasons. Hardy plant that grows in a wide range of soils and is reasonably drought tolerant. **USES** Very popular for its fruits in India.

Yellow Orchid Tree *Bauhinia tomentosa* up to 4m 🔵

Light shrub growing into a small tree. Attractive leaves divided into two lobes and light green in colour. In December–March produces bell-shaped flowers; bright yellow with deep maroon-coloured centres. Sheds leaves in N Indian cold winters. **HABITAT** Native to India, Sri Lanka and tropical Africa. **USES** Flowers rich in pollen and nectar, and attract various butterflies, bees and insect-eating birds. Certain birds and larvae of some moth and butterfliy species feed on flowers and leaves.

Touch Me Not *Mimosa pudica* 0.5m 🔵

Straggling, low-spreading shrub with spiny stem. Touch Me Not is so named because a slight touch or movement causes the leaves to fold and withdraw – a defensive action taken by plant to repel herb-eating insects and other animals. Flowers mainly stamens clustered in stalks of pink-lilac colour; bloom in rainy season. **HABITAT** Native to tropical America, and found growing weed-like in wasteland and open ground; rarely found in cultivation in India. **USES** All parts are medicinal.

Lantana *Lantana camara* 0.5–2m ℹ️

Hardy, common shrub with aromatic leaves. Leaves have finely serrated edges and are covered in hair. Small flowers appear nearly throughout the year, in dense clusters of many colours, ranging from yellow-orange-red to white-pink-red. **HABITAT** Native to tropical America. Has naturalized in many parts of the world, including India. Considered an invasive species and found growing in wasteland. Drought resistant. **USES** Colourful garden shrub that flowers profusely. Attracts many species of butterfly, and grown in butterfly gardens.

Milkweed

Indian Crocus

Phalsa

Yellow Orchid Tree

Touch Me Not

Lantana

Andaman & Nicobar Islands

Chidiya Tapu

Also called 'bird island', this is a small village situated on the southeastern tip of South Andaman Island. A carpet of rich mangrove forests, it hosts numerous species. The site is a treasure trove of mangrove forests, tidal mudflats and silvery beaches overlooking the azure-blue Bay of Bengal.

Access Chidiya Tapu is accessed by road from Port Blair, 32km away. The nearest airport is Port Blair, which can be reached from Kolkata and Chennai.
Best time to visit November–March.

KEY SPECIES Chidiya Tapu	
Andaman Serpent Eagle	Andaman Wild Boar
Andaman Shama	Indian Spotted Deer
Andaman Drongo	Indian Muntjac
Andaman Coucal	Andaman Pit Viper
White-headed Starling	Andaman Krait
Red-breasted Parakeet	Andaman Cat Snake
Long-tailed Parakeet	Saltwater Crocodile
Andaman Flowerpecker	Andaman Banded Dandy
Andaman Bulbul	Andaman Nawab

Mount Harriet National Park

Situated in Ferrargunj Tehsil of South Andaman Island, Mt Harriet is the third highest peak in the Andaman and Nicobar archipelago. The national park was established in 1969 to safeguard the biodiversity of its flora and fauna. The park is a delightful amalgamation of hill ranges, freshwater streams, dense evergreen and semi-evergreen forests, moist deciduous forests and mangrove forests, with an open seashore on its eastern side. It also has many fruiting plants, which cater to a wide range of avian species.

Access The park is 55km by road from Port Blair via Ferrargunj. There is a 15km ferry ride from Phoenix Bay to Bamboo Flat and from here to Mount Harriet by road.
Best time to visit November–March.

KEY SPECIES Mount Harriet National Park	
Andaman Wood Pigeon	Common Palm Civet
Andaman Treepie	Saltwater Crocodile
Andaman Crake	Olive Ridley Sea Turtle
Vernal Hanging Parrot	Green Sea Turtle
Andaman Woodpecker	Hawksbill Turtle
Spot-breasted Woodpecker	Andaman Cobra
Andaman Hawk Owl	King Cobra
Andaman Coucal	Andaman Crow
Nicobar Megapode	Ironwood Tree

Arunachal Pradesh

Eaglenest Wildlife Sanctuary

Nestled in the Himalayan foothills in the Kameng district of Arunachal Pradesh, Eaglenest is a part of the Kameng Elephant Reserve. Spread over $217km^2$, it conjoins the Pakke Reserve to the east and the Sessa Orchid Sanctuary to the north-east. With more than 500 bird species, it is India's top birdwatching destination. This unique sanctuary gained popularity in 2006 with the discovery of the rare bird – the Bugun Liocichla, named after the Bugun tribe who are the original inhabitants of this area. The Arunachal Macaque, another resident, was discovered in 2008. Good birding areas include Ramalingam, Lama, Bompu, Sessni and Eaglenest Pass.

Access Guwahati Airport 300km. Tezpur Airport 150km. Bhalukpong the nearest railway station (95km). Tezpur to Tenga is 135km (4–5-hour drive to the park entrance). Arunachal Pradesh entry tickets and Inner Line Permits are checked at Bhalukpong. These are issued by the DFO, Pakke Tiger Reserve.
Best time to visit November–April.

KEY SPECIES Eaglenest Wildlife Sanctuary	
Beautiful Nuthatch	Arunachal Macaque
Bugun Liocichla	Common Slug Snake
Himalayan Cutia	Green Indian Rat Snake
Ward's Trogon	Spot-tailed Pit Viper
Blyth's Tragopan	Monocled Cobra
Hodgson's Frogmouth	Bhutan Glory
Asian Elephant	Blue Admiral
Himalayan Serow	White Owl
Asiatic Golden Cat	Dusky Labyrinth
Clouded Leopard	Tiger Brown

Dibang Valley, Mishmi Hills and Roing

The Mishmi Hills, a southwards extension of the Himalayan mountain ranges, are located in the northeastern tip of India in Arunachal Pradesh. Named after the Dibang river that flows through them, they are divided into two broad sections – the lower Dibang valley, which is the floodplain of the tributaries of the Brahmaputra river, the lower foothills with Roing as the headquarters, and the upper Dibang valley that rises from the foothills to the middle ranges of Mayodia pass with Anini as its headquarters. The Arunachal Himalayan ranges consist of snow-capped mountains.

This is one of India's prime birding areas. The complex hill system with varying elevations makes it a major biodiversity hotspot. A staggering 550 avian species have been reported from this area. Many rare mammals like the Mishmi Takin, Himalayan Goral, Himalayan Musk Deer, Himalayan Serow and Mishmi Giant Flying Squirrel are found in the higher regions.

Access Dibrugarh Airport 40km.Tinsukhia Railway Station 70km. The approach to Mishmi has now become much easier with the opening of the 9km-long Bhupen Hazrika Setu over the Lohit river. Recommended access is Dibrugarh–Tinsukhia–Sadiya Ghat via NH 37–Roing–Mayodia Pass. Roing town is 65km from Sadiya Ghat and Mayodia Pass is 56km from Roing. An Inner Line Permit is required for entry into Arunachal Pradesh and can be sourced from the Resident Commissioner's office.

Best time to visit November–March

High-altitude lake, Arunachal landscape

Gopinath Kollur

Pakke Tiger Reserve

The reserve lies in the foothills of the Eastern Himalayas in the East Kameng district of Arunachal Pradesh and covers an area of 862km². It is bound by the Jia Bhoreli river on the west and the Pakke river on the east. Towards the south, it adjoins the Nameri National Park of Assam. Home to many species of rare and endangered wildlife, it is most famous for sightings of the four resident hornbills: Wreathed, Rufous-necked, Oriental Pied and Great Hornbills. Also seen here is the White-winged Wood Duck, known to be very elusive.

Access Guwahati Airport 50km and Tezpur Airport 60km. Soibari is nearest railway station (36km). By road from Guwahati to Tejpur and then to Soibari (234km). Soibari to Seijosa, which is the entry point, is 36km (2-hour drive). An Inner Line Permit for Indians and Restricted Area Permit for foreigners are required to enter Arunachal Pradesh.These can be sourced from the Deputy Resident Commissioner's Office.
Best time to visit November–March.

KEY SPECIES Dibang Valley, Mishmi Hills	
Coral-billed Scimitar Babbler	Rusty-bellied Shortwing
Hill Blue Flycatcher	Ward's Trogon
Black-breasted Parrotbill	Fire-tailed Myzornis
Dark-sided Flycatcher	Asiatic Black Bear
Grey-headed Bullfinch	Mishmi Takin
Mishmi Wren Babbler	Himalayan Musk Deer
Temminck's Tragopan	Assamese Macaque
Blyth's Tragopan	Himalayan Serow
Gould's Shortwing	Western Hoolock Gibbon
	Mithun

KEY SPECIES Pakke Tiger Reserve	
Great Hornbill	Fire-tailed Myzornis
Rufous-necked Hornbill	Tiger
Oriental Pied Hornbill	Indian Leopard
Wreathed Hornbill	Indian Hog Deer
Blue-naped Pitta	Arunachal Macaque
Jerdon's Baza	Capped Langur
Silver-eared Mesia	Malayan Giant Squirrel
Sultan Tit	Long-banded Blue Crow
Blyth's Kingfisher	Indian Orange-tailed Awl
Green Cochoa	Common Sailor

Namdhapha National Park

This park is situated in the Changlang district of Arunachal Pradesh and is located between the Mishmi hills and Patkai ranges, close to the Indo-Myanmar-China trijunction. Covering an area of 1,985km², it was declared a national park and Tiger reserve in 1983. It comprises the catchment areas of the Noa-Dihing rivers, and many streams drain into this, forming natural salt licks and small pools.

It is possible to see the four big cats in the park: Indian Leopard, Tiger, Snow Leopard and Clouded Leopard. The Namdapha Flying Squirrel is only found in this park. It is a paradise for birdwatchers as the avifauna is a unique mix of Indo-Burmese, Sino-Tibetan and Himalayan species, with more than 500 species reported. The park harbours the northernmost lowland evergreen rainforests in the world. It is also known for extensive dipterocarp forests and thick canopy covers. The vegetation changes with increases in altitude from subtropical moist forests, to temperate broadleaved and coniferous forests, to alpine meadows, finally ending in perennial snow cover. The park has extensive bamboo forests to complement the secondary forests.

Access Dibrugarh Airport 197km. Tinsukhia Railway Station 150km. By road, Dibrugarh is a 6-hour drive via Tinsukhia-Digboi-Miao-Deban. This is one of the few parks that have to be traversed by foot. To enter Arunachal Pradesh you need to obtain an Inner Line Permit from the Office of the Resident Commissioner of Arunachal Pradesh at Kolkata/Delhi/Guwahati/Dibrugarh. Best time to visit November–March.

Assam

Kaziranga landscape

Kaziranga National Park

Located in the Golaghat and Nagaon districts of Assam, this park is spread over 430km². Established in 1974 as a national park, it was declared a UNESCO World Heritage Site in 1985. Its high species diversity and visibility, good tourism infrastructure and successful conservation measures make it a popular wildlife destination. Kaziranga is at the edge of the Eastern Himalayan biosphere hotspot, with vast expanses of elephant grass meadows, swampy lagoons and marshland, and dense broadleaved deciduous forests. The mighty Brahmaputra and other rivers criss-cross the area, forming numerous small waterbodies.

Access Guwahati International Airport 220km. Tezpur Airport 60km. Jorhat Airport 95km. Furkating Railway Station is the nearest railway station (80km, 2 hours to the park).
Best time to visit November–March.

KEY SPECIES Namdhapha National Park	
Fire-tailed Myzoris	Snow Leopard
Fulvous Parrotbill	Clouded Leopard
Golden-breasted Fulvetta	Red Panda
Austen's Brown Hornbill	Asiatic Black Bear
Pied Falconet	Red Caliph
Golden-crested Mynah	Koh-i-Noor
White-tailed Fish Eagle	Wizard
Tiger	Fluffy Tit

KEY SPECIES Kaziranga National Park	
Bengal Florican	Binturong
Swamp Francolin	Brown Palm Civet
Black-breasted Parrotbill	Swamp Deer
Finn's Weaver	Indian Gharial
Baer's Pochard	Assam Roofed Turtle
Slender-billed Babbler	Russell's Viper
Great Hornbill	Glassy Tiger
Asian Elephant	Teak

Asian Elephant at Manas

Manas National Park

Manas is located in the foothills of the Eastern Himalayas in western Assam. It is a UNESCO World Heritage Site and Biosphere Reserve. Established in 1990, it is known for its spectacular scenery and rich biodiversity. Covering 950km², it is spread over the districts of Bongaigaon, Barpeta, Darrang and Kokrajhar. Several globally threatened mammals and birds, like the Pygmy Hog and endangered Bengal Florican, can be seen here. It is recognized as an Important Bird and Biodiversity Area (IBA) site with more than 450 bird species, including many grassland species like Marsh and Jerdon's Babblers and the Bristled Grassbird. The park's northern boundary is contiguous with the international border with Bhutan. The natural landscape consists of dense forested hills, tropical evergreen forests and alluvial grassland. The park is divided into three ranges: Western (Panbari), Central (Bansbari) and Eastern(Bhuiyanpara).

Access Guwahati Airport 150km. Barpeta Railway Station 50km. By road, Guwahati to Manas 150km (3–4-hour drive). Best time to visit November–March.

Nameri National Park and Tiger Reserve

Situated in the foothills of the Eastern Himalayas in the Sonitpur district of Assam, this beautiful area was notified as a national park in 1998 and covers 220km². It shares its boundary with the Pakke Tiger Reserve of Arunachal Pradesh, thereby creating a contiguous area of wilderness. It is home to 400 bird species, including the globally threatened White-winged Wood Duck. Most areas in the park are accessible on foot and recommended for birding accompanied by experienced forest guides and guards. A major attraction is a leisurely raft ride on the Jia Bhorelli river, where you may catch a glimpse of the Ibisbill and Common Merganser. The forests are tropical evergreen and moist deciduous, with cane and bamboo brakes and narrow strips of grassland along rivers with riverine vegetation. The area is drained by the Jia Bhorelli river and its tributaries like Diji and Nameri.

Access Tezpur Airport 37km. Guwahati Airport 220km (5-hour drive). Rangapara railway station 25km. Kaziranga 125km. Best time to visit October–April.

Nameri forest

KEY SPECIES Manas National Park	
Bengal Florican	Hispid Hare
Swamp Francolin	Pygmy Hog
Black-breasted Parrotbill	Asian Golden Cat
Marsh Babbler	Clouded Leopard
White-rumped Vulture	Assam Roofed Turtle
Indian Rhinoceros	King Cobra
Wild Buffalo	Tiger Hopper
Gee's Golden Langur	Continental Swift

KEY SPECIES Nameri National Park	
White-winged Wood Duck	Asian Elephant
Wreathed Hornbill	Assam Roofed Turtle
Ibisbill	Keeled Box Turtle
Great Hornbill	Indian Gecko
Oriental Hobby	King Cobra
Ruby-cheeked Sunbird	Russell's Viper
Crow-billed Drongo	Common Windmill
Hispid Hare	Common Clubtail

Dibru-Saikhowa National Park

This sprawling, picturesque park is an important biodiversity hotspot. Located in the Tinsukhia district of Assam, it is spread over 340km². Notified as a national park in 1999, it is divided into nine zones, one of which is a wetland while the others are dense forests. Initially set up to conserve the White-winged Wood Duck, it has over 400 avian species and is recognized as an IBA site. It is famous for its brightly coloured feral horses. Maguri Bheel is a large, shallow wetland famous for its rare endemic and migratory birds and for the Wild Buffaloes. It is an IBA and is known for attracting many birds from around the globe. It is bound by the Brahmaputra and Lohit rivers, with the hills of Arunachal in the north, while the Dibru river and Patkai hills lie to the south. Containing a large *Salix* swamp forest, its forests are semi-evergreen and tropical mixed deciduous interspersed with cane brakes and grassland.

Access Dibrugarh Airport 40km. New Tinsukhia Railway Station 90km. Tinsukhia town 55km.
Best time to visit November–April.

Dibru-Saikhowa wetlands

White-winged Wood Ducks

Dehing-Patkai Wildlife Sanctuary

Known as the Amazon of the east, the Dehing-Patkai Wildlife Sanctuary is located in the Tinsukhia and Dibrugarh districts of Assam. The 112km² sanctuary is part of the Assam Valley tropical wet evergreen forest and is divided into three parts: Jeypore, Upper Dihing River and Dirok Rainforest. Declared a sanctuary in 2004, it is part of the Dibru Deomali Elephant Reserve. It is the only forest known to be home to seven cat species: Tiger, Indian Leopard, Marbled Cat, Leopard Cat, Clouded Leopard, Jungle Cat and Asiatic Golden Cat. It is also a paradise for birders with over 300 avian species, both resident and migratory, found here.

Virgin deciduous rainforests are interspersed with semi-evergreen and lush green flora and exotic orchids. Jeypore is known for its abundant birdlife and recommended for birding accompanied by an experienced local guide.

Access Dibrugarh Airport 95km. Naharkatia Railway Station 8km. Dibrugarh, the nearest city, 82km. A good time to visit is February, when the Dehing Patkai festival takes place.
Best time to visit September–March.

KEY SPECIES Dibru-Saikhowa National Park	
Jerdon's Babbler	Asian Elephant
Marsh Babbler	Wild Buffalo
Black-breasted Parrotbill	Capped Langur
Swamp Prinia	Feral horse
Pale-capped Pigeon	Bengal Slow Loris
White-winged Wood Duck	Small Indian Civet
Jerdon's Bushchat	Chocolate Demon
Baer's Pochard	Blue Imperial

KEY SPECIES Dehing-Patkai Wildlife Sanctuary	
Pied Falconet	Assamese Macaque
Grey Peacock-pheasant	Bengal Slow Loris
Pale-capped Pigeon	Malayan Giant Squirrel
Oriental Bay Owl	Clouded Leopard
Bay Woodpecker	Marbled Cat
White-winged Wood Duck	Yellow Coster
Sapphire Flycatcher	Redbreast
Stump-tailed Macaque	Painted Jezebel

358

Pobitora Wildlife Sanctuary

This sanctuary lies on the southern bank of the Brahmaputra river in the Morigaon district of Assam, 30km from Guwahati. Spread over 39km², it has a high density of rhinos. It is a good birdwatching site as it attracts thousands of migratory birds annually. The riverine composition of the forests, with vast grassland and wetlands interspersed with waterbodies or jheels, make it an ideal habitat for rhinos.

Access Guwahati is well connected by train and air. Jeep safaris available outside gate.
Best time to visit November–March (avoid the monsoons, when area is prone to flash floods).

Hoolangapar Gibbon Sanctuary

Situated in the Jorhat district of Assam, this sanctuary was officially constituted and renamed in 1997. Spread over 22km², it is perhaps the best place to see the rare ape, the Hoolock Gibbon. This is an island of dense evergreen rainforest in the midst of sprawling tea gardens. Initially the forest was a green corridor extending to Nagaland, but it has now been fragmented by tea gardens and villages. It is known for its staggering primate community and has one of the highest primate densities in the world. A railway line laid in 1819 divides the park into two, which effectively limited the movement of gibbon groups, leading to inbreeding. Most of the habitat is evergreen and composed of several canopy layers. The upper canopy of the forest is dominated by the Hollong tree while the Nahar tree dominates the middle rung. The lower canopy consists of evergreen shrubs, herbs and many varieties of bamboo. The park is small and you can walk, accompanied by a guard.

Access Jorhat Airport 30km from park. Jorhat Railway Station 20km. Guwahati 250km (6–7-hour drive).
Best time to visit October–March.

KEY SPECIES Pobitora Wildlife Sanctuary	
White-rumped Vulture	Indian Rhinoceros
Grey-headed Fish Eagle	Wild Boar
Pallas's Fish Eagle	Wild Buffalo
Marsh Babbler	Indian Leopard
Greater Adjutant	Indian Muntjac
Lesser Adjutant	Asian Palm Civet
Swamp Francolin	Yellow Helen
Spot-billed Pelican	Pale Hedge Blue

KEY SPECIES Hoolangapar Gibbon Sanctuary	
Red Junglefowl	Capped Langur
Kalij Pheasant	Bengal Slow Loris
Rufous Woodpecker	Northern Pig-tailed Macaque
Collared Treepie	Malayan Giant Squirrel
Rufous-bellied Niltava	Indian Rock Python
Western Hoolock Gibbon	Indian Rat Snake
Stump-tailed Macaque	King Cobra
Assamese Macaque	Himalayan Blue Imperial

Indian Rhinoceros in Pobitora Wildlife Sanctuary

Tripta Sood

Goa

Bhagwan Mahavir Wildlife Sanctuary

This sanctuary was set up in southeastern Goa, on the border with Karnataka, near the town of Mollem in 1969 to protect the flora and fauna of the Western Ghats. It was initially called Mollem Wild Life Sanctuary and was given its present name in 1978. It has a thick canopy of tropical evergreen, semi-evergreen and moist deciduous forests, through which flow many perennial streams. It has more than 700 species of flowering plant and 128 endemic plant species.

Access Panjim, capital of Goa, 70km away. Goa International Airport at Dabolim 70km. By rail, Amravat Express, Goa Express and Poorna Express stop at Collem railway station, 6km from sanctuary.
Best time to visit October–March.

Gururaj Moorching

Malayan Night Heron

Gujarat

Gir National Park

Also known as Sasan Gir, this park is situated in the Junagadh, Gir Somnath and Amreli districts in Gujarat, near the town of Talala Gir. It is the oldest sanctuary in India and the last abode of the Asiatic Lion. In the 2015 Asiatic Lion Census, the population of Asiatic Lions in Gir numbered 523 individuals. This is a land of rugged ridges, isolated hills, valleys and plateaux covered with dry scrub and open deciduous forests. It forms a unique ecosystem not only for the Asiatic Lion, but also for a variety of mammals, reptiles and birds.

Access Junagad to Gir National Park 76km by road. Rajkot to Gir National Park 168km; closest airport. Nearest railway stations are Junagadh and Veraval.
Best time to visit December–March.

Lionness in Gir National Park

KEY SPECIES Bhagwan Mahavir Wildlife Sanctuary	
Sri Lanka Frogmouth	Indian Spotted Chevrotain
Malabar Barbet	Indian Spotted Deer
White-bellied Treepie	Wild Boar
Blue-eared Kingfisher	Malabar Giant Squirrel
Oriental Dwarf Kingfisher	Slender Loris
Asian Fairy-bluebird	Gaur
Malabar Pied Hornbill	Malabar Pit Viper
Malabar Grey Hornbill	Russell's Viper
Spot-bellied Eagle Owl	King Cobra
Brown Hawk Owl	Indian Rock Python
Flame-throated Bulbul	Malabar Gliding Frog
Yellow-browed Bulbul	Malabar Tree Nymph
Blue-capped Rock Thrush	Tamil Yeoman
Malayan Night Heron	Common Mormon
Tiger	Blue Mormon
Indian Leopard	Common Jezebel
Indian Muntjac	Mango

KEY SPECIES Gir National Park	
Eastern Imperial Eagle	Jackal
Crested Serpent Eagle	Jungle Cat
Bonelli's Eagle	Rusty-spotted Cat
Changeable Hawk Eagle	Chinkara
Brown Fish Owl	Four-horned Antelope
Mottled Wood Owl	Nilgai
Indian Eagle Owl	Indian Rock Python
Indian Paradise Flycatcher	Indian Cobra
Indian Pitta	Bengal Monitor
Ultramarine Flycatcher	Mugger Crocodile
White-rumped Vulture	Lemon Pansy
Indian Vulture	Yellow Pansy
Spot-billed Pelican	Blue Pansy
Asiatic Lion	Peacock Pansy
Indian Leopard	Plain Tiger
Striped Hyena	Blue Tiger
Honey Badger	Striped Tiger

Little Rann of Kutch

Great Rann of Kutch

The Great Rann of Kutch is a salt marsh located in the Thar Desert, in the Kathiawar Peninsula, in the northwestern part of Gujarat. It is a land of desert, salty mudflats, extensive grassland and great stretches of water in the 'dhands' (shallow wetlands) created by the monsoons. Dry-thorn forests punctuate the flat, limitless stretches of land. The deserts of the Great Rann, to the north, the grassland of Banni and the coastline along the Arabian Sea are the main birding and wildlife hotspots.

Access Dhordo, gateway to the Great Rann, is 70km from Bhuj by road. Trains operate to Bhuj from major cities in India. Bhuj is the closest airport.
Best time to visit November–February.

KEY SPECIES Great Rann of Kutch	
Grey Hypocolius	Desert Fox
Spotted Flycatcher	Desert Cat
Rufous-tailed Scrub Robin	Small Indian Civet
Marshall's Iora	Indian Desert Jird
White-naped Tit	Indian Leopard
Sykes's Nightjar	Nilgai
Short-eared Owl	Indian Pangolin
Red-tailed Shrike	Small Indian Mongoose
Red-backed Shrike	Indian Spiny-tailed Lizard
Painted Sandgrouse	Saw-scaled Viper
Greater Spotted Eagle	Common Krait
Crested Lark	Spectacled Cobra
Dalmatian Pelican	Danaid Eggfly
Macqueen's Bustard	Large Salmon Arab
Tawny Eagle	White Arab
Indian Wild Ass	Pioneer
Indian Wolf	

Little Rann of Kutch or Wild Ass Sanctuary

Little Rann of Kutch is a salt desert located primarily in the Kutch district of Gujarat. It is the largest wildlife sanctuary in India, spread over 4,953km² in the districts of Kutch, Surendranagar, Banaskantha, Patan and Rajkot. It is a salt marsh that floods during the monsoon. It has 74 elevated plateaux, or 'bets', covered with grass after the rains. This is the main fodder for the Indian Wild Ass, for whom the sanctuary was set up in 1972.

Access 130km from Ahmedabad. The nearest railway station is Dhrangadhra, 16km from sanctuary.
Best time to visit November–February are ideal for viewing migratory and resident birds and mammals.

KEY SPECIES Little Rann of Kutch	
Demoiselle Crane	Blackbuck
Common Crane	Indian Wolf
Merlin	Desert Fox
Cream-coloured Courser	Desert Cat
Sociable Lapwing	Caracal
Peregrine Falcon	Nilgai
Pallid Harrier	Indian Spiny-tailed Lizard
Montagu's Harrier	Bengal Monitor
Western Marsh Harrier	Common Sand Boa
Steppe Eagle	Indian Rat Snake
Greater Hoopoe Lark	Saw-scaled Viper
Sykes's Lark	Small Orange-tip
Greater Flamingo	Crimson Tip
Lesser Flamingo	Common Emigrant
Macqueen's Bustard	Mottled Emigrant
European White Stork	Plain Tiger
Indian Wild Ass	Painted Lady
Chinkara	

Nalsarovar Bird Sanctuary

Nalsarovar is a 120km² shallow freshwater lake, situated west of Ahmedabad in Gujarat. It is located at the junction between the Saurashtra Plateau and the mainland of Gujarat, amid the semi-arid lands of Ahmedabad and Surendranagar. It was declared a bird sanctuary in 1969 and a Ramsar Site in 2012. It is a natural shallow depression surrounded by dense reed beds, fed by rivers and monsoon rains, and is 60km by road from Ahmedabad.

Access The nearest railway station is Viramgram, 40km from Nalsarovar. Ahmedabad is the nearest airport and is well connected to major cities in India.
Best time to visit November–February is the best time to see ducks and migrant waders.

Velavadar National Park

This park is situated in the Bhavnagar district of Gujarat and is dedicated to the protection of the Blackbuck and the Lesser Florican. It is known for the largest population of harriers in the world, which are winter migrants. Primarily flat tropical grassland and acacia scrub, the grasses in the park are 30–45cm tall and provide good cover for the enigmatic bird of Velavadar – the endangered Lesser Florican. To the south of the park is the Gulf of Khambhat, whose tidal mudflats welcome migratory wading birds from Central Europe and Siberia in winter. To the north are arid areas and agricultural fields.

Access Ahmedabad 170km and Bhavnagar 65km from the park. Direct trains operate between Ahmedabad and Bhavnagar, and between Mumbai and Bhavnagar. Domestic flights operate between Mumbai and Bhavnagar. International airlines fly to Ahmedabad airport.
Best time to visit November–March.

Velavadar landscape

Himachal Pradesh

Great Himalayan National Park

Tucked amid the snow-capped Western Himalayas, this park is located in the Kullu region of Himachal Pradesh. Declared a national park in 1999 and a UNESCO World Heritage Site in 2014, it spans more than 1,711km² at an altitude of 1,500–6,000m. It is part of the Himalayan biodiversity hotspot and shelters diverse wildlife. The park lies in the upper catchment areas of the Tirthan, Sainj and Jiwa rivers, and includes the Tirthan Sanctuary. The eastern part is snowbound and has glaciers.

The area is particularly known for its prolific pheasant population and is home to more than 250 avian species. The Himalayan Monal, Koklass Pheasant and Kalij Pheasant are more common than the Cheer Pheasant and Western Tragopan, which have restricted ranges. Other rare species like the Bearded

Vulture, Chukar and Snow Partridges, Snow and Speckled Wood Pigeons, and Blue-capped Redstart, can also be found here. More than 30 species of mammal occur in the area, like the Himalayan Goral, Bharal or Blue Sheep, Asiatic Ibex, Himalayan Thar, and Asiatic Black and Himalayan Brown Bears. There are four valleys in the park and a trek of 40km in any of them takes you to the high-altitude abode of the iconic Snow Leopard. Himalayan Ecotourism organizes treks in September–October.

Access Kullu Airport 60km. The nearest railhead, Joginder Nagar Railway Station (near Mandi), is 140km away. There is no direct road to the park entry. Kulu via NH 21 to Aut, from here take divergence on the Kulu Manali highway. Take the road cut into Banjar Valley–Tirthan Valley.
Best time to visit March–June for breeding and nesting of birds; September–November for other animals as they migrate to lower altitude.

Pong Dam Wildlife Sanctuary

Located among the snow-clad mountains of the Himalayas, Pong Dam, or the Maharana Pratap Sagar sanctuary, is a lake sanctuary in the Kangra district of Himachal Pradesh. It consists of several deforested islands and is spread over 450km². The elevation of the dam is about 448m and it attracts thousands of migratory birds from the plains of India, Central Asia and Siberia. It is famous for its waterfowl diversity and over 200 avian species have been reported here.

Seen here in large numbers are waterfowl like the Northern Pintail, Mallard, Ruddy Shelduck and Bar-headed Goose. There is a healthy population of waders, like the Common Greenshank, Common Sandpiper and Temminck's Stint. A variety of raptors can be seen over the lake, including the Osprey, Tawny Eagle, Pallas's Fish Eagle and Western Marsh Harrier. Mammals like the Indian Spotted Deer, Blackbuck, Wild Boar and Indian Leopard are sighted here. Tourists visit for water sports such as rowing, canoeing, sailing and boating, and for the scenic beauty of the area. The forests and hills are covered with coniferous and deciduous forests. Many trees are found here, including eucalyptus, Jamun and Mango.

Access Closest airport is Kangra Valley Airport (45km). Pathankot Railway Station 35km. The sanctuary is about 8km from Kangra and is well connected from Pathankot and Dharamshala.
Best time to visit November–March.

KEY SPECIES Great Himalayan National Park	
Western Tragopan	Asiatic Ibex
Kalij Pheasant	Snow Leopard
Koklass Pheasant	Himalayan Tahr
Himalayan Monal	Himalayan Musk Deer
Himalayan Griffon	Himalayan Goral
Bearded Vulture	Indian Rat Snake
Golden Bush Robin	Himalayan Pit Viper
Long-tailed Minivet	Eastern Keelback
White-throated Dipper	Kashmir Rock Lizard
Chukar Partridge	Karakoram Bent-tailed Gecko
Black-throated Sunbird	Common Blue Apollo
Bharal	Yellow Swallowtail
Asiatic Black Bear	Chir Pine
Himalayan Brown Bear	

KEY SPECIES Pong Dam Wildlife Sanctuary	
Black-headed Gull	Indian Leopard
Black Stork	Wild Boar
Common Teal	Indian Muntjac
Northern Lapwing	Himalayan Goral
White-rumped Vulture	Bengal Monitor
Common Greenshank	King Cobra
Black Redstart	Indian Rock Python
White-capped Redstart	Banded Krait
Orange-headed Thrush	Yellow Swallowtail
Indian Spotted Deer	Spot Swordtail
Blackbuck	Jamun

Himalayan Goral

Kibber Wildlife Sanctuary

Situated high in the Trans-Himalayan valley of Lahaul and Spiti in Himachal Pradesh, this is the only cold desert sanctuary in India. It is spread over 2,220km² with an elevation of 3,600–7,600m. Established in 1992, it has gained immense popularity due to the frequent sightings of the elusive Snow Leopard. The Himalayan Research Centre at Kibber has played a pivotal role in conservation of this iconic animal and 25–30 of the cats are known to be living within the sanctuary. The vegetation is sparse, with subalpine and alpine pastures. However, the plants found here have been known to have high medicinal properties and are used extensively in Tibetan medicine.

Access Kibber can be approached from either Shimla or Manali by road. Shimla (Shaheed Bhagat Singh International) and Manali (Bhuntar) are the closest airports. Nearest Railway stations are Shimla and Joginder Nagar (near Mandi). Shimla to Kibber (430km), a 12-hour drive; Manali to Kibber (186km), a 5–6-hour drive.
Best time to visit May–July, when it is not too cold. Snow Leopard sightings are best in winter.

Snow Leopard

Otto Pfister

Jammu & Kashmir

Hangul

Dachigam National Park

Situated near Srinagar, this area was given the status of a national park in 1981 to protect the Critically Endangered Hangul. Located in the Zabarwan range of the Western Himalayas, it is divided into two areas: Lower Dachigam and Upper Dachigam (reachable only by trekking). Dachigam comprises several lakes, flowering meadows, waterfalls, alpine pastures and coniferous forests. The vegetation is Himalayan moist temperate, alpine pastures and alpine moist scrub. The trees are pine, Deodar, oak, birch, poplar and Chinar, interspersed with fruiting trees.

Access Srinagar is 22km away by road. The nearest rail station is Jammu, at a distance of 315km. Srinagar is the closest airport; then by car to Dachigam.
Best time to visit March–October.

KEY SPECIES Kibber Wildlife Sanctuary	
Gold-naped Finch	Bharal
Snow Pigeon	Himalayan Tahr
Alpine Chough	Asiatic Ibex
Himalayan Griffon	Red Fox
Bearded Vulture	Lynx
Red-fronted Serin	Woolly Hare
Great Rosefinch	Himalayan Wolf
Chukar Partridge	Large-eared Pika
Himalayan Snowcock	Himalayan Blackvein
Snow Leopard	Common Blue Apollo

KEY SPECIES Dachigam National Park	
Himalayan Monal	Snow Leopard
Koklass Pheasant	Ladakh Pika
Brown-fronted Woodpecker	Himalayan Marmot
Kashmir Flycatcher	Mountain Weasel
Steppe Eagle	Himalayan Serow
Orange Bullfinch	Himalayan Musk Deer
Hangul or Kashmir Stag	Himalayan Silverstripe
Asiatic Black Bear	Himalayan Common Beak
Himalayan Brown Bear	Indian Tortoiseshell
Red Fox	Common Copper

Ladakh

Tso Kar

This lake lies in the Rupshu Valley in southern Ladakh, at an altitude of 4,530m. It is connected by a stream to a small lake, Startsapuk Tso, and together they form a lake that is 9km long. The shore of Tso Kar is covered with a salt crust, but vegetation such as pond weeds, sedges, nettles and buttercups grows on the shore of Startsapuk Tso, which ensures the existence of a variety of fauna.

Access By road from Leh via Taglang La is 153km. Leh is the closest airport. It is advised to rest and acclimatize in Leh for two days before setting out for the high-altitude lakes.
Best time to visit June–September.

Tso Kar

Tso Moriri

Also called Tso Moriri Wetland Conservation Reserve, this lake is situated at an altitude of 4,522m, near the village of Korzok, on the Changthang Plateau. The lake is fed by springs and snow-melt from the mountains. Extensive marshes occur where the streams enter the lake, the water of which is brackish and alkaline. The lake is accessible only in summer, through Karzok, on the northwestern side. Tso Moriri is a remnant of a structural lake that was formed due to movements in the Earth's crust. The Tso Moriri ecosystem provides a unique landscape for the breeding of Bar-headed Geese, Brown-headed Gulls and Whiskered Terns.

Access By road from Tsokar via Polokongka la, 150km. By road from Pangong Tso via Merak, Chushul, Sumdo to Tso Moriri, 235km.
Best time to visit June–September.

Hanle

At 4,500m, this is the easternmost village of Ladakh, near Tibet, and is a habitat for rare birds such as the Black-necked Crane, Tibetan Lark and Eurasian Eagle Owl, and mammals such as the Red Fox. It has recently been opened to visitors.

Access By road from Tso Moriri to Hanle, 150km. By road from Pangong Tso via Mahe to Hanle.
Best time to visit June–September.

KEY SPECIES Tso Kar	
Black-necked Crane	Ruddy Shelduck
Hume's Ground Tit	Tibetan Wild Ass
Tibetan Snowfinch	Tibetan Wolf
Blanford's Snowfinch	Tibetan Gazelle
Great Rosefinch	Himalayan Marmot
White-winged Redstart	Tibetan Argali
Rufous-tailed Rock Thrush	Bharal
Eurasian Magpie	Ladakh Copper
Horned Lark	Western Blue Sapphire
Great Crested Grebe	Sorrel Sapphire

KEY SPECIES Tso Moriri and Hanle	
Black-necked Crane	Tibetan Wild Ass
Upland Buzzard	Red Fox
Eurasian Eagle-owl	Snow Leopard
Tibetan Lark	Pallas's Cat
Hume's Lark	Tibetan Gazelle
Twite	Tibetan Fox
Golden Eagle	Mountain Weasel
Desert Wheatear	Blue Sheep
Hill Pigeon	Royle's Pika
Brown-headed Gull	

Karnataka

Dandeli, Ganeshgudi and Anshi National Park

Dandeli Wildlife Sanctuary was set up in 1956 in the thick evergreen forests of the Uttara Kannada district in Karnataka. In 1987 part of the sanctuary was carved out to create the Anshi National Park. The latter was renamed Kali Tiger Reserve in 2015. Ganeshgudi is a jungle camp in a dense deciduous forest and is very popular with wildlife watchers and bird photographers. It is situated 52km from the Kali Tiger Reserve. The latter is located in the Western Ghats and has montane rainforests and deciduous forests of Silver Oak, Teak, bamboo and eucalyptus. Ganeshgudi has a similar habitat. The entire area is a hotspot for endemic birds such as the Malabar Trogon, White-bellied Blue Flycatcher, Dark-fronted Babbler and White-cheeked Barbet, mammals such as the Malabar Giant Squirrel, and iconic butterflies like the Southern Birdwing.

Access Anshi National Park 590km from Bangalore, 120km from Goa, the nearest airports. Anshi 60km from Karwar railway station. By road, Ganeshgudi is 120km from Goa Airport.
Best time to visit October–March.

Prakash Ramakrishna

KEY SPECIES Dandeli, Ganeshgudi and Anshi	
Great Hornbill	Asiatic Wild Dog (Dhole)
Malabar Pied Hornbill	Jungle Cat
Blue-bearded Bee-eater	Leopard Cat
White-bellied Woodpecker	Malabar Giant Squirrel
Heart-spotted Woodpecker	Malabar Civet
Brown-cheeked Fulvetta	Indian Spotted Deer
White-rumped Shama	Indian Muntjac
Indian Paradise Flycatcher	Mugger Crocodile
Asian Emerald Dove	Bengal Monitor
Indian Blue Robin	King Cobra
White-cheeked Barbet	Spectacled Cobra
Dark-fronted Babbler	Russell's Viper
Puff-throated Babbler	Saw-scaled Viper
Orange-headed Thrush	Indian Rat Snake
Malabar Trogon	Common Vine Snake
Yellow-browed Bulbul	Blue Nawab
Flame-throated Bulbul	Golden Tree Flitter
White-bellied Blue Flycatcher	Common Tiger
Tickell's Blue Flycatcher	Tawny Rajah
Brown-breasted Flycatcher	Southern Birdwing
Rusty-tailed Flycatcher	Black Prince
Blue-capped Rock Thrush	Cruiser
Black-naped Monarch	Malabar Banded Peacock
Indian Leopard	Common Pierrot
Asian Elephant	Malabar Tree Nymph
Sloth Bear	Teak
	Sandalwood

Hampi and Daroji Bear Sanctuary

The archeological ruins of Hampi, a UNESCO World Heritage Site, and the Daroji Bear Sanctuary, 20km from Hampi, in the Bellary district of Karnataka, are two important heritage, biodiversity and ecotourism sites. Craggy hills, stark stones piled up precariously over one another, sparse shrubbery, old temple ruins and caves in the Tungabhadra River Basin form the ideal habitat for the birds and other wild animals that are found here. The ruins of temples and palaces of the great Vijayanagar Empire lie scattered over 40km^2 of bare hills. Visitors might even spot a pair of Indian Leopards near the Sister's Stone, adjacent to the Queen's Bath, two well-known monuments in Hampi. The bear sanctuary is located 20km south of Hampi, where the visitors, under the supervision of the forest department, see Sloth Bears coming down the Kodipetta hill, at a distance of 3–5m from the watchtower.

Access Bangalore airport 350km and Hubli airport 143km from Hampi.
Best time to visit October–March.

KEY SPECIES Hampi and Daroji Bear Sanctuary	
Yellow-throated Bulbul	Sirkeer Malkoha
Painted Spurfowl	Sloth Bear
Painted Sandgrouse	Indian Leopard
Indian Eagle Owl	Jackal
Indian Thick-knee	Jungle Cat
Yellow-wattled Lapwing	Indian Hare
Grey Francolin	Indian Grey Mongoose
Blue Rock Thrush	Ruddy Mongoose
Red-headed Bunting	Indian Porcupine
Red Munia	Indian Star Tortoise
Scaly-breasted Munia	South Indian Rock Agama
Indian Silverbill	Brahminy Skink
Rock Bush Quail	Mugger Crocodile
Jungle Bush Quail	Saw-scaled Viper
Indian Peafowl	Indian Rock Python

KEY SPECIES Nagarhole National Park	
Lesser Adjutant	Gaur
Grey-headed Fish Eagle	Stripe-necked Mongoose
Nilgiri Wood Pigeon	Malabar Giant Squirrel
Malabar Grey Hornbill	Grey Langur
White-bellied Treepie	Black-naped Hare
Malabar Trogon	Mugger Crocodile
Malabar Parakeet	Common Vine Snake
Sirkeer Malkoha	Common Wolf Snake
Green Imperial Pigeon	Indian Rock Python
White-cheeked Barbet	Common Krait
Tiger	Painted Lady
Indian Leopard	Pea Blue
Wild Dog (Dhole)	Common Grass Yellow
Striped Hyena	Blue Tiger
Asian Elephant	Common Gull

Nagarhole National Park

This park is situated in the Coorg and Mysore districts of Karnataka. It is separated from Bandipur National Park by the Kabini reservoir. This important Tiger reserve in South India is part of the Nilgiri Biosphere Reserve. The park has thick forests, streams, waterbodies, hills and deep valleys. It has moist deciduous forests of Teak, North Indian Rosewood and Silver Oak, and dry deciduous forests. *Lantana*, clumping bamboo, Flame of the Forest and Laburnum trees are prominent types of flora.

Access Mysore airport 98km from park. Bangalore Airport 268km from park. Closest city and railway station is Mysuru (90km). **Best time to visit** October–March.

Asiatic Wild Dogs (Dholes)

Nandi Hills Karnataka

Nandi Hills, also called Nandi Durg, is a rocky group of three hillocks located in the Chickballapur district in Karnataka, 60km from Bangalore. The Yellow-throated Bulbul can be seen on the hill slopes. Several migratory birds (Pied Thrush, Blue Rock Thrush) and endemic Western Ghats birds (Nilgiri Wood Pigeon) can be seen here. Two-thirds of the Nandi Hills are covered with thorny scrub, *Lantana* and eucalyptus plantations. At the summit, original broadleaved trees of tropical moist evergreen forests survive along with cultivated species.

Access Nandi Hills is close to Bangalore (60km), which is well connected by rail and air to all parts of India. From Bangalore, a taxi can be hired.
Best time to visit November–April.

KEY SPECIES Nandi Hills Karnataka	
Nilgiri Wood Pigeon	Blue Rock Thrush
Yellow-throated Bulbul	White-cheeked Barbet
Indian Blue Robin	Shaheen Falcon
Asian Brown Flycatcher	Red Spurfowl
Brown-breasted Flycatcher	Painted Spurfowl
Ultramarine Flycatcher	Bonnet Macaque
Blue-throated Blue Flycatcher	Grey Langur
Taiga Flycatcher	Yellow Pansy
Indian Paradise Flycatcher	Common Emigrant
Pied Thrush	Plain Tiger
Orange-headed Thrush	Dark Blue Tiger
Indian Blackbird	Common Crow
Blue-capped Rock Thrush	Double-banded Crow
	Lantana

Kerala

Eravikulam National Park

This park was set up in the Kannan Devan hills of the Idukki district of Kerala in 1978 to protect the Nilgiri Tahr, a mountain goat that is endemic to the area. The park consists of high-altitude grassland interspersed with sholas or stunted montane forests. Many perennial streams criss-cross the terrain and merge to form tributaries of the Periyar river. The Anamudi peak, 2,965m high, located here is the highest peak in South India. Three major plant communities flourish here: montane grassland, forests and shrub. These features ensure the survival of unique endemic bird species such as Kerala Laughingthrushes, Nilgiri Flycatchers, White-bellied Sholakilis, Black-and-orange Flycatchers; several endemic reptiles and the Nilgiri Tahr.

NIligiri Tahr

Access Munnar 13km away by road. Alwaye the nearest rail station, 120km from park. Kochi airport 148km and Coimbatore airport 175km from park.
Best time to visit October–March.

Thattekad Bird Sanctuary

Thattekad or Salim Ali Bird Sanctuary was set up in 1983 in the Ernakulam district of Kerala, on the northern bank of the Periyar river. Situated between two branches of the river, it is an area of biodiversity of endemic birds, mammals and reptiles of the Western Ghats. The terrain is undulating and has two high peaks, Thoppimudi and Njayapillamudi. Thattekad lies at the base of the western slopes of the Western Ghats, and extensive parts of the sanctuary are hilly and covered with forests and thick undergrowth. The trees are tropical wet evergreen, semi-evergreen and moist deciduous with grassland and plantations. The best birdwatching sites are the Urulanthanni lowland area, Edamalayar Power Plant and south side of the Periyar river.

Access Kochi International Airport 45km from the sanctuary. By road Kochi 65km from Thattekad. Aluva the nearest railway station (50km).
Best time to visit October–March.

KEY SPECIES Eravikulam National Park	
Kerala Laughingthrush	Gaur
Nilgiri Sholakili	Lion-tailed Macaque
Nilgiri Flycatcher	Indian Leopard
Black-and-orange Flycatcher	Asian Elephant
Broad-tailed Grassbird	Asiatic Wild Dog (Dhole)
Nilgiri Wood Pigeon	Asian Small-clawed Otter
White-browed Bulbul	Nilgiri Striped Squirrel
Malabar Trogon	Malabar Giant Squirrel
Dark-fronted Babbler	Large-scaled Pit Viper
Malabar Parakeet	Buff-striped Keelback
Nilgiri Pipit	Anamalai Wood Snake
Nilgiri Tahr	Palni Shield-tailed Snake
Nilgiri Langur	Nilgiri Clouded Yellow
Nilgiri Marten	Nilgiri Four-ring
Sloth Bear	Golden Champak

KEY SPECIES Thattekad Bird Sanctuary	
Sri Lanka Frogmouth	Indian Leopard
Sri Lanka Bay Owl	Sloth Bear
Mottled Wood Owl	Bonnet Macaque
Spot-bellied Eagle Owl	Indian Porcupine
Malabar Trogon	Kerala Mud Snake
Jerdon's Nightjar	Collared Cat Snake
Grey-headed Bulbul	Gliding Lizard
Flame-throated Bulbul	Coastal Day Gecko
Yellow-browed Bulbul	Malabar Flash
White-bellied Treepie	Travancore Evening Brown
Rusty-tailed Flycatcher	Blue Oak Leaf
Nilgiri Wood Pigeon	Red Spot Duke
Black Baza	Rubber Tree
Tytler's Leaf Warbler	Elephant Apple Tree
Red Spurfowl	Amla

Madhya Pradesh

Bandavgarh Tiger Reserve

Bandavgarh, located in the Shahdol and Umaria districts of northeastern Madhya Pradesh, was once notorious for the relentless massacre of Tigers by the maharajahs of Rewa, whose hunting reserve it once was. The bad old days are long over and in 1993 the Tiger's habitat was finally earmarked as the Bandavgarh Tiger Reserve. With 716km² as the core zones of Tala, Magadhi and Khitauli and a buffer zone of 820km² in Umeria and Katni, the reserve covers more than 1,500km². With the Tiger corridor leading to the Panpathy Sanctuary on its northern boundary and with protected areas around it, Bandavgarh boasts a healthy Tiger habitat.

Bandavgarh lies in the highlands of the Deccan Peninsula. The valleys have tropical moist deciduous forests of sal and meadows, while the drier hill slopes have mixed forests. Along the streams are grassland where Indian and Red-headed Vultures are seen, with dense bamboo thickets in many places. The highest part of the reserve is Bandavgarh hill, which is a good place for spotting Malabar Pied Hornbills. The Raj Bahera, Chakradhara and Sehra meadows are also known for birdwatching.

Access Nearest airport Jabalpur (170km). Umaria nearest railhead (35km) on Katni Bilaspur route. From Umaria it is an hour's drive to Tala, the entry to the reserve. Katni railhead 102km away.
Best time to visit October–June.

KEY SPECIES Bandavgarh Tiger Reserve	
Malabar Pied Hornbill	Sloth Bear
Indian Vulture	Gaur
Red-headed Vulture	Sambar
Brown Fish Owl	Indian Spotted Deer
Crested Serpent Eagle	Grey Langur
Grey-headed Fish Eagle	Wild Boar
White-eyed Buzzard	Indian Rock Python
White-browed Faintail	Russell's Viper
Puff-throated Babbler	Common Krait
Black-naped Monarch	Banded Krait
Orange-headed Thrush	Checkered Keelback
White-bellied Drongo	Striped Tiger
Lesser Adjutant	Common Wanderer
Sarus Crane	Blue Mormon
Tiger	Common Rose
Indian Leopard	Baronet
Asiaic Wild Dog (Dhole)	Danaid Eggfly
Bengal Fox	Lime Butterfly
Asian Elephant	Red Spot Duke

Tigeress in Bandavgarh

Tripta Sood

Kanha National Park

Kanha National Park in Madhya Pradesh was created in 1955 to prevent the extinction of the hard-ground Barasingha or Swamp Deer. In 1973 it was declared a Tiger reserve, covering the districts of Mandla and Balaghat. It is the largest Tiger reserve in Madhya Pradesh, famed for its tall forests and meadows and its iconic resident – the Tiger. Two rivers flow through Kanha, the Banjar and Halon, both tributaries of the Narmada. The valleys are covered with sal and mixed dry deciduous forests, interspersed with meadows. On the higher areas are wet deciduous forests and bamboo. The zones of the park are Kanha, Kisli, Mukki and Sarhi.

Access Jabalpur the closest airport (175km). Nagpur airport 289km away. Jabalpur and Gondia the nearest railheads. Park well connected by road to major cities of India.
Best time to visit October–June.

Tiger

Tripta Sood

Pench National Park and Tiger Reserve

This park in Madhya Pradesh, which became a Tiger reserve in 1992, occupies the southern parts of the Satpura Range in Seoni and Chindwara districts. The forests of Pench were made famous by Rudyard Kipling in *The Jungle Book*. This is one of the most scenic and best-managed Tiger reserves in India. The reserve comprises low hills, deciduous forests of Teak, Amla and Haldu, with mixed trees of Mahua, Laburnum and bamboo thickets. Its total area is 758km^2, of which 299km^2 is the core and the rest is the buffer area. The Pench river flows through the reserve and forms a reservoir called Totladoh, which attracts many waterbirds during the winter. It has two entry gates, at Turiya and Karmajhiri.

Access Nagpur Airport 130km away. Jabulpur Airport 240km away. Seoni nearest railway station (115km).
Best time to visit October–June.

Sal forest

KEY SPECIES Kanha National Park

Indian Vulture	Indian Spotted Deer
White-eyed Buzzard	Indian Muntjac
Lesser Adjutant	Indian Spotted Chevrotain
Asian Paradise Flycatcher	Sambar
Mottled Wood Owl	Gaur
Stork-billed Kingfisher	Grey Langur
Tickell's Flycatcher	Indian Rock Python
White-browed Fantail	Indian Cobra
Indian Grey Hornbill	Common Krait
Great Thick-knee	Grass Snake
Black Francolin	Indian Rat Snake
Tiger	Common Emigrant
Indian Leopard	Lemon Emigrant
Indian Fox	Common Rose
Asiatic Wild Dog (Dhole)	Crimson Rose
Jungle Cat	Lime Butterfly
Swamp Deer	Small Grass Yellow
Four-horned Antelope	

KEY SPECIES Pench National Park

Indian Vulture	Jackal
Grey-headed Fish Eagle	Jungle Cat
Crested Serpent Eagle	Indian Spotted Deer
Oriental Honey Buzzard	Sambar
Cinnamon Bittern	Four-horned Antelope
River Lapwing	Wild Boar
Large Woodshrike	Mugger Crocodile
Asian Paradise Flycatcher	Termite Hill Gecko
Stork-billed Kingfisher	Red Sand Boa
Malabar Whistling Thrush	Common Indian Cobra
Indian Pitta	Buff-striped Keelback
Orange-headed Thrush	Common Sargeant
Plum-headed Parakeet	Common Wanderer
Painted Stork	Gaudy Baron
Tiger	Common Baron
Indian Leopard	Grey Pansy
Asiatic Wild Dog (Dhole)	Chocolate Pansy
Sloth Bear	Silverline
Indian Wolf	Striped Pierrot

Maharasthra

Melghat Tiger Reserve

Situated in the Gawalgadh hills of the Satpura Range in the Amravati district of Maharashtra, the area was designated as a wildlife sanctuary in 1967 and was given the status of the first Tiger reserve in Maharashtra in 1974 under Project Tiger. Malur village in Harisal is one of the best places in India to see the rare Forest Owlet. The reserve is dotted with high hills, deep valleys, rivers and 'nullahs' (ditches), which have water all the year round. The Tapti river and Gawalgadh ridge form the boundaries of the reserve. The vegetation is tropical dry deciduous forest, with Teak being the dominant tree species.

Access Nagpur airport 260km by road from Melghat. Badnera and Amravati the nearest railheads (127km and 110km respectively from Melghat).
Best time to visit October–June.

Tadoba National Park

Also known as the Tadoba Andhari Tiger Reserve, this park was set up in 1955 to protect the habitat of the Tiger. It is situated in the Chandrapur district in Maharashtra. It is renowned for having one of the highest densities of Tigers. The park has three wildlife areas, Tadoba or Kollara, Mohurli

Tadoba landscape

Tripta Sood

and Kolsa. It has three lakes; the largest is the Tadoba Lake; the smaller ones are Telia lake in Mohurli and the Kolsa waterbody. The Andhari river, after which the reserve is named, flows through the park. Densely forested hills cover the northern and western sides, while the southern part has meadows and deep valleys. The vegetation is tropical dry deciduous type, with Teak, Semal, Tendu, Mahua and Flame of the Forest trees, and thickets of bamboo.

Access Nagpur International Airport 140km from park. Nagpur city 140km and Chandrapur 45km away. Nearest railhead Chandrapur.
Best time to visit October–June. For Tiger sightings, April and May are the best months.

KEY SPECIES Melghat Tiger Reserve	
Forest Owlet	Indian Spotted Chevrotain
Crested Serpent Eagle	Small Indian Civet
Bonelli's Eagle	Asian Palm Civet
White-eyed Buzzard	Indian Hare
Malabar Pied Hornbill	Indian Rat Snake
Jungle Bush Quail	Arrow-headed Trinket Snake
Black-rumped Flameback	Common Krait
Indian Nightjar	Indian Cobra
Red Spurfowl	Russell's Viper
Tiger	Bamboo Pit Viper
Indian Leopard	Saw-scaled Viper
Asiatic Wild Dog (Dhole)	Common Mormon
Sloth Bear	Common Jezebel
Gaur	Striped Tiger
Honey Badger	Tawny Coster
Sambar	Mahua
Four-horned Antelope	Silk Cotton Tree
Indian Muntjac	

KEY SPECIES Tadoba National Park	
Mottled Wood Owl	Small Indian Civet
Crested Hawk Eagle	Mugger Crocodile
Grey-headed Fish Eagle	Bengal Monitor
Oriental Honey Buzzard	Banded Krait
Orange-headed Thrush	Spectacled Cobra
Spotted Owlet	Russell's Viper
Grey Junglefowl	Indian Rock Python
Barred Buttonquail	Slender Coral Snake
Savanna Nightjar	Green Vine Snake
White-naped Woodpecker	Lemon Pansy
Tiger	Chocolate Pansy
Indian Leopard	Common Lime
Gaur	Great Eggfly
Sloth Bear	Commander
Honey Badger	Teak
Asiatic Wild Dog (Dhole)	Silk Cotton Tree
Grey Langur	Flame of the Forest

Manipur

Loktak Lake and Keibul Lamjao National Park

The largest freshwater lake in India and the largest lake in north-east India, Lotak lake is situated in the Bishnupur district of Manipur. The lake covers more than 240km^2 with a maximum depth of 2.1m. Numerous hills varying in size and elevation appear as islands in the southern part of the lake. The lake is famous for its unique system due to the 'phumdis' floating on it – a phumdi is essentially a heterogeneous mass of vegetation, soil and organic material in various stages of decomposition. Phumdis form naturally when foliage floating in water piles up together over a course of many years. Their thickness varies from a few centimetres to 2m. The lake provides refuge to many bird species.

Keibul Lamjao National Park is situated on the largest phumdi, covering an area of 40km^2, and is home to the highly endangered Manipur Brow-antlered Deer, or Sangai as the locals call it, the state animal of Manipur. The floating park is the last refuge of this shy animal and the only living population of an estimated 260 animals is found here. These Manipur dancing deer have specialized hooves that are adapted to walk on the phumdis. They share their restricted habitat with Indian Hog Deer, whose decrease in population is a matter of concern.

Access Imphal Airport is 53km from the park. By road from Imphal to Moirang (30km), then to Thanga.
Best time to visit October–March.

Mizoram

Mizoram landscape

Dampa Tiger Reserve

Declared a Tiger reserve in 1994 as a part of Project Tiger, this reserve covers an area of 500km^2 with an elevation of 600–1,100m. Situated in the Manit district of Western Mizoram, its dense tropical forests are home to diverse flora and fauna. In 1994 four Tigers were reported from the park, but the 2018 census has now reported no Tiger population. Threatened mammals found here are the Clouded Leopard, Western Hoolock Gibbon, Phayre's Leaf Monkey, Binturong and Stump-tailed Macaque. Bird rarities include Mrs Hume's Pheasant. Forests of closed and open semi-evergreen and evergreen forests, and moist deciduous forest, are interpolated with steep hills, deep valleys with rivulets and natural salt licks. Bamboo is fast replacing the evergreen forests.

Access Aizawl Airport 125km (3–4-hour drive). Silchar Railway Station 180km. A Restricted Area permit is required for foreigners to enter.
Best time to visit October–April.

KEY SPECIES Loktak Lake	
Rufous-necked Hornbill	Black-necked Grebe
Wreathed Hornbill	Brow-antlered Deer
Oriental Pied Hornbill	Indian Hog Deer
Yellow-breasted Bunting	Marbled Cat
Rufous-throated Partridge	Western Hoolock Gibbon
White-cheeked Partridge	Wild Boar
Chestnut-breasted Partridge	Smooth-coated Otter
Ruddy Shelduck	Tawny Mime
Northern Hill Myna	Common Bluebottle
Lesser Skylark	

KEY SPECIES Dampa Tiger Reserve	
Mrs Hume's Pheasant	Indian Leopard
Bay Woodpecker	Clouded Leopard
Striated Yuhina	Marbled Cat
Green Imperial Pigeon	Gaur
White-browed Piculet	Phayre's Leaf Monkey
Speckled Piculet	Hog Badger
Blue Pitta	Binturong
Van Hassel's Sunbird	Lesser Bamboo Rat
Great-eared Nightjar	King Cobra
Western Hoolock Gibbon	Hill Tortoise

Meghalaya

Balpakram National Park

This park is situated in the South Garo Hills district of Meghalaya at an altitude of 910m; it covers an area of 220km². Famous for its forest-covered canyon and gorge, it is a hotspot of biodiversity known for rare flora, fauna and marine fossils. A remnant population of Gaurs and Wild Buffaloes is found here, and it also is home to a diverse primate population that includes the Western Hoolock Gibbon. Numerous species, from the Tiger to the Marbled Cat, can be seen here, and an interesting feature is the presence of a small population of Red Pandas.

As the park lies in the Eastern Himalayan endemic bird area, it is a popular birdwatching site, with more than 250 bird species. For the native Garo tribes it is 'the land of spirits' and claimed to be haunted, giving it a sacred and religious significance. The area includes the forest-covered canyon, the plateau and the surrounding forests, which are of mixed forest type with secondary regrowth of the jhum, or slash-and-burn, type of cultivation that the locals follow. Carnivorous sundew plants and many rare orchids are found here.

Access Guwahati Airport 220km. Shillong Airport 300km. Helicopter services available from both these places to Tura, 160km from park. Guwahati Station the nearest railway station. Guwahati to park via Tura, Baghmara and Hatisia (8-hour drive). Shillong to park (12-hour drive).
Best time to visit October–March.

Nagaland

Amur Falcons

Benrue

Benrue is a quaint village in the Peren district of Nagaland in the Barail range and lies 1,950m above sea level. It houses a unique community, where the minority animistic population dictates the customs and rules to the majority Christians. Benrue is a special dot on the ornithological map of the region due to its bird diversity and density. Most of the birding takes place along the roadside. The area includes intact natural broadleaved evergreen and deciduous forests with numerous Wild Cherry, oak, alder, walnut and fig trees. A rare species of bamboo believed to be the tallest in the world is found in the foothills.

Access Benrue is 130km from Khonoma (5–6-hour drive). An Inner Line Permit is required to enter Nagaland.
Best time to visit October–March.

KEY SPECIES Balpakram National Park	
Grey Peacock-pheasant	Gaur
Mountain Bamboo Partridge	Tiger
White-throated Bulbul	Red Panda
Pale-headed Woodpecker	Wild Buffalo
Black-backed Forktail	Marbled Cat
Grey-headed Parakeet	Common Vine Snake
Dark-rumped Swift	Green Pit Viper
Tawny-breasted Wren-babbler	Bengal Monitor
	Yellow Kaiser
	Bamboo Forester

KEY SPECIES Benrue	
Blyth's Tragopan	Leopard Cat
Chestnut-bellied Nuthatch	Asian Palm Civet
Yellow-throated Laughingthrush	Orange-bellied Himalayan Squirrel
Spot-breasted Parrotbill	Indian Spotted Chevrotain
Grey-sided Thrush	Small-toothed Ferret Badger
Eyebrowed Thrush	
Mountain Bamboo Partridge	Tawny Emperor
Naga Wren-babbler	Comic Oakblue
Spotted Lingsang	Naga Treebrown
	Naga Sapphire

Khonoma

Khonoma is a pristine Angami Naga village in the Japfu mountain range of Nagaland. It is situated 20km west of Kohima, the capital city, and is the first green city of Asia. Known for its fighting and hunting prowess in the past, in 1998 the village council declared a 70km² area as the Khonoma Natural Conservation and Tragopan Sanctuary, banning all hunting and logging to preserve the lush forests and rich biodiversity.

Also famous for its unique way of terraced cultivation and slash-and-burn method of agriculture, it is home to a wide variety of bird species, including Blyth's Tragopan, which is the designated state bird.

Considered one of the best birding areas of north-east India, many rare birds can be seen here, such as the Mountain Bamboo Partridge, Assam Laughingthrush, Blue-naped Pitta, Rufous-gorgeted Flycatcher and Red-faced Liocichla. The terrain ranges from gentle slopes to steep and rugged mountains, covered with lush forest land and rich in diverse flora and fauna. Khonoma's immediate habitat comprises agricultural land, land under alder trees and small patches of conifers.

Access Dimapur Airport 7km (2–3-hour drive). Dimapur Railway Station is the nearest and linked to Guwahati. Kohima to Khonoma 20km, and Kohima linked to Guwahati and Shillong. An Inner Line Pass is required for entry into Nagaland for all Indians.
Best time to visit October–March.

Odisha

Bhitarkanika Wildlife Sanctuary and National Park

The Bhitarkanika Wildlife Sanctuary was created in 1975 to protect the Saltwater Crocodile in the estuarine region of Brahmani–Baitarni, in the Kendrapara district of Orissa. It soon became a Mecca for birdwatchers as it has several rare resident bird species such as the Mangrove Pitta and Indian Skimmer, and attracts many migrants in winter. It became a national park in 1998 and a Ramsar Site in 2002. Bhitarkanika also includes the Gahimatha Beach and Marine Sanctuary where thousands of Olive Ridley Turtles nest. The habitat is mainly mangroves and tropical monsoon deciduous forests. Bhitarkanika is the second largest mangrove ecosystem in India. It also has casuarinas and grasses such as the Indigo Bush.

Access Bhubaneshwar, 170km away, is the nearest airport. Taxis available. The nearest railway station is Bhadrak, 70km from park.
Best time to visit October–March.

Herons at Mangalajodi

KEY SPECIES Khonoma	
Blyth's Tragopan	Olive-backed Pipit
Eurasian Woodcock	Leopard Cat
Naga Wren-babbler	Asian Palm Civet
Rusty-capped Fulvetta	Binturong
Grey Sibia	Indian Spotted Chevrotain
Brown-capped Laughingthrush	Small-toothed Ferret Badger
Striped Laughingthrush	Spotted Lingsang
Mountain Bamboo Partridge	Malayan Box Terrapin
Mountain Scops Owl	Jerdon's Forest Lizard
Crested Finchbill	Red-necked Keelback
Chestnut-vented Nuthatch	Indian Tortoiseshell
Flavescent Bulbul	Kohima Sapphire
Dark-rumped Swift	Blue Admiral
Eyebrowed Thrush	Tawny Mime

KEY SPECIES Bhitarkanika Wildlife Sanctuary	
Mangrove Pitta	Black-necked Stork
Brown-winged Kingfisher	Long-billed Plover
Black-capped Kingfisher	Indian Spotted Deer
Collared Kingfisher	Sambar
Common Kingfisher	Jungle Cat
Mangrove Whistler	Fishing Cat
Indian Skimmer	Wild Boar
Black-bellied Tern	Saltwater Crocodile
Oriental Darter	King Cobra
Black-necked Stork	Water Monitor
Spot-billed Pelican	Olive Ridley Sea Turtle
Greater Spotted Eagle	Tawny Coster
White-bellied Sea Eagle	Peacock Pansy
Black-headed Gull	Jamun

Avinash Khemka

Mangalajodi wetlands

Mangalajodi Marshes

Mangalajodi is a small, marshy freshwater lagoon and hamlet on the northern tip of Chilika lake, the largest brackish lake in Asia. It is situated 70km from Bhubaneshwar, the capital of Odisha. The nearest town is Tangi in the Khordha district of Odisha. The landscape is a shallow freshwater zone connected by channels that cut through the reeds and connect with the brackish water of Chilika lake. It is covered with common reeds, pond weeds and lillies, which give sufficient cover for nesting birds. Scattered Mango trees and bamboo lend charm to the habitat.

Access 70km by road from Bhubaneshwar. Khurda Road Railway station (30 km) on south-east railway on the Chennai-Kolkata route. Nearest rail station is Kalupadaghat. Nearest airport is Bhubaneshwar, 70km from Mangalajodi.
Best time to visit November–March. January is the best month for viewing waterbirds.

Punjab
Harike Wetland

The Harike Wetland was created with the construction of a barrage over the Sutlej river near the confluence of the Sutlej and Beas rivers in 1951. The Harike lake extends over the districts of Amritsar, Ferozepur and Kapurthala, and is home to many resident and migratory birds. It was declared a wildlife sanctuary in 1982 and a Ramsar Site in 1990. The entry point to Harike is from the Nanaksar Gurudwara. Vehicles can be taken up to the gurudwara, and there are birding trails that lead into the sanctuary. Birds to look out for are the Rufous-vented Prinia and Jerdon's Babbler on both sides.

Access The nearest airport and railway station is Amritsar, 60km by road. Amritsar is connected by the NH 15 (60km), Ferozepur (66km) on NH 15.
Best time to visit October–February.

Wikipedia CC

Rufous-vented Prinia

KEY SPECIES Mangalajodi Marshes	
Grey-headed Lapwing	Baillon's Crake
Black-tailed Godwit	Eurasian Whimbrel
Marsh Sandpiper	Ruff
Wood Sandpiper	Temminck's Stint
Pacific Golden Plover	Ruddy-breasted Crake
Clamorous Reed Warbler	Slaty-breasted Rail
Watercock	Jungle Cat
Oriental Pratincole	Fishing Cat
Whiskered Tern	Jackal
Ruddy Shelduck	Plain Tiger
Greater Painted-snipe	Common Jezebel
Bluethroat	King Cobra
Yellow Bittern	Water Monitor
Cinnamon Bittern	Olive Ridley Sea Turtle

KEY SPECIES Harike Wetland	
Greylag Goose	Indian Skimmer
Ruddy Shelduck	Common Snipe
Tufted Duck	Common Woodshrike
Common Teal	White-browed Fantail
Red-crested Pochard	Striated Grassbird
Common Pochard	Brown-headed Gull
Ferruginous Duck	Jackal
Black-tailed Godwit	Jungle Cat
Great Cormorant	Wild Boar
Jerdon's Babbler	Indian Gharial
Rufous-vented Prinia	Indian Star Tortoise
Black-headed Gull	Smooth-coated Otter
Black-necked Grebe	Indian Rat Snake
Hen Harrier	Tree of Heaven

Rajasthan

Jorbeer, Bikaner

Jorbeer, situated 15km from Bikaner, is a dumping ground for animal carcasses, which attract huge congregations of vultures and eagles, particularly in winter. Birdwatchers and wildlife enthusiasts visit in winter to see seven vulture species, Griffon, Himalayan, Egyptian, Indian, White-rumped, Red-headed and Cinereous, in one place. It is an IBA and Conservation Reserve. It is arid, sandy desert habitat with acacia and Khejri *Prosipis cineraria* trees, which afford perching posts for vultures and eagles.

Access The nearest airport is Jodhpur, 260km from Bikaner. Bikaner is connected by rail to Jodhpur, Mumbai, Delhi and Kolkata.
Best time to visit October–March.

Tapas mishra

Jorbeer

KEY SPECIES Jorbeer, Bikaner

Griffon Vulture	Great Grey Shrike
Himalayan Vulture	Desert Fox
Red-headed Vulture	Jungle Cat
Egyptian Vulture	Desert Cat
White-rumped Vulture	Indian Wolf
Cinereous Vulture	Indian Desert Jird
Tawny Eagle	Chinkara
Steppe Eagle	Nilgai
Eastern Imperial Eagle	Indian Spiny-tailed Lizard
Laggar Falcon	Common Krait
Saker Falcon	Saw-scaled Viper
Shikra	Spectacled Cobra
Long-legged Buzzard	Blue-spotted Arab
Yellow-eyed Pigeon	Common Jezebel
Rosy Starling	Plain Tiger
Variable Wheatear	Blue Tiger
Common Kestrel	Catechu

Keoladeo Ghana National Park (Bharatpur Wildlife Sanctuary)

This is a man-made wetland on the western part of the Indo-Gangetic Plain, in the state of Rajasthan. It lies on the path of the Central Asian Flyway of migratory birds, and is a point of congregation of thousands of migratory birds before they disperse to other parts of India. Many stay over to spend the winter, before returning to breed in Central Asia in the spring. Resident birds, like Painted Storks, Open-billed Storks and Black-headed Ibises, breed in the heronry here. Bharatpur or Keoladeo Ghana is a UNESCO World Heritage Site and a Ramsar Wetland.

The park is a mosaic of dry grassland, woodland, woodland swamps and wetlands. The principal vegetation is tropical dry deciduous forests intermixed with dry grassland. Forests are of huge Kadamb and Jamun trees in scattered pockets. Most of the woodland is open woodland with Babul, Khejri, (the ubiquitous tree of Rajasthan), and Ber, or Indian Hog Plum. The grassland has tall grasses with scattered trees and shrubs. The park is a freshwater swamp that floods during the monsoon.

KEY SPECIES Keoladeo Ghana National Park

Sarus Crane	Common Sandpiper
Black-winged Kite	Brown Hawk Owl
Indian Spotted Eagle	Oriental Darter
Greater Spotted Eagle	Great Cormorant
Dusky Eagle Owl	Nilgai
Indian Nightjar	Indian Spotted Deer
Grey Nightjar	Sambar
Black Bittern	Wild Boar
Yellow Bittern	Jungle Cat
Baillon's Crake	Leopard Cat
Garganey	Fishing Cat
Gadwal	Jackal
Common Teal	Indian Porcupine
Common Pochard	Smooth-coated Otter
Northern Pintail	Water Monitor
Northern Shoveler	Indian Rock Python
Black-necked Stork	Checkered Keelback
Painted Stork	Russell's Viper
Eurasian Spoonbill	Common Cobra
Striated Heron	Common Grass Yellow
Grey Heron	Pioneer
Black-crowned Night Heron	Small Salmon Arab
Eurasian Wryneck	White Orange-tip
Green Sandpiper	Plain Tiger

376

Access Jaipur and New Delhi are the nearest airports and Bharatpur is the nearest railway station. Both airports are a 3–4-hour drive from the park. Inside the park, motor transport is not allowed, to minimize disturbance to the birds. Bicycles and cycle rickshaws are available for hire to move about in the park. The rickshaw pullers are also knowledgeable and well-trained bird guides.
Best time to visit October–March.

Ranthambore National Park
Ranthambore, situated in the Sawai Madhopur district in eastern Rajasthan, is one of the most famous Tiger reserves in northern India, with about 70 Tigers. The park is part of a larger reserve that includes the Keola Devi Sanctuary, Sawai Madhopur Sanctuary and Sawai Man Singh Sanctuary. It is a scenic area made up of dry deciduous forests, rocky hills, thorny scrub, lakes and open, grassy meadows. Deciduous forests have trees of Teak, Jamun, Mango, Banyan, Peepal and Tamarind. Thorny scrub comprises acacia and clumps of bamboo. Small grassland areas contain waterbodies and rivulets. The biggest lake is the Padam Talao, with a former royal hunting lodge and a huge Banyan tree near it. The ruins

of the tenth-century Ranthambore Fort overlook the park. The archeological ruins have merged with the forest and Tigers are frequent visitors here.

Access The closest airport is at Jaipur (182km). The closest railway station is Sawai Madhopur, 11km from the park. Jaipur is 160km by road.
Best time to visit October–June.

KEY SPECIES Ranthambore National Park	
Crested Serpent Eagle	Ruddy Shelduck
Changeable Hawk Eagle	Tiger
Painted Spurfowl	Indian Leopard
Great Thick-knee	Caracal
Indian Thick-knee	Jungle Cat
Indian Roller	Rusty Spotted Cat
Dusky Eagle Owl	Sloth Bear
Indian Scops Owl	Striped Hyena
Common Kingfisher	Sambar
Black-rumped Flameback	Indian Spotted Deer
Indian Peafowl	Chinkara
Rufous Treepie	Blackbuck
Jungle Bush Quail	Wild Boar
Yellow-footed Green Pigeon	Northern Plains Langur
Grey Francolin	Asian Palm Civet
Black Stork	Mugger Crocodile
Woolly-necked Stork	Indian Cobra
Alexandrine Parakeet	Leaf-nosed Snake
Indian Pitta	Bronze Tree Snake
Chestnut-bellied Sandgrouse	Indian Rat Snake
Painted Sandgrouse	Common Rose
Greylag Goose	Common Mormon
	Leopard Lacewing
	Spotless Grass Yellow

Jogi Mahal, a former hunting lodge, at Ranthambore

Kheechan - Demoiselle Crane Village in the Thar Desert

Kheechen, a remote desert village situated midway between Jodhpur and Jaisalmer in Rajasthan, is the place where 15,000–20,000 Demoiselle Cranes migrate every year from August and September onwards. They arrive here from their frozen homelands in Mongolia, China, Russia and Europe. Hordes of birdwatchers and ornithologists descend on Kheechan every year in the winter to witness this amazing spectacle. The World Crane Foundation has given Kheechen the status of a World Heritage Site.

Kheechen is situated on the edge of the Thar Desert, in the Phalodi administrative area of Jodhpur district. Its habitat is arid desert with sparse thorn-scrub vegetation. Sand dunes near the village serve as a staging ground for the cranes, where they gather before they come to feed on the grain laid out for them in a fenced enclosure. Small waterbodies and ponds (Vijaysagar lake and Raatdi Naadi) dot the area, and this is where cranes and migratory waders drink water. About 25km from Kheechen is a salty landscape called Malhar Rinn, where the cranes roost at night.

Access Jodhpur 150km from Kheechen by road and the nearest airport. Jaisalmer and Bikaner 150–160km from Kheechen. Phalodi

Tal Chappar landscape

railway station 6km from Kheechen, and on the broad-gauge line from Delhi to Jaisalmer and en route to Jodhpur.
Best time to visit October–March.

Tal Chappar Blackbuck Sanctuary

This sanctuary was established in the Churu district of northwestern Rajasthan, about 210km from Jaipur, to protect the Blackbuck. Earlier it was the hunting reserve of the Maharaja of Bikaner. It is a tiny sanctuary, measuring only 8km^2. It is on the pathway of raptor migration in winter and birders visit here to see the resident and migratory raptor species as well as other birds. The sanctuary lies on the fringe of the Thar Desert and is subject to great extremes of climate – very hot summers and cold winters, when temperatures reach freezing point. The habitat is flat grassland with tropical thorn forests of acacia *Prosopis cineraria* and *P. juliflora*. Rainwater flows through shallow, low-lying areas and collects in small water pools. The birding hotspots are the sanctuary, the Gaushala area nearby, which is an important habitat for the Spotted Creeper, and adjacent villages for Demoiselle Cranes and small waders.

Access The sanctuary is 350km from Delhi and 210km from Jaipur, the closest airport. Sujangarh the nearest railway station. Chappar railway station connected to Jaipur and Ratangarh (45km to Tal Chappar by road), to Delhi.
Best time to visit Throughout the year.

Demoiselle Cranes

KEY SPECIES Kheechan - Demoiselle Crane Village	
Demoiselle Crane	Desert Wheatear
Indian Peafowl	Desert Fox
Common Sandpiper	Desert Cat
Little Ringed Plover	Blackbuck
Chestnut-bellied Sandgrouse	Chinkara
White Wagtail	Catechu

Bhanu Singh

Great Indian Bustards

Desert National Park, Jaisalmer and Barmer

This park in northwestern India is one of the largest parks, with an area of 3,162km. Most of the park is in the Jaisalmer district and the rest is in Barmer. This is the hottest and driest region in India, the Thar Desert. The area is entirely landlocked and sandwiched between the Aravalli mountains to the east, the Rann of Kutch to the south and the Indus plain to the west. The park is a vast, sandy terrain with sand dunes, scattered Khejri trees and open grassland. After brief spells of rain, short grasses appear. The desert is the home of India's most famous grassland bird, the Great Indian Bustard and a number of birds of prey, which include the Vulnerable Laggar and Saker Falcons.

Access Jaisalmer is about 20km from the park and is the nearest railway station, connected to all parts of India. Jodhpur is the nearest airport (300km).

Best time to visit October–February.

KEY SPECIES Tal Chappar Blackbuck Sanctuary

Pallid Harrier	Himalayan Vulture
Montagu's Harrier	Griffon Vulture
Western Marsh Harrier	Stoliczka's Bushchat
White-eyed Buzzard	Indian Eagle Owl
White-tailed Eagle	Chestnut-shouldered
Short-toed Snake Eagle	Petronia
Tawny Eagle	Spanish Sparrow
Steppe Eagle	Yellow-eyed Pigeon
Eastern Imperial Eagle	Variable Wheatear
Laggar Falcon	Short-eared Owl
Red-necked Falcon	Blackbuck
Oriental Skylark	Desert Fox
Eurasian Skylark	Desert Cat
Sand Lark	Chinkara
Singing Bush Lark	Wild Boar
Crested Lark	Jackal
Bimaculated Lark	Indian Spiny-tailed Lizard
Rufous-tailed Lark	Desert Monitor
Greater Short-toed Lark	Indian Rock Python
Long-billed Pipit	Common Wolf Snake
Tawny Pipit	Rounded Pierrot
Demoiselle Crane	Small Salmon Arab
Common Crane	Blue Pansy

KEY SPECIES Desert National Park

Great Indian Bustard	Himalayan Vulture
MacQueen's Bustard	Egyptian Vulture
Demoiselle Crane	White-eared Bulbul
Chestnut-bellied	Trumpeter Finch
Sandgrouse	Water Pipit
Black-bellied Sandgrouse	Desert Cat
Blue-cheeked Bee-eater	Chinkara
Cream-coloured Courser	Blackbuck
Indian Courser	Desert Fox
Black-crowned Sparrow	Indian Fox
Lark	Indian Wolf
Desert Lark	Desert Hedgehog
Greater Hoopoe Lark	Indian Desert Jird
Crested Lark	Indian Spiny-tailed Lizard
Short-toed Snake Eagle	Dwarf Gecko
Steppe Eagle	Persian Gecko
Tawny Eagle	Laungwala Toad-headed
White-eyed Buzzard	Agama
Red-headed Vulture	Sindh Awl-headed Snake
Cinereous Vulture	Desert Monitor
White-rumped Vulture	Saw-scaled Viper
Indian Vulture	Common Krait
Griffon Vulture	Lime Butterfly

Tamil Nadu

Anaimalai Tiger Reserve

The Anaimalai Wildlife Sanctuary and National Park was designated as the Anaimalai Tiger Reserve in 2007. It is located in the Pollachi and Valparai divisions, in the Anaimalai Hills in the Coimbatore district of Tamil Nadu and Udumalaipettai of Tiruppur, also in Tamil Nadu.

The park has flora typical of the Western Ghats and shelters fauna that is unique to it. Wet evergreen forests, semi-evergreen forests, montane forests, shola grassland, moist deciduous and dry deciduous forests, thorn forests and marshes are found here. Bamboo stands also occur in the original natural evergreen forest, much of which has now been converted to Teak plantations. Birdwatching and wildlife viewing occur at three main places: Karian Shola, Grass Hills and Manjampatti Valley.

Access Anaimalai is best approached from Coimbatore to Pollachi (40km), then to Topslip (35km), the entry point to the park. Coimbatore airport, connected to major cities, is 75km from Anaimalai.
Best time to visit October–March.

Mudumalai National Park

The Mudumalai National Park and Wildlife Sanctuary was set up in 1940 and is situated on the northwestern tip of the Nilgiri Hills in Tamil Nadu, at the junction of Tamil Nadu, Kerala and Karnataka. It is located 150km to the north of Coimbatore and is divided into five ranges: Masinagudi, Mudumalai, Kargudi, Thepakadu and Nellakota. Three main types of forest florish here, tropical moist deciduous, tropical dry deciduous and tropical dry thorn. Tropical semi-evergreen forests are also found in the western part of Mudumalai, where the annual rainfall exceeds 2,000mm. The trees in the park are mainly Teak, Indian Rosewood, Elephant Grass and bamboo. Plants of wild rice, wild ginger, turmeric, cinnamon, pepper and mango grow alongside other vegetation.

Access Mudumalai National Park is 240km from Bangalore, 150km from Coimbatore, 90km from Mysore and 68km from Ooty. The reserve lies along the Mysore-Ooty national highway. Mysore is the closest airport to Mudumalai, which is 90km by road to the park.
Best time to visit October–March.

KEY SPECIES Anaimalai Tiger Reserve

Wayanad Laughingthrush	Lion-tailed Macaque
White-bellied Treepie	Rusty-spotted Cat
Great Hornbill	Slender Loris
Malabar Grey Hornbill	Indian Porcupine
Nilgiri Flycatcher	Stripe-necked Mongoose
Black-and-orange Flycatcher	Ruddy Mongoose
White-bellied Blue Flycatcher	Indian Pangolin
	Indian Spotted Deer
Rufous Babbler	Bonnet Macaque
Nilgiri Wood Pigeon	Brown Palm Civet
White-bellied Sholakili	Malabar Pit Viper
Malabar Parakeet	Large-scaled Green
Yellow-browed Bulbul	Pit Viper
Heart-spotted Woodpecker	Nilgiri Keelback
Crimson-backed Sunbird	Common Emigrant
Tiger	Common Albatross
Indian Leopard	Plain Puffin
Asian Elephant	Five-bar Swordtail
Sloth Bear	Nilgiri Four-ring
Asiatic Wild Dog (Dhole)	Iron Wood Tree
Nilgiri Tahr	Mango
Nilgiri Langur	Teak

KEY SPECIES Mudumalai National Park

Malabar Trogon	Changeable Hawk Eagle
Malabar Pied Hornbill	White-rumped Spinetail
Black Eagle	Tiger
Crested Goshawk	Indian Leopard
Besra	Wild Dog (Dhole)
Jerdon's Baza	Striped Hyena
Brown Hawk Owl	Asian Elephant
Rock Bush Quail	Sloth Bear
Black-and-orange Flycatcher	Gaur
Asian Fairy-bluebird	Red Giant Flying Squirrel
Red Spurfowl	Indian Spotted Deer
White-bellied Woodpecker	Sambar
Lesser Yellownape	Spectacled Cobra
Asian Emerald Dove	Common Krait
Painted Bush Quail	Indian Rock Python
Crimson-backed Sunbird	Malabar Raven
Indian Paradise Flycatcher	Malabar Tree Nymph
Malabar Parakeet	Southern Birdwing
Yellow-browed Bulbul	Red Helen
Malabar Barbet	Blue Oakleaf
Malabar Whistling Thrush	Common Nawab
Nilgiri Wood Pigeon	Sandalwood
Mottled Wood Owl	Arjun

Clement M Francis

Anaimalai landscape

Uttar Pradesh

Dudhwa National Park and Tiger Reserve

This park is situated in the terai region of the Lakhimpur-Kheri district of Uttar Pradesh, adjacent to the Indo-Nepal border. The southern boundary is formed by the Suheli river and the northern by the Mohana river, which flows along the Nepal border. Established as a national park in 1977 by the lone effort of conservationist 'Billy' Arjan Singh, it was declared a Tiger reserve in 1987 under Project Tiger by bringing in two more sanctuaries, namely Kishanpur and Katarniaghat. The rich and fertile Indo-Gangetic Plain supports a flamboyant growth of forests and tall grassland scattered with pools, streams and rivulets. Covering 811km², it is home to many rare mammals like the Swamp Deer, Tiger, Asian Elephant, Indian Rhinoceros, Fishing Cat and Hispid Hare, and also has rare avian species like the Bengal Florican and Swamp Francolin. The Indian Rhinoceros was relocated to the park in 1984 after being translocated from Assam.

The park includes some of the best sal forests and grassland left in the terai region. The forest type is North Indian moist deciduous, nearly 60 per cent of which is Sal trees, with the remaining trees being typical of the sub-Himalayan terrain. Extensive tracts of grassland are interposed with swamps and lakes.

Access Lucknow Airport 240km. Dudhwa Railway Station 4km. Mailani Railway Station 37km. Lucknow Railway Station 220km. Shahjahanpur Station 107km. Lucknow 220km by road.
Best time to visit October–July.

KEY SPECIES Dudhwa National Park	
Bengal Florican	Asian Elephant
Yellow-legged Green Pigeon	Indian Rhinoceros
	Swamp Deer
Black-breasted Weaver	Sambar
Great Slaty Woodpecker	Indian Spotted Deer
Slender-billed Vulture	Nilgai
Indian Grassbird	Hispid Hare
Spot-billed Pelican	Fishing Cat
Hodgson's Bushchat	Burmese Rock Python
Swamp Francolin	Common Mime
Tiger	Sal

Uttarakhand

Chopta and Kedarnath Wildlife Sanctuary

Also called the Kedarnath Himalayan Musk Deer Sanctuary, this sanctuary is situated in the Chamoli and Rudraprayag districts of Uttarakhand and is spread over 975km². It was established in 1972 to protect the declining population of the Himalayan Musk Deer. Drained by the Mandakini river and its tributaries, it is at an elevation of 1,160–7,068m, with Chaukhamba being the highest peak. A rich bioreserve, this lush green forest belt abounds in high peaks, waterfalls, deep valleys, lakes, high-altitude glaciers and vast meadows. Chopta, a small hamlet and part of the sanctuary, has attracted the attention of birdwatchers from around the world for its rich avifauna of more than 300 species, including the Himalayan Monal. Tungnath, which is a short, steep trek from Chopta, is a favourite site for sighting the Snow Partridge. Wet temperate mixed forests and subtropical forests are found in the lower ranges, while higher altitudes have subalpine and alpine coniferous forests with alpine meadows. Medicinal and aromatic plants are found here.

Access Dehradun Airport 227km from Chopta. Rishikesh Railway Station 212km. By road Rishikesh to Chopta is a 7-hour drive.

Best time to visit April–June; September–November.

Chopta landscape

Alok Prasad CC

Corbett National Park and Tiger Reserve

This park is an important part of India's environmental heritage and was the first national park to be established in 1936. It is named after Jim Corbett, the famous naturalist and conservationist. It was the first area to be initiated under the Tiger Project in 1973, covering an area of 1,318km², of which 580km² is the core area and the rest the buffer zone. Located in the Nainital district of Uttarakhand, the park boasts breathtaking landscapes bound by the Western Himalayas on one side and the verdant terai region on the other. The Ramganga river and its tributaries are the lifeline of this amazing biodiversity. This is the only park in India that allows you to stay overnight in the forest rest house in the lap of nature and enjoy the rich flora and fauna it harbours. For ecotourism purposes the park is divided into different zones: Dhikala, Bijrani, Jhirna, Dhela and Durga Devi, where jeep safaris can be undertaken. Some zones have forest rest houses where night stays are allowed.

Thick forests, sprawling grassland, marshy swamps, hill streams, rivulets and lakes are all part of the diverse topography of this area, and it houses the most exotic mammalian species that India has to offer, namely the Tiger, Indian Leopard, Asian Elephant, five species of deer, Sloth Bear and crocodiles. Equally rich in avifauna, it is reportedly home to more than 600 bird species and many rare birds like the Tawny Fish Owl, Spot-bellied

KEY SPECIES Chopta and Kedarnath	
Himalayan Monal	Himalayan Langur
Snow Partridge	Jungle Cat
Koklass Pheasant	Himalayan Goral
Bearded Vulture	Bharal
Crested Goshawk	Asiatic Black Bear
Scarlet Finch	Himalayan Tahr
Fire-capped Tit	Indian Muntjac
Mountain Hawk Eagle	Red Giant Flying Squirrel
Long-billed Thrush	Royle's Pika
Chestnut-crowned Warbler	Himalayan Pit Viper
Maroon Oriole	Boulanger's Keelback
Himalayan Musk Deer	Common Woodbrown
Indian Leopard	Common Blue Apollo

Gopinath Kollur

Corbett landscape

Eagle Owl, Wallcreeper, Ibisbill, Common Green Magpie, Crested Serpent Eagle, Great Slaty Woodpecker, Pallas's Fish Eagle, Great Hornbill, Wallcreeper and Rosy Minivet. Subalpine, tropical dry and moist deciduous forests with tropical grassland and riverine vegetation are found here. Forest cover is 70 per cent and grassland cover is 10 per cent, while the remaining land is interposed with rivulets, streams, marshes and lakes. Sal, Haldu, Sheesham, Dhak (Flame of the Forest), Rohini and Peepal trees form the main bulk of the forests.

KEY SPECIES Corbett National Park	
Golden-headed Cisticola	Indian Muntjac
Spot-bellied Eagle Owl	Indian Hog Deer
Great Hornbill	Yellow-throated Marten
Hodgson's Bushchat	Sloth Bear
Common Green Magpie	Wild Boar
Yellow-eyed Babbler	Smooth-coated Otter
Maroon Oriole	Indian Gharial
Chestnut-headed Tesia	Indian Pangolin
Collared Falconet	Mugger Crocodile
Tiger	Bengal Monitor
Asian Elephant	Indian Rock Python
Indian Leopard	Indian Jezebel
Sambar	Sal
Indian Spotted Deer	Flame of the Forest

Access Delhi Airport 280km. Ramnagar Railway Station well connected by trains from Delhi. Kathgodam Station 55km from Ramnagar. By road, Delhi to Ramgarh is 6 hours. Morning and afternoon jeep safaris are available for Bijrani, Jhirna and Dhela zones. Online permits for entry/safaris into the park and for stays inside in the forest rest house have to be obtained in advance. **Best time to visit** November–June.

Kilbury Bird Sanctuary and Pangot

This birding paradise is located 15km from Nainital in Uttarakhand. It is at an elevation of 2,528m, and is home to 580 bird species in the midst of the reserved forest of Nainital. Surrounded by lush green forest of oak, pine and rhododendron, the Kilbury road is one of the most scenic and famous birding routes. Pangot, a quaint village, is known for high-altitude west-central Himalayan bird species like the Chestnut-bellied Nuthatch, Red-billed Blue Magpie, Altai Accentor, Rufous-bellied Woodpecker, Blue-throated Barbet, Mountain Hawk Eagle, Black-headed Jay,

Khushboo Sharma

Sattal Lake

Long-tailed Minivet and Black-throated Tit. The drive beyond Vinayak offers a chance of sighting Kalij, Koklass and Cheer Pheasants. Other species like the Mistle Thrush and Long-billed Thrush can be commonly seen, and many species of tit, laughingthrush, sunbird, babbler and flycatcher can also be seen. Mammals like the Indian Leopard, Himalayan Goral, Red Fox, Indian Muntjac, Wild Boar and Yellow-throated Marten are occasionally seen on this road.

Access Pantnagar Airport (80km) is a 3-hour drive. Kathgodam Station 50km. Ramnagar Station 70km. Delhi is an 8-hour drive,
Best time to visit October–March

Sattal

The Sattal Lake comprises a group of seven small, interconnected freshwater lakes and is situated in the lower Himalayan range near Bhimtal town in the Nainital district of Uttarakhand. Located at an elevation of 1,370m and surrounded by thick pine and oak forests, it forms a unique biodiversity which has an unparalleled diverse avifauna with more than 500 resident and migratory species. It is considered one of the best places to see the middle-elevation western Himalayan bird species at close quarters on walking trails, accompanied by a local birding guide. Studio Point has gained recognition for sightings of many species that gather here for feeding and drinking water. Many experts have now set up camps with hides in the area, so you need not trek far for observation and photography.

Access Pantnagar is the closest airport. Kathgodam Railway Station 27km. By road from Delhi to Sattal via Haldwani is a 7-hour drive.
Best time to visit October–March.

Rufous-throated Partridge

KEY SPECIES Kilbury Bird Sanctuary	
Koklass Pheasant	Green-tailed Sunbird
Cheer Pheasant	Indian Leopard
Kalij Pheasant	Himalayan Goral
Mountain Hawk Eagle	Red Fox
Black Francolin	Wild Boar
Hume's Leaf Warbler	Indian Muntjac
Rufous-bellied Woodpecker	Yellow-throated Marten
Blue-winged Minla	Indian Grey Mongoose
Mistle Thrush	Western Blue Sapphire
Chestnut-tailed Minla	Common Wall
Common Cuckoo	Lesser Punch

KEY SPECIES Sattal	
Kalij Pheasant	Himalayan Goral
White-crested Laughingthrush	Indian Leopard
	Wild Boar
Great Barbet	Yellow-throated Marten
Long-tailed Broadbill	Himalayan Langur
Ultramarine Flycatcher	Himalayan Pit Viper
Chestnut-headed Tesia	Boulanger's Keelback
Blue-winged Minla	Red Lacewing
Rufous-throated Partridge	Tawny Rajah
Fire-capped Tit	Indian Oakleaf
Chestnut-crowned Warbler	

West Bengal

Buxa Tiger Reserve and National Park

Situated in the Jalpaiguri district of West Bengal, this park was established in 1983 and designated as a national park in 1992. It covers an area of 760km², with elevations ranging from 60m in the Gangetic Plain to 1,750m bordering the Himalayas in the north. Contiguous with the Manas National Park, it forms part of the international corridor for elephant migration between India and Bhutan. The Jayanti and Raidhak rivers flow through the park, making it a rich bioreserve with a variety of orchids and medicinal plants. The park is a haven for elephants, bison and several species of deer. The forest watchtower is a good place to observe wildlife. Forest types include northern dry deciduous, Eastern Himalayan moist mixed deciduous and northern tropical evergreen forests, as well as moist sal savannah, tropical grassland and riverine vegetation. Sal, Teak, Shisham, Silk Cotton, Champa and Gamar trees are abundant.

Access Bagdogra Airport 185km to Rajabhatkhawa (4-hour drive). New Jalpaiguri Station 170km. Alipurduar Station 15km. By road Siliguri to Rajabhatkhawa via NH 37, 187km. Permit for entry to the park should be obtained from the forest office at Rajabhatkhawa or Jayanti, both of which are entry points to the park. **Best time to visit** November–April.

Buxa landscape

Swaroop Singha Roy CC

KEY SPECIES Buxa Tiger Reserve	
Great Hornbill	Asian Elephant
Common Merganser	Gaur
Jerdon's Babbler	Tiger
Black-necked Stork	Asian Golden Cat
Finn's Weaver	Clouded Leopard
Black Baza	Indian Spotted Deer
Jerdon's Baza	Sambar
Velvet-fronted Nuthatch	Indian Hog Deer
Chestnut-breasted Partridge	Wild Boar
Long-tailed Minivet	Asiatic Black Bear
Bristled Grassbird	Branded Awlking

Neora Valley National Park

Covering an area of 88km², the Neora Valley National Park was established in 1986 in the Kalimpong district of West Bengal. The highest point in the park is Rachela Pass at an altitude of 3,200m, which forms the boundary with Sikkim in the north and Bhutan in the north-east. The southern limit is just 183m high and consists of the Jalpaiguri forest belt.

Red Panda, Neora Valley

The Neora river flows through it, giving the park its name. This land of the elegant Red Panda has pristine natural habitat with rugged inaccessible terrain. Considered a paradise for birdwatchers, it is reportedly home to 350 bird species. Lava is a good area for birding and an experienced bird guide is recommended. The park has four main habitat types: subtropical mixed broadleaved forests, low temperate evergreen forests, upper temperate mixed broadleaved forests and rhododendron forests. Thick bamboo groves in the park are inhabited by Red Pandas. Orchids form a canopy at higher altitude.

Access Bagdogra Airport 120km from Lava (4-hour drive). New Jalpaiguri Station 105km from Lava (3-hour drive). By road, Darjeeling 81km and Kalimpong 34km. An entry permit is required from the forest office at Lava to enter the forest, and the entry point is at Kolakham, 10km from Lava. Vehicles can go only up to Zero Point, which is 13km into the forest.
Best time to visit October–March.

Mahananda Wildlife Sanctuary

Located in the foothills of the Himalayas, between the Mahananda and Teesta rivers in the Darjeeling district of West Bengal, and spread over 159km^2, the sanctuary was declared in 1959 to protect the Gaur and Tiger, which were on the brink of extinction. The variation in altitude, from 150 to 1,370m, and the variable forest types, support diverse flora and fauna. This is the largest compact block of forested habitat situated in the western route of the migratory corridor of the Asian Elephant. Latpanchar is at the highest elevation of the sanctuary and is 44km from Siliguri; it offers a good birding experience. The sanctuary is at the crossroads of two biomes, the Sino-Himalayan subtropical forests and Indo-Chinese moist tropical forests, with a small portion of the Indo-Gangetic Plain.

Access Bagdogra Airport 41km. New Jalaiguri Railway Station 35km. The main entrance to the park is from Sukhna village, which is only 12km from Siliguri. Morning and afternoon safaris are available at the gate.
Best time to visit October–March.

Mahananda landscape

KEY SPECIES Neora Valley National Park	
Speckled Wood Pigeon	Red Panda
Darjeeling Woodpecker	Asiatic Black Bear
White-tailed Robin	Himalayan Serow
Golden-throated Barbet	Indian Leopard
Gould's Shortwing	Leopard Cat
Rusty-bellied Shortwing	Hoary-bellied Squirrel
Satyr Tragopan	Himalayan Goral
Himalayan Cutia	Kaiser-i-Hind
Rufous-necked Hornbill	Krishna Peacock
Yellow-browed Tit	Bhanj Oak

KEY SPECIES Mahananda Wildlife Sanctuary	
Rufous-necked Hornbillr	Indian Muntjac
Chestnut-winged Cuckoo	Gaur
Violet Cuckoo	Asiatic Black Bear
Pin-striped Tit-babbler	Indian Leopard
Asian Fairy-bluebird	Fishing Cat
Red-headed Trogon	Wild Boar
Purple Cochoa	Common Peacock
Asian Elephant	White Orange-tip
Tiger	Silk Cotton Tree
Sambar	Sal

Sunderbans Biosphere Reserve

This reserve is located in the southeastern tip of the North 24 Parganas district of West Bengal. Established as a national park in 1984, it was declared a UNESCO World Heritage Site in 1987. This unique biosphere reserve is the largest delta covered with mangrove forests and vast saline mudflats in the world, and derives its name from the local mangrove species – Sundari. The delta, formed by the Ganga, Brahmaputra and Meghna rivers, covers 10,000km^2, of which 4,260km^2 is in India and the rest in Bangladesh. It hosts a large Tiger population and hence is also a designated Tiger reserve. This complex ecosystem is known for its rich biodiversity, especially in regard to fish, reptiles, birds and crustaceans. Many mammals are also found in the park, and form the prey base for the Tigers. Some rare birds like the Mangrove Pitta, Mangrove Whistler, Buffy Fish Owl, Goliath Heron and Brown-winged Kingfisher can be seen here.

Access Kolkata is the closest airport. Canning Station is the nearest railhead (64km from Kolkata). You can drive from Kolkata to Canning, Namkhana, Raidhiki, Sonakhali or Basanti, from where you can take a boat to the various islands: Sajnekhali, Bali, Piyali and Jharkali.
A permit to enter the park needs to be obtained from the field director's office in Canning, and guides accompany tourists in motorized launches to traverse the vast waterways of the sanctuary.
Best time to visit October–February.

KEY SPECIES Sunderbans Biosphere Reserve	
Mangrove Pitta	Olive Ridley Sea Turtle
Mangrove Whistler	Hawksbill Sea Turtle
Brown-winged Kingfisher	River Terrapin
Black-capped Kingfisher	Checkered Keelback Water
Ruddy Kingfisher	Snake
Collared Kingfisher	Red-tailed Pit Viper
Goliath Heron	White Tiger
Saltwater Crocodile	Spotted Black Crow
Water Monitor	Freshwater Mangrove

Spotted Deer at Sunderbans

Vaidehi Gunjal

Recommended Reading

Grewal, B. (2021) *A Naturalist's Guide to Birds of Nepal*. Oxford: John Beaufoy Publishing.

Grewal, B., Singh, Bhanu (2020) *The 100 Best Birdwatching Sites in India* Oxford: John Beaufoy Publishing.

Grewal, B., Bhatia, G. (2021) *A Naturalist's Guide to the Birds of India*. Oxford: John Beaufoy Publishing.

Grewal, B., Chakravarty, R. (2021) *A Naturalist's Guide to the Mammals of India*. Oxford: John Beaufoy Publishing.

Grimmet, R. Inskipp, T., & Inskipp, C. (1998) *Birds of the Indian Subcontinent*. UK: A & C Black.

Rasmussen, P. & Anderton, J. (2005) *Birds of South Asia: The Ripley Guide*. Barcelona: Lynx Editions.

Sachdeva, P., Tongbram V. (2019) *A Naturalist's Guide to the Trees and Shrubs of India*. Oxford: John Beaufoy Publishing.

Sachdeva, P., Tongbram V. (2019) *A Naturalist's Guide to the Garden Flowers of India*. Oxford: John Beaufoy Publishing.

Smetacek, P., (2017) *A Naturalist's Guide to the Butterflies of India*. Oxford: John Beaufoy Publishing.

Das I., Das A. (2014) *A Naturalist's Guide to the Reptiles of India*. Oxford: John Beaufoy Publishing.

Venkataraman, M., (2021) *A Naturalist's Guide to the Insects of India*. Oxford: John Beaufoy Publishing.

Acknowledgements

The authors would like to thank all the photographers for so generously contributing their photographs. In addition they would like to thank the following people for their help in producing this book: Amit Sharma, Arhaan Satwalekar, Arpit Deomurari, Ashok Kayshap, Avinash Khemka, Bhanu Singh, Biswarup Satpati, Clement M Francis, Dipika Sharma, Garima Bhatia, Gopinath Kollur, Gururaj Moorching, Khushboo Sharma, Kintoo Dhawan, Malika Pandey, Manoj Kejriwal, Mohit Aggarwal, Nitin Srinivasamurthy, Panchami Manoo Ukil, Rahul Sharma, Raj Kishore Beck, Ramki Sreenivasan, SarwanDeep Singh, Savio Fonseca, Sumit K Sen, Sunil Kini, Tanmoy Das, Vaidehi Gunjal, and Varun Thakkar.

We would specially like to acknowledge the contributions of Peter Smetacek for help with the butterfly section; Indraneil Das and Abhijit Das for the reptile section; Rohit Charkravarty for the mammals section; Pradeep Sachdeva and Vidya Tongbram for the trees section and Meenkashi Venkataraman for the insects information.

Finally we are very grateful to Alpana Khare for designing this book so beautifully.

Index

BIRDS

MAMMALS

REPTILES

INSECTS

TREES & SHRUBS